ALLEGIANCE

ROBERT BRENNAN

ALLEGIANCE

by

ROBERT BRENNAN

TO

UNA

A QUIET, BRAVE

AND

VERY PATIENT LADY

Foreword

A FRIEND who read the MS. said in effect :

The story is incomplete, inasmuch as you were writing only for the initiated. It deals mainly with your own connection with the struggle for Irish independence, but there is little or nothing to show the why and wherefore of that struggle.

He advised me to write a foreword summarising, in a few lines, the history of the Independence movement, and here they are.

In the year 1169 the Normans, who in a single battle had conquered England a hundred years before, invaded Ireland. They easily secured a footing on portions of the East and South coasts, but they met with persistent resistance elsewhere and more than four hundred years elapsed before they were able to occupy the whole island. Of course, they were hampered by the fact that when the Anglo-Norman conquerors had resided in Ireland for a few generations they suffered a sea change. Succumbing, no doubt, to the charm of the country and its people they, in the words of the Viceroy, became " ipsis Hibernicis Hiberniores "—(more Irish than the Irish). They adopted the Gaelic language and the Irish way of life and many of them joined the Irish in the fight against the invader.

However, Elizabeth and her successor James I found themselves in possession of all Ireland, but not in undisputed possession, for the Irish persisted in their resistance to the occupation. There was almost a continuous state of rebellion during the seventeenth and eighteenth centuries. Just before the dawn of the nineteenth century there occurred what was probably the most significant rising up to that time, because the actual fight was headed not as heretofore by native chieftains or Anglo-Irish lords, but by leaders from amongst the people. This rebellion was, strange to say, deliberately fomented by the British authorities who hoped to crush it easily and thus pave the way for the destruction of the semi-independent Irish Parliament. The rebellion of 1798 was a bitter and bloody struggle.

Owing to a miscarriage of plans the fighting was confined to only a few counties. The Irish had many initial successes and they were defeated only when the British general was enabled to bring against them a force greater than that which overcame Napoleon at Waterloo. For a war of the period the carnage was terrible, the fatalities amongst the Irish amounting to 150,000 and amongst the British 20,000.

The rebellion crushed, the Dublin Parliament, which was composed entirely of the Anglo-Irish aristocracy, was induced by bribery to vote itself out of existence and the Union with England was accomplished.

But the insurrections continued. In 1803 Robert Emmet made his ill-fated attempt to throw off the foreign yoke. The Tithe war of the eighteen-thirties and the Land war of the eighties were but phases of the struggle for national independence. The Young Ireland rising of 1848, though it was a failure, inspired the Fenian attempt of 1867, and survivors of the latter movement were to be executed in the so-called Sinn Féin Rising of 1916 which was crushed, but which, in its aftermath, partially achieved the dream of centuries, a free Ireland.

.   .   .   .   .

The original title of this book was *Personal Experience* and not *Allegiance*.

It purports to give the author's personal experience of the happenings which came under his notice during a momentous period in Ireland's history.

It is not, and it is not intended to be, a history of the period.

R. B.

Contents

		PAGE
CHAPTER ONE	. . . .	1
CHAPTER TWO	. . . .	9
CHAPTER THREE	. . . . . .	20
CHAPTER FOUR	. . . .	30
CHAPTER FIVE	. . . .	41
CHAPTER SIX	. . . .	50
CHAPTER SEVEN	. . . . . .	61
CHAPTER EIGHT	. . . . . .	72
CHAPTER NINE	. . . .	84
CHAPTER TEN	. . . .	94
CHAPTER ELEVEN	. . . . . .	103
CHAPTER TWELVE	. . . . . .	112
CHAPTER THIRTEEN	. . . . .	124
CHAPTER FOURTEEN	. . . . .	137
CHAPTER FIFTEEN	. . . . .	147
CHAPTER SIXTEEN	. . . . .	156
CHAPTER SEVENTEEN	. . . . .	167
CHAPTER EIGHTEEN	. . . . .	175
CHAPTER NINETEEN	. . . . .	185
CHAPTER TWENTY	. . . . .	196
CHAPTER TWENTY-ONE	. . . .	207
CHAPTER TWENTY-TWO	. . . .	218
CHAPTER TWENTY-THREE	. . . .	227
CHAPTER TWENTY-FOUR	. . . .	237
CHAPTER TWENTY-FIVE	. . . .	244
CHAPTER TWENTY-SIX	. . . . .	257
CHAPTER TWENTY-SEVEN	. . . .	264
CHAPTER TWENTY-EIGHT	. . . .	273
CHAPTER TWENTY-NINE	. . . .	284
CHAPTER THIRTY	. . . . .	293
CHAPTER THIRTY-ONE	. . . .	301
CHAPTER THIRTY-TWO	. . . .	311
CHAPTER THIRTY-THREE	. . . .	320
CHAPTER THIRTY-FOUR	. . . .	326
CHAPTER THIRTY-FIVE	. . . .	334
CHAPTER THIRTY-SIX	. . . . .	343
APPENDIX	. . . .	356
INDEX	. . . .	357
ACKNOWLEDGMENTS	. . . . . .	373

List of Illustrations

Robert Brennan . . . . . . *frontispiece*

Robert and Una Brennan on their wedding day . *facing page*   22

Landing the guns at Howth . . . . „ „   23

Padraig Pearse's address to the Wexford Brigade „ „   38

Eamon de Valera after the Surrender . . „ „   39

Letter from Col. French, O.C. British Troops . „ „   70

The Castle, Enniscorthy . . . . „ „   71

Surrender Order for the Wexford Volunteers . „ „   86

Group taken before the Surrender in Enniscorthy „ „   87

Prisoners leaving Athenaeum, Enniscorthy . „ „   118

Enniscorthy prisoners . . . . . „ „   119

Tumultuous welcome at Westland Row Station „ „   134

Welcome to released prisoners, June, 1917 . „ „   135

Some prisons in which R. Brennan was confined „ „ 166-7

Group of prisoners released from British prisons . „ „   182

Rathmines Sinn Féin Committee, 1918–19 . „ „   183

Group taken at Sinn Féin Headquarters . . „ „   230

Delegates to Paris Peace Conference . . „ „   231

A typical street raid . . . . . „ „   246

During the Truce, 1921 . . . . „ „   247

Michael Collins during the Truce, 1921 . . „ „   278

At Croke Park, during the Truce, 1921 . . „ „   279

Plenipotentiaries and advisers at Holyhead . „ „   294

Arthur Griffith's testimony . . . . „ „   295

British troops leaving Portobello Barracks . „ „   326

Irish troops entering Portobello Barracks . „ „   327

The blowing up of the Four Courts . . „ „   342

Erskine Childers . . . . . . „ „   343

Chapter One

*The main objective of the Irish Parliamentary Party was to win by
Parliamentary action a measure of Home Rule. It was brilliantly
led by Charles Stewart Parnell until his downfall in 1890, when the
Party split. It was reunited in 1900 under the leadership of John
Redmond.*

*The Irish language was the everyday language of the people down to
the end of the eighteenth century, when it was gradually displaced by
English. In 1893, when the Gaelic League was founded, not more
than one-sixth of the people spoke Irish.*

ABOUT the time I was leaving school, spectacular demonstrations were being held in honour of the rebellion of 1798,
the occasion being the centenary of that event. Nowhere
were the demonstrations more enthusiastic than in my
native county of Wexford, whose people had played such
a heroic part in that fight. With much playing of bands,
waving of flags and marshalling of processions, the battle-
fields of '98 were visited and there were floods of oratory.
If any of us had thought that the purpose of all this noise
was to encourage us to follow in the footsteps of the men
of '98, we were quickly undeceived. We were specifically
warned not to do so. The members of the Irish Parliamentary Party and their adherents who were the principal
speakers at these gatherings, were careful to point out that
though their aims were the same as those of the men of '98,
their methods were different. In the future, we were to
rely on the ballot instead of the bullet and we were to
return members who were pledged to sit, act and vote with
the Party who, on the floor of the British House of Commons, would wrest Ireland's rights from her cruel oppressor.

As a matter of course we all joined in the celebrations
and roared ourselves hoarse. Then we returned to our
everyday lives and the nation continued to become each
day less Irish and more English. We were not all conscious of this, but looking back now, it is easy to see that
the period from the death of Parnell down to the end of

1

the century was as dark an hour as there had been in the history of the nation. Ireland's ancient culture was forgotten, and debased English standards had taken its place. The word "literature" applied only to English literature and precious little of what was great in that literature was read. The workingman's mental recreation was provided by the cheaper English Sunday newspapers. Theatres were given up to third-rate English strolling companies or fifth-rate English music-hall troupes. The political destinies of the nation were in the hands of the warring factions which once had been the great Irish Parliamentary Party, whose members had now become mere tools of the British Liberal Party.

In the reaction which began to set in about this time, led by Arthur Griffith in *The United Irishman* and D. F. Moran in *The Leader*, we found it easy to ascribe all of Ireland's ills, political, economic and cultural, to the Irish Parliamentary Party. By directing the eyes of the nation to Westminster, and by teaching the people to rely entirely on the British Parliament for the redress of their wrongs, they had destroyed the spirit of self-reliance which should have imbued the nation, and they had induced in the people a supineness which destroyed initiative. Moreover, they had ignored the heritage of the national language and thus helped to anglicise the nation.

In all this, we conveniently forgot the great achievements the Parliamentary Party had to its credit.

When they started their once great movement, the Irish Parliamentary Party found the tenant-farmer little more than a serf. His occupation of the land depended entirely on the goodwill of the landlord. He could be thrown out at any time. The rent he paid could be raised every year and he had no redress or court of appeal. If he improved his holding his only reward was an increased rental. The assessment and expenditure, not merely of the national revenue but even of the local rates, was in the hands of the British Government. The national revenue went, of course, to London and was disbursed when and how the British Government ordained. The local revenue for each county was controlled by a body called the Grand Jury, which was hand-picked by the British-appointed officials of Dublin Castle.

The Irish Parliamentary Party had broken the stranglehold of the landlords. They had won security of tenure and fixed rentals for the people on the land. They had, indeed, begun the great movement for the transfer of the ownership of title from the landlord to the tenant-farmer. They had not won control of the national revenue but their ceaseless agitation had succeeded in having the management of the local rates transferred to the people.

We had forgotten, or had not learned all this, a fact which helped to increase the bitterness of the quarrel when, a little later, Sinn Féin opened up its attack on the Irish Parliamentary Party.

I was reared in a household which had been, for a long time, in a state of poverty. My earliest recollections were of a house in John's Gate Street, Wexford, which faced the chapel-yard and at the rear of which was a large yard with stalls which were nearly always filled with cattle, sheep and pigs. These were all the property of my father, who also owned a smart pony and trap in which the family used to drive out on Sundays.

In after years I used to wonder how my father had amassed this property, for I never met anyone who was less fitted for business and particularly for the keen hard-eyed business of the cattle and pig dealer. I have never known a more credulous man or one who could be more easily imposed upon.

Apparently he lost everything, including the house, and for a while we lived in conditions of great hardship. To ensure that the wolf, that was always at the door, would not come in and devour us, my mother took up her old profession of dressmaking. She bought a sewing-machine which she was to pay for in instalments of 2s. 6d. per week. Whenever she did not have the instalment—which was often—she used to think up the most extraordinary stratagems to mollify the collector. These were always a subject for subsequent merriment for, in spite of our troubles, or maybe because of them, everything that happened was a source of fun. My mother was never despondent and, of course, her five children had no thought of being so. Every evening she used to recount the happenings of the day with a wealth of comic detail, mostly imaginary, and all the funnier because my father believed every word. We were very poor and we were very happy.

When she was working, my mother sang and she had a great repertoire. She knew nearly all of Moore's melodies, every one of Stephen Foster's negro songs, and all the solos in *The Bohemian Girl* and *Maritana* and a hundred Irish ballads. I learned them all.

The fortunes of the family improved almost imperceptibly. We moved to a better house and then to a better one again. A great event was my winning an Exhibition worth twenty pounds in the Intermediate examinations. On this capital my mother started a little shop, sweets, candles, matches, cigarettes, vegetables, etc., and immediately our fortunes took a new turn. The shop brought in a profit of one pound a week and there we were in the lap of luxury, almost.

I got a job in the office of the County Surveyor at a salary of six shillings per week and as the hours were from ten to four I had plenty of time to spare. I attended in the evenings the Technical schools—drawing, mathematics and chemistry—and later on I passed the Matriculation examination in the Royal University. I cycled the ninety miles to Dublin and back again to save the railway fare and I thought it great fun.

I was a member of an amateur negro minstrel troupe which was invited to contribute to the half-hour concerts organised in aid of the Wexford '98 Memorial. It was explained to us that we need not give a minstrel show if we did not wish, that it might be black and white or, indeed, all white if we liked. One of our items must have been the most incongruous ever staged. Dressed in long dark pants with white shirts crossed by green sashes, we marched on to the stage carrying tin pikes. Our chorus was an English translation of " The Marseillaise." At appropriate moments in the chorus we assumed the " charge " position with the pikes. We took it all very seriously and so, apparently, did the audience, for we got a great deal of applause. My solo item was something that had the audience puzzled. A few weeks before I had picked up a copy of Dinny Devereux's penny book of '98 ballads in which there were a few songs in the Irish language, one of them being Dr. Hyde's translation of " Who Fears to Speak of '98 ? " Aided by the elementary knowledge of the language which I had gained in the Christian Brothers' school, I memorised the ballad and sang it at the concert. Though I did not realise it then, it was the first time in half a century that the people of Wexford had heard a song in Gaelic. I was the object of a good deal of banter from the lads in the troupe and they did not hesitate to imitate what they considered the barbarous sounds.

The incident was to have a profound effect on my future, for because of it I was thrown into the role of a pioneer for the Irish-Ireland movement in the district. A few days after the concert, Nicky Cosgrave, a man who had a considerable bakery business in the town, called me into his shop and told me that he and a few others who had heard the song were anxious to learn the language. He asked me to meet a few people that night. Amongst those present I remember were Nicholas O'Hanlon Walsh, M. J. Furlong and old Ben Hughes, who was the mayor of the town. Someone suggested that we should invite Dr. Douglas Hyde to come down and start a branch of the Gaelic League. I well remember the day we awaited the arrival of Dr. Hyde. As we sat on over-stuffed chairs in a genteel drawing-room, we listened to old Ben Hughes droning on endlessly about the reasons why he had sided with the Young Irelanders against O'Connell away back in the eighteen-forties. We were all a little nervous about meeting the great Dublin scholar and when Dr. Hyde entered we got a bit of a shock. Instead of the carefully-groomed, bespectacled professor we had expected, we saw a big, wide-shouldered man, carelessly dressed in homespuns and wearing a tweed cap. His broad face and heavy drooping moustache were not prepossessing, but his eyes held one. Deep grey and set wide apart, they were full of kindliness and humour. In his greetings he showed that astonishingly youthful enthusiasm which remained with him all his life, and behind

his genial manner I observed something which I later
identified as the old-world courtesy which one happens on
frequently in the remote parts of Ireland. Answering
Ben Hughes, the Mayor, he proudly stated that everything
he wore was Irish, adding with a disarming smile, " I see
you were before me in that." Mr. Cosgrave explained
rather shamefacedly that we had not secured the support
we expected for the first meeting. Dr. Hyde waved that
circumstance aside. He would rather have an audience of
twenty than five hundred. Later, after tea, I walked with
him through the narrow streets of the old town. I told
him that in our Irish lessons in school one of the texts
had been his own *Ceithre Sgéalta* (" Four Stories ") and
how we had enjoyed the exploits of Paudeen the Giant.
With unfeigned delight he recalled some of the incidents
in the story, laughing aloud and gesticulating like a boy.
I was painfully aware that the critical eyes of the town were
upon the stranger and myself, but he did not seem to
notice it. If ever he observed the ridicule which attended
his course in those days, he never gave any indication of
doing so.

Six years earlier he had founded the Gaelic League in
Dublin and day in and day out he had travelled to and fro
on his bicycle, unpaid and mostly unheeded, teaching the
language in the various classes. Already he had captured
earnest groups in Dublin and though neither he nor
anyone else realised it then, in those little classes there
were gathered the young men and women who, one day,
thanks to the spirit Hyde infused in them, were to break
at long last, after seven centuries, the stranglehold of the
foreigner on the Irish nation.

At our meeting that night we had fifty people. It seemed
a forlorn start, as our motley gathering filled only a little
space in the hall. Hyde did not seem to mind. He spoke
to us as if we were the Irish people. We could save the
soul of the nation, which was its language. He quoted
Thomas Davis to the effect that a nation's language would
guard its frontiers more surely than fortress or river. He
poured scorn voluble and scathing on the *seoinins*, the " little
Johns," who tried to ape the English. He drew a contrast

between the heroic Gaelic Ireland of the past and the shoddy
English-speaking Ireland of the present and mourned the
fact that the thoroughbred racer felt no shame in being
taken for a donkey. I could not help feeling in my youthful
superiority that his movements were *gauche* and some of his
similes too homely, but I saw that the little group was
listening and absorbing what he had to say. And of the
people who were there that night nearly one-third remained
with us to the end. When I got home I fished out his
Love Songs of Connacht and discovered for myself that this
modest and sincere zealot was a poet. The small hours of
the morning found me still enthralled by the songs which,
despised then by the intellectuals, he had garnered from
the humble workers of the fields and the fishing-grounds
in the West. It was the songs of simple beauty that held
him, such as—

> I thought often that you were more
> Like God's lamp shining to find me
> Or the bright star of knowledge before
> And the star of knowledge behind me.

Sixteen years later, when he had been President of his
beloved Gaelic League for twenty-two painstaking years,
he left the chair. The tide of politics which had always
threatened the League had at last engulfed it. The
enthusiasts who demanded that it should throw off its
non-political mask had had their way. His attitude everybody admitted was logical, holding as he did that you can
lose political freedom and regain it and lose it again, but
the language once lost could never be regained. As he left
the hall that night, behind his wistful smile was a heart
very sad and well-nigh broken. He did not realise that his
work was already done, that the forces he had set loose
were to tear down the mighty and seemingly everlasting
pillars of an alien civilisation and to set up in its place an
Ireland in line with its ancient Gaelic culture—that like
"An Craoibhin," his pen-name, the little slender branch
which by its slightest movement affects the whole forest,
he had stirred the land from end to end. He could not,

2—1893

in fact, then foresee that on a May day twenty-three years later all sections of the nation, Gael and Saxon, Dane and Norman alike, were to unite to bestow on him the proud title of the first President of a new Ireland—becoming Gaelic and all but free.

Chapter Two

Sinn Féin opposed the policy of sending Irish representatives to the British Parliament and advocated the setting up of a National Council in Dublin to direct a policy of passive resistance to the British Government.

The Irish Republican Brotherhood (the I.R.B.) was a secret oath-bound organisation founded in 1865. It aimed to set up an Irish Republic by physical force.

WE started our branch in Wexford and I was appointed teacher at five shillings per week. We began with an attendance of seventy or eighty, which dropped to twenty or so at the end of the season. A few months later another branch was started in Castlebridge and the following year one in Tagoat. I was teaching in all three until we became stronger and we were able to bring in a native speaker as teacher.

In order to spread the light, half a dozen of us used to hire a pony and car every Sunday and travel to various villages throughout the county.

We used to hold a meeting in the village we visited and tell the people of the new movement. After the meeting we would dance a four-hand reel and sing a few Irish songs. It was not all work and we got a good deal of fun out of it. Besides, we were ourselves learning. We had begun reading Arthur Griffith's paper, *The United Irishman*, learning from him the principles of Irish nationality and Sinn Féin. When Griffith himself came down for our first Wexford Feis it was a great occasion. He cycled the whole ninety miles from Dublin with a few friends, including Seumas O'Sullivan, Seumus Connolly, Tomas Ó hAodha, Seumas O'Connor and Tom Cuffe.

When Griffith decided to establish his Sinn Fein movement we organised Wexford County in the cause and became the best organised county in Leinster outside Dublin. We even succeeded, after some heartbreaking defeats, in getting a few of our members elected to the

Wexford Corporation. In spite of this, we were still a very small minority of the general public, who seemed to think we were a little mad anyway. The adherents of the Irish Parliamentary Party, enraged at our policy of withdrawing the Irish Members from Westminster, decided we were the real enemies of the country. One of the local newspapers, an Irish Party organ, openly preached the doctrine that we should be driven from the town and county.

All this time we had been hearing rumours that the I.R.B. (Irish Republican Brotherhood) or Fenian organisation, was still in existence and we got a thrill when it was whispered that some of the heads of the Gaelic Athletic Association were in it and that they were followed about by detectives. We made very discreet enquiries and, as a result, one memorable day eight or nine of us were sworn into the organisation by Sean T. O'Kelly, the locale being John Barker's house in South Main Street, Wexford.

The amazing thing about Sean T. at this time was that he was a grown man, a responsible citizen, when the rest of us seemed to be still in our boyhood. Though he was younger than many of us, and though he was as full of fun as any, he knew and talked on equal terms with bishops, while the rest of us hardly dared to speak to a parish priest and certainly not on equal terms. In one respect he was rather like a priest himself. At a gathering you always found him in a corner hearing someone's confession, or so it seemed. Everyone confided in him. He travelled all Ireland enrolling young men into the secret organisation—whose members were pledged to take up arms to establish the Republic whenever the call came. Everywhere he went Sean T. made a courtesy call on the bishop of the diocese who, to say the least, would have been very much surprised had he known of the visitor's Fenian activities.

There was an unwritten rule in the I.R.B. that women were not to be admitted into the " organisation "—the name we always gave to the I.R.B. When I was about to get married the pledge of secrecy I had given disturbed me. I felt I had no right to withhold from the lady who was to be my life partner, the fact that I was pledged to the cause.

I could tell her, however, only if she was a member also. I put this up to the authorities and was so stubborn about it that Una was sworn into the organisation by the same Sean T. O'Kelly. I was told later that only one other woman had ever been admitted. I think it was Maude Gonne.

I had seen Maude Gonne only once at that time. It was just after the turn of the century, when she came out on the stage of St. Teresa's Hall in Dublin, as an old woman in her bare feet, in the title-part of *Cathleen ni Houlihan*. I was so carried away by the beauty of the play that I ventured backstage to ask if I might be permitted to thank her. She was surrounded by a group of admirers and I had not the nerve to interrupt. I had heard she was the most beautiful woman in Ireland—I thought she must be the most beautiful woman in the world.

The effect of the play on the young men and women of the Gaelic League and Sinn Féin was profound. Many of them had already dedicated their lives to Ireland. Yeats and Maude Gonne brought into the forefront of their hearts the simple grandeur of that sacrifice. To the question which Yeats asked thirty-six years later :

> Did that play of mine send out
> Certain men the English shot ?

I can without hesitation answer " yes."

Our little Group in the I.R.B. managed to buy a German Mauser rifle and we even had some target practice with it on a few occasions. This and the distribution in the dead of night of handbills dissuading Irishmen from joining the British forces, and the hanging up of black flags for the King's visit, provided plenty of excitement, especially when we were chased by the police. One of our fellows in the I.R.B. got conscience-stricken during a mission and told his confessor—a visiting Redemptorist Father—that he was in a secret society. The priest told him to send his superior officers to see him. So Ned Foley, who was the center, and I, who was the secretary, went in fear and trembling to see the priest. He asked us what it was all about. We told him,

" Have you got many men ? " he asked.

" Not many."

" How many ? "

" About twenty or so in the town."

" Why have you not got more ? "

" We have to be very careful to get the right men."

" Have you got any rifles ? "

" One."

" You're only fooling yourselves," said the priest in a rich Dublin accent. " You should either drop this or go at it seriously. Go and get rifles and men and make your men sharpshooters. There must be lots of material in Wexford."

We were grinning with delight when we left him.

What with the Gaelic League, in which I was, by this time, a volunteer teacher, Sinn Féin, of which I was County Secretary, and the I.R.B., of which I was also County Secretary, I was kept pretty busy, but it did not seem that we were making much headway amongst the people. We were still a very small minority. Furthermore, in the absence of any programme of work in Sinn Féin to which the individual could devote himself, branches were continually falling off, so that by the time the Home Rule Bill of 1912 was introduced we seemed to be going backward as rapidly as the Redmondite Party stung into activity by our opposition was going forward.

Griffith decided to launch a Sinn Féin daily paper, and we went at the work of collecting the necessary funds. It was uphill work. Big John O'Mahony, who was a traveller for a confectionery firm, happened to visit Wexford and I enrolled his services in my collection. He complained afterwards, with great delight, that I had persuaded him to get shaved three times in one day and that we got only one pound for his torture.

The Sinn Féin daily was an evening paper. Griffith believed that since most successful continental papers were published in the afternoon, his paper was more likely to succeed if it also was an afternoon issue. This was partly the reason why it failed, because his followers were largely scattered through the country and they had no chance of getting the paper till next day.

The paper failed and our hopes ran low. On a visit to Dublin shortly afterwards, I called to see Griffith in his dingy office in No. 17 Fownes Street. In his brisk, curt, shy way, he asked me how the organisation was going, and I had to tell him that the failure of the paper had had a bad effect and that the branches and membership had fallen off sharply, whereas the Redmondites were going strong. He was quite undismayed.

" This setback is only temporary," he said. " The English are not serious about Home Rule and they will let Redmond down. Then the people will turn to Sinn Féin. It's as certain as night follows day."

His optimism was contagious. It was impossible not to feel full of buoyant hope when listening to him. He brought me to tea in the D.B.C. where he was to meet some friends and, while waiting for the latter, we played a game of chess.

We were joined by Alderman Walter Cole and O'Leary Curtis. After a while I heard a shout from the doorway and looked up to see the pale, bright face of Sean MacDermott, a man who had more personal charm than anyone I have ever known. Laughing gaily and dragging his crippled leg, he came towards us saying :

" Well, Bob, so you have joined the Green Hungarian Band."

The moment he said it, I knew he was sorry. The mocking name had been bestowed on Sinn Féin by D. P. Moran of *The Leader*, the reference being to Griffith's book *The Resurrection of Hungary—a Parallel for Ireland.*

Cole and Curtis stiffened and Griffith looked surprised.

" I'm sorry," said Sean, " you know, Griffith, I didn't mean that."

" That's all right, Sean," said Griffith, relaxing with a smile, " won't you join us ? "

" I'm sorry, I can't. I have an appointment."

I was sorry he could not join us because one of the objects of this visit was to try to close a widening breach between Sean's group and that of Griffith. Sean was one of the leaders of Cumann na nGaedheal, a newly revived organisa-tion, which had for its objective not the restoration of the

Constitution of 1782, but the establishment of the Irish Republic. It was a rival organisation to Sinn Féin. I thought I saw a way of bringing the two groups together. I failed on this occasion, but a few months later there was an amicable settlement.

As he was leaving us, Sean leaned over to me and said in a loud whisper :

" I understand that there is electric light in Carlow."

He laughed gaily as he moved away. Griffith asked what was the joke and, as his companions thought there was something sinister behind the phrase, I explained that it referred to an amusing experience I had had some years before.

" Come, let us have it," said Griffith, and I did.

I had travelled to Dublin for an examination and I was met at the railway station by three Wexford friends of mine, John Moloney, his brother Peter and Fred Cogley, all students. They were all staying at the same digs in Lennox Street and they had arranged for me to stay there also. We were hardly well inside the house when the three of them rushed to the window crying, " Here she is ! " I joined them and saw a very good-looking girl. She came up the steps of our house and entered and the attentions of all three of them were transferred to the doorway through which she could be seen tripping lightly up the stairs. They said to me :

" Isn't she grand ? "

I agreed and asked what she was like.

" Well, haven't you seen her for yourself ? "

" But what is she like to talk to ? "

They didn't know. They had never spoken to her, because they had not been introduced. She was a lodger like themselves. Her name was Kiernan and she was a native of Carlow. I thought it strange that in the course of several weeks they had been unable to strike up an acquaintance. They wanted to know how.

" Well," I suggested, " you could, for instance, run up the stairs when she's coming down and bump into her and beg her pardon, and there you are."

" But," said Peter, " what could we talk to her about ? "

" I don't know," I said, " maybe if you get talking to her you could think of something." I suddenly remembered she was from Carlow. " Why not talk about Carlow ? "

They knew nothing about Carlow, did I ?

" The only thing I know about it," I said, " is that they have electric light there."

At that time Carlow was the only provincial town in Ireland so blessed.

The next day I left the library and walked up into Grafton Street. What was my amazement when I saw Peter Moloney on the opposite side of the street standing talking to Miss Kiernan, or rather he was standing looking at her, his round, fair, innocent face like the rising sun. When he saw me he sent out signals of distress and I joined him and was introduced.

" This is Mr. Brennan, Miss Kiernan."

I looked at her and saw the bluest eyes I had ever beheld. They were paralysing. I managed to say :

" How do you do ? "

" I'm well, thanks," she said, and she was blushing too. I made a violent effort to concentrate.

" It's a fine day," I said.

" Yes," she replied.

Then I tried in vain to think of any further word in the English, Irish, or any other language. The silence was solid. At last I blurted out :

" Which way are you going ? "

She indicated the direction of Stephen's Green.

" That way," she said.

" So am I."

The three of us walked towards Stephen's Green. I tried to think of something to say and Peter's obvious embarrassment did not help me. At last I had an idea. Of course, I could not know that Peter had said it already.

" I understand," I said, " that you are from Carlow, Miss Kiernan."

" Yes."

I saw now that Peter had already said it, but it was too late to draw back.

"I believe," I said, and there was desperation in my voice, "that you have electric light there."

"Yes."

We entered Harcourt Street without another word. The perspiration was rolling off me. It was clear that what Peter was saying to himself should have blasted me from the earth. We were half-way up Harcourt Street when we saw Cogley coming down. I thanked God.

He stopped and was introduced.

"How do you do," he said and I was horror-stricken to see that her eyes had the same effect on him.

"I'm well, thanks."

He managed to say "It's a fine day."

"Yes."

After a very long pause, he said : "I think I'll go back with you."

And the four of us walked on. The silence was now fourfold. Of course, Fred got the same idea. I saw it dawning in his mind and I kicked him. This only spurred him on.

"I believe, Miss Kiernan," he said, "that you come from Carlow."

"Yes."

He knew now. It was evident from the quiver in his voice.

"I understand," he said, "you have electric light there."

"Yes."

It was terrible. There was not a word spoken till we turned into Lennox Street. John Molony was sitting on the steps of the house reading a book. I hastened on in front.

"John," I said in a tragic whisper, "don't say anything about electric light in Carlow."

And aloud he said : "What about electric light in Carlow ? "

She heard him and she passed indoors, her head held high. She never looked at any of us again.

A visit to Dublin in those dark days was like a tonic. Every person one met seemed to be a rebel of some sort and one felt it was only a matter of time until all Ireland would follow Dublin's lead. This stimulating atmosphere was not by any means confined to the political field. There were poets, essayists and artists galore and one met them everywhere. In the Library one could talk to Padraic Colum—boyish, cantankerous, enthusiastic, and invariably bursting his way out through the wrong turnstile. He had just published his first book of poems, *Wild Earth*. There, too, were James Stephens, whose strange poems were appearing in *The United Irishman* and who was not unlike one of his own leprechauns, and William Dara of *The Light on the Broom*. George Moore, who looked like a very large pink cigar, was in and out. He was contributing what we thought was a scandalous series of notes for Yeats's magazine, *Dana*. Joe Campbell showed me some of the beautiful verses which were to appear in *The Gilly of Christ*.

One night a crowd of us went to the Gaiety Theatre to protest against a play called *Sappho*. We knew nothing about the play except that Moran in *The Leader* had said it was immoral. We kicked up such a row that the play could not proceed. The police were sent for and when they arrived they threw out mostly the wrong people, amongst them a small Jew who kept yelling out that he had paid his money and wanted to see the play. One of our fellows was, however, taken to the police station, but a bunch of us called at the station and explained that he had had nothing to do with the row and that his father was a very important justice of the peace in County Limerick. We got him out.

Next day we were hilariously discussing all this on the Library steps when a fairish, thin-faced fellow came out of the Library and joined the group. He carried a mackintosh over his arm and an ash-plant in his hand. He never said a word but his attitude was so icily contemptuous that the conversation petered out and was not renewed till he took one of the group, Sarsfield Kerrigan, by the arm and walked away. I asked who he was and was told his name was James Joyce and that he had just published a slim volume of rather poor poems under the title *Chamber Music*.

Many years later I happened to be in Paris and I heard that Joyce was thinking of returning to Dublin. I rang him up and asked if I might come and see him. He asked

me to come right away.   He was almost completely blind
and felt his way about the room by touching the furniture.
He sat down and talked for over half an hour.   I soon learned
that the alacrity with which he received me was because
he thought I might have some influence in having John
Sullivan, the opera singer, invited to Dublin to give a
concert—this as a stepping-stone to an American tour
which would bring him some money.   I had no great hopes
for the project as Sullivan was, at this time, about fifty and
many thought past his prime, but I promised to do what I
could.   We talked of Dublin and it was rather pathetic to
see how eager he was for details of his old friends.   I asked
him when he was coming back.

" Not until they make some amends for burning my
book on the steps of the National University," he said
bitterly.

Æ came to Sinn Féin headquarters one day to talk
to us about banking.   It was a very clear and exact dis-
course, but Edward Martyn, who was in the chair, slept
all through it.   I left with Æ and was surprised to find
that he remembered I had sent him a story, though he had
not published it.   He recounted for me his famous vision
of the young man sowing seed across the face of the land.
He did not seem to notice that I was wheeling a bicycle
and that his headlong pace was bringing me into conflict
with the many passers-by.   We went to the vegetarian
restaurant in College Street where I was compelled to eat
a strange and unappetising dish called a vegetable chicken.

A quarter of a century later I walked with Æ through
the streets of Washington and his talk was as vivid, fresh
and spontaneous as ever.   There was not the slightest
indication that he had only a few months to live.   His
gait was, as usual, headlong and I had great difficulty in
keeping him from walking into the whirling traffic.   There
was a blimp lazily sailing in the clear air over the Capitol.
It advertised Goodyear tyres.   Æ looked up at it and
groaned :

" They even pollute the heavens with their blatant
advertisements," he said, and added : " When you and I
enter through the sacred portals of heaven we will be

greeted by an American barker yelling at us about the virtues of his own particular brand of Ambrosia."

We had walked to the waterfront behind the Lincoln Memorial when I ventured to say I had an appointment.

" Why, so have I," he said, " what time is it ? "

It was a quarter past three.

" My goodness," he said, " I was to meet Mr. Wallace at 2.15."

We got a taxi and I left him at the Department of Agriculture ten minutes later. He had kept the Cabinet Minister waiting an hour and ten minutes.

One day I went to the Gaelic League offices to see Sean T. O'Kelly. He was out for the moment and I sat down to wait. There was an earnest-looking young man sitting at a desk, absorbed as if thinking what to write. He jotted something down on a slip of paper. Then he looked up and asked me if I spoke Irish. I said " a little " and he handed me the slip of paper. The words on it were :

" Leanam lorg na Laochraidhe."

" Do you understand it ? " he asked.

" Yes," I said, " Let us follow in the footsteps of the heroes."

" Isn't it grand," he said, and I agreed. He was writing an article on this topic for *An Claidheamh Soluis*, the Gaelic League organ. When Sean T. came and fetched me, I asked who the man was and he told me it was Padraig Pearse.

Chapter Three

After the 1910 General Election the 84 Irish Nationalist members held the balance of power between the Tories and the Liberals and Home Rule seemed certain. The Orange Society in Belfast and adjoining areas set up a Provisional Government to take over Ulster in defiance of the Imperial Government if and when Home Rule should come into force.

THE home atmosphere was very unlike that of Dublin. The first enthusiasm had disappeared and trying to make any headway seemed like rolling a stone up an endless hill. This applied to everything except the Gaelic League in which we were all still strenuous workers. The yearly Feis which was held alternately in Enniscorthy, New Ross and Wexford, was easily the chief county festival of the year and it had grown to be the biggest Feis in Ireland. Moreover, it was respectable because the priests were with us. In Sinn Féin, however, matters were far different. The county branches had fallen off one by one and in the town we were finding it increasingly difficult to pay the rent of the rooms we had taken. One night we decided we should come out into the open and focus attention on our policy. The method agreed on was to hire the town hall and stage a lecture and concert. After a great deal of debate, we decided to invite Father Willie Harper, one of the few priests active in Sinn Féin, to lecture on " The Manchester Martyrs " and I was instructed to issue invitations to all the principal citizens in the Wexford area. Amongst the names given to me was that of a man named Brown from the south county who was stated to be a kinsman of Saucy Jack Barry, the Father of the American Navy. I, of course, wrote to Mr. Brown and invited him to attend. The night of the lecture arrived and, to our amazement, the hall was crowded. I was taking tickets at the door of the hall when a man in rough tweeds came towards me and asked if I were Mr. Brennan. When I replied in the affirmative, he told me in a very impressive manner that

he was Mr. Brown and he added that he was a cousin of
Saucy Jack Barry, the Father of the American Navy. I
thought to myself that the description was unnecessarily
wordy, but I conducted Mr. Brown to the supper room and
asked him if he would mind proposing a vote of thanks
to the lecturer.

"I'll do that," he said, "with the greatest of pleasure.
You have standing before you a man of patriotism handed
down from generations, a lover of liberty and a hater of
oppression."

He was going on and on when I hastily excused myself
on the plea that I had to superintend the arrangements.
Mr. Brown thereupon began to stride up and down the floor,
rehearsing his speech in a barely audible voice. Shortly
afterwards, Jem Breen, the Chairman of the branch, arrived
and when he saw Brown he approached me aggressively.

"Who's that?" he asked.

"That's Mr. Brown," I replied. "He has promised to
speak, to propose a vote of——"

"My God!" said Jem, "we're ruined."

"What, what's the matter?"

"Don't you know about him?" he asked. "Why, he's
the man who broke up the Young Men's Debating Society,
a society which was in existence for twenty-five years until
he joined it. He talked everyone blind and bothered. If
you let him get on his feet to-night, we're ruined."

He called the other members of the Committee together
and explained the situation. They all agreed I should tell
Mr. Brown he could not be allowed to make a speech. I
indignantly refused, but they were adamant, and so I
approached Mr. Brown.

"I'm sorry, Mr. Brown," I said, "to have to tell you that
the Committee had already made arrangements for someone
to propose a vote of thanks. I did not know——"

"I'll second it," said Brown.

"But they have a seconder."

"I'll support it," he said.

I went back to the others who had overheard this conversation and it was agreed that we would get Mr. M. J.
Furlong to propose a vote of thanks, Mr. Breen to second

it, and then rush on the concert so quickly that Brown would
not have a chance to get to his feet. But we reckoned
without our man. The lecturer had hardly said the last
word when he was up.

"Reverend Chairman, Reverend Fathers, ladies and
gentlemen," he began, and Mr. Furlong who had risen to
propose the vote of thanks subsided. "It gives me the
greatest pleasure to be here to-night amongst the young
priests and people of Wexford. It reminds me of my cousin,
the fearless and dauntless Saucy Jack Barry, the Father
of the American Navy."

As he spoke he flayed the air with his arms and gradually
he cleared a ten-foot circle around him. It was amusing
enough so long as he dealt with the lecture, but suddenly
he branched off.

"I am proud of Wexford," he said, "and never so proud
as when I think of our illustrious and distinguished fellow-
townsman, John Edward Redmond, leading his eighty Irish
terriers to bait the British Lion on the floor of the English
House of Commons."

For a moment we thought he was being funny, but no.

"And I'm humiliated to think that here on Irish soil we
have creatures, mean-souled, unpatriotic, ungenerous, vile
creatures who would traduce the name of that great man."

As we were the only people who were engaged in this
nefarious activity, the effect can well be imagined. The
crowd in the back of the hall, seeing the joke against us,
began to cheer the speaker vociferously. I was called to
the supper room where I found the members of the Committee pacing up and down and literally tearing their hair.
The Chairman was groaning : "Oh, Lord, think of the
Free Press (the Redmondite organ) and the laugh they will
have at us this week." Suddenly he made a run at me.
"You, you," he said, "you're responsible for this." The
members gathered round me demanding that I should go
out and stop Brown. For some time I resisted their appeals.
The proceedings in the hall were becoming more and more
hilarious. Finally, I decided to try to bring Brown's speech
to a halt. I made my way through the crowded chairs
and touched the speaker on the arm. "I beg your pardon,

Robert and Una Brennan on their wedding day in 1909.

Landing the guns at Howth from the *Asgard*, July 1914. Mary Spring-Rice has back to camera. Erskine Childers at right.

sir——" Brown turned and looked at me and pushed me away. " Stand back, young man," he said, and launched into a new peroration.

The crowd in the back of the hall yelled at me amid shrieks of laughter to leave the man alone. I retired in the utmost confusion. Later, I tried vainly on two separate occasions to stem the flow of Brown's oratory—in vain. After some time, the more staid members of the audience began to file out. We saw it was hopeless to think of going on with the concert. The performers, very irate, had crowded into the supper room and they left the building in high dudgeon. Gradually, even the ribald crowd at the back of the hall grew tired of the performance and left, but Brown kept on talking. He was near-sighted and apparently did not notice that his audience was dwindling away. Near midnight, there were only three or four of us left and we decided to tell the caretaker to turn off the lights at midnight. I was on my way home when I thought it was unfair to leave Brown to make his way alone out of the dark hall, so I went back. Paddy Bryan, the caretaker, was beginning to turn off the lights, so I went in and collected Brown and brought him down the stairs.

" How did I do ? " he kept saying.

" Fine," I said. " How are you going to get home ? "

" I have the yoke down at Harper's Lane," he said.

I went down there with him and I had to listen all the way to various passages of the speech.

" Do you know," I said, " that the Committee that got up this affair are all against the Party ? "

" You don't tell me," he said.

" I do. The Sinn Féin movement is dead against the Party and against Redmond."

" Begob a man," he said, " if I had only known that."

" What would you have done ? "

" I'd have told them what I thought of them," he said.

With Sinn Féin matters went from bad to worse, while the Irish Party's fortunes continued to rise as Home Rule seemed to come nearer. Griffith had put up a Sinn Féin candidate for a parliamentary vacancy in North Leitrim and had taken a heavy defeat, though Griffith called it a

moral victory. Years afterwards I heard Jerry Boland say
" I'm sick of these moral victories. After every one of them
I'm in jail and in debt."

As the support for the Party increased, their attacks on
us redoubled and this at a time when our numbers were
getting fewer and fewer. Sir Thomas Esmonde, who had
left the Party to join Sinn Féin and who had, as a
consequence, been subjected to the most vile abuse, suddenly,
as a result of a convention in Enniscorthy, decided to
rejoin the Party.

About this time I was employed by the County Council
as an assistant County Surveyor. More than once it was
conveyed to me that the members of the Council, who were
at least ten to one on the side of the Party, did not quite
like my political activities though they were well aware I
did not allow such activities to interfere with my work.
Indeed, some members of the Council were against me
because I was zealous in bringing venal road contractors
to account. An accident on the Deeps bridge, which
spanned the Slaney River, gave my critics their chance.
A horse belonging to a Captain Walker, a bitter enemy of
the County Surveyor's, broke a leg as the result of a faulty
plank. There resulted a Local Government inquiry and in
the upshot the County Surveyor was called on to resign.
I had not been alarmed because it was clear from my
instructions that the inspection of the bridge was not one
of my duties. Notwithstanding this, the Council passed a
vote of censure on me. I was within a month of being
married but Una and I decided at once that I should resign,
and I did so. Fortunately, the position of Wexford correspondent of the *Enniscorthy Echo* became vacant and the
editor, Mr. William Sears, who was with us in the Sinn
Féin movement, agreed to give me the job and pay me one
pound per week. Una and I made out a budget and found
that after making allowances for rent, food, clothing and
all contingencies, we would have tenpence over from my
one pound at the end of a week. Sure enough we had
tenpence left over at the end of the first week but we never
had it afterwards, at least not till very many years later.

After the arduous work I had had surveying four hundred

miles of roads on a push cycle, mostly in the depth of the winter, I found life as a reporter very comfortable. Moreover, it was gratifying to find my erstwhile enemies on the County and District Councils very anxious to be nice to me because of their fear of the press. I am glad to say I never tried to get back on them though the temptation, at times, was terrific. I had now an opportunity to indulge my flair for story-writing. I had already won a prize for a short story in a local newspaper and I had published a few stories in *Ireland's Own*. I was furious to find that the ending of one of the latter had been altered. I called on the proprietor, Mr. John M. Walsh, and he told me he had altered the story as it was too highbrow for his readers. He told me I could write the sort of stories he wanted if I tried. So I invented a quaint detective character called " Crubeen Patch " and he was an instant success. I wrote well over one hundred short detective stories in three years. I used to start each story on Thursday evening, when my last despatch to the *Echo* had been sent off and, writing continuously, finish it about four in the morning and then go down town to post it at the G.P.O. before the 5 a.m. collection, so as to be in time for publication. As each story contained about seven thousand words, it will be seen that this was hard work. The series, according to Nick Murphy, the traveller for the magazine—long afterwards superintendent of the Civic Guard—sent the circulation up from thirty thousand to eighty thousand, but I was paid at the same rate all the time, namely half a crown a column, which amounted to twenty-five shillings for seven thousand words. The money, small as it was, was very helpful, particularly as we had, unfortunately, invested in a farm. This consisted of ten acres of land and an old rambling house situated on the outskirts of the town. Una and I both had had grandiose notions of making money from poultry and gardening. Alas for our dreams ! Everything in connection with the farm went wrong, except the bees, to which I gave a good deal of attention, but even these went against us at the end when a blundering old retired army officer imported some stocks from England and with them the Isle of Wight disease, which put all bee-keepers in the area

out of business. We might have done better had I not
allowed an expert gardener to talk me into engaging his
services. He showed me on paper that there was a lot of
money to be made by providing something that everybody
was pining for, namely a glass frame for the raising of plants
from seed. We could make them for ten shillings and sell
them for double the money. We made some and advertised
them in the Dublin papers, as well as in the local press.
We never had even an enquiry. Then he said we might as
well use the frames to raise plants and sell them. So we
raised plants enough for a hundred thousand acres but
apparently nobody wanted them either, so we planted what
we could in our own garden and had to throw the rest away.
Our man was not dismayed. He talked me into building
a greenhouse for the raising of grapes and tomatoes. I
balked at the grapes but consented to the tomatoes. He
certainly gave us a bumper crop, but there was something
wrong, for in order to gather the crop we had to go into
the greenhouse on our hands and knees, so luxuriant was
the foliage. When we had gathered the crop and assessed
its market value, I found that if we had a full crop for forty-
two years, we might be able to pay for the cost of the
greenhouse.

When I sold the place the head rent due almost swallowed
up the purchase price and I still owed the bank the greater
part of the three hundred pounds I had borrowed to buy
and stock the place. Such was the stress of the succeeding
years that I was able to pay off the last of that debt only
in 1930, twenty years after it was contracted.

One Sunday in 1911, Una and I were on our way to
Mass down Summerhill, when round the corner from
Hackett's Spout a little band of boys in green uniforms
came marching. They were the Wexford troop of Fianna
Éireann which had been organised by Sean Sinnott a few
months earlier. The Fianna, an open Republican Boy Scout
organisation, had been founded two years before by
Madame Markievicz.

I had, of course, seen similar parades, but this
time there was something in their bearing which sent my
heart beating a little faster. In front of the column with

Sean was a boy with a crop of unusually fair hair. When they came abreast of us, Sean halted the column and brought the stranger over to us. I experienced an unexpectedly strong handclasp and found myself looking into the blue eyes of Liam Mellowes, full of good humour, enthusiasm, optimism and comradeship.

The boys were bound for the mountain on a route march. Later that day they came in to us for tea and thereafter Liam stayed with us nearly every time he came to Wexford. Our place was ideal for drilling the boys and he took full advantage of it. Liam's father had spent his life as a regular soldier in the British Army. Intending Liam for the same career, he had sent him to the Hibernian Military Academy. The old man had been badly cut up the day Liam told him that if he was going to fight, it would be for Ireland and on Irish soil. Liam was now giving the benefit of his military schooling to boys all over Ireland. To some of us who had been many years in the I.R.B. the prospect of a rising seemed remote, but Mellowes' optimism was infectious. We would get our chance soon he said, when England and Germany would go to war.

On the parade ground Liam was a stern, rigid disciplinarian. He drove the boys hard. Off duty he was a light-hearted harum-scarum practical joker and he was an inveterate punster. I give two classic examples of the puns of his later days, when the Black and Tans were on the rampage in their Crossley lorries, raiding the countryside. Liam and I lay side by side in a house one night when the lorries rumbled nearer and nearer and slowly passed. He whispered : " When I hear any lorry, I lay me down and dee." A few days later, the district we were in was surrounded by the raiding Black and Tans. Liam said : " Solomon in all his glory was never in a raid like one of these."

We often stayed at the Mellowes' home in Dublin and, I must say, that if there was a happy family, it was that of the Mellowes' in those days. They lived in a small, but very comfortable house in Mountshannon Road, near Dolphin's Barn. Hanging on the walls were many group photographs of British soldiers, in all of which the old man appeared. Concerning the treasonable activities of his family, Mr. Mellowes was puzzled but tolerant. The mother, however, declared that since she was a Wexford woman she could be nothing but a rebel. In the evening Liam would tramp in in the heavy hobnailed boots he always wore and give us a light-hearted and lively account of the day's doings. After tea, Liam, Barney, Fred and Jenny, the only girl, would play quartettes—piano and strings—always arrangements of Irish airs. Fred and Jenny died before the Rising and the father and mother grew visibly older, but they bore their sorrows very bravely and never complained.

One day after the great war started, I journeyed up from Wexford, and Liam and his father met me at Harcourt Street station. As we emerged into the street, a battalion of British soldiers was marching past. We stood on the footpath with hundreds of others to watch them. "Now don't you see," said the father to Liam, as if resuming an argument.

"Yes, of course I do," replied Liam testily. He was immediately aware that he had shown some temper and he turned to me with a grin.

"Father thinks the Volunteers do not put on as good a show as the British."

"You know well they don't," said the old man, "they haven't the precision, the order, the bearing or anything else. Look at the way these fellows walk."

Liam patted him affectionately on the shoulder.

"Wait till you see the way they'll run," he said.

The old man was about to explode. He turned to me gravely.

"Don't make the mistake," he said, "of under-estimating the British soldiers."

"He's afraid we are going to beat them," said Liam with a grin.

The old man must have found it strange when the Rising started and his two remaining children were out with the rebels, one away in Galway and the other with his company in Dublin. Barney told me later, when we met in Richmond

Barrack, that the old man managed to reach him on Wednesday or Thursday of the fight when the garrison of the South Dublin Union was being sorely pressed. He had crossed the canal under fire and came to say to Barney that his mother was bearing up well under the strain.

" That's not what you came to say to me," said Barney.

His father regarded him thoughtfully for a while.

" Why don't you enfilade those fellows ? " he asked.

" How ? "

" If you send a couple of men with rifles across the canal to such and such a position you can turn their flank."

" Good old Dad ! " said Barney. " We'll do it." And they did.

The old man was broken, however, and he died before Liam, who had escaped to America after the Rising, had returned.

Chapter Four

With the backing of the Tory Party an Ulster Volunteer Army was organised in 1912 to oppose Home Rule. A year later the Irish Volunteers were organised " to secure and maintain the rights and liberties common to all the people of Ireland."

The Home Rule Act was passed in 1914, but its operation was suspended until the end of the war and an amending Act was promised which seemed to foreshadow the partition of Ireland.

ONE day during the great Dublin strike of 1913, Liam Mellowes came down and asked us if we could put up two Dublin men who were fugitives from justice. We knew, without being told, who the fugitives were because the papers had given very full accounts of their depredations. They were the Two Men who had Thrown a Policeman into the River Liffey and had Hurled a Barrel in after him. They were two of Larkin's men and the Hue and Cry was out for them. The affair had occurred during one of the numerous clashes between the police and the strikers and as the policeman had been rescued it seemed to me that there was much ado about very little. We were told, however, that they were dangerous men and that the police had it in for them. We, of course, agreed to take the two men and to try to arrange to have them smuggled on a Wexford schooner to England. In due course, the men arrived. One of them, Stephen Hastings, was a big fellow, not unlike Larkin himself. He had, indeed, been requisitioned at times to impersonate Larkin so as to lead the police on a false trail. After a couple of weeks, we managed to smuggle him on board a schooner and get him away. The other man, Higgins, remained on our hands and, to our dismay, he developed a troublesome cough which threatened to betray his presence in the house. We had to keep the men in one room all the time because we had sharing the house with us a family which was not at all friendly to the cause. For several weeks we waited and though Mike Morris, the captain of the schooner

Alice T, was willing to take him on his boat, he could not sail as the weather was unfavourable.

" Just like the Armada," said Mellowes, who was now on the scene frequently, " the wind and the waves are fighting for England."

Finally, we thought it safer to send Higgins to the country for a while and Larry De Lacey found a house for him in Oulart, his native village. He placed him in the home of a bachelor, right in the village. It was the first time the little Dublin man had been in a house in the country and it was all very strange to him. His bachelor host entertained him for some time, but when night came on, the former remembered that the circus was paying its annual visit to the village and he did not intend to miss the circus for Higgins, or Larkin, or any man in Ireland. Higgins was terribly upset when he heard this.

" But what am I going to do if they come in for me ? " he asked.

" They won't come in for you," said the other, " no one knows you are here and there will be no one coming in anyway."

He completely forgot that he had a lodger—the local schoolmaster—and that the latter would be coming home while he was at the circus.

As Higgins still protested, his host handed him a billhook and put him sitting on the stairs facing the door.

" Now," he said, " if anyone comes in, all you have to do is to chop the head off of him with this."

So off the bachelor went to the circus and he was enjoying it thoroughly when he suddenly remembered the schoolmaster. He stood up in his seat and crying out, " Oh, my God, the schoolmaster ! " he rushed across the ring and out, nearly taking the tent with him. He ran all the way to the cottage and, bursting in, nearly got his own head off.

We brought Higgins back after a while and managed to get him away to England, but he was arrested shortly afterwards. He got a ten years sentence.

When the Volunteers were formed in 1913, we all joined up.

We had about fifty recruits to start with and the numbers

gradually increased. In the beginning, we drilled in a malthouse loft, our instructors being successive ex-sergeants of the British Army. One such instructor was Jack McEvoy, whose personality underwent a drastic change on the parade ground. Normally he was a quiet, unassuming citizen, obviously an ex-soldier who had served many years in tropical climes. On the drill ground, he was not merely a martinet but a tyrant. His whole appearance, manner and voice were changed. He became an inexorable, over-bearing master, dominating not merely our movements and our wills, but our very thoughts. When he spoke we trembled—all of us. He did not confine himself to drilling us. He arrested us in the middle of a movement to lecture us on the conduct of war.

" What is the greatest weapon a soldier possesses ? " he would cry, his voice ringing with seemingly suppressed fury.

" I don't know, sir," said the man he was glaring at.

" I didn't ask you," cried Jack. " No, thank God, I haven't yet lost the little bit of wit God gave me. Come on, what is the greatest weapon the soldier has ? Cannon, you say ! Artillery, you say ! I say Bah ! Bosh ! Non-sense ! I say the rifle. Give me the rifle. With twenty picked riflemen I can disable the heaviest battery of artillery they can send against me." He was pacing about like a caged lion and he suddenly stopped in front of me and bellowed, " Give me twenty picked riflemen ! "

The eye he fixed on me was baleful. It was as if I was failing in my duty in not supplying then and there twenty picked riflemen. Fortunately, when I felt I could no longer keep silence under the strain, an incident occurred to relieve me. It was a very warm night and we were all perspiring freely under the low roof of the loft. A fly had alighted on the nose of the man beside me and, as we were all standing at attention, the poor fellow could do nothing about it except jerk his head whenever he thought Jack's eye was not on him. The fly, however, was persistent. Finally, the man could stand the torture no longer and, when he thought Jack's attention was diverted, he made a hasty movement with his hand to brush his tormentor away.

Unfortunately, Jack turned at the moment and saw the movement. He was on to the delinquent like a shot.

" You," he cried, " You ! What's wrong with you ? "

" There was a fly on my nose, sir."

We all trembled for the poor fellow.

Jack took three or four strides up and down, his body taut as a stretched bow, his teeth clinched.

"A fly on his nose," he breathed, " a fly on his blasted nose ! Here's a fellow who's going out to fight the bloody British Empire and he's afraid of a goddam fly on his goddam nose ! "

On Monday, 26th July, 1914, when I entered John L. Doyle's shop, as I did nearly every morning, the place being a rendezvous for all the Sinn Féiners, John called out :

" How many men can you drill in Heffernan's loft ? "

" Well, it's pretty full now with over a hundred men."

" You'll have to get another loft," he said and handed me a paper. The news was sensational. On the previous day, the Dublin Volunteers had marched to Howth and had received a thousand rifles which were landed from a white yacht (Erskine Childers' yacht *The Asgard*). Marching back to Dublin, the Volunteers had been intercepted by a large body of police and soldiers and some of the rifles had been captured. The soldiers returning from the scene had been boohed by an irate crowd and some stones were thrown. The military fired on the crowd, killing three people and wounding many more.

The incident seemed to show that there was one law for the Orangemen and another for the Nationalists. During the spring and summer the Ulster Volunteers had openly landed tens of thousands of rifles from Germany without interference on the part of the authorities.

That evening so many recruits poured in that we had to adjourn to the Sports Field where, eventually, we had between 600 and 700 men on parade and there were not enough instructors to handle all the new-comers. This happy condition continued until the war started and Redmond began to talk of the " double duty " of the Volunteers, one duty being to defend Ireland, and the other, apparently, to defend the British Empire. Many of his followers in our ranks joined up in the British Army, others fell away and many split from us and formed the National or Redmondite Volunteers, while we, the Republican or Sinn Féin Volunteers (as we came to be called), were left with about forty men. We carried on, however, and we met semi-secretly two or three times a week in a hayloft outside the town which was lent to us by Mr. Fitzsimons. Such was the bitter feeling against us at this time that Mr. Fitzsimons ran no small risk in thus obliging us. Our whole time here was given to rifle practice.

Shortly after the war started I went to Dublin to attend a Leinster Council meeting of the I.R.B. Such meetings, at that time, were fixed to coincide with some important Gaelic Athletic fixture. This was to enable the members to travel without attracting unnecessary attention and also to allow them to take advantage of the reduced railway fares. On this occasion, the Wexford football team were playing for the Leinster semi-final. At all such important meetings of the I.R.B., a member of the Supreme Council presided and this time Tom Clarke was in the chair. As soon as the meeting was called to order, Tom said that if any of us had hitherto taken our duties lightly we were to do so no more because there was a war on now and that meant business. We would get our chance to rise before the war ended. He then asked if anyone present had been followed to the meeting-place. After a pause, the delegate from Athlone said that there had been a G-man after him at the Broadstone Station but that he had thrown him off.

"Are you sure?" asked Tom.

" I'm nearly sure."

Tom looked at the young man sitting nearest the door.

"Are you armed?" he asked.

" No."

" You?"—to the next.

" No."

I was next.

" You?"

I answered quite calmly " Yes " and I produced the ·32 calibre automatic pistol I had been carrying for some time.

"All right," said Tom, " take your place at the door and see that nobody enters."

I stood at the door and, I must say, I heard very little of what went on for the ensuing half-hour. My mind was in a whirl for I knew that in this building, The Foresters' Hall in Parnell Square, there were ten or twenty meetings going on at the same time, for the place was a rendezvous not merely for the Republican Clubs, but also for various Gaelic Athletic Clubs and other societies. If anyone were to stray into our room by mistake, what was I to do? Tom should have been more explicit in his instructions, or I should have asked for some. However, no one paid any attention to me. They were all listening to Tom.

Up to that time the G-men had been treated as more or less of a joke. They were the plain-clothes political constabulary who kept tab on all suspects. So efficient were they that later, at my court-martial, they had records to show every time I visited Tom Clarke's shop during the previous three years. It was common knowledge that one of our fellows from the West, whenever he alighted at Broadstone Station picked out the G-man who was waiting for him, and said :

" You can have the day off. I'm going to the usual spots and you can go to the races. I'll turn up in Mooney's pub at nine o'clock to-night."

It was said that the G-man generally agreed to this arrangement.

Tom's talk had much to do with these G-men. We were not to let them follow us any more. One of the delegates suggested that the Supreme Council should establish an Intelligence Service to deal with possible enemy agents within our own ranks. An old Dublin man stood up immediately and denounced the proposal.

" I saw such a thing in operation before," he said, " and it was disastrous. It culminated in the assassination of an innocent man at Seville Place and the subsequent hanging of Joe Poole, another innocent man, for his murder."

Tom agreed and said we need have no fear because our organisation was sound. The rest of his talk had to do with discipline, being prepared, getting guns and learning to shoot.

" The old enemy is in the toils," he said, " we'll get our chance now."

From the meeting I went to Banba Hall and found Bulmer Hobson. I had brought £28 10s. with me, all subscribed by our Company. It was to buy twelve rifles and 1,200 rounds of ammunition, but Hobson was able to let me have only eight rifles and 800 rounds, so I paid him £19. He gave me a permit for the guns and ammunition, addressed to a Mr. Cullen at an address in Clontarf.

At Croke Park where our team beat Dublin, so that we were all in high spirits, I collected three of our lads and we went out to Clontarf. I entered the house and Mr. Cullen and his wife helped me to select the guns from a small arsenal they had behind the kitchen. We handed the guns and ammunition over the back wall of the garden to the three lads who were waiting. I then rejoined the latter and we carried the rifles through the streets. People we passed looked at us but, apparently, did not wonder very much. Such a sight was not unusual at this time. We had tea in the North Star Hotel, just across from the station, and we parked our rifles against the table. We wondered when we were in the train whether the police would try to take the guns from us when we got to Wexford. We had arranged for some of the boys to meet us. Tom Clarke had told us not to allow our guns to be taken, so we loaded them and when the train stopped at Wexford, we got the boys into the carriage and apportioned out our eight rifles. There were several policemen on the platform but they made no attempt to intercept us as we proudly marched out with our rifles on our shoulders.

These rifles, they were really carbines, were a hasty job. We had to correct all the sights. They were made in Birmingham and took ·303 ammunition. This was about the first consignment of the 300 rifles we had in the Wexford Brigade when the Rising started, by which time, outside of Dublin, we were the best armed county in Leinster. We had started making pikes also. A man named Judge in Dublin, who had been prominent in the Howth gun-running, printed a design for a pike but it was found to be

altogether too heavy. In Enniscorthy, Seumas Rafter kept
two forges busy night and day and Pat Keegan and Jim
Cleary forged hundreds of pikes. In Wexford, Pat Furlong,
a house painter, set up his own forge behind his workshop.
We never got a chance to use the pikes in the Rising, so
that the very much-debated question as to whether they
would have been any good to us, was never settled. In the
later stages of the war we did not think of them, as we
were thinking in terms of rifles, revolvers, grenades and,
later still, Thompson guns and land-mines.

The great war was only a short time under way when
the British authorities made the discovery that Wexford
might have to be taken seriously. They had posted a
warning notice that if the Germans landed in Ireland,
the farmers were to burn their fodder and drive their
livestock before them into the midlands. We never knew
whether the notice was what it purported to be, or
just another recruiting device. Everybody in Ireland, even
the British supporters, laughed at the plan. However,
we posted up hand-written notices to the effect that if the
Germans landed they would come as friends and that we
should, in the modern American phrase, give them the
glad hand. Of course, the police raided the houses of
those suspected of posting the notices and amongst them
was the house of Larry De Lacey in Enniscorthy.

What they found in the house astonished and alarmed
them. There were literally stacks of Roger Casement's
seditious pamphlet, *Ireland, Germany and the Freedom of the
Seas*. This had been printed secretly in the *Echo* office.
In addition, they found a collection of crude, home-made
grenades—cocoa tins filled with gelignite and scraps of
iron—as well as yards of fuse and hundreds of detonators.
Two men found in the house, Jack Hegarty and Jim Bolger,
were arrested, but De Lacey escaped. Bolger was my wife's
brother and he, like De Lacey and myself, was on the staff
of the *Echo*. Hegarty had been employed in the Cork
Post Office and he had been ordered by the British authorities to leave Cork because of his seditious activities. He
had come to Enniscorthy on a visit to De Lacey, a kindred
spirit.

The discovery and the arrests created a sensation. The Dublin newspapers gave the event big headlines. The two prisoners were kept *incommunicado* and they were whisked away in the dead of night to Arbour Hill barracks in Dublin. We learned that the opinion of the police was that they would be court-martialled and shot. I got orders from the Supreme Council of the I.R.B. that I was to go to Dublin to try to secure an interview with Bolger, and Una came with me. After many futile calls on various officials, we were directed to see Major Price, the Chief of the British Intelligence Service in Ireland. He had a very sinister reputation and all our Dublin friends warned us that we were to be very careful about what we said to him as he was dangerous. I was surprised to find that he was child's play. We saw him at the Headquarters of the Irish Command, near the entrance to the Phoenix Park. He was a tall handsome man with suave and polished manners and he was even polite to the orderly when he told him he wished to be alone with us.

I said that we had come up to see Bolger and told him of the relationship. He replied that the young man was in great danger and that he might be executed. He had been found sleeping in a house which was, undoubtedly, the headquarters of the rebels in the Wexford area. I protested that I was sure Bolger had nothing to do with any rebel movement, that he was a most law-abiding citizen and that he knew nothing of what was going on in that house.

" He's in bad company," said the Major.

" I am sure he was not aware of that," I replied.

" Very well," said the Major. " If that is so, you can see him. Get him to write down the names of all those who frequented that house. If he does that, he can go home with you. Will you promise me that you will ask him to do that ? "

" Sure I will," I replied.

So we saw Bolger and when I had conveyed to him the information that the Dublin men were raising a defence fund for him and that they were going to move heaven and earth to have them tried by jury, I said loud enough for anyone who might be listening to hear :

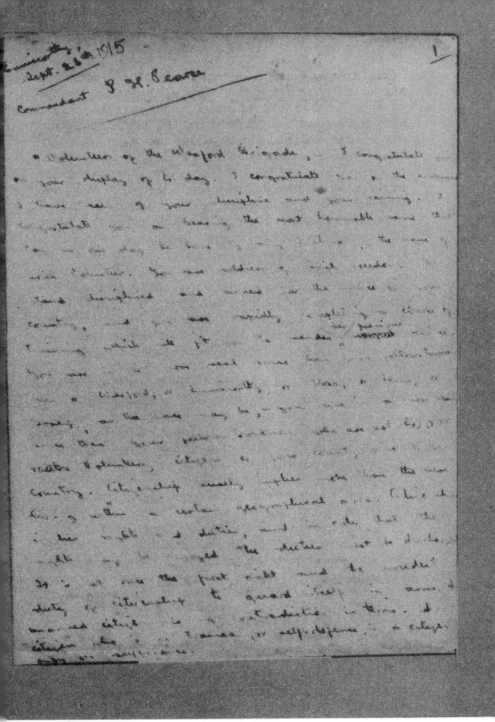

Enniscorthy
Sept. 26th 1915.

Commandant P. H. Pearse

Volunteers of the Wexford Brigade, — I congratulate ... your display of to-day. I congratulate ... of the ... I have ... of your discipline and your ... I congratulate you on bearing the most honourable name that can one day be ... , the name of Irish Volunteer. You are ... of a ... and disciplined and ... for the ... of your country, and you are rapidly ... training which will fit you to ...

You are ... and ... than you ... whether of Wexford, of Enniscorthy, or ... as the case may be, you are ... no more than your fellow-citizens who are not ... volunteers, citizens of ... country, of the ... country. Citizenship ... than the mere living within a certain geographical area. Citizenship ... rights and duties, and ... that the ... the duties must be discharged. It is ... the first right and the noblest duty of citizenship to guard itself in arms. An unarmed citizen is a contradiction in terms. A citizen who ... arms for self-defence, is a citizen ...

Padraig Pearse's address to the Wexford Brigade, Irish Volunteers,
at Vinegar Hill, 26th September, 1915.

Reproduced by courtesy of the owner of the original document, Seamus O Dubhghaill, and the National Museum of Ireland.

Eamon de Valera after the Surrender, Easter week, 1916.

" Major Price says that all you have to do to get out is to write down the names of all those who frequented that house."

He did not laugh though he knew my own name would be one of the first on the list.

" I couldn't do that," he said. " The only ones I saw there were ourselves. I always left early in the morning and got back late at night."

Subsequently, after two trials in which Tim Healy and Charlie Wyse Power appeared for the defence, the two were acquitted on all charges of treason, sedition, creating disaffection, etc. They had been charged, amongst other things, with knowing that the seditious literature and the explosives were in the house and with not informing the authorities. The jury found they were not guilty, though neither of the two men could get in or out of bed without climbing over stacks of the literature, and they could hardly move anywhere in the house without knocking over one of the pernicious cocoa tins. De Lacey's old housekeeper, shown the yards of fuse, said of course she had seen it. She had cut off a length of it to tie the little dog to the bed-post.

Tim Healy was largely responsible for the acquittal. He made it appear that Hegarty was being persecuted, not for his political activities, but for his religion. His plea was based on the fact that one of the witnesses for the prosecution, who testified that the pro-German notices were in Hegarty's handwriting, was a Belfast man who had himself, as he was forced to admit in cross-examination, preached in the streets of Cork with a Sankey and Moody band. Hegarty, said Tim, had been hounded out of his employment and out of his native city by the bigots who had come down from Belfast to insult the people of Cork by preaching against their religion. Tim made a great point of the fact that Hegarty, when he left Cork City, first went to Gougane Barra.

" This terribly dangerous man who is conspiring to bring about the downfall of the British Empire is driven out of Cork. Where does he go ? Is it to the great city where such subversive activities could be carried on ? No. He goes to Gougane Barra, the loneliest spot in all God's creation. The poet has testified to its loneliness." He proceeded to recite with great feeling J. J. Callanan's poem : " There is a green island in lone Gougane Barra."

Chapter Five

The Royal Irish Constabulary (R.I.C.) was not a mere police force. Its units, armed with rifles, occupied fortified posts in every town and village. Specially trained men kept close watch on the movements of all Nationalists. The British Chief Secretary for Ireland said that through the work of the R.I.C., he had Ireland under the microscope.

DURING this trial I had the experience one evening of seeing how severe Tom Clarke, usually very gentle in his personal relations, could be with any man who showed signs of weakening. There was a rumour to the effect that one of the big men of the I.R.B., who had been served with a deportation order, contemplated going to America. I went up to Tom's shop to see about some detail in connection with the trial. Tom mentioned the name of the man in question and asked me if I had seen him. I said I had not. Tom said he heard the man was in town and that he had sent for him. As he spoke the man entered—(let me call him Jack Smith). I knew that he and Tom had been associated in the extremist movement for upwards of a dozen years.

" Hello, Tom," he said.

Without any preliminary, Tom said :

" I hear that you are thinking of going to America, Jack. Is that true ? "

" Well, you see, Tom," said Jack rather lamely, " my affairs are not in the best of shape. If I am arrested, it will be bad. So I thought if I went to America for a little while——"

"All right," said Tom. " Goodbye, Jack."

He turned his back on Jack, who looked sheepishly at me and left the shop. Tom never spoke to him again.

Bolger was still in jail awaiting trial when one day I had an extraordinary experience. On returning from a walk, Una and I were told by our next-door neighbour that there had been a man knocking at our door several times. He was a stranger and he looked like a police officer in plain clothes. As deportation orders were being served on various suspects, I thought that this man might be the bearer of mine. Later that evening the man called. I brought him into the sitting-room and he himself closed the door.

" Can we be overheard ? " he asked.

I assured him we could not and he told me his name. It sounded like Harold. He said that I was recommended to him by Mr. Phillips, the chief reporter of the *Irish Times*, for which paper I was, at that time, the Wexford correspondent. The visitor went on to tell me that he had called first at my previous home, " Summerville," as that was the address Mr. Phillips gave him. His mission, he said, was a delicate one. As I was a reporter, I would find what he wanted me to do an easy task. No one but himself and myself would know what I was doing. He assumed I had heard the stories that were going about the activities of German submarines on the Irish coast and the rumours that they were getting supplies from the shore.

I was bewildered by all this, but I sparred for time, wondering whether he was an agent trying to trap me into some admission. I said that, of course, I had heard such stories and that I was positive that there was no truth in the rumours of help from the land, because the longshoremen were, as a rule, very anti-German. My visitor proceeded to say that what he wanted me to do was to investigate such rumours and to report to him what I found out. He said he was working for the Intelligence Division of the British Admiralty.

Naturally, I was dumbfounded, but I did not let him see it. I could not but reflect that if this proposal was genuine, the man was a very bad bungler. If he had asked the first policeman he met in the town who would be the last man he should approach with a proposition of this kind, the answer would have been myself.

" But surely," I said, " the police make such enquiries and they could keep you informed."

" I am not in touch with the police," he said. " I have had nothing to do with them since I resigned."

Suddenly it dawned on me who my visitor was.

" What did you say your name was ? " I asked.

" Harrell," he said.

" Oh, then you are Sir David Harrell ? "

" No," he said, " Sir David Harrell is my father."

" But you are the man who got into trouble over the Bachelor's Walk shooting ? "

" Exactly."

Commander William Vesey Harrell, the ex-Assistant Commissioner of the Dublin Metropolitan Police, the man who had been relieved of his post to save the face of the British Government over the butchery at Bachelor's Walk when the British soldiers had fired on the people of Dublin.

" You have my sympathy. Everybody believes you were made the scapegoat to save somebody's skin."

" That's exactly what happened," he said, " and now you can realise why I am not in touch with the police. My present work is entirely independent of them and they know nothing of my activities. I report direct to the British Admiralty."

I realised by this time that the man had made a genuine mistake. He had, for instance, gone to my former residence at " Summerville " and I recollected that that address was still being used by the *Irish Times*. Phillips, the chief reporter, no doubt knew nothing of my politics. To him, of course, I was just a provincial reporter.

Harrell went on to explain that all I had to do was to send the reports to the address he gave me in Monkstown, Dublin. I would be paid for my work as if it was ordinary newspaper work. I assured him that as there was nothing to these reports, it would be a waste of time and money, but he insisted that that was his concern. Before he left, he warned me not to say a word to anyone about his visit.

Una was aghast when I told her. She said that I should drop the whole thing right away, but I convinced her that I might be able to turn the business to account. I brought into consultation Sean Sinnott and Ned Foley, the local leaders of the Volunteers and the I.R.B., and told them my plan. I was going to get the authority of the Supreme Council of the I.R.B., to let me go ahead ostensibly as one of Harrell's agents. I would manage it so that I would win the confidence of the latter and, as time went on, we might, by working in with Germany, help to lead the British fleet into a trap. This may sound extravagant, but I managed to convince the lads, and a couple of days later I went to Dublin to lay the plan before Tom Clarke. It was the occasion of the O'Donovan Rossa funeral and, unfortunately, I failed to see either Tom Clarke or Sean MacDermott. However, I told the whole story to Sean T. O'Kelly and he promised to put the matter before Tom.

Two weeks passed and I had no word from Dublin. I had, however, a letter from Harrell asking for a report. I typed out a report saying that I heard such rumours as he had mentioned and that I had gone to Carne, Kilmore and other places on the coast and found there was no truth in the rumours. This report I sent him. A couple of days later, Sean T. came down and told me that Tom's advice was that I was to drop the whole thing at once like a hot potato.

I was terribly disappointed. I asked Sean T. if he had put forward all the arguments I had given him.

" I did," said Sean T., " and he says you are to drop it."

Not satisfied, I went to Dublin and saw Tom. He was adamant.

" The risk for you is too great," he said. " Even if you had a letter from the Supreme Council sanctioning this, something might get out in ten or fifteen years' time and all the water in the sea would not wash you clean."

I said I was willing to take that risk. He said he appreciated my motives and admired my self-sacrificing offer, but that he would not countenance it. He took me by the collar of the coat and glared at me, saying, " Drop it ! " Then he gripped me by the hand and gave me one of his rare smiles.

" We'll beat them without that," he said.

I received two pounds in postal orders from Harrell, and this went into our arms' fund. I also received a couple of further letters from him which I ignored. The strangest part of this story is to come.

The Rising was over, and I had spent more than a year in English prisons, and a spell in Cork prison. In 1918 I

was in Dublin occupying the prominent post of Chief of
the Sinn Féin Publicity Bureau when I got a letter re-
directed from my old address in Wexford. It was from
Harrell and it had been written about a week before. He
said that he would be in Wexford shortly, at White's Hotel,
and that he would look me up.

I immediately cycled out to Batt O'Connor's house in
Donnybrook to see Mick Collins. By an extraordinary
coincidence, Sean T. was there with Mick. I produced the
letter and told Mick the whole story. His attitude was very
different from that of Tom Clarke.

" You must go down to Wexford and meet him," he said.

Sean T. and I pointed out the impossibility of this course.
I was now something of a public character in Wexford and
I could not contact anyone like Harrell there without
everybody, including the police, knowing all about it and
thereafter Harrell would soon know all about me. We
agreed to get someone to act in my place, but by the time
we got our message through to Wexford, Harrell had come
and gone. I never heard from Harrell again, but Mick
put his letter to good purpose. He had Harrell's mail
intercepted, copied and re-posted. He had special techni-
cians in the post office doing such work for him. Mick
told me later that he had thus discovered all Harrell's
correspondents. He did not tell me what use he made of
the information. He probably enrolled some of them at
least in his own organisation. That was his way.

In March 1916 Pearse came to Enniscorthy and delivered
a public lecture. Our fellows attended from all over the
county. There was about this gathering an atmosphere
of impending crisis, which was heightened by the presence
of a guard of Volunteers in full uniform with rifles and
fixed bayonets, under the command of Captain Pat Keegan.
It was clear to every Volunteer who heard Pearse speak
that night that the struggle was coming very soon and, from
that time forward, we became rather grim about our preparations for the Rising. About a week later, Captain
Seumas O'Sullivan, an officer attached to G.H.Q., and
now of Limerick, came to Wexford. In the presence of the
Brigade Vice-Commandant, Sean Sinnott, he told me he had

a special order for me from Commandant Pearse. I was
to take the vacant position of Quartermaster of the Brigade
with the rank of Captain. Of course, I accepted at once,
but without elation. I had hitherto refused to take a commission. I did not like the business of soldiering and I had
strong doubts that I could ever be a good soldier. So I
had remained in the ranks. Now I was in for it, whether
I liked it or not. I had but the faintest idea what the
duties of a Brigade Quartermaster consisted of, but I did
what I could to increase our scanty supply of arms and we
had long bicycle rides nearly every night carrying guns,
ammunition and pikeheads, to the outlying towns and
villages.

For some time we had been collecting all the explosives
we could get our hands on, for the purpose of making
grenades. One day, Tom Treanor, the Assistant County
Surveyor, reported to me that there were about thirty
pounds of gelignite in a little shed in the front garden of
the courthouse. He arranged to leave the door of the
shed open for us that night. Ned Foley and I went down
about midnight to collect the stuff. We passed two policemen standing in silence in a gateway in the vicinity of the
courthouse and we had to make a detour. We managed
to get into the little courthouse garden after some nervous
fumbling with an iron gate. We had to be careful to make
no noise for fear of awaking the caretaker. It was fairly
dark and it was with difficulty we managed to keep off the
gravel walk. We got safely to the door of the shed when
misfortune befell us. Ned, thinking that the door opened
inwards, pushed it, and the lock clicked shut.

"Bedambut," said Ned.

He tried, in vain, to open the lock with various keys and
a penknife. We were both frozen into immobility when we
heard the ponderous feet of the two policemen approaching.
They stopped just outside the little gate.

"Be janey mack they have us," whispered Ned. I
clutched his arm, as much to steady my own nerves as his,
and I remember saying to myself that they must be strange
and wonderful men who take up burglary as a profession.
After what seemed an hour—it was really three minutes—

the two policemen moved away. When the sound of their footsteps seemed sufficiently remote, we moved away also.

Next day, I decided to get the stuff before it could be removed to the quarries that evening. So, at midday, I went down to the courthouse and asked one of the County Council clerks, Seumas Cadogan, for his key to the shed. I knew he kept his bicycle there. He looked at me for some time, a question on his lips. He did not ask it, but he handed me the key with a wry smile. I went to the shed and boldly entered it and picked up the gelignite, which was in a large brown-paper bag. It was much heavier than I expected and it grew heavier with every step I took. As I left the garden, I knew that the eyes of Seumas were on me from the window overhead, but I knew he would say nothing. As I walked along the quayside, I reflected that it was a most unusual thing for me to be carrying a brown-paper parcel and that it would be considered even more unusual if I were to be seen carrying it up the long lane that led from the quayside to my house. So I decided that I would not take the lane but that I would march boldly up Main Street. When I turned into Main Street, I felt that everybody must be looking at me and my brown-paper parcel, which by this time had become a ton weight. Almost the first person I met was the County Inspector of Police. This old fellow, knowing that I always avoided even a nodding acquaintance with any of the police, used to amuse himself by stopping me whenever he met me and jibing me good-naturedly about my pro-Germanism. He always had the same joke. I would be under the bed when the Germans came. He waddled over to me now, his eyes on my parcel.

" What devilment are you up to now ? " he asked, with his disarming smile. A few yards behind him, two members of his force were patrolling the street, their eyes also on me.

" You've a great chance now," I said to the Inspector, " this is a parcel of gelignite."

He burst into a loud guffaw and turned into John L. Doyle's newspaper shop.

" D'ye hear this, Doyle," he shouted, " this blackguard, Brennan, is going around with a parcel of gelignite ! "

I walked on past the two glowering policemen and got

my parcel safely home. But I arranged for the lads to take it away that night. I allowed that the Inspector would see through the joke when the loss of the gelignite would be reported. As it happened, it was never reported.

During all this time I was carrying on my ordinary work as, of course, were all the Volunteers. In the course of my duties as a reporter, I had to attend meetings of the public bodies and of the Courts and hardly a day passed but I had to report fulsome and false speeches lauding the British and reviling the Huns, heaping scorn and ridicule on the Sinn Féiners, the cowardly poltroons who looked on callously while little Belgium was being martyred. This was, of course, because all the councils were manned largely by followers of Redmond. But we managed to get some fun even out of this. On one occasion during a public meeting at the Redmond Monument, Peter French, the local M.P., was vigorously denouncing the enemies of the Party. He paused and raised his hand.

" The policy of the ostrich," he cried, and paused again.

A man in front of me who was very enthusiastic, concluded that the ostrich must be against the Party.

" To hell with him," he cried.

One day at the Quarter Sessions, the County Court Judge gave in himself an example of how war passions will transform the best of us. He was normally a kindly and courteous man with a very keen sense of humour. He had just adjourned a case to the following sessions, when the defendant, a poor old woman, in descending from the witness box asked when would the next sessions be held.

" Next September, ma'am," said the Judge, beaming at her.

" Oh, plaze God," she said, " the Germans will be here by that time."

She was already half-way to her seat before His Honour recovered from his astonishment.

" What's that," he cried, his face convulsed with fury, " bring her back here."

The poor woman was brought back.

" What's that you said ? " he shouted. " Did I hear you say that please God the Germans will be here by that time ? Why, madam, you might as well say the devils out of hell will be here by that time."

He launched into a terrific tirade against the Germans and then went on to deal with the Americans, the people who were " too proud to fight," an allusion to a famous statement of President Wilson's. Finally, he said he had reconsidered the adjournment of the case and it went against the defendant. The poor old woman was almost stunned. As she passed the press box, however, I heard her mutter :

" Well, maybe I'm right at that. Maybe by that time they will be here."

The poor people, particularly in the rural districts, had no fear of the Germans, despite all the propaganda. The old regime had not been particularly kind to them and perhaps a change would be for the best. But it was not that thought which influenced them so much as that if the Germans should come, the old oppressor would have been already beaten. Mellowes and I had an experience which showed that this was the idea.

We had been travelling in a motor car through Wicklow, over the route Mellowes hoped the Wexfordmen would take to reach Dublin when the Rising should come. Something went wrong with the car in the hills and two of the lads who were with us decided to walk to Bray to get help. Mellowes and I, having a couple of hours to wait, climbed a hill. Away up high we came to a farmer minding his sheep and we stopped to chat with him awhile. We praised the wonderful view of the sea and the mountains.

" Won't it be grand for the Germans when they see it," said the farmer. I remarked to him that he could not have been reading the papers for, according to them, the Germans had the most nefarious designs on Ireland and particularly on the Irish farmers.

" Why, they'll take all your land," I said.

" Well, we haven't very much," he said, " and we haven't had it very long. And in any case if the Germans get here, I'll know they'll be after batin' the other fella."

Mellowes was jubilant as we came down the hill. He kept repeating :

" ' They'll be after batin' the other fella.' There's poetry in them there words."

Chapter Six

Eoin MacNeill, Chairman of the Volunteer Executive and Chief of Staff, favoured defensive action only. Other Executive members determined there should be a Rising before the war ended, if only to redeem the National honour. MacNeill discovered their plans three days before the Rising was timed to start.

ON THURSDAY, April 20th, 1916, it was my turn to cover the Petty Sessions at Taghmon, seven miles from Wexford. The day was three days before Easter Sunday, but I did not think of that till afterwards. I went down to the office of Mr. M. J. O'Connor, solicitor, who was giving me a lift in his car. As we motored along Selskar Street, I saw a lady amongst the people who had arrived by the mail train from Dublin. I did not know that she was the bearer of a message that was to alter not only the course of my life, but that of everyone I knew.

O'Connor, at that time, was probably one of the most influential men in Ireland. He was the power behind the throne, the confidant and advisor of John Redmond. Through his influence, his brother James had become Solicitor-General for Ireland. I had occasion to say very little on the journey as O'Connor talked all the time, his subject being the futility of Sinn Féin and the Sinn Féiners. His shafts were pointed, but they were nearly always witty too. Nothing could shake the absolute determination of the Sinn Féiners to keep on talking about fighting. They were ready to die to the last man—in bed. Perhaps he should say that they were ready to die to the last German. God had given me some intelligence but, apparently, not enough to enable me to see on which side my bread was buttered.

" Not by bread alone—" I ventured. He laughed.

" I said butter, too."

We got back to Wexford about four o'clock and Una met me at the door.

" Have you heard the news ? " she asked, with elation. " You are going out on Sunday."

I cannot say that I was elated, but the relief the news brought was certainly tremendous. The last month had been a terrible strain, particularly since the order issued by MacNeill, the Chief of Staff, that we were to defend our rifles on any and all occasions, which meant for most of us, inviting war on our own homes. I saw Commandant Sean Sinnott immediately and he confirmed the news. The girl I had seen that morning in Selskar had brought him a message from Pearse. Ostensibly it was an order for furniture to be delivered on a certain date. Decoded, it meant that the Rising would start on Sunday at six o'clock.

Thursday night brought disquieting news, a rumour that all was not well in Dublin, because MacNeill was against the Rising. We were all very glum and we were particularly so the next day when a dispatch rider from Kilkenny arrived with the definite news that the Kilkenny Brigade would not come out since there was disagreement in the staff at G.H.Q.* As Kilkenny was to work in with us, this was a serious blow, but we determined that if a start was made in Dublin we would be in the fight. The succeeding three days were hectic, what with rumours and alarms and our feverish efforts to remedy our poor preparedness.

Sunday morning, however, dawned bright and fair. A shrewd observer in any of the Catholic churches might have guessed that there was something afoot because of the numbers of our fellows who received the Sacrament. As Una was to be out in the Rising as well as myself, we had brought our daughter Emer, then nearly six years old, to Coolnaboy, to stay with her grandmother. Una said goodbye to me on Sunday morning and set out for Enniscorthy where we were to meet again when I arrived with the Wexford Battalion.

We took advantage of the fact that there was a hurling and football fixture at Wexford Park and we ordered our lads from Wexford and vicinity to mobilise there at 5.30.

*It is only fair to say that the surviving leaders of the Kilkenny Volunteers know nothing of the contents of this dispatch. The Kilkenny men were mobilised under arms on Easter Sunday night and again on Easter Monday night only to be disbanded each time on the orders of General O'Connell.

We were to set out for Enniscorthy at six o'clock. Earlier
on Sunday I had the task of notifying such of our men as
had not yet received the mobilisation order. I was dismayed
to find that several had made up their minds not to come
out. I had underestimated the effect of the disastrous
rumours we had heard of dissension at G.H.Q.

At five o'clock I was at the Park Gate making a mental
note of the little groups that were assembling here and
there in the Sports Field and on the roadway outside, when
Myley Redmond, a lieutenant in one of the Wexford Companies, came racing up on his bicycle.

" The whole thing is off," he said, " Commandant-
General O'Connell is in town. He says the Rising has been
called off."

" Where's General O'Connell ? " I asked.

" He's down in Sean Sinnott's house."

I cycled down to Sean's house, where O'Connell confirmed Myley's message. The whole thing had been called
off. I said we had heard that MacNeill was against the
Rising, but what about Pearse and Clarke and the others.

" They wanted to go on," said O'Connell, " but they all
agreed to call it off."

There was nothing we could do but stand around sunk
in the deepest gloom. I thought it was the end because
now we would all be arrested and there would be no chance
of doing anything in our time. They were all talking, but
I was afraid to say anything for fear I should begin to cry
while they thought I was being strong and silent. I walked
down to my mother's house, forgetting I had a bicycle.
Two policemen followed me, but I barely noticed the fact.
I was utterly deflated and I suppose that because of the
reaction I was showing the effects of the strain I had been
under, for my mother asked me what was the matter. I
told her, and instead of upbraiding me, she said :

" Never mind. God is good. You'll find everything
will come out for the best. Go upstairs and say a prayer
to the Sacred Heart and then lie down and get a sleep.
You are dead out."

I lay down but could not sleep. A line of Rooney's kept
running round and round in my brain :

All the bright dreamings we cherished
Went down in disaster and woe.

At nine o'clock a messenger arrived to say an order had been received from Pearse postponing the Rising.

Next morning, the Dublin papers carried MacNeill's order cancelling all movements of Volunteers over the week-end. The *Independent* stated that the order had been published in the later issues of the Sunday edition. In the late-news column there was a report that a mysterious stranger had been arrested on the Kerry coast. He had presumably landed from a submarine, as a collapsible boat had been found in the vicinity. I guessed it was Casement.

Una returned from Enniscorthy on the morning train. She said the opinion there, too, was that now there would be wholesale arrests and that meant goodbye to the Irish Republic.

However, at two o'clock, John Barker sent for me.

" Did you hear," he asked, " that Dublin has been cut off for the past two hours ? "

" What do you mean by cut off ? "

" There are no telephones or telegrams. No one can get in touch with Dublin. I had it from the *Free Press* office."

I hurried down to the newspaper office and learned from Willie Corcoran, the proprietor of the *Free Press*, that the news was correct. He knew nothing definite, but there were rumours that those damn fool Sinn Féiners were fighting. I rushed down to Stafford's workshop.

" Dublin is out ! " I said to Sean Sinnott.

" If so," said Sean, throwing down the saw he was using, " we're out too."

He told me I was to find Lieutenant Myley Redmond, get him to mobilise the lads for nine o'clock that night and help him to do so. Later in the evening I was on my rounds when I got word I was to go at once to Sean Sinnott's house. I did so and found General O'Connell there. He had been to Borris in the meantime. He said we were not to stir. What had happened was that Connolly had made a mess of things by going out at the head of a handful of the Citizen Army men. The Volunteers were standing firm. He said he had got this news in a dispatch he had

received at Borris. I argued that the Volunteers would
never allow the Citizen Army to go out alone. By this
time they too would be out. He was positive they were not.

" Well if you are right," I said, " there should be a train
in from Dublin in an hour or so. There should be news
then."

He agreed and we all adjourned to my house where
Seumas Doyle, the Adjutant of the Brigade, who had come
from Enniscorthy, was waiting for us. I set out for the
railway station just before ten o'clock when the Dublin
train was due to arrive. As soon as I stepped outside the
house, I saw there were groups of the Royal Irish Constabulary standing about here and there in the vicinity.
I was surprised to find I was quite cool. I had my revolver
ready to hand and I was determined to fire should they
attempt to arrest me. I counted the number of police within
view. There were twelve, but I noticed others lurking in
the doorways. I returned to the house and told the others.
It was urged I should not go out alone, but I held that if
two or more of us appeared, they would be more likely to
try to take us.

" They probably know you are all here and have the
house surrounded, so they will be in no hurry to fight outside over one man, and in any case they are probably
waiting too for the news the train will bring."

When I entered the railway station, there were few people
about. The station-master, Mr. Farrell, and a plain-clothes
policeman named Sloan, were talking in the office.

" What time will the train be in, Mr. Farrell ? " I asked
cheerfully.

" What time will the train be in," he echoed, " maybe
you could tell me."

" What's up ? "

" What's up ! These bloody friends of yours in Dublin
are shooting up the place."

" Good Heavens, you don't say so ? "

Sloan spoke up. " It's a bad business, Mr. Brennan,"
he said.

" You should not complain," I said. " You have been
following me about for the past couple of years and you

won't have to do it any more. To-morrow you'll get a
chance of taking a shot at me, with you behind one ditch
and me behind another."

"Well, Mr. Brennan," he said with great sincerity,
"whatever happens, I would like you to believe that I
never did you any harm and I never will."

I turned to the station-master.

"You would never think," I said, "that he has probably
given them enough evidence to hang me."

"Damn it, man," said Farrell, "this is no laughing
matter. This is gone beyond a joke. And who the hell
is talking about hanging anyway?"

After some coaxing, he told me that there was a train
on the line, that it was making slow time, and that it might
be in by two o'clock, not before. I returned home rather
jubilant. If the Citizen Army alone had gone out, they
could not have caused such dislocation. As I approached
my house, I saw that the police were still about.

"Good night, men," I called to them, and got no reply.
They must have noticed my awkwardness in opening the
door. I had to use my left hand as I had my revolver
grasped in my right-hand pocket. Inside the house, all
except O'Connell shared my view of the Dublin situation.
We argued over the question till shortly before two o'clock,
when I set out for the station again. As the street lamps
had now been extinguished, it was pretty dark, so I walked
straight from the door onto the roadway and kept in the
middle of the road. I did not want to be grabbed at from
a doorway. The police did not speak, but one or two of
them coughed derisively.

Only the station-master, Farrell, and the detective, Sloan,
were at the station. They had no more news, they said.
The train arrived in about ten minutes. A lone passenger
alighted. She was an old woman who sold apples and
oranges from a basket. She ran down the platform yelling :
"Oh, let me get home! The murderin' rascals! Let
me get home!"

I ran to the guard's van.

"What's up, John?" I said to John Doyle, the guard.

"What's up!" he said jovially. "Why, the Sinn

Féiners are up. They've taken the railway station and the post office and everything. They've taken Dublin Castle ! We had to get a permit from Countess Markievicz to get this train out."

Sloan, who had followed me into the van, asked in a frightened voice :

" Have they taken the Castle ? "

" Sure they have," said John, " they've taken everything."

The detective and I went through the exit together, both running. A surprise awaited me at the house. The police were gone. To make sure, I scouted round a bit. O'Connell refused to believe the news. He suggested that my enthusiasm accounted for some of the details. Somebody's enthusiasm, or imagination, must have been responsible for the bit about Dublin Castle, as we afterwards found out, but the invention was not mine. Finally, O'Connell said that whatever the position was, he was not going to countenance any movement until he got a definite order from Dublin, and that he was going to bed. He did. The rest of us, after a consultation, decided to start as soon as we could get the fellows mobilised. Before leaving for Enniscorthy, Seumas Doyle decided to have another try with O'Connell and, after a while, he came downstairs to say the latter was getting up and that he was coming out with us. He was going to Enniscorthy with Seumas. Before they left, we sent a man to Rosslare Harbour to wreck the railway line at the viaduct so as to hamper the movements of any reinforcements for the British who might be coming from England by that route.

At six in the morning, Sean Sinnott and I started out for the rendezvous, John Furlong's house at Skeeterpark, on the side of the Three Rock Mountains. It began to rain as we pushed our bicycles up the steep hill past the reservoir. It was a persistent drizzle and we were soon wet to the skin. It was a depressing start. We were cheered, however, when we came to Tom Fielding's house. Tom was the Lieutenant of the local company. His uncle, Phil Doyle, was in the yard " spronging " manure into a cart. He was a retired contractor and builder and he had always been a strong supporter of John Redmond.

" God bless the work," we called out. Phil leaned on his "sprong" and stared at us.

" You too," he said. " What's up ? "

" Dublin is up," said Sean, and I added, " Dublin Castle is in the hands of the Irish."

" The Lord be praised," said Phil, taking off his hat. He turned to the house and called : " Tom ! Tom, come out ! Get your gun and come out."

Tom came running out and we had to tell him again. He shouted in delight and Sean told him we were on our way to John Furlong's house.

" Jack [his brother] and I will be there in two shakes," said Tom.

As we were mounting our bicycles, Phil Doyle called out :

" Tare an' ouns, you're not going like that. Come in and have something."

" We haven't time," said Sean.

" Well, the blessings of God be on you," called Phil. He had forgotten all about the Parliamentary Party.

When the little mountain road brought us to the main road—the Duncannon line—neither of us knew whether John Furlong's house lay to the right or left. We saw a young lad of about twelve outside a labourer's cottage and we asked him where John Furlong lived. He said he did not know. This was unbelievable for we knew the house must be only three or four hundred yards away.

" Do you know anybody of the name of Furlong around here ? " asked Sean.

" Not around here. There are Furlongs across the other side of the mountain in Barntown."

We mounted our machines and rode off, but we had not gone twenty yards when the boy hailed us. We dismounted and he ran up to us.

" You wouldn't be Captain Sinnott ? " he said to Sean.

" Yes, that's who I am."

"Aw, now I know," said the lad, with a wide grin. " Why didn't you tell me who you were. You might be anybody, the police or anybody. Sure I know where John lives. Why wouldn't I ? It's the second next house you come to on the left."

We thanked the boy and rode on. When we entered
Furlong's haggard we saw John and his mother in the
kitchen. John came to the door and his mother peered
over his shoulder.

" Hello, boys," called John.

Sean jerked his head, beckoning him.

" I want a word with you, John," he said.

" Come on in," said John, " you can shout out loud
anything you have to say here." He grinned broadly and
asked : "Are we going out ? "

" We are," replied Sean.

" I thought so by the look o' you," said John cheerfully.
His mother felt our clothes.

" Glory be to God," she said, " the creatures are drowned.
Take off your wet clothes and dry them at the fire." There
was a blazing fire of furze branches. The old woman
went on :

" So you are going out. Thanks be to God I lived to see
this day."

This old woman had three sons and all three of them
were going out to risk their lives or liberty in what had for
ages been a forlorn cause and her words were : " Thanks
be to God I lived to see this day." In my own experience
in 1916 I encountered hundreds of women whose men—
husbands or sons, brothers or lovers—were involved and,
with one or two exceptions, no woman tried to hold her
man back. This is a different picture from that of the
querulous, weeping women one sees depicted in story, stage,
and screen versions of the various Risings. I suppose there
is more dramatic value in the picture of the man going out
despite the wails of his adoring wife or sweetheart.

Mrs. Furlong gave us dry socks, and we dried ourselves
piecemeal at the roaring fire and ate a hearty breakfast.
After a while the lads began to drop in and one of the first
was the boy we had encountered on the road. He proudly
carried a huge fowling-piece on his shoulder. John Furlong,
who had heard our story about him, began to rag him.

" So you nearly sent the Captain astray, Tom."

" Indeed an' I didn't," said the boy, sitting down at the
fire and holding the gun between his knees. " I was only

gaugin' them. How did I know but what they might be peelers comin' for you."

"And what are you going to do with that big gun ? "

"Ah, John," he protested, " you know well enough. Didn't you promise me that when we were going out you'd give me a carbine for the fowling-piece. You know well enough you did."

" But who told you we were going out ? "

The boy's face fell.

" Don't say you're not going out ! "

"And if we were itself, you're too young to come with us."

" I'm not. I'm thirteen."

I broke in. " What does your mother say ? "

" She said I'm big enough to go out with yous. She says sure if I can't do anything else, then I can boil the spuds for the fighting men."

" It's damn few boiled spuds we'll get," said John with a grin.

Pat Furlong, John's brother, who had cycled out from town, told us to leave the boy alone and the boy, Tom Stafford, showed his gratitude by standing up and gravely saluting.

Perhaps I better tell the story of Tom Stafford's capture here. After the Rising, when we had surrendered, the police carried out a very thorough drive in the neighbourhood of the Three Rock Mountains. They were searching for the arms which they believed had been hidden there. During the raid, Tom Stafford was taken outside his mother's house by two policemen and told he would have to divulge the whereabouts of the arms. Tom said he knew nothing about them. The sergeant said that if he did not tell he would be shot.

"All right," said Tom, " shoot away."

" Very good," said the Sergeant, " you're leaving me nothing else to do." He ordered the constable to level his rifle at Tom. " Now," he said, " if you don't tell me before I count ten, it will be too late." Tom looked towards the window where he could see his mother. She was kept inside the house by another policeman. He heard her voice, faintly, " Tell them nothing, Tom." The sergeant began

to count very slowly. He halted at nine and said to Tom :
" Well now is your last chance." Tom said, " Why don't
you shoot ? " The sergeant motioned to the constable to
lower his rifle.

" It's no use," he said.

When the police had gone away, Tom's mother took him
in her arms. She was crying.

" Were you afraid they would kill me, mother ? "

" I was," she replied ; " but I was more afraid you
might tell."

" Much chance of that," said Tom.

The moment he arrived, Pat Furlong got busy. He
brought down from the loft pike-heads and shafts, and
proceeded to put the pikes together. He had hammered
on the heads of thirty or forty when he looked up at me
with a grin.

" There's not many living men," he said, " who can say
they have struck as many blows for Ireland as I have."

All that long dreary rainy day the boys kept coming in
from districts all over South Wexford. The Rathangan
and the Bannow men had cycled some fifteen miles in the
drenching downpour. As soon as they arrived, they collected carts and horses from the neighbouring farms for
the march to Enniscorthy, and there was only one case
where there was an unwillingness to give.

Chapter Seven

The Rising, originally fixed for the 23rd of April, began in Dublin on the 24th. British artillery wrought great destruction on the city, the centre of which was in flames when the insurgents surrendered on the 29th

SEAN SINNOTT returned to Wexford during the day to make a survey of the situation in the town. This was because Lieutenant Myley Redmond had reported that the police had withdrawn from the streets, apparently expecting an attack. Later, Sean sent me word that it would be risky for the Wexford men to venture out before nightfall as they might be surrounded and their guns taken.

During the evening, the neighbouring boys and girls dropped into Furlong's house and there was a real old-fashioned hooley. If any of them feared disaster and woe from the coming events, they showed no sign of it. There was the care-free lightheartedness one always finds in a dance in the Irish countryside, the same good friendly repartee and even the same lugubrious songs. One boy sang an interminable ballad entitled " The Grand Dissolving View."

We had set ten o'clock as the zero hour to start for Enniscorthy. We had hoped to be able to take Killurin Police Barracks on the way, but we knew that would be difficult now as the element of surprise was ruled out. These barracks, as subsequent events showed, were substantial structures capable of being defended by a few men against heavy odds, unless they were taken by surprise.

At a quarter to ten, we all knelt down and Pat Furlong, invoking a blessing on our efforts in the coming struggle for the freedom of our country, gave out the Rosary. The prayers were finished and we were forming up to march off when someone shouted that Myley Redmond had arrived with a despatch. Myley ran in at the same time and said out loud :

" General O'Connell has sent an order from Enniscorthy : ' Don't stir. Dublin is smashed. The British landed

61

a division of troops in Kingstown yesterday and the fight
is lost.' "

There was nothing I could do but dismiss the men even
had I wished to do otherwise.   I could see that the effect
of the message was disastrous.   I addressed the men, saying
that the news might be true and it might not ; that they
were to return to their homes and safeguard their weapons
and maybe I would be able to send them a different message
on the following day.   I have never seen men more disconsolate as they went their various ways.

In the morning, I cycled down the hill into Wexford
and, as Una had again gone to Enniscorthy, I went to my
mother's house for breakfast.   When she saw me she said :

" You're not out ? "

" No."

" Why not ? "

" We were sent back."

"And your lads in Dublin are fighting with their backs
to the wall."

Now, she had always been against my getting mixed up
in the movement.   Over and over again she had inveighed
against my participation.   " There will be nothing for you
in it," she said, " but heartbreak and misery.   The people
you are fighting for will stand by and see you hanged or
jailed.   Look at Robert Emmet.   The people deserted him.
Look at Parnell.   You're not the sort to take this up and
get out of it easy.   Give it up in time."

And here she was now upbraiding me for not doing what
God knows I was longing to do.

" What happened ? " she asked.

" There were orders and counter-orders.   There is no
one to give us the order to go out."

" Why don't you give the order ? "

" I have no authority."

Then she said :

" Go up there to the room and kneel down in front of
the Sacred Heart and you'll get your authority."

I did not tell her what I meant to do—to get to Enniscorthy and see what could be done there.   It was the only
place in Wexford where we now had a chance.   We had

three hundred men there. I was amazed to learn, from all
we could hear, that Dublin was still fighting gallantly and
that there was no sign of surrender. I heard that Una
had arrived from Enniscorthy and I went home. To my
surprise, General O'Connell was there, after travelling
with her from Enniscorthy. O'Connell and I had a bitter
quarrel and he left. Subsequently, someone told me that
he was on his way to the South Station to take a train for
Waterford. I cycled to the station and found him just as
the train was about to start. I asked him not to try to stop
the Waterford and Kilkenny men from joining us if we
rose. He said he would have me court-martialled. As
the train steamed out I was threatening to have him court-
martialled. Of course this was mutiny, but I did not see
it like that at the time. And, indeed, the action of the
insurgents in Dublin might have been construed as mutiny
also, but the Irish people condoned it if such it was.

From Tony Mulvey—(Mr. A. J. Mulvey, afterwards
M.P. for Tyrone)—a fellow-reporter who was in our confidence, I learned that a strong detachment of British troops
were on their way from the Curragh to Wexford and also
that reinforcements for the British were coming from
England via Rosslare to attack Dublin. This news made
it imperative for me to get to Enniscorthy. Instead of being
confined to barracks, as they had been the previous day,
the police were now swarming all over the place. I feared
an attempt might be made to arrest me before I could leave
town. Any attempt to procure a car I knew would invite
arrest and to cycle out might lead to the same result. I
prepared my usual news report for the *Echo* and, with
Mulvey, I went down to the railway station to send it on
the Dublin-bound mail train, which was the usual procedure. Having registered my letter, I remained chatting
with Mulvey and a few other people who were waiting for
the train to depart. Constable Sloan and several other
policemen were on the platform. I knew they were closely
watching me and I made a pretence of not seeing them.
The guard blew his whistle and the train began to move.
It was already well under way when I jumped on the foot-
board of the train, opened a compartment door and stepped

in. The look of surprise on the faces of the policemen was comical.

The sensational news they heard in Wexford next morning was that Enniscorthy was Up and, of course, they attributed the blame, or the credit, to me. It belonged more to Seumas Doyle and Sean Etchingham and their Enniscorthy comrades.

The moment I arrived in Enniscorthy, I found that everybody was of the opinion that we should come out, orders or no orders. Seumas Doyle, the Adjutant of the Brigade, told me that Etchingham was in town. He had met him on the bridge, about to cycle to Dublin to get into the fight. Doyle, Etchingham, Seumas Rafter and a few more of us met and decided to act at once regarding the news I had brought of reinforcements for the British from the south. We sent two men out to take up sections of the railway line so as to prevent any British troop movements from the south. After a couple of hours, word came in that these two men had been ambushed by the police from Oylegate and that, after a gun battle, they had been captured. We immediately sent out orders to mobilise the Volunteers. Towards nightfall, Brigade Commandant Paul Galligan arrived from Dublin, whither he had gone for instructions. He had seen James Connolly and the latter told him we were not to leave Wexford County, but we were to prevent, as far as we could, any reinforcements for the British passing through our territory. Galligan at once confirmed our action in mobilising. The town was occupied without incident, the police retiring to their barracks. Some three hundred men reported at once for duty and we made the Athenaeum our headquarters. Seumas Doyle wrote and posted the notice proclaiming the Republic. A train arrived from Wexford and we took possession of this and held it under steam ready for the emergency of our being ordered to Dublin. We posted a notice ordering in all arms in possession of private citizens and it was surprising to see the motley array of weapons which resulted. The country houses, whose owners were unwilling to comply with this order, were raided by our men and all arms found collected. Within a couple of hours the Cumann na mBan, under the command of Mary White, had organised very efficient food kitchens and first-aid stations.

Michael De Lacey undertook to form a volunteer police force, and such was its success that not a single disorderly incident occurred during the time of our occupation. We issued food tickets to the families of the men who were out and ordered the shopkeepers to honour them, and I heard of no instance in which there was any abuse in this matter. On a report that some of our men were beginning to indulge in liquor, we closed all the public-houses and made it a penal offence for anyone to sell liquor. One offender was arrested and had the keys of his premises confiscated. Indeed, there was such an absence of disorder during the whole period that when, several days later, we had agreed to surrender, a deputation consisting of the Chairman of the Town Commissioners and several private citizens came along to us to voice their admiration and praise. Mr. Roche, whose castle adjoining the Athenaeum we had occupied, also came along to assure me that he had found everything in the castle undisturbed. I am dwelling on this because after I came out from prison, I was shown a magazine article written by Moira O'Neill which gave a fantastic and mischievous account of our depredations.

We did not try to take the police barracks. Our men fired a few shots to isolate the building, which we hoped would surrender owing to lack of provisions before we should evacuate the town. We were anxious to get the arms and ammunition it contained.

Commandant Galligan occupied Ferns and the surrounding area. The police vacated this section and were concentrating on Arklow. We got word that British forces, to the number of two thousand, had arrived in Wexford and that they had outposts as far as Ferrycarrig bridge, three miles north of the town. Recruits were pouring into our ranks so fast that we could hardly handle them, not merely from Enniscorthy, but from practically every town and village in North Wexford. Apart from this, we were constantly getting messages, like the following from the priest at Marshallstown : " I have two hundred men assembled in Marshallstown. We have fifty shot-guns and the rest have only pitchforks. We are all ready when you want us."

A comical incident I recall in connection with the " separation " women—the name given to the wives of the men who were fighting in the British forces and who were getting a separation allowance from the British authorities. A deputation of them came to us and pointed out that as the post office was closed, they could not get their allowances. We decided that they should get permits for provisions similar to those given to the families of our own men. Shortly afterwards, I overheard two of them talking as they came out of a provision shop carrying parcels. I expect that the allowance was more generous than they had been getting, because one of them said to the other :

" Glory be to God, Katie, isn't this a grand government."

On Friday, a deputation of three, consisting of Rev. Father Fitzhenry, Adm., the Chairman of the Town Commissioners and Mr. Buttle, a prominent local merchant, asked to be allowed to go to Wexford for the purpose of discussing terms with a Colonel French, the Officer Commanding the British forces there. We told them we would allow nothing of the sort. They then asked for permits to leave the town and, of course, we could not refuse this. They returned on Saturday bearing with them a special edition of one of the Wexford papers which contained, in block type, an account of Pearse's surrender in Dublin. They said they had discussed the situation with Colonel French, who was very anxious to come to terms with us. The deputation was satisfied that the terms would not be too severe.

We refused to consider the matter on the grounds that, firstly, we had no knowledge that Pearse had surrendered, apart from a newspaper report and that we were sufficiently acquainted with British methods to know they would stoop to such a device to undermine our morale, and, secondly, we were going to fight it out anyway.

The deputation asked me if I was willing to take the responsibility of having the town of Enniscorthy shelled. They were aware the British had field-guns and that they would shell the town if we resisted. I assured them they need have no fear because we would not defend the town, we would take to the hills.

In all this we had several things to consider. One was genuine doubt about the Dublin surrender and another was that even if the news were true, we had a group which included Pat Keegan, Mat Holbrook, Jack Lacey, Jim Cleary, etc., who would not surrender lightly, if at all.

When the deputation withdrew, we debated the whole matter for a long time and finally decided that we should hold out for a verbal order from Pearse. Accordingly, I wrote a letter to Colonel French stating that if it were true that Pearse had surrendered and was now a prisoner in the hands of the British, it would be an easy matter for them to arrange that two of our officers should see him. If this were agreed to, Captain Doyle and Captain Etchingham were ready to go to Dublin for the purpose. This epistle had a real international tone, being addressed from Irish Republican Headquarters, Enniscorthy, to Colonel French, commanding the British forces in Wexford.

Here I might mention one of the two characteristics which differentiated the Easter Week Rising from all previous attempts during one hundred and twenty years. There was no disposition to try to avoid the consequences of defeat. To none of us did it occur that we should try to escape. In all previous attempts when our people were beaten they scattered and fled the country, in many cases, no doubt, in the hope of lying low for the time being and renewing the fight later. I have tried to find a reason for this difference and the only thing I can ascribe it to is the new spirit of independence in the individual inculcated by the teachings of the Gaelic League. The other characteristic I might also mention, and that was that we had laid the ghost of the informer. In every previous rising, the British Government had been kept well informed. This time they were completely blinded. All our officers, and many of the men throughout Ireland, knew of the impending Rising on the Thursday of the previous week and yet Dublin Castle was taken completely by surprise by the event.

The deputation carried this letter to Wexford and they

returned late on Saturday night. To our amazement, they carried a letter from Colonel French agreeing to our proposal, thus disposing of any doubt we may have had about Pearse's surrender. The letter set a new headline by giving us our military titles and even alluding to " Commandant Pearse." I had been hoping they would not fall in with our demand and thus give us the excuse of retiring to the hills and continuing the fight as so many of our men wanted to do. There was now nothing for it but to let Seumas Doyle and Etchingham go to Dublin, and they set out straightway for Ferrycarrig where the British were to take them over. The deputation had said that Colonel French had taken it for granted we would not attack any British posts while awaiting the return of the two officers and we had agreed to this.

On Sunday morning I was at my post in the Athenaeum when Jack Lacey, one of the most active of the militant group in Enniscorthy, came in to me in a state of the most violent agitation and dashed his cap to the ground.

" In the name of God ! " he cried, " is this what we've been working for for the last three years ? "

" What's up ? " I asked.

" Come here," he said and led the way to the front door.

There was great commotion in the street. An open motor car was drawn up in front of the Athenaeum and an angry crowd, many Volunteers amongst them, surrounded it. There were cries of " Pull them out and lynch them ! " Seated in the car, which bore a white flag, were four persons. One was Father Owen Kehoe, the parish priest of Camolin, an old friend whose sympathies were with us ; the other three were plain-clothes policemen, one of whom everybody recognised as a special political detective who had recently been transferred from Enniscorthy. He had a particularly bad reputation. As I reached the door, I saw this man, who was white with fear, make a significant motion. His hand stole towards his inside breast-pocket. I realised he was reaching for a revolver and that there was no time to be lost. If he fired nothing could save him and his comrades. I saw one of our officers trying to keep back the crowd. I addressed Father Kehoe in a loud voice.

" What's the meaning of this ? " I asked.

" I don't know," he replied. " I was asked to accompany these men to see you under a flag of truce."

I turned to the Volunteer officer :

"Arrest these men ! " I said loud enough for all to hear. " Place them in the guard-room and report to me."

Now there was no guard-room, and the officer knew that as well as I did, but he behaved as if there was. He beckoned to two of his men and they hurried the occupants of the car through the doorway and down the hall. He placed them in a dressing-room at the rear of the premises, left his two men on guard and returned to me.

" You did that well," he said, " but do you think we ought to keep the priest down there? He wants to speak to you."

" I'll see him after a while."

" What are you going to do, court-martial them ? "

" I'll court-martial you."

" For what ? "

" For not disarming them."

" But they had no arms."

"All right, we'll see. Bring them up here."

In a few moments they all filed into the room.

" Disarm these men," I said to the Volunteer officer.

" Hand over your guns," he said.

Two of them sheepishly produced their revolvers and handed them over.

" What about you ? " I said to the third.

" I've no gun," he said and turned to me. " My name is Barney McGovern, I'm the District Inspector at Arklow. I was directed to come here and give you this order from Commandant Pearse."

He handed me a paper which purported to be a written order from Pearse telling us to surrender or disperse. I read the document and handed it back to him. I said :

" We are aware of the contents of this document. Two of our men have gone to Dublin to see if it is authentic. Meanwhile there is an armistice between our forces and those of the enemy, but I do not think that will prevent me from dealing with your two men here as they deserve. I have no option but to detain you all here under guard pending their trial."

" My God ! " said McGovern, " what for ? "

" For transgressing the laws of war by coming in here under a flag of truce while bearing arms."

" Good heavens ! " said McGovern, "you don't mean it."

" You'll see," I said, " as soon as I can convene the court-martial I shall have them tried and shot."

None of them pointed out that I was sentencing them before trial. Instead, Father Kehoe said :

" Could we go to Mass ? We're all Catholics."

I agreed, on their giving an undertaking they would not try to escape or communicate with anyone. They had a strong escort to Mass and back to the Athenaeum. Father Kehoe sent a message saying he wanted to see me. When he came in he asked me whether I was still determined to shoot the two policemen. I replied that I was.

" There's only one point I would put," he said, " what good would it do our cause ? "

Then I was forced to show my hand.

" To-morrow," I said, " if this order of Pearse's is authenticated we shall have to surrender, at least so far as the officers are concerned. Our men will be left unprotected. Their lives may be forfeit because of the evidence those two men will be able to give. I cannot take that chance."

" Let me speak to the D.I. about this," he asked.

" That will do no good."

" Let me try."

"All right."

After a while, the D.I. sent word he wanted to speak to me, but I let him wait for two hours. Then I allowed them to hear a rumour that the court-martial was assembling. I got a note from the D.I.

" For God's sake," it said, " let me talk to you."

I had him brought in and the poor man was desperately in earnest.

" I have never broken my word," he said, " but I'm not asking you to take my word. I'm willing to go down on my knees in the presence of the priest and swear that

Wexford, April 29th, 1916.

Sir,

I am in receipt of your communication ... and the same ... by no superior authority.

I am desired to inform you that if Cmdon James Doyle and Captain James ... whether surrender themselves to me at the R.I.C. Barrack ... Wexford I will send them up to Dublin under military escort ... to their communicating with Commandant Pearse ... they will proceed by Motor Car from Wexford to Dublin. The ... will be met at ... Bridge by ... military ... and conducted to ... known body ...

I herewith enclose a copy of the terms ... these conditions now laid ... to-day ... upon ... lines.

I have the honour to be

Your Obedient Servant,

R. A. French
Colonel,
O.C. British Troops Wexford.

Capt. Robert Brennan.

Letter from Colonel French, O.C. British Troops in Wexford, to Captain Robert Brennan, arranging interview with Commandant Pearse after the Surrender in Dublin, April, 1916. It will be noted that the "rebel" officers are given their military titles.

[National Museum of Ireland]

The Castle, Enniscorthy.

neither of these men will give any evidence direct or indirect or divulge anything of what they have seen here."

I pretended to hold out and finally I went through the process of relenting.

I gave them an escort out of the town and I am glad to say that the D.I.'s promise was kept.

Nothing that I did during the Rising caused me as much subsequent embarrassment as did this incident. Barney McGovern, the District Inspector, apparently gave a glowing account of what he called my magnanimity and, when I returned to Wexford the following year, policemen I had never known used to stop me in the street to tell me how much they appreciated my action in saving the lives of Barney McGovern and his two men.

Late that night, Seumas Doyle and Etchingham returned. They had interviewed Pearse in Arbour Hill Barracks and he had confirmed the order. Seumas said Pearse was very grave. He had said to him, apparently as one reason for the surrender, " They (the British) shot down women and children in the streets. I saw them do it."

Chapter Eight

Owing to MacNeill's countermanding order, the Rising was confined to Dublin and two or three other isolated districts.

OF course, there was nothing we could now do but surrender, but I tried to get the condition that whereas the six officers amongst us would surrender unconditionally for themselves, the men should be allowed to go unmolested. The deputation carried a letter to this effect to Wexford and when they returned they said this condition had been granted but Colonel French had said he could not give them a letter embodying it, and this caused me to doubt if it would be carried out.

Meanwhile, we had a very tough job persuading the Enniscorthy men to agree to surrender. They wanted, rightly or wrongly, to fight it out in the hills. Finally, we succeeded in convincing them that we had to obey Pearse's explicit order.

It was arranged late on Sunday night that we were to assemble at 2 p.m. on the following day for the formal surrender. We had got an undertaking that the military and not the police would take the surrender. Colonel French kept the letter of his undertaking by taking the surrender himself, but we were almost at once handed over to the police and marched off to the police barracks. There were six of us, namely, Seumas Doyle, John R. Etchingham, Seumas Rafter, Michael De Lacey, Dick King and myself.

Perhaps here I should refer to the fantastic account of this affair published at the time in the *Irish Times* and, later, repeated in every book I have seen on the Enniscorthy Rising, even in Dorothy Macardle's usually meticulously accurate book, *The Irish Republic*. It stated that the British advanced from Wexford under cover of an armoured train which had been christened " Enniscorthy Emily," that the rebels, outfought in the town, retreated to Vinegar Hill where they finally surrendered. The fact was that the British did not enter the town until twelve hours subsequent

to our decision to give up and that we never even heard of
" Enniscorthy Emily."

After a short delay we were brought to Wexford by road
with a heavy police escort. The news of our coming had
evidently got out, for George's Street barracks to which we
were bound was surrounded by a large hostile crowd
composed, in the main, of people whose relatives were
fighting in the British forces. The crowd left no doubt in
our minds as to what they wanted done to us. Through
the window of the barracks I could see my mother's house
across the street. While the Head Constable was searching
us, I asked the County Inspector if I could speak to my
mother. He said I could not without the consent of the
military, who were in charge. I left the matter so. We
were brought out to the cars again and whisked off to the
military barracks. As we entered, I was surprised to see
a number of the Redmondite Volunteers in green uniforms
mingling with the British soldiers. They joined the British
in jeering at us.

We were placed in a sort of block-house standing in the
centre of the barrack square. There was but one room and
someone had thrown a heap of straw on the floor. The
only light came from a small window. A policeman with a
drawn revolver stood with his back to this. Outside there
were soldiers with fixed bayonets all around our building.
We lay down in the straw and Etchingham, who was
irrepressible, started to compose several limericks about
the Redmondite Volunteers we had seen. In a little while,
Sean Sinnott was put in with us ; he had been arrested that
morning. I fell fast asleep. Some time afterwards I was
awakened. It was pitch dark, but someone came in with
a bicycle lamp and in its light we saw gleaming mugs of
tea and a basket of bread and butter.

" Hello, Mr. Brennan, how are you doing ? Take some
of this tea and bread and butter."

It was Sergeant Collopy, a police officer who had no
reason to love me. I had many times refused to speak to
him and I particularly disliked him because of his supposed
officiousness. He was now here tó heap coals of fire on my
head.

" I had to fight to get this stuff in to you," he said.
" These fellows would starve you if they could."

I thanked him and took the provisions. We all found
we were very hungry. The Sergeant, kneeling on one knee,
leaned over to me.

" Whisper," he said, " I shouldn't tell you this. They're
going to court-martial you and shoot you in the morning."

" Thanks, Sergeant," I said. " What time is it ? "

" It's midnight," he said, and added : " You're taking it
very easy."

" What way can I take it ? " I asked, " but thanks for
the news all the same."

" Father Mark Byrne tried to get in to see you," he said,
" but they wouldn't let him."

" But surely," I said, " they'll have to let us have a priest
anyway before they shoot us."

" Make sure you insist on that," said the Sergeant.

When he had gone I began to doze again. I realised
only now that I had been ten days practically without sleep.
Suddenly the door opened and there entered two orderlies
carrying a small table, a chair, some candles, pens, ink and
paper. When they had lighted the candles and placed the
pens, etc., in the correct positions, they made way for a
procession consisting of the Resident Magistrate, the District
Inspector of the Constabulary and a couple of military
officers, one of whom, an impertinent young fellow, conducted the proceedings.

My name was called. I raised myself on my elbow in the
straw but did not get up. The officer read a document
from which it appeared I was charged with waging war
against His Britannic Majesty's forces, with conspiring with
the enemy in time of war, with creating disaffection amongst
His Britannic Majesty's loyal subjects, and so on, and so on.
The officer asked if I had anything to say and I replied that
I had not.

Seumas Doyle was called next and there was a like result.
Then they called Etchingham's name. He, too, was charged
with waging war on His Britannic Majesty's forces, with
conspiring with the enemy, creating disaffection and rebellion, etc. Had he anything to say ?

Etchingham raised his head.

" Is there any reason," he asked, " why you would not let us out under the First Offenders' Act ? "

The rest of the proceedings lost their gravity so far as we were concerned, while the court became more and more irate. As they left, the young officer blew up.

" You swine ! " he cried, " I'd like to take you all out right now and finish you off."

We felt he would have done it, too, if he had had the authority, and the strange thing is that this young officer was, according to Seumas Doyle, three years later fighting in the ranks of the I.R.A. in Dublin against the British forces.

I was dozing again when I heard Etchingham, who after all, should have been as sleepy as I was, launching into a speech, addressed to the solitary policeman who, presumably, was still with us, though we could no longer see him because of the darkness. Etchingham dwelt on the fact that the war was being fought in the interests of small nations. It was the policeman's duty to defend small nations. Mr. Asquith had said so. Why, therefore, did not the policeman go up to Enniscorthy to defend the small nation we had proclaimed free. He should do his duty.

King spoke up.

" For God's sake, Patsy, will you shut up and let us go asleep."

" I can't," said Etchingham, " and you should not be trying to sleep when there's a dead man in here with us."

" Who's the dead man ? "

" That policeman is dead."

" Nonsense," said King.

" Oh, he's dead all right," said Etchingham, " I've been talking to him for the best part of two hours and no living man could stand that without answering back. It's a terrible pity. Think of his poor old mother wondering where's her wandering boy to-night and she not knowing that he's after dying in an ould stable in Wexford Barracks, and that he's not even lying down but standing up against the wall stiff and stark——"

" He's not dead," said King.

" Oh, he's dead all right," said Etchingham.

"All right," said King, " I'll find out whether he is or
not "—and he began to move in the straw, whereupon, to
show he was not dead, the policeman began to shuffle his
feet on the concrete floor.

.   .   .   .   .

Somebody punched me into wakefulness. There was a
grey light of dawn coming through the little window. Some
of the fellows were on their feet.

" Get up," said Seumas Doyle.

" What's up ? " I asked, " are they going to shoot us ? "

" I don't know," said Seumas, " they're taking us out
anyhow."

The door opened and we could see a file of soldiers with
rifles. An officer beckoned to us to come along. Nothing
more terrifying than handcuffs, however, awaited us when
we emerged. We were marched down to the South Station
surrounded by a squad of police. O'Hara, the District
Inspector, was in charge. As soon as the train started he
removed our handcuffs and told us we were bound for
Waterford Jail. He was a quiet, decent man and he did
not relish his present job one bit. His wife was a personal
friend of Madame Markievicz's and Madame had appeared
in some dramatic productions organised in Wexford by the
D.I. When we arrived within the portals of Waterford
Jail, Etchingham held up the proceedings by formally
proposing a vote of thanks to the D.I. for his courtesy and
kindness. After a few flamboyant sentences, he turned
gravely to me and asked me to second the vote. Before
I could reply, Seumas Doyle blurted out angrily :

" Look here, Patsy—you're going too far with this play-
acting."

" It's too bad," said Etchingham, " I'm always being
misunderstood."

O'Hara shook hands with us, as if he were seeing us for
the last time. He had confided to me his fear that we
would not escape the firing squad.

We all called Etchingham " Patsy " because for years
he had been writing a column in the *Echo*, after the style of
" Mr. Dooley," called " Patsy Patrick." He had been a

jockey in his younger days and afterwards had become a very able journalist. For years I read every line he wrote in his " Gorey Notes " and his " Patsy Patrick " column. He had the real journalist's flare for turning everything he saw and heard into interesting reading matter. One day in Enniscorthy at a football match I said something about Diogenes. He asked me who Diogenes had been and I told him all I knew about the old philosopher. The following issue of the *Echo* contained a long dissertation by Patsy Patrick on Diogenes and the latter's opinions on the current Irish political situation. Etchingham was one of the best sports writers in Ireland and, notwithstanding his poor health, the extent and variety of his activities were amazing. He was a member of almost every local council and he seemed to revel in being the central figure in all the squabbles which are a feature of such councils. He had hundreds of friends all over the county and, indeed, all over Ireland, but he had also many bitter enemies, particularly in his native Gorey. He did not try to placate them ; indeed, he stung them into fury with his biting sarcasm and boisterous raillery and he was not at all scrupulous about his methods of attack. Once, during a heated debate in the Gorey District Council, Etchingham rose up and said he could afford to ignore the attacks made on him by a man who had let his old poor father die in the poor-house. That was about the worst taunt any Irishman could throw at another. Half a dozen members had attacked Etchingham on a question on which, for once, right seemed to be on their side. None of them knew who was the one Etchingham referred to and there ensued an embarrassed silence during which Etchingham got away with the point he had been making. Afterwards, I asked him which of them had let his father die in the Union.

" I don't know if any of them did," replied Patsy, " but I was in a tight corner and I had to get out of it."

Seumas Doyle said to me : " I never could make out whether Patsy was in earnest or not about the fight until I met him on the bridge of Enniscorthy with a bicycle. He was going to cycle to Dublin to get into the fight there, as it seemed nothing was going to be done in Wexford."

There are a hundred stories about Etchingham's ready wit and about the mischievous pranks he played on friend and foe alike, but few realised his gay light-heartedness concealed a spirit strong as steel. His health never was good, but no one ever heard him complain. In Dartmoor Jail he nearly died of starvation because he could not eat the coarse food supplied but, again, he did not complain. Instead, he composed funny songs about the two ounces of margarine he was allowed and about other items on the menu. In years and appearance he was considerably older than the rest of us but he was far more youthful in spirit than any of us. Only in the last few months before he died did I notice a change and then Patsy was a broken man. It was clear that the execution of Liam Mellowes—they were devoted to each other—had smashed him and he talked of nothing else. But an hour before he died, Seumas Doyle called to see him. Patsy knew he was dying but he contrived to make a joke out of the fact that he was dying of the same disease which had killed President Wilson. " It's apparently an honour reserved only for the most distinguished men," he said.

In Waterford Jail we were drawn up in line and subjected to the most ridiculous medical examination I have ever heard of. Without divesting us of a single garment, an aged doctor with a flat felt hat, which he did not remove, literally skipped from one of us to another stabbing a stethoscope to our chests.

" It's only a genius can do things like that," said De Lacey. "Any doctor could examine you the other way."

The warder who registered our names, ages, weights, etc., was inquisitive about our arms.

" Did ye give them up ? " he asked.

We were being wary and lied that we did.

" That's a nice bloody how-d'ye-do," he said. " Now the English can come over and conscript the whole goddamn lot of us."

The first time we were allowed out for exercise we had ample evidence that the promise we had got, that our men would be unmolested, had been broken. We saw filing out into the exercise ground practically every able-bodied

man in Enniscorthy and many who were not able-bodied.
Next day, the original six of us were taken out and handcuffed. We were told we were being removed but were not
informed of our destination.

" The English seem to be very fond of handcuffs," said
Etchingham to the warder who was fastening his. " Why
didn't they tell us so that we could have brought our own
along."

" That's right," said Seumas, " we had plenty of time
in Enniscorthy waiting for them to come and take us,
when we could have walked away."

" Our honour was our handcuffs then," said Seumas
Rafter with a grin.

We thought we were to go alone but soon we saw that
all the other prisoners were being brought along too. The
train journey was a long drawn out affair and we realised
we were bound for Dublin. We stopped at nearly every
station to take on more prisoners. There were only prisoners
and soldiers on the train. It seemed that the journey would
never end but, at last, someone said we were at Kingsbridge.
It was pitch dark when we alighted. We were lined up
between two files of soldiers with rifles and fixed bayonets,
all very grim. An English voice came from somewhere :

" If there's any attempt at escape, shoot at once. Let
them have it ! "

We shuffled off through the dark gloomy streets. The
soldiers' nerves were on edge for whenever one of us acci-
dentally stumbled or bumped into one of them, they cursed
savagely and threatened to use the bayonet. The English
voice repeated its warning from time to time. We all hoped
no one would try to escape. We could see nothing but the
dim outline of high walls and buildings. The air was full
of gloom and there was a smell of smoke from the charred
ruins of the city. Finally, we were halted and a great gate
swung open. We entered a barrack square which we soon
learned was Richmond. We were herded into various
buildings and served with rations of tea and hard biscuits
as we entered. Our building was a large single chamber.
It was the first chance we had of talking to the Enniscorthy
men we had left behind. We learned from them that as

soon as we were in custody, the police and military raided
practically every house in the town and made wholesale
arrests.   Irwin, the manager of the *Echo*, and Sears, the
editor, told me that everybody employed on the *Echo* had
been taken, including the commercial staff, the reporters
and printers, and even the messengers.   It seemed to be a
bad joke that the military had also served on the proprietors a notice suspending publication of the paper indefinitely.   It was nearly a year before publication of the
paper was resumed.   We slept on the floor that night and
soon discovered that the place was crawling with lice.

Next day, some more prisoners came in and all of them
were known to someone with the exception of one man.   He
knew no one and no one knew him.   He seemed ill at ease.
Then someone noticed that his boots were newly polished
and pointed out that he could not have been in the fight.
The whisper went around that he was a spy.   Whenever
he joined a group, the men quietly moved away.   The poor
fellow sat down by himself, looking very self-conscious.   I
thought it unfair and joined him.   I told him who I was.
He brightened.

"I know about you," he said.   "My name is Joe
Mooney."

"There was a Joe Mooney," I said, "who contested a
seat in the Dublin Corporation in the Sinn Féin interest."

"Yes," he said, "I'm the culprit."

"Then you know Griffith?"

"Sure I do and Dan McCarthy and Sean MacDermott
and all the boys."

"How is it that your boots are so clean?"

"When the surrender came I managed to get away and
I went home and cleaned up.   Then an old one came along
and said the British soldiers had been fired on from my
house in Meath Street.   So they took me."

I told him the others had taken him for a spy.

"No!" he said, and after a pause, "I suppose it's natural
enough.   I never met anyone here before, but if any of the
Dublin fellows were here, you'd see."

I vouched for Joe and we became great friends.   Two
years later when it was practically impossible to get supplies

of petrol which we badly needed for transportation in the elections all over Ireland, Joe managed to supply all our needs.

Someone passed around a much-read copy of a Dublin evening newspaper in which there was an official British announcement to the effect that Pearse, MacDonagh and Tom Clarke had been executed the previous morning. We all wondered at this, for one of the soldiers had told us that dozens had been shot. Some new prisoners came in and they had a list of sixteen of the leaders who they said had already been executed. Sean MacDermott's name was on the list and so we were agreeably surprised to find him still very much alive a couple of days later. The original six of us had been transferred from one room to another and, finally, we were put into a large room which was very crowded. There were some Dublin men, including Gearoid O'Sullivan, Barney Mellowes and Sean MacDermott. I told Sean I had been praying for the repose of his soul.

"It won't do a bit of harm," he said with his old gay laugh, " I'll probably need those prayers to-morrow."

It wasn't surprising to find that Sean was the most popular man in the room. He " had a way with him " and he had even charmed the guards into allowing him to go to the canteen to buy stuff for us. From the Dublin men we learned that the court-martial was sitting every day and that two or three executions were taking place every morning. Sean went out to go to the canteen. He did not come back and, from the windows, we saw him limping across the barrack square with an escort. They were bound for the building where the courts-martial were sitting. On the steps of this building there was a group of men, amongst whom I recognised Harry Boland and Jack Shouldice. They were awaiting trial.

At midday, two soldiers carried a huge bucket of soup into the room. A powerfully-built sergeant-major super-intended the operation. I recognised him at once as Tommy Gorman, a Wexfordman who, in my childhood days, had been a resplendent figure in the gorgeous uniform of the British Lancers. His people lived in the street where I was born. I told him who I was and he recalled the names of some of his old-time neighbours. He was very good-humoured about it and, at the same time, very condescending towards me. It was clear that he did not want to discuss present-day politics.

Later that day from the windows we saw a large number of prisoners being lined up in the barrack square. They were, someone said, bound for a concentration camp in England. Some of our Wexford comrades were there and they waved goodbye to us as they were marched off. Barney Mellowes told me that another batch had been sent off the day before and that Sean MacDermott had been amongst those lined up. Just before they were marched off, however, two of the G-men walked along the line and took MacDermott out.

To our surprise, Sean came back to us in the evening. The trial, it seemed, had been only a preliminary hearing for the taking down of evidence. The court-martial was to come later.

Sean and I lay side by side that night after lights-out. He told me the whole story as to why and how the plans for the landing of the arms from Germany had gone wrong. The story is substantially as it appears in Dorothy Macardle's book *The Irish Republic*. Once his story was interrupted. Someone had switched on a light in the room. Immediately a floodlight from the barrack square was turned on us and a voice cried : " Put out that light ! "

Sean said quietly : " Put out the light and lie down everybody." The order was obeyed. There was a confused whispering in the room. Sean's voice was tense as he said :

" Quiet ! They're only looking for a chance to massacre ye. Go to sleep, everybody." He whispered in my ear : " We must save all the men we can to carry on."

" You think there's a chance for you, Sean ? "

" Not an earthly," he said. " I know I'm going."

He was not at all bitter about MacNeill. " We all did the best we could," he said and these were almost the same words MacNeill himself used when speaking to me of Pearse and MacDermott a year later in Lewes Jail.

" You're satisfied, Sean ? "

" I am," he said serenely, " we put up a great fight. The lads were grand. We have awakened the old spirit. You'll see."

As I was silent, he said :

" I mean I hope you will. You're thinking you may not be here to see it?"

" Yes."

" You're reconciled ? "

" Sure I am."

" I can see that," he said. " It's a great life, Bob."

They took him away from us in the morning. He shook hands with us all.

" I've given away all my souvenirs," he said to me, " I've only a penny left." He scratched his initials on the penny and gave it to me. They later found it secreted in my clothes and confiscated it.

Chapter Nine

General Maxwell had a pit dug in Arbour Hill Barracks to receive the bodies of 150 men he intended to execute. After fourteen of the rebel leaders had been executed on various dates between May 3rd and May 12th, the executions ceased owing to the indignation aroused in Ireland, England and especially the United States.

NEXT morning, the six of us were brought over for our preliminary hearing. To my surprise, the examining officer was a barrister whom I had met frequently at Wexford Quarter Sessions. He was a friend of Charlie Wyse Power. I asked him how Charlie was. A long time afterwards, Charlie told me that my innocent query nearly cost him his liberty, if not his life. The police officers from Wexford gave their evidence and it appeared that the only real evidence against us consisted of my letters to Colonel French regarding the surrender.

Next day came the court-martial. Outside the building we encountered several of the police witnesses. They were anxious to be friendly. I utilised the service of one of them to send a letter to my mother. The poor man used this fact afterwards when the tide had turned, to prove he had been in our confidence all along. While we were waiting, an English soldier had a talk with Seumas Doyle. I overheard Seumas refusing him something. " What does he want ? " I asked.

" He's a Catholic," said Seumas, " and he wants my rosary beads as a souvenir."

" Why don't you give it to him ? "

" I may want it myself," said Seumas.

" You'll never want it half as bad as he does," said Etchingham.

The English soldier joined in the laugh.

" You may not believe it, chum," he said, " but I have a great deal of respect for you fellers."

" Your heart is in the right place," said Rafter, " but your rifle isn't."

After a long wait we were ushered up a couple of flights of stairs and along a narrow passage. Here, I encountered the second Wexfordman in the British forces. He was standing at a door with a rifle and fixed bayonet and he glowered at us. His name was Martin and he came from Bride Street.

" Hello, Martin," I said cheerfully, " how are they all in Bride Street ? "

His reply was unprintable and when Etchingham gently reproved him, he threatened to use his bayonet. He was the special orderly on the door of the court-martial chamber.

At length we were ushered into the presence. Three very weighty, not to say, beefy men, resplendent in uniform and decorations presided, in a room so small that the six of us crowded the floor-space. A precise gentleman, also in uniform, who stood at the side of the bench, read the charge " waging war on His Majesty's forces, etc., etc." He then read the evidence which had been taken down the previous day.

I don't know what I had expected, but the demeanour of those men surprised me. They apparently took their position very seriously, which was not to be wondered at considering they were imposing death penalties day after day, but there was an air of righteousness about them which was astonishing. How could there be righteousness when there was no right ? The same thought was in Seumas Doyle's head. He whispered to me, wonderingly : " These fellows actually believe they're right."

I replied : " What they need is a course in Irish history."

" That would be a long way round," said Seumas, " and it's a bit late now."

Meanwhile, they were a machine which could only kill or refrain from killing.

My thoughts wandered.

> I see a broken body on the ground
> The English guns have silenced Padraig Pearse
> With heavy tread the soldiers march away
> Their work is done. A poet now lies dead.

No longer will they see him in the West
Around the little cabins of the poor
Nor will he walk again in Kilmashogue
Or sail in Bealadangin by the sea.

But far and near beyond those granite walls
His song is stirring in the people's hearts.
The people whom he loved have heard his song
The poet's words are rising to their lips.

The Judge Advocate finished reading the evidence and
asked had we anything to say. No, we had nothing to say.

"Like Wolfe Tone," murmured Seumas, "we have no
wish to delay the court."

The Presiding Officer said : "We have heard the charges
and the evidence and the sentence will be promulgated in
due course."

We were about to file out when the Judge Advocate
addressed me :

"At the preliminary hearing," he said, "you stated
there had been several people arrested in Enniscorthy who
were not connected with the uprising. I am instructed by
the court to say that an officer will wait on you and ask
you to write down the names of such people. Their cases
will be specially considered."

We filed out and immediately began to debate whether
we should give such a list or not. The idea of complaining
about the wholesale arrests had originated with Seumas
Doyle and Micheal De Lacey who thought we might be
able to get the older men released, as well as people like
Irwin and Sears who could get the *Echo* going again. Now
we were in a fix. If we wrote down any names at all, we
were thereby implicating in treasonable activities all the
others. However, when the appointed officer came around
we gave him half a dozen names and added that there were
hundreds of others who were unknown to us and who
consequently could not have taken any part.

We were lined up with many other prisoners in a roadway
leading to the exit in front of a wooden hut whence an
officer came from time to time with slips of paper. The
names of six of us were called and we took our places at

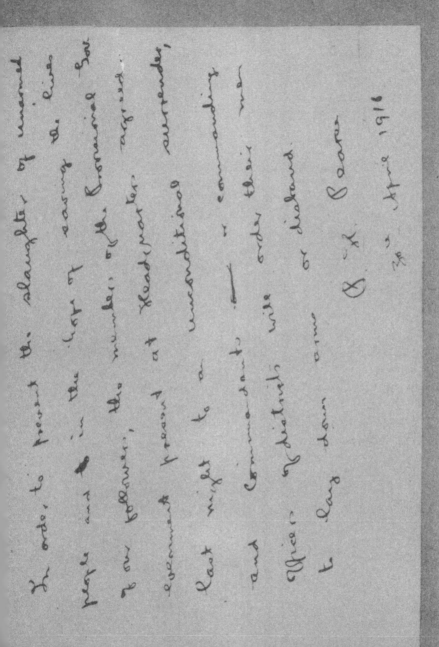

In order to prevent the further slaughter of unarmed people and in the hope of saving the lives of our followers, the members of the Provisional Government present at Headquarters have agreed to an unconditional surrender, and the commandants of the various districts in the City and Country will order their commands to lay down arms.

(Sd) P. H. Pearse
30th April 1916

Surrender Order for the Wexford Volunteers given by Padraig Pearse in Arbour Hill Prison, 30th [National Museum of Ireland] April, 1916, to S. O Dubhghaill and S. R. Etchingham.

Group taken before the Surrender in Enniscorthy, 1st May, 1916. *Back row* : Una Brennan, Michael de Lacey, Eileen Hegarty. *Front row* : Seamus Rafter, Robert Brennan, Seamus Doyle, Sean R. Etchingham.

the head of the file. The British sergeant, who indicated our places, said to me, not unkindly :

" You know what this means ? "

" I have a fair idea," I replied.

" You're for it," he said.

" So it seems."

" You're a bally game lot," he said, without enthusiasm.

King said : " What the hell do they expect us to do—start roaring and bawling ? "

An escort formed up beside us and we were marched out into the street. Little groups of people gathered here and there, gazed at us curiously as we walked the few hundred yards to Kilmainham Jail. Opposite the jail gate a ballad singer in front of a public-house was singing " It's a Long Way to Tipperary."

" You never said a truer word," said Patsy.

Kilmainham was the gloomiest jail ever built. To make it gloomier, they had moral mottoes inscribed over the interior archways : " Cease to do evil, learn to do well," etc. We were each put in a separate cell in which there was no furniture of any kind save a stinking bucket in one corner. I began to take off my clothes with the idea of trying to rid myself of the vermin I had picked up in Richmond Barracks. I stopped when I heard a click and saw an eye at the spyhole in the door. A voice said :

"Are you from Wexford ? "

" I am."

" Wait there a minute," said the voice. As if I could do anything else but wait there.

The door opened after a few minutes and a weather-beaten man in the British uniform entered. He was very grave and seemed prematurely aged. His regiment was the Royal Irish.

" What's your name ? " he asked. I told him.

"Are you a son of Bob Brennan ? "

" I am."

" Did you ever hear of Anthony Doyle, the lime-burner ? "

" Yes, he lives just outside the town near Drinagh."

" I'm a son of his."

There was an awkward pause. The poor fellow was

terribly agitated. I thought : " This is the third Wexford-man in British uniform I've met here."

" This is terrible," he said. " You know where you are ? "

" I can guess."

" These are the condemned cells."

" I thought that."

" You're not takin' it hard."

" What's the use ? "

" Maybe they won't go on with it," he said. " They say Asquith is going to stop the executions."

" Do you know George Holbrook ? " I asked.

" Sure I do, well. It's often he gave me a shave."

" Don't you think he's a philosopher ? "

" He's certainly a comical fella."

" Well, George says you might as well die of a Tuesday as of a Wednesday."

" I dunno about that."

He stepped nervously to the door and peeped out into the hall. Turning, he said :

" I thought I heard wan of them prowling around."

" Who ? "

" Wan of these English bastards. Is there anything I can do for you ? "

I asked him if I could have a bath. He said it was impossible.

" Could you get me a bucket of water and a towel. We all picked up a lot of lice in Richmond Barracks."

" I'll see what I can do."

He locked the door and went off. In five minutes he was back with a bucket of water and a greasy towel.

" It's the best I could do," he said, " I'll be back."

He locked the door again and I stripped naked and washed as well as I could.

When Doyle came back, I asked him if he would get me some paper and envelopes. I had a pencil.

" I'll see," he said. " I have to be careful because these English have eyes everywhere. If I don't come back before I go off duty, you'll understand."

He did come back, however, and he had several sheets of paper and a few envelopes for me.

" Don't write any to-night," he said, " because they'll be watching you. Write your letters in the morning before the guard comes on at six o'clock. If I can manage it, I'll post your letters for you."

I knew the risk he was running and I thanked him.

" That's all right," he said, " I wish to God I could do more for you."

He went off and I put in some time getting rid of at least the more conspicuous of the vermin. Then I lay down on the floor and slept soundly. Daylight was breaking when I woke. I sat up immediately and started to write my letters. I was in the middle of a letter to my mother when I heard a movement in the hall downstairs. There were sounds of men marching and doors opening. I thought a new batch of prisoners had arrived and I went on with my letter. A few minutes later, I realised that something more sinister was afoot. The marching men were now in the yard outside my cell. Suddenly there came a queer silence. I could see nothing because the cell window was too high and, in any case, the vents in it were pointed skywards. I heard the click of the rifle-bolts as the cartridges were shot into place. Another silence, and then a loud volley.

After a pause, I went on writing my letter. I told my mother that I had just heard the volley which killed Sean MacDermott and I prayed that the Lord might have mercy on his soul. Maybe, I said, we should be praying not for him, but to him. I heard the confused noise of men moving off the ground outside and voices low and indistinct. I went on to deal with the subject about which I had been writing to my mother. I stopped. The noise in the hall downstairs was repeated. This time, I waited, tense. I followed the movements of the men out of the hall and into the yard outside. Again, there was the click of the rifles, the awful pause, and then the volley. This time it was a ragged, sickening volley. I went on with my letter.

When the door opened shortly after six o'clock, Doyle appeared. He seemed to be out of breath. He opened his mouth once or twice to speak, and then said :

"Are you all right ? "

" Sure I am."

" Somebody told me there had been executions this morning. I don't sleep in the prison. They were pulling my leg, I suppose."

" There were two executions," I said. " I think one of them was Sean MacDermott."

He stepped to the door and looked down into the hall.

" Yes," he said, " his cell door is open. How did you know it was him ? "

" I just guessed."

I did not tell him how I knew it was Sean. I knew as well as if I had been there with him. One moment he was alive and the next he was dead, and yet I felt no break in our companionship. We were still together. Death was no break, it was a continuance in another phase.

But I was troubled to know who had been the second. I asked Anthony Doyle to find out.

" It may be de Valera or Tom Ashe," I said.

" I'll see," he said. He turned at the door and said with a wry smile.

" I'm glad it wasn't you."

He was gone for a good while. When he came back, he said : " It was a man who wasn't in the prison at all. James Connolly. He was in a hospital somewhere. They carried him in here on a stretcher."

That day we were shifted downstairs to the cells the dead men had occupied. I was only a little while there, when a soldier opened the cell door and entered. He had spotted my black pigskin leggings and he wanted them. He was a tall heavily-built Saxon, a private.

" Come on, take them off," he said.

" Why ? "

" I want them, that's all. You'll have no use for them to-morrow."

I did not care whether he got the leggings or not and if he asked civilly for them, I probably would have given them to him. Now I was determined he should not have them.

" I'm sorry, I can't give them to you," I said.

" Why not ? "

" I promised them to the sergeant-major."

This was a long shot. I did not even know there was a sergeant-major. The Saxon's face fell.

" Oh," he said, " was he in here ? "

He backed out without another word.

Later, when Doyle slipped in to see me, I told him of the incident.

" That fella," he said, "is a dirty bastard. He's robbing all the prisoners."

" I'd like to let you have the leggings," I said, " I've nothing else to give away."

He brushed the matter aside.

" I'm not thinking of that," he said, " I'm thinking of you all the time. I can't sleep a wink. I wish to God you were out of it."

The poor man was terribly upset. It seemed to me he was visibly growing older.

" Look here," I said, " those others died well, didn't they ? "

" Sure, they did. Even these damn English say they never saw men die so game."

" Well, we must all go sometime, and isn't it a fine way to go when you are in a mood to go out and face death cheerfully, when you are reconciled, and not afraid."

" I wish to God you were out of it," he said sadly. He took my letters, concealed them in his clothes, and went off.

A couple of days passed and there were no executions. Then, one day I realised suddenly that I was very hungry. I concluded it must be past dinner-time. As breakfast consisted only of a pint of tea and eight ounces of bread, we welcomed dinner, such as it was, at midday. I rang my bell, but nothing happened. I rang again, and again. At last a voice answered me through the door.

" What's up with you ? "

" What time is it ? " I asked.

" What the hell is that to you ? "

" What about dinner ? "

" Shut up," said the speaker. He went on to tell me what he would do to me if I didn't keep quiet. The conversation must have been heard by the other lads, for all at once they began to ring their bells, but as nothing happened, we grew tired and the clamour died down. Later, I heard someone shouting it was four o'clock and this fact seemed to increase my hunger. I felt famished. I heard the doors being unlocked and when mine was opened, Anthony Doyle was standing there, his face white as chalk.

" The officer is here with the sentences," he said.

" What about my dinner ? " I asked.

" Did you hear what I said ? You are going up to hear your sentence."

" I can only think of how hungry I am," I said.

He shook his head as if to say I was hopeless.

We were marched into the huge dim hall. There must have been forty or fifty of us. I was first in the line. A dapper little officer, looking very important, stepped forward and glanced at the papers in his hand. He called my name.

" Here," I said. He read a document. It appeared that I had been charged with waging war, etc., etc., that the court-martial had found me guilty and sentenced me to death and that the general officer commanding had reviewed the evidence and the verdict and had confirmed the sentence. He then passed on to De Lacey. A similar sentence. The same for Doyle, King, Rafter and Etchingham. The next man got life imprisonment, and the next ten years, and so on.

I find it hard to describe my feelings at that moment. I had not been without hope that we would escape the death penalty, particularly during the past few days when there had been no executions. Thus, the sentence was heavier than it would have been a week earlier. I knew, however, and this gave me great joy, that I was not afraid and that I would walk out to meet death as easily as the others had done.

Then came the anti-climax. The little officer returned to me and read another document to the effect that the general officer commanding had been pleased to commute my sentence to five years' penal servitude. He went on to De Lacy to say the same thing. I got a shock. I had not wanted to die, not by any means, but I had been screwed up to a high pitch. I felt as a man would who, having been relieved of an immense burden, had had it placed on his shoulders again.

Etchingham made some joke and I dutifully smiled, but I was still a bit dazed when I got back to my cell door. Anthony Doyle was there, his face bright with joy.

" I'm glad," he said, " I'm terribly glad. That five years is nothing. Here," he said, and pushed a big loaf into my hands. I told him I could not eat and asked him to give it to the other fellows, but he looked so hurt that I broke off a piece. It was an hour afterwards that I remembered Etchingham's joke.

" That death sentence," he had said, " saved our lives."

He meant that if the English had had the sense to execute no one but to kick us all out, our political opponents would have ridiculed us to death.

Chapter Ten

Prime Minister Asquith, stating that the old machinery of government in Ireland had broken down, said the time had come for a new departure.

The British Ambassador in Washington reported that Britain could not count on American help or sympathy. " The attitude towards England has been changed for the worse by recent events in Ireland."

NEXT morning we left that horrible place and were taken to Mountjoy Jail, where we were treated to the luxury of a warm bath and clean clothes, even though they were prison clothes. After the squalor of Kilmainham, the cell I was put into seemed beautiful. The only reading matter, however, was the Bible. (" The English," said Etchingham, " are always leaving bibles lying around for their enemies to trip over them.") I was glad when the door opened and a cheerful, if anaemic warder came in. He left the door ajar and took the only stool, leaving me standing.

" How are you feeling ? " he asked.

" Fine."

" You're glad they didn't shoot you ? "

" Sure I am."

" They're finished with their shooting," he said, with a grin. " You've put the fear of God into them. They're going to give Ireland Home Rule now."

"Again ? "

"Again," he laughed. "Asquith said so in the House of Commons last night. They're going to put it in force at once. I have to laugh."

And he did.

He gave me more news. The men who had been sent to concentration camps in England the night before had been surrounded by cheering crowds on the Dublin quays. The deportees had cried out such things as " Stand fast by the Republic,"—" We're coming back to fight again," and so on, and the crowd went wild.

" Think out something good to say," he counselled me, " something good to shout out. The papers will print it."

94

He got up to go.

" Home Rule to-morrow ! 'Clare to God ! I have to laugh." He laughed again as he went out.

My next visitor was not so pleasant, though he should have been more so, being a priest. He, too, took my stool. (These must be Mountjoy manners, I thought.) He discoursed airily on the futility of our fight. We were dreamers and visionaries, not wise enough to be as dangerous as we would like to be. The British had shown wisdom in not executing more of us.

"As they had every right to do ! " I said.

" Oh, no, I'm not saying that."

" But I am," I said. " Surely if they have a right to be here, they have every right to protect their power here by shooting those who would undermine it."

He waved the point aside disdaining to argue with me.

We were allowed out for exercise next day in a spacious yard where there were more than one hundred prisoners marching round and round, single file, in circles. We saw many old friends there. We were not supposed to talk and every now and then a robust warder yelled out to remind us of the fact, but we talked all the same. I was behind Harry Boland and he heard my account of Enniscorthy and he told me of the Dublin fight. Later, Tom Ashe dropped in behind me and I got a thrilling account of the fight at Ashbourne. I recalled later that both Tom and Harry pointed out to me a morose-looking man, serious for his years, with extraordinary long legs and a head that was small for his large frame. It was de Valera.

De Lacey devised a rough and ready way we could communicate with each other while we were locked in separate cells. It was a code to be tapped out on the hot-water pipe which ran the length of the cells. One tap was for A, two for B, and so on. E, however, was a stroke and every fifth letter was an additional stroke. Thus, the letter D was four taps, while W was four strokes and three taps. I memorised it and practised it all one afternoon.

Una came to see me the following day. We had our interview in the same cage in which she and I had seen her brother a year earlier. She was learning the path to

the jails. Before the troubles were over, she might have
been a guide to nearly all the jails in Ireland. She brought
me a great deal of news about the situation in Enniscorthy
and Wexford generally, and I was anxious to pass it on to
De Lacey and the others as soon as possible. So the moment
I got back to the cell, I started tapping out a message to
De Lacey. It took me half an hour to tap out.

" I had a visit from Una."

The reply took nearly as long :

" Who is Una ? "

Evidently De Lacey's code had passed into other hands.
I dropped the code.

      •   •   •   •   •

There were a dozen of us on the boat journey to England,
a long choppy crossing, followed by a seemingly interminable train trip. One time in the darkness of a foggy night
we were halted at a station. We had been warned to keep
the blinds drawn. Tom Ashe lifted a corner of the blind
and a policeman looked in. Tom got great satisfaction
from the fact that the policeman said :

" Is Eireannach mise."

Dick Hayes* had little patience with Tom's ready
enthusiasms.

" I can't get much consolation from that," he said.

They both, however, got great amusement recalling a
line in a recent Abbey play :

" It's unpatriotic to say we were bet."

Both of them had got life sentences but they were not
worried. We all took it for granted we would be released
together. Ashe had a greater store of Irish songs than
anyone I had met up to that time. I was delighted to find
I had two airs he did not know. He memorised them.
He told us many stories of his experiences in America,
whither he had gone a few years earlier to collect money
for the Gaelic League. Amongst them the following :

On the first day he arrived in New York, he was advised
to call on a wealthy Irish-American who might be good for

---

* Dr. Richard Hayes, afterwards film censor, director of the Abbey Theatre,
and author of *The Last French Invasion* and other historical works.

a big subscription. He was warned he would have to use all his blandishments in order to succeed. He got an appointment and found his way to a hotel which was as high as the cliffs of Moher. As he entered the lift, he began to whistle softly in order to tune himself up for the coming interview. As they were passing the third floor, the lift-boy, without turning round, said :

" That's not right."

" What's not right ? " asked Tom.

" If that's the ' Little Red Lark ' you're trying to whistle, it's not right."

" Why not ? "

" ' The Little Red Lark' goes like this," and the lift-boy whistled a bar or two.

" You're wrong," said Tom. " If I don't know the ' Little Red Lark,' I'll swim back to Ireland."

" Then you'll swim."

" Maybe," said Tom, " it's the ' Foggy Dew ' you're thinking of."

" No, it's not. The ' Foggy Dew ' goes like this," and he whistled another bar.

" That's one version of it," said Tom. " That's the one some people sing ' The Jackets Green ' to. Listen to this one," and Tom gave a couple of bars.

" That's not ' The Foggy Dew ' " said the boy, " that's 'As I Roved Out.' "

By this time, the lift had gone right up to the top of the building and out into a little box on the roof. They could see out before them the beautiful stretches of New York harbour, but neither of them took any notice of the view. They compared notes and had arguments on " The Wind that Shakes the Barley," " Spailpin a Ruin," " The Return from Fingal," and many other Irish airs. Half an hour passed and Tom suddenly remembered his appointment.

" Glory be to God," he said, " I'm ruined. There's a man on the tenth floor waiting for me for the past half-hour."

" That's nothing," said the boy, " think of all the people who are waiting for me on the ground floor."

" Well, let's go down," said Tom.

" If it's all the same to you, we can go on talking," said the boy, " your friend will have given you up and I'll be sacked anyway."

" You won't," said Tom.

" Sure, I will. Listen to that buzzer. It's going like that for the last half-hour."

" You really mean you'll be sacked ? "

" I wish I was as sure of heaven."

" I tell you what," said Tom, " I'm going to see Mr. Blank and he's been staying in the hotel a long time."

"As long as I remember."

" Well, if he said a word for you ? "

" It might help."

They went down to Mr. Blank and found him in good humour. He was so delighted by the story Tom told him that he not only gave him a big cheque but he went himself to see the manager about the lift-boy. The manager had fully made up his mind to sack the boy. Instead, he complimented him on his skill in entertaining the visitor. He even took him out of the lift and gave him a job at the Reception Desk, where, as he said, he would have to keep his feet on the ground.

One of the soldiers in our escort, with a sense of humour, gave us an English weekly magazine on the cover of which was a cartoon showing Asquith distracted over a jigsaw puzzle. The puzzle was the map of Ireland in pieces.

Finally, we arrived in Plymouth, where we were loaded into lorries. On bumpy hard seats we were whirled through a pleasant wooded country and then into a high desolate region of grey rocks and furze moorlands. Having read many of Eden Philpott's books, I recognised the Devon Tors. We seemed to be on top of the world, but also we seemed to be climbing all the time. De Lacey said we would have built a cathedral up there instead of a prison.

When it seemed we would never get to our destination, we suddenly rounded a corner, drove through a little street and entered the gloomy portals of Dartmoor Prison. I had read descriptions of the place in many novels and detective stories, but none of them was a bit like the real thing. That may have been because we were housed in an old wing which had not been occupied for several decades. We were lined up in a vast, dim hall where there were flights of black iron steps leading up to galleries five stories high. Facing us, not two feet away, was a line of warders, staring at us in grim silence, each of them having a baton swinging by a leather thong from the right wrist. I remember wondering whether they were selected for their noses, for it seemed to me they had the biggest noses I had ever seen. After a very cursory examination by the doctor, we were marched to the bathroom and told to undress, this being the preliminary to a most revolting personal search. Then we had a bath and were given ill-fitting convict clothes, after which we were measured, weighed, finger-printed and photographed. We were placed in separate cells. I had ceased to be a person and had become convict No. Q. 103, as the cloth badge on my cap and right sleeve indicated.

Hearing sounds of marching men in the yard, I climbed on my stool and looked out through the window. There was a crowd of convicts marching around in a circle in single file, while several warders watched them, with batons swinging. I thought the convicts were the most villainous lot of men imaginable. I did not realise till some days later that they were some of our own comrades who had arrived earlier. The prison haircut, the unshaven chins and the convict garb, had changed them into the most criminal-looking types. My survey was interrupted by a voice hissing through the door :

" Get down off that stool ! "

I got down and, since there was nothing else to do, I paced the floor—five short steps to and fro, to and fro. I failed to warm my feet, so I took off my shoes and, pretending I had a skipping-rope, I began to skip. It was my first skipping exercise in several years, but before I left that prison I had become adept in a dozen different skipping steps and I could go on indefinitely without becoming winded. My feet became warm and I was putting on my shoes again when I heard the cheerful voice of Harry Boland just outside my cell. He was replying to a warder who was giving him orders regarding the polishing of the steel rail of the staircase. As he started polishing, Harry began to sing :

> It was a long time before the Shamrock,
> The green isle's loved emblem,
> Was crushed beneath the weight
> Of the Saxon lion's paw.

A shocked voice said : " Silence ! "

" What's up ! " asked Harry.

" You're not supposed to sing here."

" That's funny," said Harry, " in Ireland we encourage a fellow to sing. He works better when he's singing."

" Well, you can't sing here."

" Oh, all right," said Harry. A few minutes later be began to whistle, but this was stopped also.

" You must keep silence here," said the warder.

Of course, Harry knew this very well, but he asked the warder why.

" Why what ? "

" Why must we keep silence ? "

" Because it's the rule."

" But why is it the rule ? "

" Well, because it's the rule."

" Well, it's a rotten rule," said Harry, " and someone should tell the Governor, or whoever is responsible for it."

" You must stop talking," said the warder.

" Couldn't I see the Governor about it ? "

The warder began to get cross.

" I told you to stop talking."

" Well, ain't a fellow supposed to have any rights ? Can't I see the Governor ? "

" You can put down your name to see the Governor to-morrow morning."

" Oh, that's good," said Harry. " Thanks."

I couldn't see them, of course, but I knew Harry was smiling his disarming smile.

" But if I were you," said the warder in a more amiable tone, " I wouldn't see him about that rule."

" Why not ? "

" He can't alter it. These orders are made by the Prisons Board."

" Oh, I see."   After a pause, " But couldn't I see them ? "
" No."
" Why not ? "
" Because nobody can see them."
"And do they ever see us ? "
" That'll do. Shut up."
" It's funny," said Harry, " that a bunch of people who
never come here can——"
" That'll do, I think you've done enough cleaning. Come
along."
" But I've only just started."
" No matter. Go back to your cell."
" Oh, all right," said Harry, " if that's the way it is."
As he was going back to his cell, I heard him saying :
" There's no spirit of co-operation around here."

The same warder came in to my cell a few minutes later.
He showed me how to fold the bedclothes. One had to
fold each of the two sheets, blanket and quilt three-fold and
hang them neatly over the bedboard leaning against the
wall. At dinner recess, one had to undo the whole thing
and roll the bedclothes into a neat cylinder which was then
placed at an angle on a high corner shelf. Also, he told
me to keep my tins polished ; and the asphalt floor was
to be kept shining. Later, he came in again, with sacking,
needle and thread and instructed me how to make sandbags. I was glad to have something to do and I managed
to turn out my quota.

We were kept in close confinement for a month and
then we were all assembled on the floor of one wing, seated
on stools, three feet apart, and we worked at sandbags,
mailbags and light harness straps. It was deadly monotonous, four hours in the morning, four hours in the afternoon. Any attempt at communicating one with another
was quickly suppressed. Anyone caught talking was brought
before the Governor and sentenced to not less than three
days in solitary confinement on bread and water. Some of
the lads were sent down there and they did not like it.
Two of the Galway lads were particularly unfortunate.
They had just arrived in the prison and did not know the
ropes. They were only a couple of hours in their cells,

which adjoined each other, when they noticed everything was very quiet in the hall. It was the silent hour, which succeeds the serving of the midday meal, when all the prisoners are locked in. The newcomers did not know there was a warder in the hall, moving about on padded soles. So one of them knelt down at the door of his cell and said through the ventilation slit which slanted downwards :

" Hello, Jimmy, are you there ? "

" I am, Tommy," replied Jimmy from the other cell.

" How are you ? "

Of course, Tommy had just left Jimmy a couple of hours before and he did not need to enquire for his health. He merely craved for some companionship.

" I'm well," said Jimmy, " how are you ? "

" I'm all right," said Tommy, " have you any news ? "

This question was, of course, equally unnecessary because Tommy knew all the news Jimmy had anyway. The warder intervened at this stage. He hammered on both doors, told them to shut up and reported them. They went to the dark cells for three days and when they came back, each of them looked as if he had seen a ghost.

Chapter Eleven

By mid-1916 it was clear that Germany would win the war if America did not intervene. To mollify American opinion, Lloyd George offered Redmond immediate Home Rule. The scheme was angrily rejected by Redmond's followers because it involved partition.

AFTER a while we were transferred, during working hours, to a large workshop. It, also, had not been in use for a long time. It had been built from ships' timbers for French prisoners in the time of the Napoleonic wars. A great portion of the low roof was glass and when the hot weather came, as it did very soon, the heat in the place was stifling. Here, instead of stools, we sat on backless benches, making bags. There were over sixty of us there, with three or four warders pacing up and down, swinging their eternal batons.

We were little more than a month in the place when we had our first excitement. One evening, after we had been locked in our cells, I heard the sound of marching men in the yard. I quickly climbed on my stool and was surprised to see a small group of prisoners being marched in, amongst them Eoin MacNeill, Sean McEntee, Austin Stack and Con Collins. In spite of the silence rule, news always got about and next morning there was an air of suppressed excitement. We were lined up in the dark central hall for inspection, standing in dead silence, with the grim warders facing us. Down the iron stairs in the middle of the hall came a small body of men, the first being Eoin MacNeill. We were all conscious that the prisoners had mixed feelings about him, as he had prevented the Rising from being what it might have been. To our amazement, de Valera stepped out from our ranks and faced us. His voice rang out :

" Irish Volunteers ! Attention ! Eyes left ! "

The command—a salute to MacNeill—was obeyed with military precision.

" Eyes front ! " Again the command was obeyed and de Valera stepped back into the ranks, leaving us all a bit dazed by his amazing chivalry and courage. This was rank

mutiny, one of the two offences involving corporal punishment. De Valera was marched off to the separate cells.
We did not know what was going to happen to him. As it
turned out, nothing did, except that he was returned to
us in the afternoon. The Governor had wisely decided that
harsh measures would not mend matters.

We had been a few weeks in the workshop when one day
Principal Warder Thomas Stone called me aside and asked
me if I thought I could fill the job of assisting the instructor
in cutting the materials for the bags. I realised I owed the
offer to De Lacey, who, by playing up to the vanity of the
Principal Warder, had succeeded in gaining his confidence
so far that he had been placed in charge of the stores. It
was De Lacey who supplied us with needles and served out
our numbered scissors. This he did with an air of concentration and gravity which deceived no one but the warders.
He contrived, at the same time, to convey such scraps of
news as he managed to pick up. So when I was called on
to take a special job, I knew De Lacey was behind it and I
readily agreed. It meant that instead of sitting for four hours
at a stretch on a hard bench, I could stand at a counter and
move about. The instructor, an energetic little officer with
a brisk manner, showed me how to cut the material. It was
pulled taut along the counter to the required measurement
and then slit with a knife inserted in a steel groove. It was
easy, but the instructor worked me nearly to exhaustion
during the first couple of days. We worked in almost complete silence. On the third day, as I worked, I heard a
voice say :

" Which is MacNeill ? "

I was so startled that I stopped working and looked up.
The instructor said sharply :

" Now then ! What's the matter with you ? Get on
with your work."

When I did so, he whispered, keeping his face averted
from me :

" Now, don't look up this time. Just tell me, which is
MacNeill."

I worked away and as I did I located MacNeill. Then,
speaking without moving my lips—as we all learned to do

very quickly—I told him that MacNeill was the second
man from the left in the third bench forward. The instructor looked at him.

" He was against the Rising, wasn't he ? "

I dried up at once. If they wanted information, they
would have to look for it elsewhere.

" I don't know," I said.

" You're being cautious," said the instructor and I knew
he was smiling to himself. " I don't blame you." After a
long pause, he said : " Did you know James Connolly ? "

" I did."

Then the officer surprised me, when without pausing for
a moment in his work and, apparently, without paying
any attention to me, he said :

" I spoke on the same platform with Connolly in Salford.
He was a great man."

He spoke with evident conviction, but I was still on my
guard, until he told me that his people came from Ireland
a long way back, that he had a great love for Ireland and
that they had tried to keep him out of our workshop because
he was a Catholic. He asked me if the Chaplain passed
on the Irish papers he was receiving for us.

" No," I said, " I didn't know he got any papers for us."

" He does. He gets two or three Irish newspapers every
morning and they are intended for you fellows."

I said that if he could get hold of the papers, read them
and tell me what was in them, it would be a great help.
He undertook to do so, but it was long afterwards I learned
that he had failed to get the papers from the priest and that
he had himself subscribed for them through London.
Thereafter, we were kept informed of the day's news from
Ireland and as, up to that time, we had been completely
cut off, this was a great boon. Every day our friend would
give me a summary of the news. I would then go up to
De Lacey's desk with a slate on which I had an account of
the number of bags cut. I dictated the figures to De Lacey
and though there was a warder standing only a few feet
away, I managed to convey the news at the same time.
De Lacey took it down in shorthand on a slate and in a few
minutes he had succeeded in circulating whatever news

there was throughout the room. It was surprising, however, how the news changed in its travels. One day there was news of a minor naval engagement in the North Sea. Three British patrol boats and a mine-sweeper had been sunk. I gave out this news at ten o'clock. By twelve noon, it returned to me via Davy Kent. The British losses had become three battleships and a whole fleet of cruisers.

Life in the prison was deadly dull and the routine maddeningly monotonous. In the early morning, when the prison bell rang and the cells were opened, we held up our sheets for inspection to show we hadn't hanged ourselves with them during the night. From that time until lights out at eight o'clock at night, every minute was planned with the same deadly regularity, day after day. We were under surveillance for every minute of the twenty-four hours. Often during the night, an officer moving on noiseless feet in the corridor outside, would apply his bull's-eye lantern to a disc in the doorway, illuminating the cell while applying his eye to the spy-hole. After breakfast—porridge, cocoa and bread—which, like all the meals, was served to each man in his cell, we were paraded for search in the exercise ground and we could always tell in advance what the warders were going to say. For instance, the beefy warder in charge of our squad, would say each morning :

" Halt ! Left turn ! Extend on the left ! Unbutton ! " Then, looking along the line, he would always wave his baton and say, no matter whether the line was straight or crooked, " Back a bit on the left."

One day I whispered to Dick Hayes : " How can you explain the fact that a wooden-headed people like these could keep us in subjection for seven hundred years ? "

" That's easy," he said, " if you get twenty Englishmen into a room, one of them, by the grace of God, has an idea and the ability to voice it. So they all do what he says. But if you get twenty Irishmen together, everyone of them can think of a brilliant plan, any one of which might succeed, if only they would all accept it."

In spite of the silence rule, we did manage to pass an odd joke now and again. One day in the exercise ground, when the misty rain which came in from the moors was

beating in our faces—the skull cap affording no protection—
I overheard Dick Hayes addressing a Galway farm labourer
who was beside him. Dick purposely exaggerated the Irish
idiom, saying :

" Is it how that it is the way that you forgot your umbrella?"

Without a pause, or the suggestion of a smile, the other
replied :

" No, but it is how that it is the way that there are three
ribs broke in it."

The efforts of the fellows to get around the silence rule
were ingenious, but not usually successful. Etchingham,
however, seemed to be very lucky in this respect. One was
not allowed to speak even to a warder, except on a matter
of discipline, but there was a loophole here which Patsy
took full advantage of. He was always asking the warders
for guidance on this, that and the other, and he got in a lot
of conversation.

One day, during lockup, we had the usual visit from a
Visiting Justice. He happened to be a gentleman named
Colman, of mustard fame. He appeared at the cell door,
preceded by a warder and, announcing who he was, asked
if there were any complaints. Usually the answer was in
the negative. Etchingham, however, noticed that Mr.
Colman was attired in riding garb and when the usual
question was put, he said :

" No, it's not what you might call a complaint, but I'm
worried about a colt."

"A colt, what colt ? "

" Well, it's a colt they have at home and I'm afraid they'll
sell it. You see, it's a thoroughbred, and I think the people
at home don't realise its value."

He launched into an account of the pedigree of the colt
and he named nearly every Grand National winner in the
preceding twenty-five years. There followed a long discussion between Colman and himself about famous horses
and jockeys. This was a subject dear to Etchingham's heart,
as he had himself been a professional jockey in his early
days. It appeared that the colt in question might be sold
for twenty pounds, whereas it was worth certainly twenty
times that sum.

" But why don't you write about it ? " asked Colman.

" Well, I can't. I'm not entitled to a letter for four months."

" But the Governor would give you permission for a special letter."

" Oh, I dunno. I doubt it and I don't like to be turned down."

" Well, I tell you what I'll do. I'll see the Governor myself and get the necessary permission for you."

" Good man ! " said Patsy, " that's fine. Maybe I'll do as much for you some day."

Thereupon Etchingham got permission for a special letter. The reply, when it came, required an answer, and the correspondence continued for quite a long time.

One day nearly a year later, when we had been transferred to Lewes Jail, I asked Patsy how the matter of the colt had fared.

" What colt ? "

" The colt you were writing home about."

" Oh, that colt. Well, as a matter of fact, I sold that colt myself fifteen years ago."

Phil MacMahon was always getting into trouble for talking. He used to think up the most atrocious conundrums and he had to get them across to someone. One day he was trying one on Austin Stack, but because of the vigilance of the warders, he could only say two or three words at a time between long pauses, so we had gone half a dozen times round the circle before Phil got it out. It was :

" What has become of all the young men who used to move in Gaelic League circles ? " Answer : " They are now moving in prison squares."

I heard Austin say with a groan, " Great God Almighty ! "

We were allowed two books from the Library every week. We were even allowed to select our own books but that did not necessarily mean we got the books we selected. In fact, I hardly ever got the book I wanted. Austin Stack, apparently, had the same experience, for one day when I was on orderly duty, I saw written on his slate : " Give me any two books you like except novels written by Miss M. E. Braddon."

On another occasion, Dick Hayes was in a towering rage. He and I were scrubbing the corridor and he managed to tell me the cause. Someone at home had sent him a copy of Francis Thompson's *Hound of Heaven*. The chaplain had stopped it and when Dick asked him why, he had replied :

" Wasn't Francis Thompson one of the fellows who were shot in the Rising ? "

We had been about four months in the place when we scored a victory. My officer friend came into the workshop and down to our counter in a state of suppressed delight.

" There's a hell of a row going on," he said as soon as we started working. " It seems that the *Cork Examiner* has published a letter, two columns long, giving particulars of your treatment here, with the most minute details. It must have been written by one of the prisoners, but the mystery is how it got out. Do you know ? "

" I do," I said, " but I can't tell you."

" It's great work," he said, " it has never been done before in Dartmoor. Tommy is in a fearful wax."

Tommy was Principal Warder Stone. He was one of the vainest men I have ever known and he seemed to have been created for his post. For instance, he always knew when one was going to talk. Often, just as I was about to do so, I would hear a voice behind me :

" Now then, Brennan, keep that tongue of yours quiet."

This morning, he came over to me as soon as my instructor had gone.

" Look here, Brennan," he said, " I've always tried to treat you fellows decently, haven't I ? I never had a man up for report."

This was quite true and I admitted it.

" Well," he went on, " some of you fellows have been up to tricks. There has been a letter published in the Irish papers and it must have been written by one of the prisoners. Do you think that's fair to me ? "

I expressed my surprise at the news.

" Do you know anything about it ? "

" Is that a fair question," I asked. " Do you think if I did know, I would tell you anything about it ? "

He went on to say we were not treating him fairly and that if he were removed from the " party " and if, for instance, the Wasp replaced him, things would not run so smoothly.

" That's quite right," I said.   " Maybe some of us would like that."

" You don't know what you're talking about.   They can ride you to death if they try."

" Maybe."

"Are you going to write anything about this place when you get out."

" I might."

" I hope you'll be fair to me."

I suddenly remembered that Etchingham was dying to get off the hard bench where he was sewing, so I told Stone that Etchingham was planning to write a book on the place. Next day, Etchingham was taken off the bench and put to work at a sewing-machine, out of which he seemed to get a great deal of enjoyment.

As for the *Cork Examiner* letter, it had been a painstaking and prolonged job.   It was De Lacey's idea.   We had no pens, pencils, ink, or paper and a letter had to be written, and in spite of three personal searches every day, a cell search every night, a special cell search every week and surprise searches now and then, it had to be kept carefully until it could be smuggled out by a visitor.   It seemed impossible, but we managed to do it.   Three or four paces behind my counter there was a sort of sentry box which was used by the Principal Warder now and again when he had to sign reports.   There was a bottle of ink there but even if I could get into the place unobserved, I could not take the ink bottle because its loss would be noticed before our plans were complete.   So we decided I should take the ink and not the bottle, if I got a chance.   We had to have a container.   At the time, we were supplied with half an ounce of margarine with breakfast and this was served in small tins little bigger than a thimble.   De Lacey held back one of these tins and he concealed it in one of the watering cans which were carried over each morning to supply drinking water to the workshop.   He went into the

recess in the workshop to fill the watering can and he left
the margarine tin concealed in the place. Diarmuid Lynch
retrieved the tin and left it on his counter behind some bags.
Gerard Crofts, carrying supplies of canvas from Lynch to
me, brought the tin with him. As there were three warders
on duty all the time watching us, we had to be careful at
every step. I worked very hard cutting material till I had
a huge pile on my counter, then, under cover of these, I
took the tin and crept on my hands and knees to the sentry
box, poured the ink into the tin and crept back. We then
had to reverse the process and we did this so successfully
that the ink lay in the bottom of the watering can in the
recess in our hall that night. Just before lock-up, when
the cell search was over, De Lacey suddenly remembered
he had got no drinking water for the night. He asked Stone
to let him get some and the latter agreed. De Lacey
brought his can to the recess and brought back the little
tin containing the ink in the bottom of it, pretending it
was full of water. He had managed to manufacture a nib
from some materials in the drawer of his counter. He
wrote the letter that night. We had to keep it for nearly
three weeks until Diarmuid Lynch had a visitor. It was
explained to Diarmuid that he would see his visitor in a
room but that he was on no account to approach him.
Diarmuid was searched as he left the exercise ground for
the interview, and he was searched again before he entered
the office. In a corner of his pocket handkerchief which he
held aloft in his hand during the search, he had the precious
letter. As he entered the office and saw his friend, Diarmuid
conveniently forgot his instructions and he stepped im-
pulsively forward.

" Why, hello, Seumas ! " he cried, as he shook hands with
the visitor.

" Now, now," cried Stone, who was superintending the
interview, and the two parted. The letter, however, was
now in safe hands.

One immediate effect of the publication of this letter was
that the officers showed more respect for us.

Chapter Twelve

Two by-elections held in Ireland early in 1917 *were lost by the Irish Parliamentary Party and won by Sinn Féin, a clear indication of a profound change in Irish public opinion.*

It was nearing the end of the year when there occurred a major incident. Some of us had been getting six ounces of bread extra because we had been losing weight. We shared this boon by passing the extra loaf every alternate day to someone who was not on the special list. One day when we returned from the workshop, de Valera stepped into his cell, seized his extra loaf and tossed it across the dim hall into Jack Macardle's cell on the opposite side. Jack was waiting for it and caught it neatly, and the two doors closed. Usually, this procedure was pretty safe as it was very gloomy at that end of the hall. However, this time a lynx-eyed warder, who was very officious and who was standing on the bridge on an upper floor, saw something passing through the air and he raced down and opened Jack's cell just as the latter had taken his first bite of the loaf. Jack and Dev were hailed before the Governor and sentenced to three days' solitary confinement on bread and water. Dev promptly went on hunger strike.

But for one or two friendly warders, we would not have known of this, for both men had been removed to another wing of the prison. Some of us wanted an immediate general sympathetic strike. I heard that Austin Stack was against this and in the next line-up I managed to get beside him. He was dead against the idea and warned me not to go further with it. The time had not arrived he said. I always found it very difficult to get Stack to take action in such cases, but when he did it was even more difficult to get him to stop.

On the following day, two other men were absent from the line-up, Dr. Dick Hayes and Desmond Fitzgerald. We learned later that, with Dev, they had been removed to

another prison. There was no little feeling over the dispute
as to whether we should take action or not. We did nothing,
but discipline became noticeably more slack and our fellows
grew more daring.

One day an entirely unpremeditated demonstration on
our part threw the whole prison system out of gear. There
was more than a touch of frost in the air as we went round
the exercise ring. Some of the younger prisoners found the
lagging, dragging pace too slow and there were audible
exhortations from some of them to " step out." Suddenly,
I saw one of the men taking a sudden short run and getting
in front of the man who had been ahead of him. I saw a
puzzled look on the warder's face. He knew something
had happened but could not make out what it was. Then
the same man did the same thing again. His example was
followed by Frank Thornton who passed me and stepped
in front of me. I made a run and regained my place. Like
a flash, the movement was taken up all round the ring and
soon, to keep our places, we were all running, the older
men retiring to the inner circle. It started with a trot, but
in a little while we were all racing madly, yelling and
shrieking like wild Indians. It was a spontaneous outlet
of emotions pent up for months. The warders, aghast and
panic-stricken at this unprecedented conduct, retreated to
the various exits from the exercise ground and summoned
the armed guard who were usually on duty only during
fog. The guards came running, muskets in hands, but we
paid no attention to them. We continued galloping round
and round till we got the signal to fall in and we did so
boisterously laughing and cheering. When we got the
order to march off someone cried " Double " and we ran
to the workshop followed by the panting warders.

That was definitely the end of the rigid silence rule.

My warder was jubilant when he came in.

" The news is all over the place," he said. " The Irish
are up. There is terrific excitement."

Half an hour later Stone came in. He was very agitated.
He strolled around for a while and then came over to me.

" Say, Brennan," he said, " can you tell me the meaning
of all this ? "

" It's only a bit of fun," I said, and added : " We're getting tired of the place."

" Was this thing prearranged ? "

" I'm sorry, I can't tell you."

" You mean you don't know."

" I mean I'm not saying."

" Are you one of the leaders ? "

" You don't expect me to answer that."

" Is there likely to be another outburst ? "

" That wasn't an outburst. You'll know what an out-burst is when you see one."

" I've tried to be good to you fellows," he said. " I think I'm entitled to some co-operation."

In the afternoon he came back again, and asked was there anything I could suggest to ease the situation.

" You could bring de Valera back," I said.

" I can't do that. I've nothing to do with it. Is there anything I personally can do ? "

" Well," I said, " you might prevent murder by removing some of those warders."

" Which of them ? "

I indicated the three warders then in the room. One of them was the man who had reported de Valera and Macardle ; the other two were fond of making trouble.

"Are there any officers you would prefer ? "

This was going too far. I might get some of the decent ones victimised.

"Any of them," I said, " so long as you take those three away."

The three warders were taken off that evening and we did not see them again. They were replaced by three easy-going men who did not seem to mind our talking so long as there was no superior officer about. One of them, indeed, used to keep watch at the spyhole in the door and warn us when the Principal Warder was coming. Things were much easier from that time on.

Early in December, they told us we were being removed to another prison where we would have the special privilege of being allowed to talk during exercise and of sending and receiving fortnightly letters. Up to that time, we could receive one letter every four months. We were told we could travel in civilian clothes if we gave an undertaking not to try to escape. We refused to give the undertaking, so we made the journey in convict garb and in chains, five men to a chain. At Tavistock railway station, where we had a wait, Dick King asked me to lilt a reel and as I did so he climbed up on a table in the waiting-room and danced a reel. The other men on the chain had to sway with his movements and go through the most extraordinary contortions so as not to get the chain snarled up. As it was, Con Donovan nearly had his arm broken when the chain suddenly twisted. We laughed uproariously, while the warders and the few waiting passengers present looked on in round-eyed wonderment.

Otherwise it was not a pleasant journey and it lasted a long time, right across the South of England. Whenever any man had occasion to go to the lavatory, all five men on his chain had to go with him as the warders carried no keys to the chains.

My warder had told me that if he was not sent with us, he would leave the prison service. He did not come with us and he left the service. A few years later he was arrested in a round-up of Sinn Féiners in London and sent with about one hundred prisoners to Mountjoy Jail in Dublin.

Our new abode, Lewes Jail in Sussex, seemed to be a beautiful place after the experience of Dartmoor. The cell floors were of wood and there were hot-water pipes and, though they were never hot, they looked good. The lighting of the cells, too, was infinitely better. I had been only a short time in my cell when the door opened and a man in civilian dress entered. He said he was the Governor and he hoped I would be comfortable. This, I said to myself, is a policy of killing us with kindness. The Governor was a very quiet, gentle-spoken man and though he seemed to be young, his hair was quite white. We learned later that he had spent three years as a spy in the Madhi's camp while the British were conquering the latter's territory.

The Governor asked if I needed anything. I asked for writing materials and a typewriter.

"A typewriter!" he exclaimed. He could not have been

more surprised had I asked for a machine-gun. He said
he would ask permission to give me the writing materials
but he knew the typewriter was out of the question.   In
reply to his queries, I told him I wanted to write a few
stories and we got talking about books.   He told me he
took a keen interest in mathematics and said he was worry-
ing over a problem which had appeared in the Cambridge
magazine.   He had been over a month working at it and
he had found a solution which he knew must be wrong
because, if it were right, the ice age must still have held
Sussex as late as the ninth century, which, of course, was
absurd.   He asked me if I were good at mathematics.

" I'm not bad," I said, " but I don't think I could solve
your problem.   There is a man here, however, who could,
I think.   His name is de Valera."

He hurried off to Dev's cell.   Next day I asked Dev how
he had got on with the problem.

" I solved it," he said, " but it took me over an hour."

" But the Governor said he had been over a month at it."

" Yes," he said, " and he might have been at it for ten
years if he had continued to forget, as he did, that the square
root of a positive may have a plus or minus value.   He
thought only of the plus value."

" I'm glad you sent him to me," continued Dev, " because
he is going to let me have Poincare's work on Quaternions in
four volumes.   I have been wanting it for a long time."

" Quaternions," I said, " I can't remember what they
are, but I think they were invented or discovered by Rowan
Hamilton."

" That's right."

" Well, what are they anyway ? "

" It's hard to explain," said Dev, " but it's like this.
You take a point in space—or say, take a point in a room.
In the ordinary way you can locate that point if you know
its distance from two walls and the floor or ceiling.   Now,
quaternions will indicate the location of that point by one
symbol instead of three measurements."

This left me up in the air, so I changed the subject to
talk of Rowan Hamilton himself.   He was that rare genius
who was an infant prodigy and remained a prodigy when

he was no longer an infant.   He might have been but was
not a hateful child.   Born in Dublin in 1805, he read
Hebrew at the age of seven.   Before he was twelve, he was
not only a master of all the European languages and of
Latin and Greek, but he had a knowledge of Syriac, Persian,
Arabic, Sanskrit, Hindustani and Malay.   At ten, he knew
nothing of mathematics but, happening on a Latin copy of
Euclid, he studied it and within two years he had mastered
not only it, but every work on mathematics then written.
He was self-taught.   In his eighteenth year, he entered
Trinity College and in all the examinations he took first
place.   Apart from his languages and mathematics, he
twice gained the Vice-Chairman's prize for English Verse.
He was an orator, scholar, poet, metaphysician, mathe-
matician and natural philosopher.   When he was about
twenty he was made Astronomer Royal for Ireland and he
took up this position in Dunsink Observatory, where he
remained for the rest of his life working out many mathe-
matical problems of the most abstruse kind.   He foresaw
clearly, though he did not name it, the theory of Relativity
later set down by Einstein.   One day, in his old age, walking
down the road near Dunsink he came on an ancient villager
sitting on the bridge wall.   And the ancient villager said :
   " What is it you are doing to-day, Mr. Astronomer
Royal ? "
   " I am," he said, " multiplying the North-East by the
South-West."
   When I told Dev this, he said :
   "And that is exactly what he was doing."
   Nearly thirty years later, in 1943 to be precise, I had
occasion to call on Albert Einstein in Princeton University.
I had been commissioned by the Irish Government to invite
him to the *colloquium* about to be held in Dublin under
the auspices of the Institute of Advanced Studies.   The great
man came into the room where I was waiting, dressed in
an old tweed suit, the coat of which was buttoned high
across his chest.   He wore no collar or tie and his heavy
boots were actually tied with pieces of twine.   His kindly
Hebrew eyes twinkled under a mass of grey hair which
pointed to the four winds.   He was pleased to receive the

invitation and sorry he could not accept it because his health prevented him from travelling. I told him the story of Dev and the prison Governor and he was highly amused. We talked of Hamilton and I told him he had said on one occasion that he was multiplying the North-East by the South-West and that Dev had said : " That's exactly what he was doing." Dr. Einstein said : " Of course it was," which again left me up in the air.

In Lewes we met many old friends because all the Irish prisoners from Portland, Dartmoor, Maidstone and other prisons, were brought together there. There were over one hundred and thirty of us. We talked all the time in spite of all efforts to stop us and we made wonderful plans about how we were going to carry on the fight when we got out. In addition, we were all studying various subjects, particularly languages, French, German, Spanish, Italian and, of course, Irish. Pierce Beasley held examinations for the Fainne.

It is curious that after the silence of Dartmoor I should have so quickly tired of talk, but after a few days in Lewes, I welcomed the evening and silence of my cell. I had got my writing materials and I completed two full-length mystery novels before we left the place.

We were split up into various parties assigned to carry out the work of the prison. There were about thirty of us in the workshop, where we made hearth rugs and doormats, the former on looms, the latter on upright frames. Etchingham was given a loom and the warder instructed him how to make the rug.

" Do I have to make that ? " he asked, looking at a completed rug.

" Yes," said the warder.

" I'm afraid they've selected the wrong man," said Etchingham, " I've only got five years to do."

Vincent Poole, a Citizen Army man, almost precipitated a general row within the first few days in Lewes. He was in the workshop with us and he began to sing " The Green Flag." When the warder had checked him a few times, he suddenly got up from his seat and yelled at the warder :

" What's this about ? I might as well be in jail ! "

[Micheal Mac Eochaidh, O.S., An Gleann]

Prisoners leaving Athenaeum, Enniscorthy, after the Surrender, 1st May, 1916. Amongst the prisoners may be seen Robert Brennan, Sean R. Etchingham, Richard King, Michael de Lacey, Seamus Doyle, and Seamus Rafter. The Rev. Patrick Murphy, M.S.S., may be seen in the background.

Enniscorthy prisoners, Dick Donohue and Tom Doyle, being escorted to Kilmainham Jail after 1916 Rising.

Whereupon he was brought before the Governor and sent to the cells. He went on a hunger strike. He even refused to let the warders enter his cell and when they tried to put him in a strait-jacket, he beat them. A section of the prisoners wanted a sympathetic strike in his favour, but de Valera had had a Prisoners' Council elected and they decided against it. There was a very strained atmosphere, however, until Poole was returned to us.

In the workshop, after a short while, discipline became so lax that we strolled about where we liked and there was very little work done. Most of my time was spent in Slattery's loom. He was giving half a dozen of us a series of lectures on science and chemistry. After his lecture, we would adjourn to Jack Plunkett's loom and he discoursed on Dante and Italian literature. There were individual talks on such subjects as hand carving, poster illustrations, gardening, music, etc., and I gave a series of talks on bee-keeping.

On the exercise ground, Eoin MacNeill was giving Sean MacEntee, Con Donovan and myself a series of lectures on Ancient Irish History. Without a textbook, or even a notebook to which to refer, he gave us a series of sixteen lectures in the most complete detail, covering some ten centuries of history. One day, our lecture was rudely interrupted. One of our comrades, who had more curiosity than tact, pushed his way in between MacNeill and myself. He put his arm very familiarly around MacNeill's shoulder.

" Say, Mac," he said, " why did you stop the Rising ? "

MacNeill stopped and glared at him. Then, putting his hands on the other's chest, he pushed him away with no little violence.

" Go away from me ! " he cried, and the man went off looking very much astonished.

Principal Officer Stone had come with us from Dartmoor and the poor man was very much distressed at the lack of discipline in the new prison. His vanity, however, was still colossal. One day he conducted half a dozen of us to the baths for our weekly immersion. Etchingham was in the next bath to mine and he was giving me an account of the death of poor old Mrs. Webb in Gorey.

" She was a hundred and three," said Etchingham, " and I saw her dancing a jig last year."

As there was a four-foot wall between us and as the noise of the lads splashing in the baths was considerable, he had to talk very loud. Stone intervened :

" Now then, Etchingham, not so loud."

" I'm only telling him," yelled Patsy, " about old Mrs. Webb. She has just died at the age of a hundred and three and I saw her dancing a jig last year. Now, what do you think of that, Mr. Stone ? "

" Well," said Stone, " some people carry their years well. What age would you think I am ? "

" I suppose you'd be around thirty-five," said Patsy.

" You wouldn't think I'm fifty ? "

" Why, Mr. Stone," said Patsy, sitting up in his bath in amazement, " nobody would ever take you to be more than thirty-five. You're a wonderful fine man."

" Oh, you should have seen me twenty years ago. I tell you the girls used to look at me."

" I'm sure they're doing that still," said Patsy.

"And even though I'm fifty, there are very few of your fellows would give me ten yards in a hundred."

" I bet they wouldn't. Do you know, Mr. Stone, there must have been a great moon the night you were born."

" Why do you say that ? "

" Well, you know, we have an old saying in Ireland, ' no moon, no man.' "

Afterwards, Seumas Doyle said to Patsy :

" I never heard that old saying, ' no moon, no man.' "

" Neither did I," said Patsy.

After a while, I was transferred to the cleaning squad and life became much more interesting. There were five of us and Harry Boland was our leader. We took our orders from Harry and not at all from the warder, though we never had any trouble with the man generally in charge of us, a little fellow named Gallop. Amongst other un-official duties, Harry supplied us with extra bread. We had our own men working in the kitchen and every morning, knowing the time the cleaning squad was passing the kitchen window, one of them was waiting with a string of half a dozen six-ounce loaves. As Harry passed the window, the loaves were shot forward and Harry took them and slipped them under his jersey. It was so quickly and so neatly done that even I, who was following Harry, failed more often than not to see the operation. As opportunity offered, Harry divided the loaves amongst us and we concealed them under our oxters. One day, because someone was ill, Dick Hayes was assigned to our squad. We had passed the kitchen window and we were swabbing a little yard when Harry pushed a loaf into Dick's hand. Dick held the loaf in his hand and gazed at it as if it were some strange insect.

" What am I to do with it ? " he asked blankly.

Before Harry had time to reply, the warder strode across, looking very angry.

" What's up ? " he asked.

Harry grinned at him.

" Dr. Hayes is a newcomer," he said.

The warder turned to Dick.

" Put that thing under your jersey," he said dryly.

One of the things the cleaning squad had to do was to purloin an Irish newspaper which, by the time it passed through over one hundred hands, was in shreds. We got the newspaper from the priest's room. Each morning, the five of us went down to clean the entrance hall on which opened the offices of the Governor, the priest and the steward. We swept the hall as a preliminary to scrubbing it and I had to fill the coal scuttle in the steward's room. I had also to create a diversion so as to enable Harry to get into the priest's office unobserved. Gallop always fell for the ruse. He had got very chummy with us and he had even picked up a few Irish phrases, such as, " Dun an doras," " Eist do bheul," etc.

One morning I went as usual into the steward's room and upset my bucket of coal with a clatter. Gallop came to the door.

" What's the racket ? "

" I spilled the coal."

" What's wrong with you ? You're always spilling something."

" Well, this is not the sort of work I'm used to."

Gallop returned to the hall and I followed as soon as I had cleaned up the mess. I took my brush and started sweeping.

" Bfuil se agat ? "—(Have you got it ?) I said to Harry.

" Ta,"—(I have), he replied.

Gallop had heard me. He walked over to Harry and tried to repeat the phrase I had used.

" Will shay gut ? " he said.

Harry laughed.

" Ta," he said.

Gallop went into the priest's room and saw that the newspaper was gone. He turned towards us and said :

" Ta, by God ! "

He did not give us away, however, and we continued to get the paper until the priest forestalled us by having it delivered elsewhere.

Harry had the first look at the paper as, of course, he was entitled to. One day, as we were all returning to our cells for dinner, he astonished us by yelling from his doorway :

" Russia is out of the war, boys. That's one leg off o' the pot."

The place rang with cheers and cries of " Up the Rebels ! " We had another demonstration when Joe McGuinness, one of our fellow prisoners, was elected M.P. for Longford. That night we celebrated the victory with a concert to which nearly everyone contributed. The singers, standing on stools in their cells, sang out through the windows. Some of the efforts were deplorable but we had a few good voices, including those of Gerard Crofts, Seumas Hughes and the brothers Tommy and Charlie Bevan who had been with the O'Mara Opera Company. Crofts had the cell immediately beneath mine and every night he would give us a few songs from his vast repertoire. His voice was never very powerful but he was a real artist and he could make any and every old song sound beautiful.

Fergus O'Connor was a prisoner who was always planning some trick or another. If when you pulled down the lever on your loom all the intricate threads snapped, or if you found the mouth of the bag you were making sewed up, it was ten to one that O'Connor was the cause of it. One day I saw him going about from place to place in the workshop with a ball of jute. There were a dozen huge, upright wooden frames for making jute mats lined along the workshop floor. Fergus put the ball through the tops of one frame after another till the whole lot were linked by the cord. Then he tied the string to the end of a long heavy form. I was surprised that Hawke, the very officious officer who was on duty, did not spot him and I wondered what the outcome would be. At last, Hawke spoke to Fergus asking him why he was not making his mat.

" I had to get some jute," said Fergus and, at the same time, he jerked the cord behind his back. Down went the heavy form with a clatter and down with it went all the big frames from one end of the room to the other. The noise was terrific. When it subsided, Fergus said to Hawke :

" Now look at what you're after doing."

Chapter Thirteen

In April 1917 the U.S. entered the war pledged to the principle of government by consent of the governed for all nations, great and small. The British endorsed this principle in words. Their treatment of Ireland was becoming embarrassing in view of these words.

FOOD is an elemental thing and, I suppose, its most frequent symbol is bread. It was a tiny loaf of bread which had precipitated a crisis in Dartmoor and again in Lewes a similar loaf was the beginning of a lot of trouble. Harry Boland and Dick King one day passed through the prison kitchen in charge of the warder Hawke, whom none of us liked because he was always looking for trouble. There had been two six-ounce loaves on the kitchen table before they entered. They were gone when they left. They were missed almost at once and the warder in charge rushed up and told Hawke, who ran immediately to King's cell. He found King eating one of the loaves. Harry and Dick were had up before the Governor and sentenced to three days in solitary. As they were leaving the Governor's office, Harry turned and said to the Governor :

" If any ten of your men can put me into a solitary cell, I'm willing to go there."

He hurried to the end of the main hall and stood with his back to an iron-barred gate.

" Now," he said to the Governor and the warder who had followed him, " send for your ten best men."

There was a hasty conference and it was decided that Harry and Dick should go to their own cells. When I was passing Harry's cell, I shouted encouragement to him.

" Go away," he said, " don't interrupt my thoughts. I've started the contemplative life."

This was funny coming from Harry than whom there were few more active or vigorous. He went on hunger strike. The Chaplain, on a visit to him, absent-mindedly offered him a chocolate.

" Get thee behind me, Satan," said Harry, with a grin which was always infectious. The Chaplain grinned also.

When Harry and Dick rejoined us, we decided to worry the warder Hawke till he died or resigned. We got our chance a few days later when Hawke was on duty and it came to the turn of Harry and myself to bring round the breakfast which normally consisted of a loaf, a pint of cocoa and a pint of porridge. However, because we were on half-bread rations, owing to the shortage caused by the war, we were given a kippered herring three times a week.

There were thirty-four men in our cell block and an equal number of loaves came up from the kitchen in a wooden tray. Hawke walked in front and Harry followed, pushing the tray along the handrail. The warder opened a cell door, took a loaf from the tray and handed it to the prisoner and passed on to the next cell. As he did so, Harry took a loaf in his right hand and jerked it behind his back into the cell past the head of the astonished prisoner. The movement was as quick as a flash. It had to be, because immediately following Harry came another warder and myself. I was toting a big bucket of cocoa from which my warder measured out a pint for each prisoner. Harry repeated the operation several times. When he got to the home stretch, Hawke looked at the tray.

" Why," he said, " there are only three loaves."

" That's right," said Harry, " and there are two, four, six, eight cells to do." He looked at Hawke with his sunniest smile. " It doesn't seem possible."

" There were thirty-four loaves brought up," said Hawke. " I counted them."

" Something wrong with your arithmetic," said Harry.

Hawke had to send down for five additional loaves. This meant serious trouble for him.

When it came to serving out the kippers, Harry took the tray. Hawke went in front, as before, and opened the cell door. Then he lifted the kipper on a spoon and transferred it to the plate the prisoner was holding. Before the prisoner had time to close his door, Harry had taken a kipper by the tail, slung it round his back and into the cell as before. He had to be more careful this time, as Hawke was watching

him closely. Nevertheless, he managed to get rid of four
of the kippers. To say Hawke was flabbergasted when he
reached the final cells, is to put it mildly. He gazed at the
tray, gasping like a fish himself.

" What's wrong ? " asked Harry innocently.

" There are only five kippers."

" Well ? "

" We have to do nine cells more."

Harry looked up and counted the cells.

" Begob that's right," he said, " that's funny."

" But I counted thirty-four," said Hawke.

" Nonsense," said Harry. " Where are they ? "

Of course, Hawke had to send down for more kippers,
which was another black mark for him.

The climax came when we were serving the porridge.
Harry had gone back to his cell and I was lugging the
bucket of porridge around. The warder served this by
plunging a long-handled scoop into the porridge and
measuring out a pint into each prisoner's mug. When we
came to Harry's cell the latter, instead of presenting a mug,
had one of the pint dinner tins. Hawke ladled out his
porridge and the tin was only three parts full.

" Excuse me," said Harry, " this tin holds a pint."

" What do you mean ? "

" It's only three-quarters full and I'm entitled to a pint."

" Well," said Hawke, " I was never very particular
before, but I'm going to be now."

" There's no need to grouse about it," said Harry.

" That's right," I said, " every man is entitled to a pint
of porridge."

" You keep out of this," said Hawke to me.

" Come on," said Harry, " be a sport."

" I'll show you," said Hawke, and the fool of a man,
instead of filling the tin and leaving the matter so, took the
tin from Harry and emptied it into the bucket with the idea
of measuring the exact fill of the scoop. Of course, by this
time, the tin was slippery and it escaped from Hawke's
fingers and fell into the bucket.

" Now," said Hawke, glaring at Harry, " look what
you've done,"

ALLEGIANCE 127

"You mean what you've done," said Harry.

Hawke began to swear as he fished the tin out of the bucket of porridge. By the time he got it out, he had some porridge on his sleeve, on the breast of his tunic and on his chin. The warders always tried to keep their uniforms spick and span and, of course, the poor man was, by this time, in a terrible rage. His language was unprintable.

"Now, now," said Harry, reprovingly, "that's not nice talk."

"And all for nothing," I said. "I've never before heard it disputed that every man is entitled to a pint of porridge."

"If you say another word——" said Hawke to me, and stopped.

"But I'm only saying," I said, "that every man is entitled to a pint of porridge."

"Shut up," said Hawke.

"As a matter of fact," I said to Harry, "I think it is on your cell card in there."

Harry went back into the cell and took down the card.

"Here it is," he said. "Look, read it for yourself, Mr. Hawke. Breakfast one pint of porridge, and that shows Mr. Brennan is right. Every man is entitled to a pint of porridge."

Harry finally got his pint of porridge and we moved on to the next cell when Hawke had done his best to remove the stains from his tunic. The next cell was occupied by Willie Corrigan.

"Isn't that right, Willie," I said.

"What?"

"Every man is entitled to a pint of porridge."

"Oh, sure," said Willie at once, "every man is entitled to a pint of porridge."

"If you don't stop that at once," said Hawke to me, "I'll put you back in your cell right now and report you to the Governor."

"All right," I said, "you'll be quite within your rights, but I'm sure that the Governor will hold that every man is entitled to a pint of porridge."

We continued round the cells and if I repeated the phrase once I must have said it fifty times. Finally, Hawke could

stand it no longer. In a loud voice he commanded me to
" shut up."

Stone had come into the hall downstairs. His tenor
voice came floating up.

" What's the matter, Mr. Hawke ? "

" It's nothing, Mr. Stone," I said, " only a misunder-
standing. Mr. Hawke doesn't seem to realise that every
man is entitled to a pint of porridge."

" Why, of course," said Stone, " every man is entitled to
a pint of porridge."

Hawke applied for a transfer that night and we never
saw him any more. Years later, when I was Under-
Secretary for Foreign Affairs and Harry was the Irish
Envoy to the United States, he used to send me long official
reports. At the end of every one of them, in his own handwriting, were the words : " Every man is entitled to a pint
of porridge."

It is curious to recall now how easily and naturally
de Valera stepped into the leadership. Apart from the
fact that he was the ranking survivor of the Dublin officers,
he became the leader of the prisoners in Dartmoor from the
day he gave the salute to MacNeill. In Lewes he became
the leader of us all, without any consultation, debate or
election—there was an election later, but long before that
he had become " the chief." Whenever any proposal was
made or discussed, the first question everyone asked was :
" What does Dev think of it ? " Even at that early stage,
there was the contradiction that though we found him
tantalisingly conservative, we were all looking to him for a
lead. We finally got it from him.

The officials in Lewes found that the more concessions
we obtained, the more liberties we took. In the workshop
particularly, after a little while, no one paid the slightest
attention to an order from the officials. For instance, Tom
Doyle, one of the Enniscorthy prisoners, was making jute
door mats on a frame. He discovered that some balls of
jute were a shade darker than others and by skilfully utilis-
ing the two shades, he produced a mat which had a neatly-
designed harp in the centre. The difference in shades,
however, was so delicate that the design could be seen

only from certain angles. Tom was very proud of his
artistry and he lingered over the last remaining rows of
his mat. We were all wondering if any of the warders
would notice the design. One day, Stone came along and
saw it. He was aghast. He asked Tom what was the
meaning of it.

" The meaning of what ? " asked Tom.

" That design."

" Where ? "

Stone brought him to a point from which the design was
plainly visible.

" That's curious," said Tom. " It must be in the blood.
My great grandfather was a famous harper."

The Governor was brought on the scene and the mat was
sent to the scrap heap. Tom started another one and this
produced a shamrock and at the same time it was found
that the mats the other fellows were making all had various
emblems, such as round towers and wolf dogs, some of
them very bad. The lads blamed the whole thing on the
prison officials who failed to supply jute of a uniform shade.
The mat-making was stopped.

Some of the fellows started growing moustaches. The
prison officials objected, to no effect. Before the matter
came before the Governor, Dev heard about it and he
ordered the moustaches to be removed. He said if there
was going to be a row it would be about something worth
while.

When the election of a Council was held, Dev's selection
as chief was almost unanimous. Only Tom Ashe and a
few others opposed him. He did not at all resent the
opposition, but when the election was over he did very
strongly object to the efforts of the minority to nullify the
decisions of the Council. His attitude then, as later, was
that of a constitutional autocrat. He would allow the
greatest latitude in discussion and, generally, he managed
to talk us all into his way of thinking by his clear, common-
sense arguments. When, however, he was likely to fail
in this, he did not hesitate to throw his own personality
and worth into the balance against all opposition. In
other words : " You can talk about this as much as you

like, the more the better and from every possible angle. In the last analysis, if you don't agree with me, then I quit. You must get someone else to do it." And they never could afford to let him quit. Many years later I was present on an occasion when there were two thousand delegates from all over Ireland gathered at a convention in the Mansion House. Dev was in a hopeless minority on the question at issue. That question was the introduction of special legislation to grant a pension to General O'Duffy who had been relieved of his position as Police Commissioner. With the exception of the half-dozen people on the platform, everyone of the two thousand people present was against the proposal and the speeches in opposition were greeted with general applause. Dev was, or seemed to be very angry when he rose to speak. He said that in the ordinary course, O'Duffy, as a Civil Servant, would have been entitled to a pension. Because, however, certain legislation had not been enacted, he was not so entitled at the moment. Were they to be mean enough to take advantage of a flaw in the law because they did not like the man in question. There was some applause at this, but it was very half-hearted. Then Dev threw down the trump card I have seen him use so often. He said, in effect : " You are perfectly free to have your way in this matter but you will have it without me. You can get someone else to take my place." And, because they knew they could not let him go, knew that he was a head and shoulders over everyone else, they had to let him have his way.

Matters in the prison reached such a stage that the authorities decided to call a halt. We were lined up in the Central Hall and a man from the Home Office read a document which was to the effect that we would still be allowed the privilege of talking during exercise but that otherwise we should conform to the prison rule of strict silence, and all orders of the officers were to be obeyed without question. When the visitor finished reading the document, Dev started to reply. He meant to voice a demand on behalf of all of us that we should be treated as prisoners of war but, before he had said three words, the visitor sharply interrupted and said no one was entitled to speak on behalf of the prisoners and that if any of us had any representations to make, we should individually ask for an audience with the Governor. We were then marched to our cells.

That evening, I got a note in Dev's perfectly neat handwriting to the effect that the time had arrived to make a formal demand that we be treated as prisoners of war, or political prisoners, and that he intended to present this to the Governor at our next parade. If the demand was denied, we should refuse to work as convicts or to associate with convicts. We had been expecting some such move as this, as we had previously learned he had been in touch with the people at home and they had agreed to the proposal. Next morning, we were all agog as we were marched out to the exercise ground. When we were lined up for searching, word passed along the line that we were not to march off until Dev had given the word. The Governor evidently expected some trouble for he made one of his rare appearances on the exercise ground. He looked rather pathetic in his light grey suit, his white hair and his still young face with the pallor of death as always. The search over, the ranks closed. Stone gave us the order to march off. We stood still and I saw Stone's face tense and white. Dev stepped forward and handed the Governor a paper. " I am demanding," he said, " that we Irish Volunteers should be treated as prisoners of war."

The Governor took the paper and did not reply. Dev went on :

" We refuse any longer to accept the status of convicts."

The Governor still said nothing and Dev stepped back into the ranks. Stone and the Governor exchanged a few words in a whisper. The hundred and twenty odd prisoners stood in absolute silence. Stone turned to the warders.

"All right," he said, " take these men back to their cells."

So back to our cells we marched and we were not let out again. On Saturday, however, we were asked to give an undertaking that if we were allowed to go to Mass on Sunday we would not avail of the opportunity to try to escape or to make a demonstration. In accordance with our new policy, we refused to give this undertaking, though the loss of Mass was a very serious matter for the men, most of whom received the Sacrament every Sunday. This incident was subsequently distorted out of all shape and was quoted by the Home Office as evidence of our ungodliness. When I got to Parkhurst Jail, a week or so later, the Chaplain there gave a fantastic account of the affair and described de Valera as an atheist and an anti-Christ. As a matter of fact, on that Sunday morning when we were supposed to be so ungodly, we all answered the Rosary given out by a man in each cell block.

On Monday we got word from Dev that he had given the prison authorities three days to meet our demands. At the end of that time, if we were still locked in, we were to start breaking up the prison, beginning with the windows the first night, the spyholes in the doors the second night, the lamp screens the third night, and so on. On the night the ultimatum expired, I gave the signal for our block by singing " God Save Ireland," which was enthusiastically chorused by all the lads in the wing, after which we proceeded to break the windows, amidst a great deal of noise and cheering. The people of the town, hearing the commotion, assembled around the jail. On the second and third nights, we carried on as instructed, and then we were left to our own devices as to what to break next. We started taking the brick walls apart—a slow job for the first brick but easy after that—and before I left, three of the cells in our block had been made into one by the removal of the walls.

Jimmy Brennan, who had been acting as the priest's orderly, had been ordered to carry on with his usual duties of serving Mass and looking after the chapel. One morning here turned with the news that Dev, Tom Ashe and Eamon Duggan had been removed from the prison. On the following morning, we heard Harry Boland's voice in the hall.

" I'm off, boys," he cried.

He stopped at my cell door.

" Keep the flag flying ! " he yelled in at me.

" I've no flag," I said.

" Keep it flying whether you have or not," he shouted, and we all gave him a great cheer. He refused to go on a chain and they handcuffed him after a terrific struggle. He was whirled off to Maidstone Prison in Kent in an open car. He had previously written a note to his mother and he tossed it from the car.

" What's that? " asked Stone, who was sitting beside him.

" Your death warrant," said Harry.

The note was picked up by a woman walking the road. She read :

> If it is a mother who finds this note, will she send it to my mother, Mrs. Boland, at 15 Marino Crescent, Clontarf, Dublin, to tell her that her son Harry is being taken from Lewes Jail to God knows where.

The woman sent the note to Mrs. Boland and said she had a son fighting at the front and she had sympathy for another mother whose son was in peril. The note was printed on a handbill in Dublin and circulated throughout Ireland.

Harry was only half an hour gone when my cell door opened and two warders advanced cautiously into the cell holding a wooden barricade in front of them. Behind them came two others with batons aloft. The two latter suddenly pounced, one from each side, and grabbed me. The others dropped the shutter and caught my legs. We all went down in a heap.

" Let me up," I said, " and I'll walk."

They let me up and I walked. I yelled encouragement to the others as I was marched out. I got a glimpse of Eoin MacNeill as I passed his cell. The dignified historian and University professor was sitting up on the window sill with his feet out through the window. He had put his bare feet out through the bars and then put his boots on so that he could not be dragged from the cell.

Down in the office, five of us were put on a chain and taken in a bus to the railway station. While we were sitting in the railway waiting-room I saw a man on an opposite seat whom I took to be Michael Staines, but as he took no notice of us, I allowed I was mistaken. It was Staines, as we learned shortly. He had been sent from Dublin to

watch developments. As soon as the train started, Tommy
Bevan who, with his brother Charlie, was on the chain,
produced, from some mysterious hiding-place in his clothing,
a tuning-fork. He struck this on the chain and carolled :

" Doh, mi, soh, doh !—what's it to be boys ? "

We started a chorus and when it was concluded one of
the warders, an old man named Dyan who was in charge,
said it was very good.

" You can sing as much as you like in the train," he
added, " but when we come to a station you'll have to
keep quiet."

He was a very decent, kindly old man who had clearly
selected the wrong profession. The other warder was a big
healthy, burly fellow. One day when he had been more
than usually officious, Harry had told him quite truly that
he should have been at the front. He did not like us. I
told Mr. Dyan that he was a very decent man and we did
not want to get him into trouble, but we were going to sing
at every station we came to.

" Don't," he appealed, " I'll have to report you if you do."

" Sure you'll have to report us," I said, " if you don't
do it, we'll report ourselves. We don't know where we're
being taken to but we're going to let everyone know who
we are."

The poor old man was terribly distressed, but his appeals
were in vain. The train pulled up at a station and we
alighted. It was a huge place with a vaulted roof. One
of the fellows saw a name.

" It's Brighton," he said.

Dyan said we would have to go around to another
platform.

"All right," I said, " give us the note, Tommy."

We had agreed on " God Save Ireland " as the only
Irish national song the English would recognise. Tommy
gave us the note and we burst into song as we marched up
the platform. There were only seven of us but we sounded
like seven hundred in the great vaulted chamber. People
came running from all sides and before we got round to
our proper platform, the warders had to force a passage
for us through the crowd. We got into the train. Then I

Tumultuous welcome at Westland Row Station for released prisoners, June, 1917.

Welcome to released prisoners, June, 1917. Amongst those on side-car are (1) Harry Boland, (2) Jack Shouldice, (3) Robert Brennan, (4) J. J. Burke, and (5) J. J. Derrington.

saw Staines again. An excited little man with a Cockney accent was asking him questions about us. The little man forced his way to the carriage door and asked if we were Irish prisoners.

" Sure we are," I said. " We're here because we were fighting for the freedom of a small nation, as you're supposed to be doing."

" It's a bleedin' shyme," he said. " I'll get you some newspypers."

Several people had crowded close to the carriage and Paul Galligan slipped a note to Staines. One of the warders pulled down the blinds, but through the slit I saw the man with the Cockney accent coming back with the newspapers. I thrust my free hand out and took the papers. The burly warder snatched at them but I managed to get them behind my back. We had a grand struggle during which the blind flew up. The spectators crowded round, crying out what a shame it was to beat a manacled prisoner like that. The train started off just as the warder retrieved the newspapers and received a chorus of boohs from the crowd.

Poor old Dyan mopped his brow.

" It's hard lines on you, Mr. Dyan," I said, " now, you see, you'll have to report us."

" It's awful," he said.

" Don't worry," I replied, " they are going to wallop us in the new place, anyway, because we broke up Lewes Jail. What is coming to us from your report won't make it any worse."

Towards evening, we arrived at a city. We alighted and were hurried along a platform to a steamer. Lounging about were many men in uniform who jeered at us. We boarded the steamer and Dyan hurried us below decks. We passed a woman, leading a child. She was pregnant and, as we appeared, a look of horror came into her face. She drew her child back as if she feared contamination. To her we were criminals, enemies of society, outcasts. The steamer was a small ferry boat, plying between the mainland and the Isle of Wight. We sat on a bench by the wall in the bar-room which was crowded with men in uniform, the blue of the sailors, the khaki of the soldiers.

" What's it to be ? " asked Tommy Bevan, producing his tuning-fork.

" Let them have it," said his brother Charlie, " ' The West's Awake.' "

So we gave them " The West's Awake."

> Sing oh hurrah, let England quake,
> We'll watch till death for Erin's sake.

From the time we started to sing, the others had fallen silent. They glared at us malevolently. As we finished the chorus, a British non-commissioned officer came forward belligerently.

" I'd like to kick your heads off," he said, " I'd like to take you on right now, you dirty swine ! "

" I'm on a chain," I said, " if I wasn't, you wouldn't say that to me."

A red-headed soldier stepped in front of the officer. He spoke in a rich Dublin accent :

" I'm not on a chain," he said, " why not take me on ? "

The N.C.O. turned to say something to him. " Come on," cried the red-head, " take me on."

At the same time he swung and struck so violently that the N.C.O. was lifted clean off the floor before he fell. In a moment there was pandemonium.

Mr. Dyan hurried us from that part of the ship.

Chapter Fourteen

Tom Clarke, one of the leaders of the Rising who was executed, had previously endured fifteen years of English convict life. He once said to the writer : " If they ever put you in, do everything they tell you to do. If not, they will kill you or drive you insane."

THE Isle of Wight was flooded with late evening mellow sunshine. We drove through a countryside of green hedges, pleasant and peaceful, snug and prosperous. There was no sign of war, nor of any trouble at all until we came to the gates of Parkhurst Prison. We marched through an exercise ground of vast extent, black and white, black asphalt, whitewashed walls.

The doctor was a Dublin man who thought the tuning-fork was a great joke but that our prison conduct was a ghastly mistake. As he plied his stethoscope, he said to me :

" You'd better take it easy here. It's not a bad place. If you go against the rules, they'll break you up."

Outside in the hall while I waited for the doctor to finish with the others, I sat beside a grizzled, elderly lag. He talked through the side of ugly, thick lips. He learned I was one of the " Sin Fin " and asked why we had broken up Lewes Jail.

" We didn't like it," I said.

" You'd better like this place," he said, " it's easy here, but they'll kill you if you kick up. Chum of mine got rough and after six weeks of it they took him off to Broadmoor— (jail for insane criminals). This is the easiest place of them all. I know. I was in Portland and Dartmoor."

" What's your sentence ? " I asked.

" Life." There was a swagger in his voice. " It was over my girl. I didn't mean to do her in."

I learned later that it was a very brutal killing. He would have been hanged but that there was a doubt about provocation. He said they were thinking of letting him out to join the army. He knew the so-and-so army he was going to join.

137

"But I imagine you're over age," I said.

"What do you think I am?"

"Well, say sixty."

"I'm not forty," he said. "I was twenty-four when I came in."

As compared with Lewes, the cells in this jail were poor, grimy and ill-lighted. We were again in a wing long disused. By climbing on my stool to the window, I found my eyes on a level with the ground where twenty or more prisoners were marching around in a ring. There were some strange specimens amongst them. One, who bore ankle irons, carried the spare of the chain on his arm. Another, a very tall personage who thought he looked distinguished, wore a monocle. Yet another was skilfully juggling a number of stones which he had picked up. He had as many as six in the air at one time. The warders were bored. They paid little or no attention to the lags. My door opened and I climbed down off my stool. The visitor was an aged, weather-beaten chaplain. He told me he was Father Conway.

"You're an Orangeman, aren't you?" he said. I replied that I was not. He was surprised not by the reply, but by the mildness of it. He thought I should have hit the ceiling at the suggestion. He told me his father had been born in Ireland but he had never been there himself. The Irish, he said, were a great people in their loyalty to the faith and in the honour in which they held the clergy. He had heard we had trouble in Lewes, but, no doubt, that was because we had been treated badly. We need have no fear in Parkhurst because we would find things fairly easy. I thanked him and he left.

A warder opened the door and beckoned to me with a jerk of his head.

"Hair cut," he said.

"Who's cutting it?" I asked.

"Wot?" His eyebrows went up in surprise.

"I said who's cutting my hair?"

"Why," he said, "we've a special barber all the way from London, come specially for you."

"What I mean," I said, "is that I will allow only one

of my own comrades to cut my hair and we must have a machine of our own not used by the convicts."

" Well, I like that," he said. " Come along."

" Sorry, I can't," I said.

" You know it means a report."

" Sure," I replied.

He closed the door. I had not told him that one of our fellows had contracted a loathsome disease in Dartmoor from one of these clipping-machines.

That was Saturday. On Sunday morning we went to Mass. There were only twelve of us, I found, in the prison. Somebody whispered that the others were scattered in various prisons throughout the country. All twelve of us were seated together in the front pews. When we marched out of the chapel, we emerged on the vast exercise ground. There were about fifteen hundred prisoners lined up on parade and, for the first time, we had a view of the funny sailor-like uniforms worn by the preventive detention prisoners.

George Plunkett, who was behind me, whispered :

" We're not exercising with them."

" I know," I said, and asked if he would give us the order to fall out.

" No, " said George, " you're first in the line. You give it."

We were marched across the square and into line with a section of the convicts. It was a beautiful, sunny morning and the Governor, wearing a new, gaily-ribboned straw hat, was standing out in front. As we came to a halt, I said to the warder in charge of us :

" I want to speak to the Governor."

The warder said : " No, no. You can't do that. You put your name down."

I shouted to the Governor : " Mr. Governor," I said, " I want to speak to you."

As if moved by a machine, the heads of all the convicts turned in our direction. The Governor frowned and glared at me.

"All right, officer," he said, " carry on."

" Extend on the left," said the officer, " unbutton."

I stepped forward and turned to face our men. They were standing stockstill and they seemed to be far more at their ease than I felt.

" Irish Volunteers ! " I cried, " two paces to the rear ! March ! "

They fell back and I regained my place. The Governor was waving his arms.

" Officers ! " he cried, " surround those men ! "

The other convicts were moving restlessly and chattering. The warders came running with batons swinging.

"All right," I cried to the Governor, " I'll march them off."

" To the separate cells," cried the Governor.

I gave the boys the order to march and, led by a warder, we passed the long lines of astonished lags. Some looked frightened, some delighted, and all terribly excited.

My separate cell was almost completely dark. The only light came from a square of thick pavement glass, high up in the rear wall. There was no furniture and nothing movable. A raised portion of the floor was the bed and a circular block of wood sunk in the floor served both as stool and table. After about an hour's solitude, I rang the bell. A warder peered in through the spyhole.

" What about something to read," I asked.

" Nothing doing," he said. " You can ask the Governor when you're brought before him."

" When will that be ? "

" Can't say. To-morrow maybe."

I spent a gloomy Sunday.

In the afternoon a warder came and told me to undress. He took away my clothes, giving me instead two sheets and a blanket. When I asked him for an explanation, he merely said it was half-past four.

" Time to go to bed ? " I said.

" Just that."

He was a large plain-faced, unimaginative, taciturn man. He double-locked the door when he left. No matter how I manipulated the bedclothes, the boards were still hard and they got harder as the night went on. At six in the morning, a different warder opened up and handed me my clothes, taking away the sheets and blanket. Then he gave me a small basin, made of papier mâché, and poured a pint of water into it. He handed me a slice of soap and a dry towel. He was facetious.

"Hope you enjoy your bath," he said, adding that I had better hurry up, as he would be back for the basin, etc., in a few minutes. Answering my question about the basin, he said it was made of papier mâché so that I couldn't break it and cut my throat.

Shortly after breakfast, the usual cocoa and bread—the last I was to enjoy for some time—the Governor came in. I knew it was unusually early for such a visit.

"I'm sorry you made that demonstration yesterday," he said. "Maybe if I had had a word with you beforehand, it might have been avoided. Do you realise it is a serious offence ? "

"I expect so."

"You could be charged with mutiny," he said, "and that would mean the lash, but I'm not going to have that done. In fact, if you agree to abide by the rules and get your men to do likewise, it may be possible to overlook the whole thing."

"I'm sorry," I said, "but I can't do that. We refuse to be classed as criminals any longer."

"I have nothing to do with that. I have to carry out my duty."

"And so have I."

He said he was anxious to avoid punishing us and warned me that we did not realise what we were in for if we continued to disobey the rules. They had but to carry on the ordinary machinery of the prison and, in six weeks' time, we would be dead or insane.

"Now, where did I hear that before ? " I asked myself, and I added aloud, " Why, the old lag said the same thing."

"What old lag ? " he asked.

"Never mind."

"Have you thought of your wife and children ? "

Una had given birth to a second girl, Maeve, when I was in Lewes. But how the mischief did the Governor know anything of my wife and children ? I did not then know that alarming reports of the outbreak in Lewes Jail had appeared in all the Irish papers, or that the relatives of the prisoners had been instructed to send telegrams to the various prisons. To the Governor's query I replied :

" I'm sure they would disapprove if I adopted any other course."

The Governor, looking very worried, went away. A few minutes later, my warder appeared and put down my boots at the door.

" Exercise," he said.

"Are we to exercise with the convicts ? "

" Why not ? "

" Sorry," I said, " I can't do that."

Two hours later, I was brought before the Governor and charged with refusing to obey orders. He said in a mechanical voice :

" Three days' confinement, Number One diet. Two hundred and forty marks' remission. Three months' class."

On the way back to my cell, I asked the warder to explain the sentence.

" No. 1 diet," he said, " means bread and water."

"And the remission marks ? "

" You lose remission marks. You'll stay in a month longer."

"And the class ? "

He indicated the red star on my cap. " You lose that too. For the next three months you will not be a first-class prisoner."

I tried to enjoy my first meal of bread and water, and I'm afraid I failed. The old priest, Father Conway, came in. He thought our demonstration on the exercise ground was funny, but now that we had made our position clear, we should conform to the rules. Seeing he was making no impression, he asked me who " this fellow de Valera " was. I told him and asked if he knew where de Valera was.

" I don't know," he said, " and I don't care. Imagine," he continued, " a man with a fine Irish name like Brennan being led by a fellow called de Valera."

I asked him what he had against Dev and he said he was an atheist and an enemy of religion. He had prevented us from going to Mass in Lewes Jail. I tried to give him the facts but he would not listen to me and he lost his temper. In return, I had the ill grace to quote the Commandment about bearing false witness against one's neighbour. As he continued his tirade against Dev, I said :

" Our fellows are in a tough spot here. You could do a good deal to help us, but if you keep on like this, you can only make our condition worse."

The poor old man left.

Later, the Chief Warder came in. He was in a very sarcastic mood. He said :

"Am I right in thinking you are one of the fellows who want to break up the British Empire ? "

" Sure," I replied.

" Think you can do it ? "

" Certain."

" You refused to have your hair cut ? "

" Yes."

" Still refuse ? "

" Yes."

" You won't change your mind ? "

" No."

"All right. I'll have your hair cut for you."

So he sent in four hefty warders and I was foolish enough to resist them. We had a rough and tumble on the floor and the warders got their uniforms all dusty and rumpled and, of course, that made them mad. They finally got my head on the block and held it there while one of their number got the machine into my hair. Then, instead of cutting it, he prised the hair out. In fact, he nearly scalped me. Then they went into Colm O'Gaora's cell next door and I knew, by the sounds, that the process was being repeated. I was pretty well exhausted by the struggle and I lay down on the floor, but I sat up when I heard the door opening. It was the Chief Warder.

" Well, we cut your hair," he said.

" You did," I replied and, reflecting that the war was going badly for them, I added : " Wouldn't you like to cut Hindenburg's hair ? "

His language was awful. I waved to the warder standing at the door.

"That will be all for to-day," I said. "Take him away and lock him up some place far from the society of decent men."

The Chief Warder went out. I heard his footsteps echoing down the hall. The warder opened the door and put in his hand and grasped mine.

"Blimy, sonny," he said, "I'd give ten years of my life to say as much to that swine."

We were only ten or twelve days in Parkhurst, but they were easily the worst days I had ever had. One morning, when I had got my third sentence—we were taken to the Governor every couple of days—the doctor came in and spent a long time examining my heart.

"Part of the plan to break down resistance," I said to myself. He said I was making a mistake in refusing to take exercise. I needed fresh air and exercise. I told him we had refused only because we would have had to associate with the convicts. That afternoon the warder brought my boots.

"Exercise," he said.

"Not with the convicts."

"No," he said, "come along."

He brought me outside into a small exercise ground. The air was like wine. Two of our lads, Brady, a man of sixty, and Norton from north County Dublin, were already there. Brady came over to me and we walked around chatting. Norton joined us.

"None of that," said the warder.

We ignored him. He came over to us and said if we didn't obey the rules against talking, we would have to go in.

"All right," said Mike Brady, "we'll go in. We might as well be in jail as where we are." So in we went.

From an old ventilator in the wall of the cell I fished out a large number of buttons which some unfortunate prisoner had concealed for some extraordinary reason. I drew a checker-board on the floor with the piece of soap they gave me in the morning. By beating the soaped design with my jacket, I got some semblance of black squares and white. So, with the buttons I played games of draughts

against myself, but this form of amusement grows monotonous because you know every move the other fellow is
likely to make. I tried making up limericks, but this
was tantalising, because having completed three or four,
I could not recollect the first and best ones. Then, though
I fought hard against the thought, my mind reverted to
the big intellectual men of the Fenian period who had
been driven mad in prison. Was I really mad already?
I got on my knees and I realised it was the first time in my
life I had really prayed. Two hours later, I lay flat on the
floor, bathed in perspiration, but happy. There had come
into the cell a real Presence Who had brought peace.

Shortly afterwards, a young priest came in. He was a
Cork man, named Aherne. We had quite a chat and he
asked me to be patient with Father Conway because he
was an old man and he did not understand us. He said
two of our lads had been brought to hospital but all the
others were in good form.

That night I woke up suddenly and the black mood was
on me. I was going mad, I thought. I jumped up and
paced up and down the cell. I felt the walls were too close
to me and tried to push them back. I fell on my knees
and tried to pray, but my thoughts raced round and round.
After some time I found I was sitting on the plank, talking
aloud to myself.

"Get hold of yourself. Quick, quick! Hurry up! Get
hold of yourself!"

"I wish to God I could. I can't!"

"Of course you can. Get hold of something which will
take your mind away from this."

"Impossible. The machine which would enable me to
do so is out of gear."

"It is not. You could not talk like this if it was."

"Is that true? Is that true?"

"Of course it is. Now transport yourself to another
scene. Make up a story."

"About what?"

"About anything."

"No, not about anything."

"Well, something real then. What about that series

of sketches about Danny Dwyer and the days of your childhood ? "

" Yes, yes.   But I can't write them down."

" No need.   They will stay with you.   Anything you compose now will stay with you.   Go ahead.   Go back to John's Gate Street in Wexford and the chapel-yard thirty golden years ago."

" All right, here goes."

That night I composed " The Early Days of Danny Dwyer " in sixteen episodes.

Chapter Fifteen

In 1917 *Lloyd George set up a Convention to "find a solution to the Irish Question." This was really a ruse to deceive American opinion, as Lord Birkenhead later admitted. To give the scheme an appearance of reality the remaining Irish prisoners in convict prisons were released.*

ONE day I was conducted to the Governor's office, without knowing why. I had received a sentence on the previous day and, generally, two or three days elapsed between sentences. The warder did not know why either. As we walked through a long hall, a door at the other end opened and five prisoners filed in, followed by a warder. As they approached, the warder halted them and made them face the wall, this being the usual practice when two parties of prisoners met. One of the five prisoners, a very tall, dark man, whom I took to be a Hindu, turned his head as we approached. He waved his arms in the air and cried out, apparently as an encouragement to me :

" Hi ! Hi ! Sin Fin."

His warder raised his baton and struck him on the back of the neck and the man howled in pain. My warder hurried me on. In the hall outside the Governor's office there were two of our fellows, Jack Plunkett and Jack O'Brien, in opposite corners facing the wall, each with a warder in charge.

" Hello, Bob," called Jack Plunkett.

" Hello, Jack," I replied.

O'Brien turned round. He looked sick.

" When are we going to break up this joint ? " he asked.

" Take it easy, Jack," I said, " I'll tell you when."

I was pushed into the Governor's office and halted inside the door. The Governor's desk was behind a screen. Outside, I could hear Jack Plunkett whistling the " Soldier's Song." Jack O'Brien started to sing it. I heard the warder cry :

" Stop that ! Turn your face to the wall."

" I'll turn my face where I like," said O'Brien.

147

The Governor came from behind the screen, his face red with anger.

"Stop that damn row," he shouted. Seeing me, he beckoned me over and resumed his seat.

"I sent for you," he said, "I want you to stop all this nonsense. No, wait," he went on, as I was about to speak, "I want you to realise the Government has good intentions so far as you fellows are concerned. I am not in a position to tell you what they are, but I do know you will not have to serve your five years."

He waited.

"I could have told you that long ago," I said.

"But you don't know they have ordered civilian clothes for you. That's a good sign, isn't it?"

I said nothing though, of course, I felt considerably relieved.

"So now," said the Governor, "I want you to behave yourself for the rest of the time you are here and get the others to do the same. Have I your word for that?"

"I'm sorry," I said, "but we'll carry on just as usual."

"You know what it means?"

"I'm learning."

"All right," he said, "you can go."

The argument between the two Jacks and their warders was still going on.

"Good men," I said, "keep it up."

Before I reached my cell, my escort said:

"Blimey, but you're a rum lot."

"You think so."

"You're upsetting the whole blooming place."

"No!"

"Swelp me. The separate cells are full up."

This was good. If the fifteen hundred prisoners were feeling our influence and getting out of hand, they couldn't keep us long. I was in a mood to cheer and I enjoyed my bread and water dinner and sang all the afternoon. Next day, I was up before the Governor again, this time on the usual charges of refusing to obey orders, etc. The charges were duly heard. The Governor again talked to me seriously.

" I think you should know," he said, " that you won't be long here."

" I'm glad to hear it."

" Yes, that's right. I don't suppose it will be more than a couple of months or so."

" Good."

" So I hope now you'll see reason. Naturally, you will want to be in good shape when you are getting out, and I'm asking you to forget everything that has happened and make a fresh start. I'll wipe out all the penalties if you give me your word you will obey the prison rules for the rest of the time."

I was sorry I couldn't, I said.

" Not even if I say you are going out in a month or so ! "

" No."

"All right," he said, " three days Number One, two hundred and forty marks remission."

Back in my cell, I was just sitting down to my bread and water, when I heard the cell doors being opened. The young Cork priest opened mine.

" Great news," he said, " you are going out. I'm so glad. Please don't make any demonstration."

" Why, of course not," I said.

" I'm thinking of the convicts," he said. " They're in a bad mood and a demonstration might start a riot."

I stepped into the hall. Our fellows were lining up. The Governor came down the stairs at the head of the wing and, without any preliminaries, said :

" I have to tell you that Mr. Bonar Law announced in the House of Commons last night that you are to be released immediately. You leave at once for Pentonville Prison in London, where you will be fitted with civilian clothes. Goodbye."

He turned his back and walked off. The lads stood completely motionless, without a sign of jubilation or even excitement. The Chief Warder stood in front of us, literally gnashing his teeth.

" Back to your cells," he said, " you leave here in ten minutes."

Maurice Brennan, who was beside me, said :

" Will I tell him what we think of him ? "

" It's not worth while," I said.

Back in my cell I reflected how simple life could be if we were satisfied with only the things we need. We had nothing to pack. In our pockets were all we were allowed to carry, a rosary beads and a pocket handkerchief. I rang my bell and the warder appeared.

" Could I have a prayer-book ? " I asked.

"A prayer-book ? "

" I want to take one out as a souvenir."

" Sorry," he said, " I can't let you have one. You ask the R.C. feller." He meant the Roman Catholic chaplain.

" But I won't see him. There's no time."

"All right," he said, " I'll see."

He went off and brought me a prayer-book. I thanked him warmly. I knew he was making himself a party to the heinous crime of purloining prison property.

" It's all right, sonny," he said, " I'm glad you're going out, but I'll miss you. I won't ever forget how you took that swine down "—a reference to my encounter with the Chief Warder.

So we marched out into the wonderful sunshine of the Isle of Wight and to a railway station. In the train somebody produced cigarettes and I smoked one, but there was no taste to it. I wondered why I had suffered so much from being deprived of tobacco fifteen months before. We all laughed and sang songs, somewhat hysterically, all the way to London. Here, a surprise awaited us. Night had fallen. We were put into buses with glass sides and, as soon as we emerged into the street, we became aware of a hostile crowd who pelted our buses with stones. This occurred at various points along the route to Pentonville Prison. There were curses and cries of " Down with the pro-Germans." One of the warders whispered to me that the crowd was infuriated because there had been a Zeppelin raid on London the night before, but he did not explain how the crowd knew of our arrival in London and of the route we were to take. The demonstrators were thick outside the gates of Pentonville.

We found it a filthy place, at least the wing was in

which we were located. Many of the fellows spent the night pacing the floors stark naked, because the place was crawling with vermin. Next morning, at Mass, we saw all our old comrades and heard an Irish priest deliver a fine sermon on the purpose of life. Soon afterwards, we all met in an exercise ground, where there was no restraint of any kind. We were being fitted out with civilian clothes, amidst a lot of noise and laughter. As each piece was fitted, we handed over the corresponding convict garment, but I managed to smuggle out my convict cap, as did some of the others. J. J. Walsh surprised us by bringing out his whole convict garb under his new suit. A few of us managed to make our way to the spot where Casement was buried and we knelt to say a prayer.

Our reception in Dublin was so overwhelming that some of the lads collapsed. It was during the excitement of that first day home that I first saw Mick Collins. I had heard of him before. Tom Ashe had, in Lewes Jail, shown me a letter from him, dealing with future policy. It had seemed to me amateurish and pretentious, and I said so. Later, Joe McGuinness told me several times I should know Collins who, he said, was a tremendous fellow. When I first saw Mick, we had just had a group photograph taken on the Mansion House lawn. I heard my name mentioned and, turning, I saw Seumas Doyle talking to a quick-moving, energetic, vigorous, hefty young man with a heavy jowl and a face which was too pale. His quick eyes darting here and there, he brushed back a lock of hair from his forehead, and asked :

" Where is he ? "

Seumas indicated me. The man came over to me and said :

" You are looking after the Wexford fellows ? "

" If Seumas says so, yes," I said.

He had a roll of notes in one hand and silver in the other. He said that the fares to Enniscorthy amounted to so much, and I found out later the sum was correct to a penny. He added that he was giving me five shillings, in addition, for each man, to cover incidental expenses. As he handed me the money, he looked into my eyes as if appraising me.

With a quick smile, he shook my hand and turned to someone else. I noticed the tremendous strength of his shoulders.

" Who is he ? " I asked of Seumas.

" Michael Collins," he said.

" I don't like him," I said.

This initial dislike of Collins, I never quite got over. I tried to do so later, because I had a lively appreciation of the great work he was doing and of the risks he ran. His energy was terrific and his self-confidence unbounded. Though he was dynamic, he was never flurried. He built up from nothing at all an almost perfect intelligence department. His secret agents were to be found later in almost every British institution up to the highest level. His memory for detail was faultless and his office system, harried though it was by having to remain underground and subject to constant raids, was well-nigh perfect.

Any one of his departments—Intelligence, Finance, Army Organisation and Communications—would have taxed the ability and time of a very able administrator, but Collins managed them all without apparent effort. Not merely that, but because he was impatient of delays, he encroached on the domain of nearly every other government department and thus spurred his colleagues to greater effort. I knew all this and yet I could not bring myself to like him. Perhaps it was because he was ruthless with friend and foe ; because he could brook no criticism or opposition. He drove everyone hard, but none harder than he drove himself.

Some of his admirers give Collins all the credit for such success as we had. I think this is a pity. It is true that without him Sinn Féin could not have achieved the success it did in the time it did, but this is not less true of Eamon de Valera or Arthur Griffith. For instance, Collins could never have brought about the unity of the Republicans in 1917, or that of all classes in the nation in 1918, as de Valera did ; nor could he have voiced the nation's will so brilliantly and so persuasively as did Arthur Griffith.

Collins had really little political *savoir-faire*, and this was clearly shown when, after 1916, he almost wrecked his own cause by trying to capture a young and fast-growing national movement by secret devices. He had great faith in the secret conclaves of the few, as if he despised the intelligence of the many.

A few weeks after our release, I went to Dublin and stayed a few days with the Bolands. I found the brothers sharply divided on the question of Mick. Jerry said he was a braggart and a bully.

" He's nothing of the kind," said Harry.

" You haven't seen as much of him as I have," said Jerry, who had been interned with Collins. " In the camp, if he didn't win all the jumps, he'd break up the match."

Jerry got up and, imitating Mick, strode about the room boastfully, heaving his shoulders and tossing his head.

" Never mind," said Harry, " he's young. He'll get over that. He's a great fellow."

This attitude of Harry's puzzled many of his friends. Intellectually, he was far in front of Mick and in political acumen, he was also far ahead. I judged that Harry, who had never aspired to be a leader, but who did like to be a good lieutenant, was at this stage courting Mick so as to form a link between the I.R.B. and Dev, to whom he was already devoted. But, that Harry became tremendously attached to Mick later on, there is, of course, no doubt.

Dev, at this time, was forming a platform wide enough to hold us all together and he had early decided to bring MacNeill back into the ranks, to the dismay of all those who thought the Professor should be ostracised for the part he played in Easter Week. " Don't forget," said Dev, " that the clergy are with MacNeill and they are a powerful force." Similarly, Dev was working night and day to get Brugha and Griffith in step. They had been at loggerheads before Dev came out of prison, so much so that Brugha had threatened that if Griffith stumped the country for Sinn Féin, he would get the Volunteers to stop him. This, during a violent scene at the improvised national executive headquarters. Because of Dev's attitude towards the moderates, some of Collins's adherents were already sneering about the " constitutionalists." Of course, little of this appeared in public. To them there was presented a united

front. At the Clare election all sections were on the Sinn
Féin platform. There were hectic discussions as to what
policy to present at this election. Dev settled the matter
by coming out openly for the Irish Republic without
qualification. He said to me, " Some of the young fellows
have told me it is a time to be cautious, to go slow. The
old men, on the other hand, said ' Make no mistake. Nail
your colours to the mast.' I listened to the old men. No
one need ever tell me to go slow. What I want is someone
to tell me to go forward."

I told him that Griffith's motto was " moderation in
everything." He said :

" That's funny. It's my motto, too."

During the summer, the Oireachtas was held in Waterford
and we all foregathered there. Dev outlined a plan to
save the language by working outward from the Gaeltacht
through the Breac-Gaeltacht to the English-speaking districts. The plan was on military lines.

Diarmuid Lynch, who had come down from Dublin,
had a message for me. The Supreme Council of the I.R.B.
had decided that they were going to control the Volunteers.
So that there would be no mistakes in future, we were to
see that our secret men would control all possible units.
I told him I was against the plan because it would bring
about that dual control which had been disastrous in Easter
Week. We all had learned that de Valera and Cathal
Brugha had decided (separately) not to continue membership of the I.R.B., and thought it should be disbanded, but
Collins was keeping it on.

The Sinn Féin Ard-Fheis promised to be the battleground between the moderates and the extremists and we
all knew the test would be decided by whether de Valera
or Griffith won the presidency. Before I went to Dublin
for the Ard-Fheis, I got an order from the I.R.B. to see
Collins before the Convention. In one of the houses on
the west side of Parnell Square, I found a regular queue
of men from all parts of the country. Mick, sitting at a
table, handed me a typed list. It was the ticket the
Wexfordmen were to support for the National Executive.
A Louth man who filed out of the room with me, began

to laugh and, when I asked him why, produced another list which he had got from Darrell Figgis. Griffith headed the latter list ; Dev headed the list Collins had given us. At the Ard-Fheis itself, Harry Hanrahan exposed the whole procedure of the rival caucuses, amidst almost general applause. It was apparent that most of the delegates had decided to ignore both tickets and to vote for the people they knew. The big test, as between Dev and Griffith, did not come, however, because, to the surprise of practically everybody, when the question of the election of President was reached, Griffith rose and proposed Dev, whom he described not merely as a great soldier but a great statesman. We then discovered that Dev had found a formula to satisfy Brugha (who wanted a clear-cut declaration for the Republic) and Griffith (who had been insisting on the old Sinn Féin programme). Dev's formula declared the object of the organisation was the achievement of the Independence of Ireland as an Irish Republic and added that when that had been achieved, the people would decide on the form of government they wished to have. In his speech, Dev said that if they decided to have a king, he would not come from the House of Windsor. The election of the Committee was a defeat for Collins, as most of the men on his list were beaten. He was almost defeated himself.

The Volunteer Convention, which was held later in the year, gave the I.R.B. another opportunity for a trial of strength and this time they were more successful. They captured nearly all the Council seats. The main item on the agenda was the election of a Volunteer executive. I put forward the contention that the whole procedure was wrong. What we should do was to elect one man who would select his own headquarters staff and control the policy of the Volunteers. I proposed Dev for the position. Thus, there would be no danger of dual control or confusion. Dev got up and asked me if what I intended was that this man should have the decision of peace or war. I said " yes." Dev said he would not take a post of such responsibility for all the wealth of Ireland and thus defeated my attempt to set up the first dictatorship in modern Europe.

Chapter Sixteen

*In the face of the determined opposition of Dublin Castle, Sinn Féin in
1917 and 1918 built up a political organisation such as has never been
equalled, as well as a Volunteer force which lacked only arms to make
it an effective National Army.*

*Despite warnings from America the British Government decided
to apply the Conscription Act to Ireland.*

THE extraordinary change over in public opinion was
obvious to all of us as soon as we returned from England.
We had left an Ireland beaten, baffled and sullen. We
came back to a land proud, gay and resurgent. It was a
beautiful summer and the countryside seemed to have
especially clothed itself in the national colours, orange,
white and green. The police were kept busy hauling down
the national flag from impossible positions on telephone
poles and buildings. I had gone back to my old job as a
reporter and it was a particular delight to report the
rescinding of the resolutions which had been passed by the
various public bodies the previous year, condemning the
Rising. During the whole summer we laboured hard on
the national plebiscite demanding that Ireland's case should
be heard at the Peace Conference.

I was soon to discover that my fears regarding the interference of the I.R.B. in the Volunteer movement were
justified. I had refused to take command of the Wexford
Brigade, because I thought the job was too much for me,
so M. W. O'Reilly headed the Brigade and I took over
the Wexford Battalion. Pending the usual elections, I
appointed temporary officers. One of the lieutenants refused to carry out the orders of his superior officer because
the latter had not gone out in the Rising. He told me he
was taking his orders from individuals in Enniscorthy. I
suspended him, but he was subsequently reinstated by an
officer from headquarters while I was in Cork Jail. Similar
events were happening in other commands and those who
wished for a single control for the army were becoming
very downhearted.

One day I woke up in a cell in Cork Jail and my first words were :

" 'Clare to God, here I am again ! "

I had been arrested the previous day on a charge of parading men in military formation and dressing in uniform. Count Plunkett had visited Wexford and I had paraded the Wexford Battalion in his honour. Sean Sinnott and Pierce Byrne were also in custody. On the way to Cork Prison, we taught our police escort some rebel songs. It was dark when we got to the prison and, as I was being escorted to my cell, I was surprised to hear a reel, " The Soldier's Joy," being played on a mouth-organ. Down at the end of a long hall, I saw figures dancing in a dim light.

" What's that ? " I asked.

" They're having a dance," said the warder as he opened my cell door.

" Who are they ? "

" The prisoners—your chums." Seeing my astonishment, he added : " Oh, they have a good time here."

" Can't I join them ? "

" Not till to-morrow."

He went off, but almost immediately the door was opened again and another warder came in.

"Are you from Wexford ? "

" Yes."

" Will they win on Sunday ? "

I guessed immediately he was talking about the Wexford football team which had held the all-Ireland championship for three years and which was playing Dublin for the Leinster championship on the following Sunday.

" No, they won't," I said.

" Why not ? "

" They're not training."

" God blast them," he said, " sure they could bate Dublin with one hand."

His name was Kavanagh and he hailed from Gorey. I found next day he was distrusted by the prisoners, but I told them I would depend on him for anything we wanted done. As it transpired, I was right.

Next day, we were introduced to the other prisoners.

There were about sixty of them, mainly from Cork and Kerry. They had a limited form of home rule in the prison. There was no work and from early morning till dark there were football and handball matches in the narrow exercise ground, as well as Gaelic classes. At night, there were dancing, story-telling and singing. Most of the excellent food was sent in by the prisoners' friends. All the men were awaiting trial and, as soon as the trial was over, they were transferred to some other prison. Two days subsequent to our arrival, the officer in charge elected by the men was brought down for preliminary trial and, as it was expected he would be removed at once, there was a new election and I was placed in charge. My lieutenants were three men who were subsequently to meet tragic deaths at the hands of the British : Terence MacSwiney, who died in Brixton Jail after a hunger-strike which lasted for seventy-three days ; Tomás MacCurtain, the Lord Mayor of Cork, who was murdered in his own house by the British forces ; and George Clancy, Mayor of Limerick, who met a like fate. These dread events could not be foreseen, however, and we had a pleasant time enough in Cork Jail until news came in that Austin Stack was leading a hunger strike in Dundalk Jail with a view to securing political treatment. Immediately, his fellow-Kerrymen amongst us began clamouring for a sympathetic hunger strike on our part. Before that happened, however, a number of us had been brought down for a preliminary hearing of the charges against us. A young military officer presided and took down the evidence. He had a very nasty temper which he could not control and we did not help him. One of the prisoners rolled the charge sheet he held into a cylinder and, pretending it was a bugle, he put it to his lips and began to hum the " Soldier's Song." We all followed suit and we gave a fair imitation of a bad brass band. The officer yelled at us to stop but we merely changed the tune to " Kelly of Killaan." The little man began to take it out on the police witnesses. One of them was testifying that he had heard me giving military orders to the battalion and had seen me dressed in a uniform and wearing my overcoat in review order.

" What do you mean by review order? " asked the officer.

" Oh, just review order."

" Oh, just review order ! Well, what is just review order ? "

Apparently this was a police term not known to the military.

" Well, review order."

The officer laid down his pen and glared at the policeman. " How did you get into the police force? "

" I beg your pardon, sir."

" Where are your brains ? I'm trying to write this evidence down and you are talking jargon. Will you explain what is meant by review order ? "

" Well, just—— " The policeman stopped in time and swallowed hard. The officer looked as if he was going to explode.

" It was this way, sir. His overcoat was rolled up and placed over one shoulder."

" Oh, is that all ? "

" No, sir. It was under the other."

" Under the other what ? "

" Under the other oxter."

" My God ! Is there any superior officer here ? "

" No, sir. I'm in charge of the Wexford witnesses."

" God help us ! What am I to write down ? "

" That's for you to say, sir."

Of course, all this contributed greatly to our merrimernt. We re-enacted the scene for the crowd that night.

The strike situation was becoming serious. In vain the leaders pointed out that we had no grievance. We had no excuse for a strike. The Kerrymen, however, demanded a poll on the question and we were forced to concede it. Sixty per cent. voted for the strike. I ordered that it should be a real strike and that all food should be removed from the cells; this because there were rumours that a previous hunger strike in Cork Jail had been a fake. From one cell thirty-six pounds of butter were cleared out. There were ordinary prisoners in an adjoining wing of the prison and they got the food. One of them ate so much during the transfer of the food that I thought he would die. He was so stuffed that he was hardly able to breathe and he could not speak at all.

All the leaders had been against the strike, but, of course, they accepted the decision loyally. Terry MacSwiney, finding some of the younger men indulging in their usual wild football games, advised them to desist and conserve their strength. " This may be a fight to the death," he said, " and we must stick it as long as possible." He was a very serious, quiet man, but he had a keen, if slightly sardonic sense of humour. He had no ear for off-colour stories. One night one of the Limerick men, McInerney, staged an impromptu court scene involving a breach of promise action. It was extremely funny, if somewhat coarse. I noticed that Terry stole away in the middle of it. I found him in his cell painstakingly writing in the dim light in one of his many neat notebooks. It was an unfinished poem and he read it for me.

" You're not enthusiastic," he said, when I did not comment.

" I'm not a great judge of poetry."

" That means it's very bad," he said with a wry grin; " just as I thought," and he tore it up.

One day when the strike had been going on for three or four days, I found him in his cell with his bare feet on the cold hot-water pipes.

" What on earth are you doing ? " I asked.

" Hush," he said, " the doctor is coming round. I want him to find my feet cold. It's a sign of heart disease."

He laughed heartily. In an adjoining cell, MacCurtain was in bed, reading a story by Maurice le Blanc. He was a very cheerful man, full of quiet fun. When I asked him how he was feeling, he pretended I was the doctor.

" Oh," he said, " I'm terrible bad, doctor. The aches and pains I do be having would kill a mountainy pony. And there's a fluttering around my heart that wakes me up in the middle of the night." He suddenly grew serious and asked if I had been in to see George (Clancy).

" I'm going in there now."

" I'll go with you," he said.

Clancy had not been in good health when he came in, notwithstanding which he taught language classes all day. He was one of the best Irish teachers I had ever met and, in his enthusiasm, he worked terribly hard. He had had one bad fainting fit and he could not sleep. We found him in pretty low spirits, idling over a newspaper. MacCurtain did not ask him about his health but, instead, said he wanted to take down a story George had told a few nights previously. George immediately began to tell the story in his beautiful Gaelic *blas*. He had heard it from a woman in Kerry. It concerned a hard-hearted woman who refused shelter to the Blessed Virgin, the Child and St. Joseph when they were travelling the roads. The woman's husband surreptitiously followed the travellers and brought them back to the shelter of a hut.

"An fear min agus an bhean bhorb a chur Iosa Chriost in a luighe sa colg." (The gentle man and the rough woman who put Jesus Christ to lie in the straw.)

MacCurtain was busy with his pencil and pad and George went on to another story. His woes were forgotten, and I could not help thinking that MacCurtain was a good physician.

The prison doctor was very nervous and so was the Governor. They feared that they might have on their hands another tragedy like that of Tom Ashe who, a few months earlier, had died in Mountjoy Jail as a result of forcible feeding during a hunger strike. We played on their nerves by pretending all sorts of illnesses. When the strike was only five or six days old, we arranged that one of our fellows should collapse and be carted off to hospital, but before he could do so, another man actually did collapse. The doctor, in a panic, recommended our immediate release. We were served with notices that we should all return within a month, but, of course, no one paid any attention to these.

Shortly after I got back to Wexford, Una and I returned from a walk one evening and, on opening the door, were confronted by our small maid with a poker in her hand. She explained that a policeman had called and she had driven him out. She was still explaining when there was a

discreet knock on the door. On opening it, Police Sergeant
Collopy pushed his way in, closed the door and brought me
to the rear of the hall. He produced from various pockets
three hundred rounds of ·303 ammunition.

" I was down in Cork to-day," he said, " and that god-
damn fella Kavanagh made me take this to give to you.
He got it from a soldier. Now, will you tell him not to use
me again. I tell you flat, I won't do it."

He was referring, of course, to the Wexford warder in
Cork Jail.

" Indeed you will, Sergeant," I said ; " don't worry."

" But suppose I'm caught ? "

" No one will catch you. No one will know only you
and me and Kavanagh, and he won't talk."

" What are you going to do with this stuff ? You're not
preparing for another rising ? "

" Sure we are."

" Glory be to God ! "

Shortly after the new year, I attended a Sinn Féin Ard
Comhairle meeting in Dublin. During the proceedings,
Dev called me to the chair and told me they were thinking
of establishing a Sinn Féin Press Bureau. He asked if I
knew of any newspaper man who could take charge of it.
The salary would be all they could afford, about three
pounds a week. I promised to try and think of someone.
Outside the Mansion House I met Desmond Fitzgerald.
I asked him if he would like the job and he said he would
jump at it. So I advised him to go and see Dev. That
night, when I got back to Wexford, I mentioned the matter
to Una.

"Are you sure he didn't mean you ? " she asked.

" Good Lord, no," I said, " if he did, he would have
said so."

Thinking over the matter, however, I concluded he might
have meant me so, next day, I wrote him and said if he
wanted me I was at his service. At the same time, I wrote
to Fitzgerald telling him what I had done. A couple of
weeks later, I was notified of my appointment and I packed
for Dublin. On the journey north, my fellow-passengers
and I had an opportunity of seeing Sinn Féin in action.

At Wicklow Station there was a great crowd of people cheering. The demonstration was in honour of Tom Cullen, the local Volunteer Commandant, who had been arrested that morning. There was an escort of police to take him to Dublin. They boarded the train, but it did not start. The driver, fireman and guard all refused to work a train carrying prisoners. We were held up for six hours while the authorities and the railway executives stormed, and all Wicklow town was *en fête*. Finally, the prisoner was taken by road and the train proceeded.

I was only an hour in No. 6 Harcourt Street and I had started working in the Secretary's office, when Dev sent for me. He said I was to work in his office because he did not want " them " to control the publicity. " Them " meant not so much Griffith as Darrell Figgis plus Griffith. Figgis was getting a strong hold on the Sinn Féin organisation through the fact that he was General Secretary. He was a right-winger and Dev did not want the publicity run by either the right or the left wing. He asked me if I had any idea as to how publicity could be secured. I said that the first thing should be a weekly column of Sinn Féin notes and news supplied to all the provincial papers, and the next a number of brief pamphlets setting out various aspects of the Sinn Féin case. He said, " all right, go ahead." I wrote my first column and handed it to him. He immediately took up his pen and began to make alterations. He took so long over it that I began to lose patience.

" Don't do that," I said, " just tell me what's wrong with it and I'll rewrite it."

" There's a lot of overstatement," he said. " I prefer understatement."

I rewrote the column, leaving out many of my adjectives and superlatives but, even then, he got busy with his pen again, this time on the diction. I endured this for a long time and finally blurted out :

" Look here, Chief, I'm writing journalese, not literature. We have to post this to-day if it's to be in time for this week's papers."

"All right," he said, smiling at my impatience, " let it go."

I was to learn that he never saw a draft submitted by

anybody but he must alter it. Every day, for a couple of weeks, we had the same set-to, and then I decided to get out the stuff and not let him see it till it was in print. I was gratified by the results. I had expected that not more than half a dozen provincial papers would use the material. In the first week we had thirty papers and the number gradually increased.

One day Una, who with the children had joined me in Dublin, came into the office to see me. She sat on the table at which I was working. Dev came in suddenly. He frowned severely on seeing, what he thought, was one of the girls from the Cumann na mBan office, which was on the same floor. Una, in spite of all her troubles, still looked about nineteen. Dev came right to the point.

" Look here," he said, " you shouldn't be coming in here."

" Why not ? " she asked.

" Do you know Mr. Brennan is a married man ? "

" Well," she said, " I ought to," and she explained the situation. He laughed heartily and ever afterwards, whenever he met her, he recalled the incident with glee.

Conscription was in the air. The British Government rushed a Conscription Act for Ireland through Parliament and the Irish Party left the House of Commons in disgust and returned to Ireland. Dev seized the occasion at once, in a typical manner. He saw Larry O'Neill, the Lord Mayor of Dublin, and had no difficulty in persuading him to call a conference in the Mansion House, to which he invited leaders of the Parliamentary Party, of Sinn Féin and of Labour. It was an immediate success. As we devotees of Sinn Féin expected, de Valera dominated the proceedings, as William O'Brien, M.P., later disclosed. Everybody in the country was against conscription, but there was a big difference of opinion as to how the menace might be met. A large section of the clergy, backed by the press, was calling for passive resistance. Dev drew up a pledge to be taken by the people in every parish on the following Sunday. There was no mention of passive resistance in this. It pledged the people to resist conscription by the most effective means. Dev pointed out that this phrase would leave the fighting men free to fight and the English would pause, knowing what to expect, whereas if the English thought they were going to meet only passive resistance, they would go ahead with their plans and the result would be a fight anyhow, since many were in no mood for passive resistance. He got his pledge through the conference unaltered and then rushed a deputation to Maynooth, where the Bishops were holding their annual meeting.

As the members of the deputation filed out of the Mansion House we put them into the waiting cars. When there was only one car left we found to our dismay that John Dillon and Tim Healy would have to share it. Well aware of the bitter feeling that existed between the two men, Harry Boland approached Tim and said :

" I'm afraid you'll have to share a car with Mr. Dillon. I hope you don't mind."

" Well," said Tim, " as the Yank said : ' I can eat crow, but I don't hanker after it.' I guess I've got to eat crow this time."

It was feared that the Bishops might counsel passive resistance to meet the menace, but their statement banished these fears. It said : " The Irish people have the right to resist by every means that are consonant with the law of God."

Every Sunday morning I went in to No. 6 to have a look at the mail. On one such morning I found a young man standing outside the door. He had a bicycle with a sack strapped on the back of it. As it had been raining heavily he was wet through. When Joe Clarke, the caretaker, opened the door to us the young man entered the hall and said he had cycled forty-five miles from a village in Offaly.

" We had a meeting there last night," he said, " and we decided to meet the menace of conscription by passive resistance and (pointing to the sack) they sent me in for a bag of bombs."

Joe, without commenting on their novel idea of passive resistance, gravely explained that we had no supplies of bombs ready to hand and advised the young man to get in touch with the leaders of the Volunteers in Edenderry.

The Mansion House Conference decided that the Lord Mayor should go to Washington to present Ireland's case against conscription to the President and Congress of the United States. Dev set to work drawing up the case and Father Tim Corcoran, S.J., sat in with him on it. I spent a great deal of time in the National Library fishing out material to annotate the case. The document was unfinished when Dev was arrested, as I showed in my preface to the pamphlet, *Ireland's Case Against Conscription*, by Eamon de Valera, published by Maunsel.

The Volunteers in general were hoping that the British would go ahead with their conscription plans. They would have cheerfully faced a fight in which they would have the backing of the whole Irish people, but there was a great deal of misgiving when rumours began to fly that the Volunteers would strike first, without giving the British time to complete their conscription plans. One day, I called on Michael Staines, then Quartermaster-General, to see about getting some guns for Wexford. A chance remark of his suggested that some action was imminent.

" When is it to be ? " I asked.

" Oh, possibly next week."

" That's curious," I said, " Dev doesn't know anything about it."

" How would he know ? "

" Well, he's the President of the Volunteer Council, isn't he ? "

" I know he is."

I retailed the conversation to Dev who, very much perturbed, sent for Cathal Brugha, the Chief of Staff. The latter damned the I.R.B., and went off to have a showdown with Collins. If any action had been intended, it was called off.

PARKHURST

[*Fox Photos*

Some of the prisons in which Robert Brennan was confined .

DARTMOOR

[*Associated Press*

[A. Begsley

[Irish Independent

WATERFORD

KILMAINHAM

ARBOUR HILL [Irish Press

Some of the prisons in which Robert Brennan was confined.

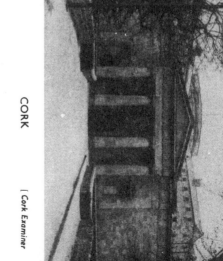

CORK

MOUNTJOY

[Cork Examiner

[Irish Times

Chapter Seventeen

The Conscription Act for Ireland was passed by the British House of Commons on April 16th, 1918. The Irish closed their ranks, resolved to fight. In the upshot the Conscription Act was never enforced and the will of the Irish people for the first time in almost a century and a half prevailed.

FOR a few days before the event, there had been rumours that wholesale arrests were to take place. Collins, who had already set up the nucleus of his Intelligence organisation, said that the arrests would take place on the 17th or 18th of May. The matter was discussed at the Sinn Féin Executive and it was decided that the members should not go into hiding, or resist arrest, but every member appointed a substitute. On the night of the 17th, under pretence of the discovery of a German plot, the British Government made nearly a hundred arrests. They included Dev, Griffith and, indeed, nearly the whole Sinn Féin Executive, as well as many leaders of the Volunteers in Dublin and throughout the country. I thought I was on the list for arrest, but I did not know it for certain till some six months later. The following night, the substitute Executive for Sinn Féin met, and I was asked to take on the position of Director of Elections, in addition to that of Publicity. Thereafter began the busiest period of my life. I worked sixteen to eighteen hours a day, Sundays included, for the next six months. There was an enormous lot of work to be done in setting up the election machinery and in writing and editing vast numbers of handbills and pamphlets. I was lucky to enrol Frank Gallagher for publicity. He was and is a prodigious worker, painstaking and sincere and already he had a vast quantity of publicity material ready for the printer. He and I turned out handbills by the score and many pamphlets.

The election machinery turned out to be so efficient that, when I entered Gloucester Jail six months later, and while the election was still three weeks off, I was able to give the

prisoners there an exact forecast of the results. The credit
was not mine. It was in a large measure due to the splendid
election scheme which was the work of James O'Mara and
Dan McCarthy, and which was based on a directorate
system. The Sinn Féin executive for each constituency
appointed a Constituency Director of Elections, who became
responsible to the General Director of Elections at Dublin
headquarters. The Constituency Director set up his staff
consisting of five sub-directors in charge respectively of
finance, organisation, canvassing, publicity and transport.
This organisation was repeated in each geographical sub-
division, right down to the townland or street. Once it
was set up, it worked almost like clockwork. The responsibility was placed on an individual and the old vexatious
committee system, with its divided responsibility and endless talk, was eliminated. Every week I received reports
from one man in each constituency—based on reports from
his internal organisation—covering all the activities I have
mentioned, so that at any moment I had only to glance at
a page in a penny copybook to see how a constituency
stood. The work of setting up this organisation was carried
out by four men whom I selected : Paddy Ryan, Jim Flood,
Seumas Doyle and Eamon Donnelly, their areas roughly
corresponding to those of the four Provinces. As we did
not know when the election would be called and, as time
was all important, we gave them six weeks to get the job
done. On their first visit they got the constituency headquarters to elect a director, instructed him in the scheme
and saw that he appointed his staff. One day only was
allotted for each constituency. On his return visit, if the
local director had not made good, it was understood he
would be replaced. Only in two cases was it necessary to
supplant a director. The country was so enthusiastic that
there was no lack of workers. In addition to preparing the
way for the election by publicity, canvassing and collecting
the necessary funds, the machinery was being set up to get
the voters to the poll and to see that they were protected by
agents and sub-agents in the polling booths.

    Almost every day, James O'Mara came in for a few hours
and his help and suggestions were invaluable. For instance,

when the organisers had got the machinery set up, I thought
I should make a general tour of inspection, but I feared
leaving headquarters for so long.

"All right," said James, " we'll have the constituencies
come to you instead. Don't write. Send them wires."

So wires were sent to the various constituency directors
to attend at 6 Harcourt Street on a certain day. James
was responsible for the hocus pocus which followed. He
would meet the director at the door, signalise he was to be
quiet and lead him to a corner desk. The man, learning
he was brought to Dublin merely to make a report, was
invariably indignant and then James would caution him
to be quiet again and would enable him to hear what was
going on at my desk, where another director faced me. He
would overhear some such conversation as this :

I : " Well, let us see now. You have all the sub-directors
appointed. What about your canvass ? "

Director : " We haven't started yet."

" Say, how long is it since you were appointed ? "

" Three weeks."

"And you haven't even started your canvass ? "

" Well, we only got the last of the district men appointed
yesterday."

" Look here, do you think you've years to do this job ? "

" Well, we could start the canvass to-morrow."

" You're losing too much time. Send a wire and start
it to-day."

"All right, sir."

" When do you think it could be completed ? "

" Well, say a couple of weeks."

" Too long."

" Maybe with a hell of a push we could have it in ten
days."

"All right. I'm marking the date with a red line. You'll
give me the figures by that date. Now let us get on.
Finance : You'll want seven hundred pounds."

" Yes."

" How much have you got ? "

" Well, we haven't——"

" Good God, man ! Don't say you haven't started. Why

there are men who went through blood and fire to free
Ireland and you are getting a chance they never got. Look
here, do you want to keep on this job ? You can get out
of it, you know."

" Oh, for God's sake, sir, don't do that. Look, I'll get
the collectors out first thing in the morning. I'll have that
seven hundred pounds inside two weeks or die getting it.
Give me a chance."

By this time, of course, James's friend was reduced to a
pulp. Invariably he appealed to James to let him go
before facing me, promising he would come back in a week
with a fine report, but James was adamant and the poor
man had to go through the same ordeal as his predecessor
at my desk.

It was wonderful how this worked and the men went
back to their constituencies galvanised into activity and
filled with burning ardour to get the work done.

A few weeks after the German plot arrests, O'Leary
Curtis, an old friend of Griffith's, came to me with a strange
story. A fisherman, walking on the strand in a remote
region in Mayo, had been hailed by a man in a boat who,
speaking with a foreign accent, had told him that there
were a number of rifles in a cave in the vicinity. The man
in the boat then rowed out to sea. The fisherman went to
the cave to investigate and saw the rifles there. He hurried to
a man in the nearest village whom he knew to be connected
with the Sinn Féin movement and told him the news. This
man, without making any investigation on his own account,
had come direct to Dublin to report the matter but, owing
to the arrests, he had been unable to make any contacts
and he was shy of coming to Sinn Féin headquarters. In
the street he had met O'Leary Curtis, whom he knew, and
had told him the story, giving him a section of an ordnance
map on which he had marked the location of the arms.

I hurried off to Collins with the story and the map and
a few weeks later Mick told me they had got a few rifles,
about twenty, as well as some ammunition, in the place
indicated, but he did not know what the explanation was.

Shortly after this event, I had a mysterious visitor. She
was a large, blonde lady, about thirty years old. She asked

if I were Mr. Brennan and, when I said I was, she said she would like to see me alone. I nodded to Micheal Nunan, who was in the office, to leave us and when he did so, she locked the door.

" I have to be careful," she said, " I have an important message. I come from German headquarters in Belgium."

She mentioned her name and said she was the wife of a well-known supporter of Sinn Féin in Belfast. She asked if she could be put in touch with the headquarters of the Volunteers. I told her I might be able to do this but I should know more about her mission. Thereupon, she opened a little case she had and set up a very small, but powerful microscope. She extracted from beneath the buckle of her garter a tiny scrap of film, not more than a quarter of an inch square. She put this on the plate and asked me to look into the microscope and read it. It was a typewritten sheet of paper containing fourteen questions, such as, what was the strength of the Volunteers in Ireland, their armaments, their strength in England, and so on. The sixth, or seventh question was whether the Volunteers in London were in a position to destroy power plants and railway junctions in England. The document stated that for every such attempted act of sabotage, the sum of one thousand pounds would be paid, and for every such successful attempt, the sum of five thousand pounds. This struck me as being so stupid, that I jumped to the conclusion that my visitor was a British, and not a German agent. Anyone should have known that, at that time, we were willing and anxious to carry out all the sabotage we could in England and that money would not be an additional inducement. Without saying anything, however, I went through the whole list of questions, making a mental note of them. The lady then told me she had a formula for a secret ink, which she was anxious to hand over to the proper person. I told her to go back to her hotel and await a message from me.

I reported that evening to Mick and I told him of my suspicions. He said he would see the lady next day and I sent Micheal Nunan to conduct her to the house Mick had selected for the meeting. This particular house had not been raided up to this time, but a few days later it was visited and, thereafter, it was systematically raided every other day.   Of course, this tended to strengthen my suspicions, but when I next saw Mick, he told me that the lady was a bona-fide agent of the Germans and that he was using the invisible ink she gave him.

During this period, though he was very much on the run, Harry came bustling into the office nearly every day, if only for a few minutes.   Sometimes he was disguised as a priest and he loved the masquerade.   He was always in the highest of spirits and his coming in was like a breath of fresh air.   He had a desk but he never sat at it for more than a minute or two.   He was very much interested in seeing that the right men—the fighting men—would be selected for the various constituencies, and I knew he was working closely with Mick on this.   Mick also came in now and again, but only when it was absolutely necessary.   He wore no disguise and he was always taking a chance for we all knew the office was closely watched.   He was an untiring worker. No matter how much he was on the run, he was in his office at eight in the morning and he opened all the mail himself.   So thoroughgoing an intelligence officer was he himself, that he opened all letters which passed through his hands, whether they were for friend or foe.   I remember that, at a later stage, Miss Fitz (Anna Kelly) made a bitter complaint because letters written to her by Frank Gallagher from Mountjoy Jail, which came by the underground route, had been opened by Mick.   When I mentioned this to Tommy Dillon, he grinned and said :

" Well, Mick is the Director of Intelligence, isn't he ? "

Whenever Mick and Harry wanted to attend a meeting of the National Executive, the meeting was held not in 6 Harcourt Street, but somewhere else.   One such meeting was held in a building at Croke Park, the Gaelic Athletic Association Headquarters.   Mick and Harry were nearly an hour late.   They had come by a roundabout route to avoid the police touts.

" Hurry up," said Mick, dominating the scene as he entered.   " Go ahead with the agenda.   We may have to get out quick."

We raced through the agenda, but once or twice Mick

held the business up because he did not like the decisions.

" I thought you wanted the business done in a hurry," said the chairman, Alderman Tom Kelly.

" I want the business done right," snapped Mick.

" This proposal of yours," said Tom, " is going to mean a terrible lot of work for someone. Who's going to do it ? "

" I'll do it," said Mick.

He was ready to take on any amount of work at any time and he did it all efficiently.

Tom said, jokingly :   " That's right, we'll leave it all to the gunmen."

The term " gunmen " was being used by everybody, themselves included, to indicate the Volunteer chiefs, or those who believed in physical force. The speaker had intended no malice or disparagement, but Mick was on his feet.

" Never mind that ! I won't stand for any jeering remarks about the Volunteers. They know what they're about and they'll do the work assigned to them. They deserve something better than cheap sneers."

He pretended to be in a towering rage.

" Keep your hair on," said Tom Kelly, " there is no one sneering at the Volunteers, or anyone else."

Mick was on his feet again, but he was interrupted by a young man who came in hurriedly and whispered something to him.

"All right," said Mick, and beckoned to Harry. He turned to the chairman :

" I'm sorry, Tom, we have to get out."

As Mick and Harry went out, still whispering to the young man, one of the members who was panicky jumped up and said :

" Let's break up the meeting."

" Why ? " asked Tom, coolly.

" The police must be coming."

" Well, let them come."

" But they'll take us all."

" Sure they will," said Tom. " Next business."

The business proceeded for a while and the same member whispered to me :

" Would they think bad of me if I left ? "

" Not at all," I said and I turned to the chairman.
" Mr. Blank has to go. Isn't that all right ? "

" Sure it is," said Tom, " go ahead."

Mr. Blank got up, bowed awkwardly and left. The rest
of the business occupied nearly an hour, but the police did
not come and there was no sign of them as we were leaving.
Mr. Blank came in to me next day. He was very much
abashed.

" What did they say about me ? " he asked.

" Not a thing."

" You despise me, don't you ? "

" Good Lord, no, not at all."

" I can't help it," he said, " when I get in a panic like
that, I have to run away."

" Sure you have," I said. " If the rest of us don't run
away, it's because we haven't got the courage to."

He said he would be my friend for life.

Harry came in one day with a letter he had received from
Austin Stack, who was in Belfast Jail. It was to the effect
that if we did not have a candidate for Leix or Offaly, he
would suggest that we should put forward the name of a
young fellow who came from the area and who was, at
that time, also in Belfast Jail. He was a lawyer named
Kevin O'Higgins and he was a nephew of Tim Healy.
None of us had ever heard of O'Higgins but when the Leix
Director of Elections came up to see me, I sold him the
idea after considerable persuasion and Mr. O'Higgins
received the nomination and the seat. In view of later
developments, it seemed ironic that but for Austin Stack,
Kevin O'Higgins might not have been in public life.

Chapter Eighteen

America had entered the war on the stated principle that its outcome should ensure self-determination for all nations great and small. The British had, willy-nilly, pledged themselves to the same principle. The Irish now looked to the Peace Conference where they hoped to show that the demand for the Irish Republic was backed by eighty per cent. of the Irish people.

A PARAGRAPH in the newspapers one day, concerning the scarcity of silver coins of certain denominations in England, put an idea into James O'Mara's head.

"Look here," he said, "we'll make England shell out silver to us. Get your men in the country to whisper there's a silver shortage coming. The people will draw silver from the banks and stow it away. The English will have to send silver over to save the banks."

So the word went out. The result amazed us. Within two weeks there was a serious silver shortage all over Ireland. The banks announced that large quantities of silver coin had been sent in from England but these, also, quickly vanished. A week later, it looked as if business was going to be paralysed because of the scarcity of silver. So we decided to call off the dogs and, in a few days, everything was normal again. I asked James why he had done this. "It's no harm to try out everything," he said, and added : "So long as you don't let it get out of control."

When, late in June, I returned from the Cavan by-election, which we won easily, I was able to show O'Mara that the result approximated very closely to the returns we had had from the constituency and this meant that, if our other returns were equally accurate, we would sweep the country in the General Election.

"That's right," said James, "the election is as good as won. And," he added, "the Germans are losing the war."

"Think so ? "

"Yes. The Americans are only getting into their stride."

He went out, but came back in a few minutes and asked :

"What next would you do if you had won the election ? "

" Get a couple of men over to the Continent to prepare the way for our being heard at the Peace Conference."

" How much would it cost ? "

" They would have to stay an indefinite time, one in Geneva and one in Paris or the Hague—say a thousand pounds each."

In the afternoon he came in and laid a loosely-tied paper parcel on my desk.

" There are eighteen hundred pounds in English banknotes in that," he said.

He pulled an old black cotton glove from his pocket. It was bulging and heavy.

" There are two hundred sovereigns in that," he said. " That makes two thousand. Get your two men out and tell no one where you got this money."

He gave me a sidelong, quizzical look, turned on his heel and went out.

I got down to the problem at once. I had to find two men who could get out and who could, without carrying any documents, present a convincing claim as to why Ireland's case should be considered by the Peace Conference. The problem of getting the two men out was a difficult one ; any chance of getting passports in the usual way was out of the question. I consulted Frank Gallagher. He told me that Rory O'Connor had a blank passport which he had had forged the previous year. He brought me this, but when we examined it, we decided it would be dangerous to use it as it was not sufficiently convincing. Paddy Sheehan, at that time de Valera's secretary, and acting General Secretary of Sinn Féin, suggested that P. S. O'Hegarty would be a good man to send out. I asked P. S. if he would go and he said he would think it over.

On the following day, Harry sent me word that Mick Collins wanted to see me that night in Gavan Duffy's house. I went along and was surprised to find that, in addition to Mick, there were present Harry, P. S. O'Hegarty and Paddy Sheehan. Mick lost no time beating about the bush. He said :

" P. S. tells me you want him to go to the Continent."

" That's right."

" To prepare for the Peace Conference."

" Exactly."

" Well, I think that's nonsense, and he agrees."

" I don't think it's the time," said P. S.

" How are you going to finance them ? "

" Well, P. S. probably told you."

" He said you had two thousand pounds. Where did you get it ? "

" I can't tell you that."

" How do we know but it came from an enemy ? "

" You'll have to take my word for that. I know the man is a friend."

" What's the mystery about then ? Why can't you tell us his name ? "

" He asked me not to."

" That's very funny."

" I don't think it's funny. I don't know why you asked me to come down here. If P. S. won't go, I'll have to get someone else."

" Don't you think the National Executive should have something to say to this ? " He turned to Sheehan. " The Executive hasn't considered it ? "

" No," said Sheehan.

" It's curious," said Mick, " that you haven't brought it before the Executive."

" Not at all," I said, " it's just what you would do in the circumstances. It will probably take me a couple of months to get my men and have things in shipshape for them to go. I will then report to the Executive and I've no doubt I'll get their sanction. If I reported it now, the whole thing might get out and then the scheme would fall down."

" Who gave you the money ? "

" Listen, Mick. There's no use in you going on like this. I'm not going to tell you or anyone else."

Harry spoke for the first time.

" Look here, Bob," he said, " Mick thinks, and we agree with him, that we want the money worse for guns."

" Is that it ? " I asked Mick.

" Sure, what else ? "

" Well," I said, " you can't have it. I got the money

for a certain purpose and it's going to be used for that purpose."

" This is god-damn nonsense," said Mick.

"Another thing," I went on, " if you want to, you can stop this. I know that. But, if you do, I'll give the money back."

They argued with me for over an hour, without getting any further, and then Harry said :

" What's the use ? He's not going to give in. Let him have his god-damn Peace Conference. Come on and have a drink."

On the following evening, to forestall any repercussions from this meeting, I reported my plan to the Executive and asked them to refrain from seeking any details till I had the plan ready. They agreed.

A few days later, Frank Gallagher introduced me to a man who, he thought, would fill the bill as one of our emissaries. I shall call the man Jean Christophe. I had known him by repute as a scholar. His father had come from the continent to Ireland at an early age, and had spent his life in Dublin in a professional capacity. I found that Jean was extremely shy, sensitive and serious-minded. He was whole-heartedly on the side of Sinn Féin and I found he was also extremely well informed on the question. I agreed with Frank that he was the right man, particularly as he could speak several European languages and, above all, because he was in a better position to get out than anyone else. It seemed that Arthur Balfour had taken an interest in his work on ancient manuscripts and that they corresponded from time to time. He anticipated he would have little difficulty in getting Balfour's help in securing a passport, ostensibly to pursue his studies in Paris and Rome. I gave him a great deal of material bearing on Ireland's case for independence and asked him to study it so that he could afterwards write an appeal to the Peace Conference on the subject.

I had occasion to see Mick the following day. I told him I had found one man to go to the Continent and I asked him point-blank if he would put any difficulties in the way.

" Not at all," said Mick, and asked who he was. I told him.

" Let me see him before he goes," said Mick. I said I would and I arranged the meeting next day.

A day or two later, I accompanied Frank to his digs again to see Jean Christophe. The latter told us he had seen Mick and then he asked me this question :

" If any instructions I get from Mr. Collins cut across yours, what am I to do ? "

I asked him what he meant.

" Your instructions," he said, " are that I am to enlist all the help I can in the cause of Ireland, to find out where the Peace Conference is to be, to try and influence by letters and interviews representatives of other nations at the Peace Conference with a view to having Ireland's representatives admitted. Now, Mr. Collins has asked me to do as follows : If I find there is no chance of Ireland's voice being heard, I am to write a letter to him to say there is no chance and to advise a rising in Ireland as a demonstration to impress the Peace Conference."

Frank and I were dumbfounded, but we both impressed on Christophe that he was to carry out his first duty. As to the second, so far as we were concerned, he was to use his own judgment.

I did not see Christophe again till the spring of the following year, when I had returned from Gloucester Jail. One day I was sitting in my office in Harcourt Street, deep in conversation with a visitor. Cathal Brugha came in and entered a little room off mine, which he sometimes used. Someone else came in and went into the same room shortly after. I did not notice who it was but, some time later, the same person returned and passed close to my desk. Something in his appearance caught my attention. He seemed to be in a daze. As he went through the doorway, I saw it was Jean Christophe. I got up and went to the door but already he had vanished down the stairs. I went into Brugha's office.

" Was that Jean Christophe ? " I asked.

Brugha glowered at me.

" It was," he said, " what about him ? "

" What about him ? " I asked, recalling some loud voices of a few minutes earlier. " you were having a row with him."

" Why not ? " said Brugha, " the fellow is an English agent."

" He's nothing of the kind," I said.

" No," said Brugha, scornfully, " maybe you don't know what he did. He had the cheek to write from Paris to say there was no chance of our being heard at the Peace Conference and that the only thing for it was a rising."

" Well, " I said, " he got instructions to do that very thing from Collins."

"And what right has Collins to give instructions like that? That is this damn I.R.B. again."

" That's not the point," I said ; " the point is that Jean Christophe was merely carrying out his instructions and you've no right to call him an English agent."

" Haven't I ? Who but an English agent would write a letter like that ? "

" But, Collins told him to do it."

"And what right had Collins to do that ? "

And so it went round and round in a circle.

I wanted to go and see Jean Christophe, but I did not know where I could find him. Next day, however, Frank Gallagher came in and told me that Jean Christophe was in the depths of despair because Brugha had called him an English agent. He feared he might be shot. I told Frank of my conversation with Brugha and I undertook to see Mick. Mick, however, dismissed the whole thing with a wave of his hand.

" To hell with him," he said.

" Wait, now, Mick. I gave Jean Christophe certain instructions. You gave him others. He carried out my instructions all right. So I've been told. He carried out yours too."

" He bungled the whole business." said Mick.

" How ? "

" Never mind."

" Do you know," I said, " that Christophe is in despair, that he's afraid he'll be shot because Brugha called him an English agent ? "

" Brugha is talking through his hat. And tell that bloody fool there's no fear of his being shot."

"Couldn't you tell him that?"

"I've plenty to do. Go to hell!"

I reported this conversation to Frank and he went off to see Dev, but the latter refused to interfere.

Jean Christophe left Ireland and so far as I know he never came back.

Late one Sunday night a visitor arrived at my house after I had gone to bed and I had to get up to receive him. It was Eamon Donnelly, our election organiser for Ulster. He had heard that the National Executive had decided to allow certain constituencies to go by default, constituencies in which there was such a strong Unionist vote that we had no chance of winning. The moment he had heard this he had set out hot foot for Dublin to see me.

He said the policy of not contesting every seat was all wrong. If we were to present our case to the Peace Conference we should be in the position of giving that body the entire Irish vote for the Republic. We could not do that if we denied the Republican voters of any constituency the right to vote. Moreover, we would by implication be conceding to the Unionist faction the right to rule a section of the country which should be subject to rule by the whole Irish nation.

I told him that the decision of the Executive had been taken because the contesting of the Unionist-held seats would run into many thousands of pounds, that there was no chance at all that the funds could be raised locally and that the cost would fall on the National Executive, whose exchequer was already excessively strained.

We argued for more than an hour and, finally, Donnelly won, as I knew all the time he would. I told him that I would not only bring his plan before the Executive but that I would back it for all I was worth.

On the following night I raised the question and after hours of debate and in spite of the most violent opposition (mainly on financial grounds) the proposal to contest every seat was carried.

To most Irishmen, the partition of the country was and is a hateful thing. To Donnelly, it was more than that. It was nothing less than monstrous that an Irishman should not be free to travel in his own country, north, east, west and south without let or hindrance. From 1920 when the partition of Ireland was first effected to the day of his death, Eamon Donnelly worked day and night to right this wrong. In 1931, I think it was, I saw him angrily face his old friend, de Valera, at a Fianna Fáil Ard-Fheis in the Mansion House on this issue. He thought that Dev was not moving fast enough in his endeavour to end the monstrosity of the partitioned Irish nation.

I am not one of those people who think that partition has any future. I think it will end sooner than most people imagine. It is, as Donnelly held, a monstrosity and in nations, as in nature, monstrosities are short-lived. When it is ended and the unity of Ireland has been achieved, I am sure that the contribution Eamon Donnelly made towards that end will not be forgotten.

Donnelly was one of the quickest-witted men I have known. I have heard and could give many examples of this trait of his. I will give only one. There was a monster demonstration in Ennis on the anniversary of de Valera's dramatic arrest there by the Free State forces. There were people from every county there. Donnelly and I were strolling through the streets and I introduced him to a lot of people, including three Wexfordmen, two of whom were lame. The third had a slight limp. Donnelly turned to me and said :

" Every bloody one of these Wexfordmen is lame because their grandfathers were wounded in 1798."

On November 11th, 1918, the screaming of sirens and the pealing of the chimes of Christ Church Cathedral announced the armistice. As if at a signal, Grafton Street became bedecked with Union Jacks. Crowds of separation women—the women who were drawing separation allowances because their husbands were in the British forces— poured into the streets and formed processions headed by the Union Jack. In a little while it became less an expression of thankfulness for peace than a jingo demonstration against Sinn Féin Dublin. A dense crowd, singing British war songs, collected in front of Sinn Féin headquarters and attacked the building. The police made faint-hearted

Group of prisoners released from British convict prisons, June, 1917. Taken outside Mansion House, Dublin.

[National Museum of Ireland

Rathmines Sinn Fein Committee, 1918–19: Tom O'Connor, Robert Brennan, Wm. Sears, Joe MacDonagh, George Daly, Tom Cullen, Seamus Dwyer, Paddy Little, George Irwin, Sean Doyle (The Spark), Mrs. Richard Mulcahy, Mrs. E. Kent, Miss ffrench-Mullen, Dr. Kathleen Lynn.

efforts to disperse the mob, which grew larger by the hour. In the evening, reinforced by many hundreds, they attempted to set fire to the building. A section of the Third Battalion of the Volunteers was called out to defend the building and a very lively fight ensued. The Volunteers saved the building and extinguished the fire, beating back the attackers. A few companies of British military then came along and occupied the street.

Next day my office was a wreck. Though I was on the third floor, every window had been smashed and the place was miserably cold. My files were scattered all over the floor and trampled on. As I was trying to restore some sort of order and, at the same time, take in the contents of the morning mail, Seumas O'Kelly came in. When Griffith had been arrested, Seumas, who was the editor of the *Leinster Leader*, had come up from Naas to edit Griffith's paper, though the doctors had warned him that Dublin was dangerous for him because of the condition of his heart. Seumas was in great distress. He had just come through Grafton Street where, he said, the Union Jacks flying from the top windows were so huge that they slapped the passers-by in the face.

" I thought I'd never again see the like of that in Dublin after 1916."

To distract his thoughts, I gave him a bundle of draft handbills which a correspondent in Tipperary had sent me. They were very striking and were curiously worded. Harry came bustling in, giving an amusing and highly exciting account of his hand-to-hand encounters of the night before in the defence of the office. Seumas enjoyed the recital. He handed me one of the handbills and said :

" This fellow must have been reading Whitman."

He then made a curious sidelong movement and placed his hand on the table, closing his eyes. I jumped up.

" Is there anything wrong, Seumas ? " I asked.

" I'm all right," he muttered between clenched teeth.

Harry ran over and caught him in his arms as he went sliding to the floor. He was unconscious but breathing heavily. The ambulance came and took him to the hospital where he died during the night.

In the afternoon I went out to see and condole with
Seumas O'Sullivan, the poet, who, at that time, was still
working in his pharmacy in Rathmines. I knew that he
was Seumas O'Kelly's closest friend in Dublin. We talked
of our dead friend and we both cried without shame.

Chapter Nineteen

Under the Defence of the Realm Act, the British Government was empowered to arrest and detain without charge or trial any person committing, or suspected of committing or being about to commit an offence against the State.

ONE day about three weeks before the election, I was working on a huge pile of letters on my desk, when the door opened and a tall man, whose sinister face seemed familiar, looked in. He was breathing fast, as if he had run up the stairs. Micheal Nunan, who was working at another desk, looked at the man and said aloud :

" G-man."

The man, whom I now recognised as Wharton, one of the most active of the G-men, entered the room and closed the door behind him. He came over to my desk and started examining some of the papers on it.

" What's up ? " I asked.

He gave me a sidelong, jeering look, but did not reply. Just then, one of the girls from the lower office ran in, crying :

" There's a raid, Mr. Brennan. They're all over the——."

She saw the G-man and backed out, leaving the door open. Across the landing I could see another G-man in the opposite room. Wharton went over to him and they held a whispered conversation. Then he returned to me.

" Your name is Brennan," he said.

" Yes."

He went over to a map on the wall and pointed to Wexford.

" Do you know this area ? " he asked.

"A little," I replied.

" No one is to leave this room," he said and went out.

" Do you think he's on to you ? " asked Micheal.

" Not at all," I replied. I wasn't uneasy as I had been coming quite openly to the place every day for over six months and, if I had been wanted, they could easily have picked me up at any time. My appointment to a position at

185

Sinn Féin headquarters had been no secret, as the Wexford Corporation, for some strange reason—the majority of the members being anti-Sinn Féin—had passed a resolution congratulating me on the fact, and this had been published in the Dublin papers.

" You wouldn't think of trying the roof ? " said Micheal.

" That might work," I said, " if they had not seen me here, but I'm sure there's nothing to worry about."

In a few moments Wharton came back with Inspector Smith.

" I think we want you," said the latter.

" For what ? " I asked.

" Never mind," he said, " come along."

" I think you are making a mistake," I said, but without any conviction. " I suppose you are aware that I am the Director of Elections and that——"

" Shut up," he said and pushed me out of the room. Micheal ran after us with my hat and coat. When we reached the street, they hoisted me into a covered lorry and Smith, Wharton and another detective clambered in. The staff had all assembled on the front steps and Joe Clarke, the caretaker, called for a cheer for me, which was heartily given. A number of people came running from the direction of Stephen's Green, some of them shouting imprecations at the G-men. Someone hurled a stone which struck the side of the lorry and I saw a man in handi-grips with two uniformed policemen.

" They're getting rough," said one of the G-men, drawing his revolver.

"About time," I said.

The third G-man turned to face me, an ugly sneer on his lips.

" You don't think they'd hurt us," he said.

" I don't know about you," I said, " but I wouldn't like to bet on the chances of your two friends here."

" Shut up," said Smith, glowering, and I thought it wise to take his advice.

I did not mean to be prophetic, but Wharton and Smith were both shot down in the streets within a few months, the latter fatally.

After a few hours in a grey, dark cell in the Bridewell, I was removed to Arbour Hill Prison where, as I shortly discovered, I was the only civilian prisoner. All the others were soldiers belonging to various regiments. I heard them being paraded in the hall outside my cell and marched out. I found out from the Orderly that every day, loaded with full kit, they were brought on route marches through the country, as part of their punishment. I had been in the prison a couple of hours when a young lieutenant, with a wisp of a moustache, came to my cell and told me I was allowed to smoke for half an hour each day, if I so wished, and that I was to have half an hour's open-air exercise each day, but if I attempted to speak to any of the other prisoners the exercise permit would be cancelled. The young man seemed extremely bored.

" Where am I to smoke? " I asked.

" You can come along now," he said and led the way to a reception room near the front entrance. It was across the hall from the room where, four years earlier, I had interviewed my brother-in-law, Jim Bolger.

The officer gave me my cigarettes—everything had been removed from my pockets in the Bridewell—and I asked him to have one. He declined to take it but helped himself to one of his own. I stood at the window looking out on the front yard and entrance gate and we talked, or rather I talked for, though he was civil enough, I found it hard to drag a word out of him. For his edification, I told him that the prison we were in had had an association with Irish rebels for at least a century and a quarter and that Robert Emmet had been confined there.

" How jolly," he said.

Thus encouraged, I proceeded to give him some more items of Dublin history, but he was not responsive. I changed the subject and asked him how he liked the Phoenix Park.

" Rather jolly," he thought.

I advised him to take advantage of his stay in Dublin and go to see the Museum, particularly the gold ornaments, some of which dated back to the ninth century.

" How jolly," he said.

It began to dawn on me that he was not giving me and my subject the attention that was necessary and I thought he might be in love or something. I asked him how he had liked France and I knew the answer before he had given it. It was rather jolly.

I went on talking. I spoke of England and Francis Thompson and Shelley and Henley, of the Sussex Downs, the beauty of the Thames at Richmond, of Kew Gardens and Epping Forest. I even dragged in the Devon Tors and Eden Phillpotts and the Isle of Wight. Did he not think them beautiful?

" Jolly good," he said.

I refused to be discouraged and kept on. I spoke of madrigals and catches, of maypoles, coffee-houses and Dr. Johnson. I lamented the passing of the stage-coach. Suddenly, out of the blue, came the remark :

" I'd rather like to go to Russia."

I was so surprised that I almost stopped talking. Russia at that particular moment was not exactly a pleasant place. Red armies and White armies and allied armies were making havoc of the place.

" Why ? " I asked.

" It would be jolly," he said.

So I talked of Russia, of the czars, of the steppes and Siberia, of Mackensen's brilliant strategy at the Mazurin Lakes, of the Ukraine and Kurdistan. I told him of a book written by an American on a journey he had made from Haifa through Asia Minor and Persia and up through Turkestan. He did not appear interested, so I switched back to literature and the arts. Had he read Dostievski? He had not. Turgenev, Tolstoy and Maxim Gorky brought no awakening of interest. I spoke of the ballet, of Pavlova and Karsavina. I even tried a feeble joke about the last-mentioned lady, saying that she really came from Cahirciveen and spoke Russian with a Kerry accent and that the stage name she had taken—Cahirciveena—had been changed by the Russians to Karsavina. I thought he would say it was jolly funny, but he didn't. Finally, when I had said everything I could think of regarding Russia, I asked him point blank why he wanted to go there.

"It would be jolly to get out of this hole," he said and looked at his watch. He had let me smoke for an hour and had not bothered to notice that I had transferred several cigarettes and matches to my pocket.

In the exercise ground, next day, I had to walk to and fro on a cinder path. My guard was the original sergeant-major type. In an open shed near by, several military prisoners were at work cutting up timber for firing. They were curious about me, but cautious. The one nearest my path had a horrible scar on his face and neck, as if he had been burned by acid. After three or four turns, I approached my sergeant-major.

"This walking up and down is a silly business," I said. "You walk up and down with me and we can talk."

He fixed me with a belligerent eye.

"You carry on," he said and added, as an afterthought, "or you can go back to your cell."

The prisoners grinned and I returned to my path. At the western end, it led past an iron-barred gate, leading to a large grass plot with a few trees. On the other side of this plot beyond the prison wall, I could see a few houses like artisans' dwellings. I wondered whether the people who lived in those houses were with us. After a while, my sergeant-major went over to talk to the guard who was in charge of the military prisoners. As I passed near the bench where "scarface" worked I dropped a cigarette and when I turned at the end of the path I saw it had disappeared. As I came back again I heard the old familiar prisoner's whisper :

"You're a toff. Got a match?"

On my next journey, I dropped a couple of matches and I noticed down the line of the prisoners a quickening of interest. I had made up my mind that I had lost my freedom too lightly and that I should use such material as was at hand to try an escape. When my half-hour was up, my guard came over.

"Time to go in," he said.

"Look here," I said to him, nodding towards the iron gate, " will you tell me why that place is locked up? "

"Why do you ask? "

" Because," I said, " I've an idea they dug a grave in there for me."

" Nineteen-sixteen ? " he asked.

" Yes," I said. " Were you here then ? "

" I'll show you something," he said and pulled from his pocket a whistle on a chain. " Pearse (he called it Perrse) gave me that. Come here. You can see from the gate where they are buried. I was here at the time."

He pointed to a distant corner of the plot, but I could see nothing only the green grass. I knew, of course, that they had all been dead before being brought to Arbour Hill but I refrained from asking how a dead man could have given him the whistle. When I got back to my cell, there was evidence that my friends had discovered my where-abouts. There was a " sent-in " dinner on a tray with a cloth, but though I searched every morsel of food, there was no sign of a message. About an hour later, the orderly opened my cell door and told me there was a visitor for me.

" Who is it ? " I asked.

" Search me," he said. He brought me to the end of the corridor where my young lieutenant was waiting.

" We'll go in here," he said, showing me into a larger and airier cell.

" Who is the visitor ? " I asked.

He consulted a slip of paper.

" Youna Brennan," he said.

I was about to correct his pronunciation when Una came in, looking very thin and pale. Her fourth baby was only a few weeks old. My young lieutenant very kindly walked to the other end of the cell and turned his back. She told me she had found out where I was after endless enquiries all day and all night and that Countess Plunkett, finding her almost exhausted from the search, had insisted on driving her around in a cab which was waiting outside. Having failed to get any information from the police, or at any of the military barracks, she had finally called on Major Friend at his old headquarters and he had permitted the visit. She brought me some clean underwear and a suitcase, fearing I might be deported. I tried to reassure her on this point, but I knew my voice carried no conviction. Before we realised the interview had begun, it was over and she had gone.

Next day, I tried to further my plans for escape. Passing the wood shed, I dropped a few more cigarettes and, as my sergeant-major conversed with the other guard, I drew nearer and nearer to the wood shed in my peregrinations.

"Any news ? " asked " scarface," and as I returned again and again I told him what I had heard from the orderly, that there was an idea they would be all sent to Russia.

" Why ? "

" They're sending a lot of troops to Russia."

" Why ? "

" To stop the revolution."

" To fight ? "

" Of course."

The conversation had to be resumed next day.

" We're not going to Russia."

" You'll have to go."

" No fear ! "

" What are you going to do ? "

" You tell us."

" Listen. You are marched out every day . . . with full kit. . . . When the gates are opened, throw yourselves on the guard—disarm them. . . ."

" If we had a few of your fellows in here ! We can't trust the crowd here."

" You can trust a few. . . . Get me out of my cell. . . . I'll lead the way to the city . . . and find shelter for you."

I had some hopes for success but, as it happened, the attempt was never made. On the following day I was allowed out for exercise but, in the afternoon, I was told to pack my bag and I was brought to a rear entrance to the prison and put into a van. Three soldiers, a sergeant and two privates, got in with me. They had great difficulty in preventing their fixed bayonets from buckling against the roof. Through the little window I could see we were being driven through familiar Dublin streets and that we were heading eastward for the docks. At O'Connell Bridge we were held up by the traffic.

" Where are we going ? " I asked the sergeant.

" You'll find out," he said, and the two privates laughed. Through the little window, I scanned the faces of the good-humoured people passing by in the street, but there was not one I knew. Not one of them gave more than a passing glance at the military van. At the North Wall we went down the companion-way of an ancient steamer and I was hurried below—much further below than I had ever been before. My three guards and I found ourselves on the bulkheads of the boat. There were two other military men with another prisoner in uniform. I gathered that he was a Canadian soldier who had been arrested for deserting. The wretched place we were in was semi-dark and there was little head-room. It was difficult to find a position on the curving timbers which one could maintain for even five minutes without suffering extreme discomfort. There was little conversation because neither the soldiers, nor the other prisoner, gave me any encouragement to talk. After what seemed hours, we became aware that the ship had put out to sea and after a while she began to pitch badly. We all got very sick and we kept on being very sick. The Canadian, after one very violent bout, revealed a rich fluency in bad language. He consigned the ship to the bottom of the sea, and the Army, the Allies and the British Empire to the nethermost depths. To show his impartiality, he consigned the Germans there too. The English soldiers were too sick to take any notice of him. After what seemed a very long interval, during which I must have dozed, I heard my sergeant say that he was dying and he certainly looked very bad. He was a small thin man with pale, sandy hair which did not tone with his now green complexion. The place stank. I pointed out to him that at least we were all entitled to some fresh air and that he ought to bring us up on deck. He was afraid some one, whom he called the R.T.O., would report him.

" What you want," I said, " is a drop of whiskey. If I could get on deck I might wangle a drink."

He shook his head dolefully. I went on to point out we were now somewhere in the middle of the Irish Sea and that there was no chance of my escaping. It took me a long time to win him but, finally, he agreed to allow his two men to conduct me to the lower deck. They were not to go out on the deck themselves but were to allow me to do so. I promised I would keep within their view. The air itself was intoxicating after the foul atmosphere down below. The boat still pitched heavily and the clear, salt spray stung my face. There were a few soldiers clinging to the bulwarks here and there and fewer civilians and none of them took any notice of me. Nearly ten minutes passed before a steward happened along. I spoke to him and my heart beat faster when I heard his grand Dublin accent.

"Listen," I said softly, "I'm a prisoner. They are taking me over to somewhere in England. My guard is over there by the hatch."

"Great God above," he said, and then quickly : "What do you want me to do. I'll do anything I can. My brother Jim—Jim Doherty, maybe you know him, was out in 1916. Maybe when we get to Holyhead I could help you to escape."

I explained that all I wanted at the moment was some whiskey. He was doubtful if he could get it; because of all the military on board the bar had not been opened.

"Never mind, I'll manage something," he said, "even if I have to break open the bar."

I handed him a pound note and he seemed doubtful about what he should do with it as he went off. He was gone for what seemed a long time and I could see that my guards were getting fidgety. At last, my friend reappeared and, with a jerk of his head, he went down the hatch and we followed. He drew me aside and handed me a full bottle of whiskey, giving me back my pound note at the same time. "Tony,—he's the barman," he explained, "got it for me and he wouldn't take a penny for it when he heard it was for you."

I protested, but he refused to take the money.

"Are you sure we couldn't try a getaway at Holyhead ? " he asked. "I've lots of friends there."

I said "no" and tried to express my gratitude. He undertook to call to No. 6 Harcourt Street next day when he got back to Dublin and tell them that he had seen me.

No conjurer pulling a rabbit out of a hat ever created

a greater sensation than I did when I produced the bottle of whiskey in that filthy hole.   I became a benefactor to the race.   At that time, no soldier travelling could be served with a drink and war conditions still prevailed.   My guards became my warmest friends and even the Canadian began to feel a little less unfavourably disposed towards the human race.   We boarded a train at Holyhead and I promptly fell asleep.   Some hours later, my sergeant roused me when we had to change trains.   The new compartment we got into was crowded and it was obvious that the other passengers were puzzled by our appearance.   It looked as if I was a prisoner, but they could not understand the friendly terms my guard and I were on.   A brisk little man, sitting directly opposite me, was bursting with curiosity.   He took advantage of something I said to ask if I came from Ireland, and when I said " Yes," he declared he was glad to hear that conditions were improving over there and that my countryman, de Valera, was about to be released.

" It's the first I heard of it," I said.

" I'm sure I read it in some paper yesterday," he said.

" I must tell him that," I said, " I'm on my way to join him, I think."

" Oh ! " said Mr. Brisk, his eyes popping.   He opened his paper and began to read. '

A man in the corner who had a beard like Charles Dickens', turned to look at me.

" You mean you're a prisoner ? " he asked.

" Yes.   These gentlemen are my escort."

" What is the sentence ? "

" There was no sentence."

" No sentence !   What were you charged with ? "

" There was no charge."

" But, but, there must have been a charge in the warrant."

" There was no warrant."

" What about your lawyer ? "

" I was not allowed a lawyer."

" Were you not brought before a judge or a magistrate ? "

" The secret police arrested me, threw me into prison and the military shipped me off to England.   Even now I don't know where I'm going."

Another man spoke up.

" But they must have something against you," he said.

" Of course they have," I answered. " They know I'm a Sinn Féiner, like nearly everybody else in Ireland—just as they know you're a Sinn Féiner—meaning England for the English."

" Why, it's outrageous," said the man with the beard. " These are the methods of Czarist Russia."

Mr. Brisk had lowered his paper. His eyes popped from one of us to the other.

" Is this true ? " he said to the sergeant.

" You bet it's true," said the sergeant. " You ain't got no idea wot it's like. If a kid sings ' The Soldier's Song ' down O'Connell Street the 'ole bloomin' garrison is turned out. Ain't that so, Jimmie ? "

Jimmie, one of the other soldiers, nodded gravely.

" It's God awful," he said.

" I tell you," said the sergeant, " it ain't no bloomin' 'oliday."

Mr. Dickens was blazing with indignation.

" Would you mind giving me your name and address, sir," he asked.

" Certainly," I said and gave him the particulars. " I would be glad if you would send my wife a post card to say you saw me. She doesn't know whether I'm dead or alive."

" I'll do that with pleasure," said the man, " and, moreover, I'm chairman of the shop stewards in the factory I work in in Leeds and I'll bring the whole thing before them and we'll see what our M.P. has to say about it. It's enough to make any Englishman ashamed."

My sergeant, thus encouraged, gave horrid details of the night raids on the dwelling-houses.

" It's a bloomin' nightmare," he wound up. His hearers clicked their tongues in sympathy and I began to feel like a martyr.

Chapter Twenty

In the General Election of 1918, Sinn Féin, which was pledged to the establishment of an Irish Republic, won 73 of the 105 Irish seats. " No English Party," says Dorothy Macardle, " had ever received a majority so overwhelming as the Irish people had given to Sinn Féin. It is doubtful if in the whole history of parliamentary institutions a decision so nearly unanimous had been given to one party."

VERY late that night we arrived in Birmingham, where we had to wait several hours for a train. The station was crowded with soldiers, all returning from the front. I brought my escort to the buffet to treat them to a cup of coffee. Some of the milling soldiers there recognised my sergeant and there were enthusiastic greetings, introductions, enquiries, reminiscences. My sergeant, still under the influence of the man from Leeds, began to tell them all of the iniquitous work the troops were required to perform in Ireland.

" Why, look at this man," he cried, pointing dramatically at me, " 'E's a white man, ain't 'e ? Don't tell me, I know it. Me and my mates know it. Well, 'ere 'e is going to some bleeding prison in England and 'e don't know where, but I can tell him now, it's Gloucester. Well, 'ere 'e is, dragged out of 'is bed, away from his wife and kiddies, and all for wot ? Nobody knows, because see there's no trial, no warrant, no sentence, no judge; just like Russia and the Czar. Well, if that's plying the gyme, I'm a mug, we're all mugs."

All this, and much more, he shouted out while I, very much embarrassed, stood there surrounded by sympathetic Tommies, who all agreed it was " a god-damn shyme." By and by, his friends had to rush off to catch their trains and there were boisterous goodbyes which I had to share.

The four of us sat on a bench on the platform and smoked. It was one o'clock in the morning, but there were lots of people about. The excitement over the end of the war was plainly still in the air. Some girls were ostentatiously

196

parading up and down in our vicinity and, after a while,
the two privates joined a couple of them and chatted a
while. Then, with apologetic glances at the sergeant, they
moved on up the platform where it was dark.

The sergeant told me his life story, and there wasn't much
to it. He worked in a wire factory, was married and had
two children, a boy of five and a girl of six. They were
the grandest kiddies in all the world. The wife was a
topper. When he was called up her heart was broke but
she took it like a hero, she did. And she was true to him,
she was. He was going to make up to her for all she had
been through since he was called up. Luckily, he had
missed being sent to the front, not that he would have
shirked it. Luckily, too, he had been promoted sergeant
only two weeks after being made a corporal. He wasn't
going back to the wire factory, but he was going to start a
wire factory of his own—in a small way, of course, at first.
There was nothing about wire-making he had to learn. And
he was going to give his little woman a good time to make
up for——

For some time, a comely maiden had been giving both
of us the glad eye. She was strolling up and down a few
yards in front of us and I could see that my companion was
finding it more and more difficult to keep his mind on his
story.

" Nice piece," he said.

" She looks inviting," I replied, speaking the literal
truth.

" I wonder if you wouldn't mind," he said.

" Not at all," I replied.

The lady received him almost with open arms and the
two of them adjourned to the nether depths of the platform.
So here I was left alone and desolate on the platform of
Birmingham railway station with no one to look after me.
I stood up to stretch my legs and stroll about. Gradually,
I approached the entrance to the station. There was only
a ticket-checker at the entrance to what seemed to be an
overhead bridge which led, I supposed, to the city. At the
farther end of the bridge there were two military policemen. There was nothing, apparently, to prevent my

walking out. I tried to recall the address of the only man
I knew in the city—my old friend Peter Moloney. Do what
I would, I could only recollect the word Edgbaston. Now,
I reflected, if I go out I will find myself in a strange city
with no place to go, very little money, and an accent that
will betray me if I ask questions. Within a few minutes my
absence will be noticed here and the alarm will be out.

I turned and went back to the bench. I smoked three
cigarettes before the sergeant came back. He was almost
running.

" Oh," he said, " you're 'ere. I was afraid you might
think of skipping."

" Well," I said, " as a matter of fact, I did. I went out
and came back again."

" Good 'eavens, why ? "

" I don't like Birmingham."

" You're a toff," he said.

When we got to Gloucester it was five o'clock in the
morning. It was very dark when we left the station. The
station-master had told us that it was easy to find the jail.
We had only to walk straight ahead, take the second turn
on the left, and first on the right, and there we were. The
streets were woefully dark. The war ordnances forbidding
street lights were, apparently, still in force. We took what
we thought was the second turn on the left and first on the
right but there was no jail. I was lugging my heavy bag
and they were carrying full war kit, and when we had been
walking for nearly half an hour without coming on the jail,
we were all rather cross. The darkness was stygian. One
of the soldiers suggested getting back to the railway station,
so we retraced our steps but we could not find the station.
If we had been in darkest Africa, we could not have been
more utterly lost. The first rays of dawn were beginning to
show when we came to a canal bridge.

" I'm not going any further," I announced and made my
way down to the bank of the canal. The others followed
and discarded their kits and threw aside their guns. We
all stretched out luxuriously on the slope and soon the
soldiers were fast asleep. Half an hour elapsed while the
sky brightened and the sun rose pink, crimson, golden. I

looked at my companions. The younger of the two privates
was only a boy. Instead of being in this drab uniform, he
should have been off skylarking or playing football. The
second was mean, thin-lipped and crafty. He had contributed nothing to our conversation during all the time
we had been together. The sergeant was sleeping soundly,
no doubt dreaming of his wire factory. Again I considered
leaving them but I banished the thought. Already I was
bound up with them for all time. I might escape for the
moment but——

A man carrying a lantern still lighting came over the
canal bridge. From my angle, he seemed cowled like a
monk.

" Hey ! " I called and he stopped, staring at us.

" Do you know if there's a jail about here ? "

" Yeh," he replied and pointed over my head. " You
can see it from here. It's just around the corner."

" Thanks," I said, and turned to find the sergeant
sitting up.

" The jail is just around the corner," I said.

He woke his companions and they donned their kits.
I got my bag and we tramped around the corner. Right
enough there was the jail with a big, open space in front
of it. The sergeant worked the big knocker, awakening
echoes in the empty space. After a little while, a wicket
door opened high up in the wall over the great iron-studded
door.

" Yes," said a voice.

" I have a prisoner here," said the sergeant.

" You're too early," said the voice and the wicket was
slammed shut.

The sergeant knocked again—the sound of the echoes
in the great square was dismal. The wicket opened.

" It's only six o'clock," said the voice. " We don't open
the prison on Sunday till seven," and the wicket was
slammed again.

" Well, that's the limit," I said, in a rage. Already my
companions were preparing to squat down on the ground,
presumably to wait for the place to open. I went at the
knocker and banged it. There was no answer, but I kept

up the bombardment. Several minutes elapsed before the wicket opened again.

" Open the door," I yelled, " I'm not going to wait here another hour."

" Sorry," said the voice, and the little door was shut once more.

" You'll be sorrier before I've finished," I shouted and began on the knocker again.

" Take it easy," remonstrated the sergeant from his position on the ground. " It's no use. They won't open up."

I kept on knocking while I yelled at the sergeant :

" It's not good enough. We did find this damn jail and now they won't let us in."

Suddenly the incongruity of the position began to dawn on me and I was about to desist when the little door opened again. The voice was thoroughly angry this time and it advised me to go to a warm place.

" We can't stay out here till seven," I cried.

" Well, go round to the police station," said the voice, " it's just around the corner."

" Come on," I said to my escort, and led the way to the police station. A very large and imposing sergeant beamed on us when we entered the day room, in which there was a huge fire. The soldiers lay down promptly and went to sleep again. The police sergeant asked me if I was a Sinn Féiner and his pronunciation was perfect. I mentally noted the fact that he was Irish and began indulging in the old trick of discovering his native place from his accent. He told me I would find congenial company inside, that Hunter, Griffith and McEntee were fine fellows. He knew one of the warders who spoke constantly of them. When, in answer to his question, I told him my name, I noticed a curious flickering in his eyes. I made a long shot.

" Wasn't your mother's name Brennan ? " I asked.

" How did you know ? "

Suddenly I had placed his accent. It was Geashill.

"Are you long over here ? " I asked.

" Thirty-two years."

" Did you ever go back to the old spot ? "

" How did you know I came from over there at all ? "

" Tell me," I said, " I never can remember, whether Geashill is in Leix or Offaly."

" Why, it's in Offaly, of course—now how the mischief——? "

His amazement was comical.

" Well, that's the best—tell me, how did you know ? "

" We've a good Intelligence Service," I said. " Who is the warder you're so great with ? "

" Come, come, none of that," he said.

" Never mind," I said, " if I get a chance of passing a letter out to you, you'll post it for me."

" Listen, sonny," he said, " it would be too dangerous for me. I've only a few more years to put up to get my pension."

" None of the fellows will give you away," I said. " Can't you trust your warder friend ? "

He put his fingers to his lips, as footsteps sounded outside and two policemen entered. They wore storm helmets and one carried a lantern. They exchanged heavy greetings with the sergeant and seemed to take no notice of me or the sleeping soldiers. One of them made laborious entries in a heavy report book, while the other sat at the fire apparently sunk in deep contemplation. I tried to talk but I got no encouragement and, after a while, the sergeant, who was uneasy, glanced at the clock and roused my sergeant, telling him that it was nearly seven and that by the time he got round to the prison, the gates would be open. They were indeed open when we got there. My sergeant was plainly affected when we said goodbye. I followed the warder through the inner door and the old familiar round began with a bath, which I thoroughly enjoyed.

The prisoners were anything but overjoyed at my arrival, for my coming blasted their high hopes of immediate release, which had been predicted in the papers. They had their bags packed ready to go home. I was glad to accept Griffith's invitation to join the mess which he and Joe McGuinness shared. A.G., as we called him, was the prisoners' spokesman and he was easily the most cheerful man amongst the dozen internees.

" It was lucky for you you were arrested," he said,
" you must have been overdoing it, for you look all
in."

He insisted on my remaining in bed for the first few days
and he and McGuinness brought me my meals. They
were all thirsty for election news and I told them we were
going to win seventy-three seats. They thought it a joke,
for we held at the time only five seats, whereas the Parliamentary Party held seventy-four seats, and the Unionists
twenty-six. I actually gave them a list of the seats we would
win and a forecast of the voting figures. A few weeks later,
when the election was over and the returns came in, they
found that my figure of seventy-three seats was correct,
but I had made two mistakes, which cancelled each other.
Pembroke in County Dublin, which I had marked for a
loss, was won, and Waterford City, which I had marked to
win, was lost. Moreover, the poll figures which I had
given them were in most cases amazingly accurate.

Many of the newly-elected members were in jail ; in our
own little group in Gloucester jail we had seven M.P.s.—
Griffith for East Cavan ; McEntee, South Monaghan ;
McGuinness, South Longford ; Fitzgerald, Pembroke ;
Hunter, Mid-Cork ; Pierce McCann, Mid-Tipperary and
Clancy, North Sligo. Needless to say, we had great rejoicings
and many speeches.   We had applied to the Governor to be
allowed home to cast our votes on the day of the election
and A.G. had solemnly warned the Governor that if our
application was refused, we could claim that the election
was void.   The British Government, of course, ignored our
application and this led to my perpetration of one of the
atrocious conundrums which were in vogue at the time :
" Why is this place unlike a beehive in the springtime ? "
Several answers were given—" Because being Republicans
we can't have a Queen,"—" Because there are more cells
than we can fill," and so on. The correct answer was :
" Because we were not allowed out for the pollin'." They
were going to kill me for it.

One day Griffith told me that from the top floor of the
prison one could glimpse the outline of Gloucester Cathedral
and we climbed the three flights to the higher reaches.

From the end window we saw the outline of the Cathedral in the evening light. A.G. talked of its beauty and its history, which he seemed to know very well. I gathered he had visited it some time or other. I expressed surprise at his enthusiasm for something so decidedly English as the Gloucester Cathedral. He reminded me that I did not exactly despise Shakespeare and Shelley, alluding to a spirited debate we had had the night before.

There was no opera which I had seen, up to that time, which was strange to A.G. Now and again he used to sing snatches from *The Barber of Seville* or *Faust*, but never for an audience. He had a rather poor baritone voice, but he whistled very well. He was a typical Dubliner in his fondness for Wallace and Balfe and, as for drama, he knew his Congreve, Sheridan and Goldsmith very well. He had a keen appreciation of Shakespeare and of Beaumont and Fletcher. He knew and loved every melodrama that had been produced at the Queen's Theatre, Dublin, for a generation. Synge, he really hated. " Imagine," he would say, " the mentality of a man who suffers no shame in confessing that he listened through the chinks in his bedroom floor to the women talking in the kitchen of a Wicklow farmhouse."

A.G. told us a curious and interesting thing in connection with Yeats's play, *Cathleen ni Houlihan*. The poet read the MS. of the play for A.G. and said he felt that the end was not rounded out as it should be, or sufficiently dramatic. As it stood then, the ending was bald. Michael, abandoning his bride-to-be, had gone out of the house to follow the Old Woman and Brigid had taken into her arms the weeping Delia, the forsaken bride. Yeats said he knew there should be a last line, but he could not get it. Griffith said : " Why not have the father ask the young boy something like this : ' Did you see an old woman going down the road ? ' and have the boy reply : ' I did not, but I saw a young girl and she had the walk of a queen.' " Yeats at once accepted the suggestion, only putting in the word " path " instead of " road."

"And why did he use the word path instead of road ? " I asked.

"I don't know," said A.G. "He said the line over several times before he made the change. Perhaps the poets can explain it."

I have related this story to several poet friends of mine and they all doubted it, but I knew Griffith very well. He was the most unassuming and modest of men and he would never have dreamed of making a claim of such a nature if it was unfounded.

In some respects he was the narrowest of puritans. One day someone who had given him a novel of Compton Mackenzie's, asked him what he thought of it. He turned on his questioner savagely. "Filth," he said, "it has everything that appeals to the lowest English taste : adultery, a suggestion of sodomy, and tears for the poor prostitute." I was surprised, for I had also read the book and thought it rather harmless. Griffith's modern admirers who complained so much about the absence of freedom in literature under our various governments, either forget or are ignorant of this facet of Griffith's character. I am sure that if A.G. had had time to set up a censorship, it would have been far more stringent than anything we have experienced.

A.G. was not always happy in his choice of friends and Darrell Figgis is a case in point. When Figgis first appeared on the Irish scene, he knew so little of Ireland that he thought a terrible brogue and the frequent use of " sure," " begorra " and " bedad " represented the last word in Gaelicism. He was quick to learn, however, and he was one of the most acquisitive men I have ever met. He went in for politics very seriously shortly after his arrival but, despite untiring efforts to turn on charm, he made enemies more easily than any man I knew. His assertive manner and his unbounded egotism had a lot to do with this, but he had, in addition, a trait which, in Ireland, would damn a much greater man. His meanness in money matters was so pronounced and so obvious that it became almost proverbial. I knew an otherwise admirable public representative who failed to retain his seat, merely because at the end of a long day's campaigning, he gave his driver sixpence for a tip. In spite of everything, Griffith stuck to

Figgis. I asked him point-blank why he did so, and he told me the following story :

One day in Wakefield, or some other English prison in which he found himself after the 1916 Rising, Griffith and his comrades were being transferred to another jail, as were also some other Irish prisoners who had just arrived. A prison officer at the door examined the belongings of each prisoner as he passed, to make sure none of the prison property was being removed. Just in front of Griffith was a prisoner with a red, pointed beard, green eyes and a commanding manner. It was Darrell Figgis. He was carrying a bag, which he had opened for the officer's inspection. The latter took from the bag a plate, on which there was plainly stamped the broad arrow and the name of the prison.

" This belongs to the firm," said the officer, putting the plate on one side.

" I beg your pardon ? " said Figgis.

" I say this belongs to the firm," repeated the officer.

Figgis took up the plate and held it aloft.

" Do I understand you to say I have stolen this plate ? " he asked.

" No, not exactly," said the officer, " I merely said it belonged to the firm."

" If," said Figgis, " what you say is true and it belongs to what you call the firm, and if you find it in my bag, the only possible inference is that I have stolen it. Is that what you say ? "

" I say it belongs to the firm."

"Are you accusing me of stealing ? "

" No, but you are making a mistake in taking it."

" I'm making no mistake. I say the plate is mine and I am taking it with me. If you insist on retaining it, it is tantamount to a charge of stealing against me."

The officer made no reply.

" I will not," said Figgis, putting the plate back in the bag, " ask you for an apology. There can be an apology only from an equal. I bid you good day."

The astonished officer allowed him to close the bag and go out.

" I allowed," said Griffith, " that the man who was capable of dealing with English officialdom like that, was worth having."

I gave Griffith a copy of *The Economic Case for Irish Independence* by Darrell Figgis, which had been put on sale at one shilling a copy, a week or so before I was arrested. I asked Griffith to go through it and tell me what he thought of it. I did not tell him I was furious when I read it, because three-fourths of the book consisted of Griffith's own articles, lifted, without acknowledgment, from his paper and the remainder of material I had written and published at Sinn Féin Headquarters, again without acknowledgment. A couple of days later, A.G. gave me back the book.

" What did you think of it ? "

" Not bad," he said.

I turned to Joe McGuinness. " Listen, Joe," I said, " Figgis has lifted the contents of that book from work which A.G. has slaved at and which I have slaved at. Not merely does he not ask permission to use it, but he does not even acknowledge the sources, and he sells it for Mr. Figgis's benefit at a shilling a copy, and A.G. says it's not bad ! "

" Well," said A.G. " don't you think it's good to see someone getting the public to pay for it."

It was not merely his partiality for Figgis that was exhibited in this attitude. He was most unselfish and he never cared who got the credit if the work was done. He actually shunned personal publicity. If anyone attempted to curry favour with him by flattery, his suspicions were at once aroused, but his vanity showed itself otherwise. One could not say, " I think you are a great man," but one could say, " Sinn Féin is the greatest political plan yet devised to achieve the independence of Ireland," and get away with it. In his standards of conduct for other people, he was very lenient to his friends and merciless to his enemies. Once, within five minutes, I heard him referring to two men, both of whom indulged in liquor rather too freely. The first, a friend, he described as " taking a drop now and again," the other, a foe, he called " a drunken scoundrel."

Chapter Twenty-one

Following the election, the forty-seven Sinn Féin deputies who were still at large (thirty-six being held in English prisons) met openly in Dublin and set up the Parliament and Government of the Irish Republic known as Dail Eireann.

THOSE who saw Griffith only in his moments of relaxation in the Bailey or Mooney's, might easily form the opinion that he was an easygoing man of middle-class tastes, who liked a good glass of whiskey and a good yarn. He never talked politics, or shop, on those occasions and, indeed, he preferred to let the others do the talking. During all his adult years, except the last few, he slaved for four days of the week at his paper which, for a long time, he not merely wrote, but set up as well. His associates could tell the day of the week by his mood. Monday serious and earnest; Tuesday morose and aloof; Wednesday cranky and ill-tempered; Wednesday night unbearable; Thursday smiling and brisk once more. He put the paper to bed on Wednesday night and then, after a shave and brush-up, he sought his cronies in some pub and relaxed. It was almost painful to see him writing his leading articles, those magnificent editorials which were sowing the seeds of nationality in little groups of young people throughout the country. He would seize a wad of copy paper and start writing, his stub of pencil gripped tenaciously, digging into the paper, and his foot stamping the floor now and again. Half-way down the page he would change his mind and, without tearing up the page he had written, he would turn the whole wad of loose sheets right over, and start again. Often he did this half a dozen times before he would get his subject properly under way. When he ended, his eyes showed the intense mental strain to which he had been subjecting himself. His pockets were a joke in the office. They were all filled with letters, notes, memoranda and clippings, and when he wanted to find something, he would empty one pocket after another, dumping the contents on

the table higgledly-piggledly, and then try to stuff them all
back in one pocket. He never knew in which pocket his
money was and, very often, he did not know whether he
had any money or not.

For some strange reason, since we were not allowed any
spirits in the prison, we had been discussing the relative
merits of the various brands of Irish whiskey, and A.G.
told us that whiskey that was made in the pot still was
whiskey and anything that wasn't, was not whiskey. The
Dublin distillers, catering for the expert taste of Dublin
drinkers, had a craft which had gained something in every
generation during two centuries or so. For instance, the
Jameson people maturing their whiskey in sherry casks
found that up to the twentieth, or twenty-first year it gained
in flavour, and after that period it began to deteriorate.
By a careful series of trial and error, they had decided the
final date on which the whiskey was the last word in per-
fection and they kept a supply of this liquor for family use
and for a few connoisseurs who could appreciate the product.
Once he had performed some service for Andrew Jameson
and had been rewarded by the present of a half-dozen
bottles of this liqueur whiskey. It happened that on the
same evening he had a visit from an old friend, John Quinn.
A.G. produced the whiskey and he and John drank " a
bottle or so." Some time after midnight, John decided to
go home and A.G. saw him as far as the corner. John
had to travel from the north side into the city and right
across to the south side, a distance of about four miles, and
there being no public conveyance at that hour, he had to
walk. Griffith returned to his home and, shortly afterwards,
he became aware that the wind was rising. It continued
to rise and it developed into a storm. As a matter of fact,
it was the worst storm that had been experienced in Ireland
for a generation, the storm of 1903. It blew down about
half the trees in the Phoenix Park and on the sea-front at
Clontarf, it wrought such havoc that the fronts of many of the
houses were blown away and, in the morning, one could see
from the street the bedrooms from the first floor up. Griffith
could not get his mind off his friend, John Quinn. No
mortal who was out in that storm could survive it. The

worst of it was there was nothing Griffith could do about it. Next morning, as he made his way with difficulty into the city, he realised that the storm had been even worse than he had thought it. He intended going out to Rathmines to see if John had got safely home, but something prevented him. About lunch-time, he walked down Grafton Street and who did he see but John himself. Griffith ran to him and all but embraced him.

" My God, John, I thought you were dead."

" Why ? " asked John.

" On account of the storm. I wondered how you could get through it."

" To tell you the truth," said John, " I never noticed any storm. I do remember going over the canal bridge at Portobello on my hands and knees but, beyond that, I saw no signs of any storm."

" What I mean to say," concluded Griffith, " is that the makers of Dublin whiskey have learned something during the two centuries they have been making it."

Griffith could never concede that the Rising of 1916 was the turning-point in Irish history. To all of us who had been through the period, there was no question but that the Rising was responsible for changing a people, whose sense of national honour had all but vanished, into a disciplined and determined nation whose sons were willing and ready to march as one man into any danger in defence of a sacred right. A.G. could not and would not see that. The change was inevitable, he said. It was bound to come sooner or later. The Rising had hastened it a little. That was all.

He had a personal grievance about the Rising. He told me that soon after the outbreak of the Great War he had attended a secret conference at which there were represented Sinn Féin, the Gaelic League, Labour, the Irish Volunteers and the I.R.B., and there it had been agreed that Ireland should rise if (a) England attempted to enforce conscription, or (b) there should be a German landing. It had been further agreed that if neither of these contingencies arose and the war was coming to an end, there should be a further conference to decide whether any action should be taken. The second conference had never been held and Griffith considered that all parties to the first one had been badly treated. In the week preceding the Rising, he was in constant touch with MacDermott, who worked in his office, and though he had seen that Sean was unusually active and that he was receiving many visitors, he had had no inkling that an immediate Rising was contemplated. He was very sore at the fact that Sean had not trusted him. If he had been consulted, he would have been against the Rising, but when it started, he was strongly of the opinion it should have been made general.

On Easter Monday he decided to try to persuade MacNeill to call out all the Volunteers throughout Ireland. He got on his bicycle with the idea of finding MacNeill, but he discovered he could not get across the city on account of the fighting. On Tuesday, he determined to get to MacNeill at all costs and he cycled out on the north bank of the Liffey, intending to cross some of the bridges to the west of the city. He crossed the river at Lucan and made his way back on the south side and found MacNeill. The agony he experienced on his way out from the city, he described to me. He feared he might be taken and that it would be represented he was running away from the fight. On his way back to the city, he was almost happy and he had made up his mind that the Rising should be made a National one at all costs. MacNeill agreed to issue a call to the nation but, later on, other counsels prevailed. The city was already all but encircled and it was felt that the spreading of the fighting to the country would lead only to a greater holocaust and a national calamity.

Though he had been an early member of the revived I.R.B. Griffith later set himself absolutely against physical force. He visualised a disciplined, well-directed nation marching forward to its goal on passive resistance lines. He held that this was a safer and more certain way of beating England.

On a day in January, 1919, the news of Soloheadbeg made the front pages of the English newspapers. Seumas Robinson, Dan Breen and three companions held up two armed constabularymen who were conveying a load of gelignite to a quarry. The R.I.C.-men had resisted and had been shot dead and Robinson and his companions captured their carbines and the gelignite. It was the first bloody encounter since the Rising. I made no secret of my admiration of Seumas and Dan and their companions, but A.G. was scathing in his comments. He was sure that this action did not have the sanction of Dail Eireann, which had been set up a day or two before and, consequently, it was nothing short of outlaw action. But even that was not so important as the consideration that England could always beat us if we chose her own weapons.

" If this sort of thing goes on," he said, " we will end up by shooting one another."

He told us the story of Joe Poole, to illustrate the evils of physical force. Poole belonged to one of two rival factions into which the I.R.B. had split some thirty years before. A member of the opposing group, who was a stone-mason, had been seen going into Dublin Castle. The fact was that he had legitimate business there, but the other group concluded he had become a spy. He was secretly tried, in his absence, and sentenced to death. Poole heard of the decision and, believing as he did that the man was innocent, he set out to warn him that the firing party was lying in wait for him. Joe took the wrong road at Seville Place and missed his man, who walked into the ambush and was killed. Poole was arrested and tried for the murder of the man whose life he had endeavoured to save. He kept silent and was found guilty and hanged. Griffith gave us the impression that he was somehow connected with Poole's activities on that fateful night, though he must have been very young at the time. At any rate, he knew Poole well and the affair made a deep impression on him. I heard him refer to it many times.

In view of his convictions on the question of physical force, one can get a clearer glimpse of his splendid loyalty during the succeeding years. The fight between the Volunteers and the British forces grew more and more bloody and Griffith did not budge. The struggle between his loyalty to his fellows and his detestation of the deeds done by the Volunteers in their gallant and unequal fight against the constabulary and Black and Tans seared his soul. Very few guessed at his feelings and none heard him complain. Only on one occasion did I get a glimpse of the burden he was bearing and that time he was near breaking-point. I shall tell of it when I come to it.

The argument about physical force became very hot one night and Pierce McCann, who was all but a pacifist, and Ginger O'Connell, who was anything but one, nearly came to blows. Griffith decided to change the subject and asked me how I had found Fred Murphy the last time I was in Wexford. I replied I had found Fred quite well, as usual, and Griffith asked me to tell the others what I knew of him.

When I was a young man, it struck me one day that Fred never changed. He was a tailor, very sprucely dressed, very polite and he knew everybody and everybody knew him. Now and again he helped to organise local concerts and amateur theatricals and whenever a professional company came to town, Fred always knew some member of it. He seemed to be about forty-five. One day I said to Thady Hayes, who was then a man of about sixty :

" Do you know, Fred Murphy never changes. When I was a little boy, going to school, Fred was exactly the same as he is to-day."

" That's nothing," said Thady, " when I was a little boy, going to school, Fred Murphy was the same as he is to-day and, what's more, my father, God be good to him, told me that when he was a youngster Fred was the same then, and my father would be ninety-three if he was alive now."

" That's nonsense," I said.

" Is it nonsense ? " he said. " Well, if you don't believe me, just you go down and ask Ben Hughes about it."

Now, Ben Hughes was over ninety at this time. A man highly respected, he had been Mayor of the town several times and he was editor of the *Wexford Independent*, a small conservative sheet. He had once told me he had never agreed with Daniel O'Connell and that he had taken sides with the Young Irelanders against the Liberator. So the next time Ben came to the office where I worked in the County Council building—he was the contractor for the printing—I took occasion, as adroitly as I could, to bring up the question of Fred Murphy.

"It's funny," I said, "but Fred never seems to grow a day older."

"I've always wondered about that," said Ben. "I remember when I was a youngster going to school Fred was exactly the same as he is to-day."

"Why," I cried, "that can't be the case."

"It can't," said Ben, "but it is. Not only that, but my father, who remembered the Wexford men coming back from the battle of the Three Rocks in 1798, told me many times that when he was a youngster Fred Murphy looked exactly the same."

"But that would make him a hundred and fifty," I said. "It's impossible."

Ben shook his wise old head. "So I thought," he said.

"But has no one ever made any enquiries?"

"Sure we made enquiries," said Ben. "We made enquiries many times but they never got us anywhere. You go and ask Fred himself and see how far you'll get."

"I can't believe it," I said.

"Would you have time to come over with me to my office and I'll show you something?"

"Certainly," I said.

We had only to cross the lane at the rear of the Courthouse to Ben's office. He searched about amongst the newspaper files for some time and finally lifted out one.

"There is a file of the *Constitution*—the paper which preceded the *Independent*—for the year 1819," he said. "Have a look at it."

I turned the pages of the old, dog-eared, dirty volume. It was, indeed, the file for 1819, its curious type and unemotional headings making a strange contrast with the flaring headlines in the newspapers of to-day.

"What is this leading to?" I asked.

"Did you ever see Fred playing the part of Dick the Dandy in a play called *The Would-be Gentleman*?"

"I did not," I said, "but I heard him mention it."

"Well, I saw him play it," said Ben, "and he did it

pretty well. The play is a very poor adaptation of one of Molière's masterpieces."

He was searching through the file.

" Here's what I'm wanting," he said and pointed to a notice in the advertising columns. " Read that."

I read the notice. It was to the effect that Signor Luigi Fernandi, Professor of the Renowned Menapia School of Terpsichore, Elocution and the Dramatic Arts, wished to acquaint the nobility and gentry of Wexford and surrounding districts that yielding to the requests received from many distinguished patrons the performance of *The Would-be Gentleman* given by the Menapia Dramatic Class would be repeated in the Wexford Assembly Rooms on the 19th day of February 1819 under the distinguished patronage of the Ladies and Gentlemen of the Highest Station in the County, etc.

" What I want to show you," said Ben, " is that the name of the gentleman who played Dick the Dandy in that play was Fred Murphy."

" Well, after all," I said, " there are more Fred Murphys than one."

" We are talking about only one Fred," said Ben, returning the file to its place.

" But this is so extraordinary," I said, " that someone should try to get to the bottom of it."

" Life is too short," said Ben.

After this conversation, I decided to try to draw Fred out about the past. We had many conversations, but I could never corner him. He spoke freely about the past, but only as anyone else would, except that his knowledge of detail was wonderful. One period of Irish history that seemed to interest him most was that of the Norman invasion. He was particularly bitter about Strongbow. There was nothing too bad to be said about him. One day I discovered the reason, or thought I did. There had been a local performance of one of Gilbert and Sullivan's operas and a local girl, named Eva Cousins, had had a great success in it. Next day, I met Fred in the street and we talked of the opera.

" Wasn't Eva wonderful ? " I asked.

A strange change came over Fred. He seemed to be transfigured, as casting up his eyes, he said :

"Ah, Eva ! She was divine. No woman has ever lived who——"

He caught himself up and seemed confused.

" I'm speaking of Eva Cousins," I said.

" Oh, yes," said Fred, absently, " I thought for a moment——."

He broke off and with some commonplace remark, left me, but I had pierced his secret. He was the original Fergus MacMurchadha, or Fred Murphy, Eva's kinsman and lover, the man to whom she had been betrothed before her faithless father forced her to marry Strongbow, the invader, in Selskar Abbey, in the year 1172.

"And you mean to say he's still alive?" said Pierce McCann.

" Sure he is," I said. " If you go to Wexford anyone will point him out to you."

" I can vouch for that," said Griffith, " my brother-in-law, who is a Franciscan priest, was recently in Wexford and he saw Fred Murphy and talked to him and he's as hale and hearty to-day as ever he was."

He went on to instance similar cases in history, such as the deathless St. Germain who wandered about Europe for centuries, who was an intimate of Charlemagne in the tenth century, and a friend of Louis XV in the eighteenth, of the mysterious Major Fraser, who did much the same thing ; of the Ancient Roman who could not die, and of the Wandering Jew.

Pierce McCann was looking at A.G. open-mouthed.

" You don't mean to say you believe all that ? "

Griffith looked at him blandly. " Why not ? " he asked.

Pierce could think of no reply.

In spite of the fact that they hardly ever agreed on anything, Griffith was genuinely fond of Cathal Brugha. The two men had many similar characteristics. They were both unmistakably native Dubliners—a very distinctive type —both small men with extraordinary physical strength, both good and enthusiastic swimmers and both impossibly headstrong at times. In the days succeeding the Rising and before the historic Ard-Fheis of 1917, they came near the breaking point several times. Griffith was striving very hard to keep Sinn Féin to its original purpose and policy, with its immediate aim the restoration of the Constitution of 1782, its means, passive resistance. Brugha, willing to adopt the name Sinn Féin—which had been forced by press and public on the Volunteers—would have nothing to do with the Constitution of 1782 and scorned passive resistance. Griffith was not unlike a game little terrier who finds his offspring surprisingly developing into a very large and angry lion. The quarrel was very bitter at times and once Brugha faced Griffith across the table and said if he wished to stick to his programme he could go to the country and he (Brugha) would take the platform against him with the Volunteers and sweep him out of political existence. De Valera, of course, saved the day with his formula " The aim is the Republic but after independence is achieved, the people can decide by vote what form of government they want," which enabled us all to work together.

In spite, as I say, of their differences, A.G. had always a warm corner in his heart for Brugha, and more than once I heard him defend him in his absence, paying tribute to his single-mindedness and whole-hearted sincerity. A few times I heard him refer to Brugha's heroic fight in 1916 when, wounded almost to death, he kept on firing and directing his men. I was not near Griffith in his last days, but I am sure that the amazing heroism of Brugha in his last lone stand against the armed forces Griffith had sent against him, must have made the latter's heart bleed.

A.G. always hotly denied his final aim was the Constitution of 1782. One night in Gloucester there was an argument bearing on the significance of the word Saorstat, which had appeared in some statement issued in Dublin. A.G. said instead of the word " Poblacht," which was being used for Republic, they should substitute the word Saorstat, which to us would mean " Republic " and to the English " Free State." It was the first time I had heard the latter expression. We need not, said A.G., care what the English called the country if we were satisfied we had got what we

wanted. Tom Hunter, who was no diplomat, said bluntly :
" What about your King, Lords and Commons, A.G. ? "

" That's right," said Pierce McCann, " you were always
in favour of the restoration of the dual monarchy."

" Begob," said Tom Dillon in my ear, " Now we are
going to have it."

A.G. turned on Pierce. " When did I say that ? " he
asked, and there was thunder in the air.

" Why, you've always said it," said Pierce, " in every
issue of *Sinn Fein* and *Nationality* and in *The Resurrection of
Hungary.*"

" I told you before," said A.G., truculently, " that you
have not yet learned to read. I never said anything of that
kind. What I said was that the Irish people should refuse
to treat with England till she had conformed to the Act in
which the English Government renounced their claim to
legislate for Ireland and declared inalienable the right of
the King, Lords and Commons of Ireland so to legislate."

"Ain't that the same thing ? " asked Pierce, innocently.

" It's nothing of the kind. When you say you refuse to
treat with England until they restore a certain kind of
regime, it does not mean that that regime is your final aim."

" So under your plan we could go on to a republic ? "

" Under my plan, as you call it, your hands would not be
tied. You could go on to anything the Irish people wanted."

Chapter Twenty-two

In February 1919, a great Irish Race Convention in Philadelphia demanded that President Wilson should voice Ireland's right to self-determination at the Peace Conference. The U.S. House of Representatives, by a vote of 261 to 41, advocated the application of the same principle in respect of Ireland.

IT has often been stated that Griffith was antagonistic to the labour movement. The charge is not true. He deplored, certainly, the Irish trade unionists' headlong tendency to rush into a strike on the slightest provocation and he also was bitterly hostile to the Larkin type of labour leader, whose aim was not true trade unionism at all but a sort of proletarian dictatorship through the instrumentality of one big union dominated and directed by one man.

Griffith was himself a staunch trade unionist. All the time he was a working printer in Dublin, he was a loyal and trusted member of the Dublin Typographical Provident Society, one of the most rigid trade unions existing in Ireland—so rigid, indeed, that when we were starting the *Irish Press*, the D.T.P.S. refused to allow us to bring in printers from the provinces until every man on their books, no matter what his age, qualifications and physical condition, had already been employed. One of the conditions imposed was that the men brought in, even from Bray, only a few miles outside the city, had to take out temporary membership cards in the D.T.P.S., and had to surrender these if they lost their positions in the *Irish Press*, a natural insurance against allowing Dublin to be overcrowded with idle members of their trade. This union was so well run and was so far from being an employers' union, that during the period I had to negotiate with it, its members were receiving an average of £1 per week in wages more than the Belfast printers. I have frequently heard Griffith praise the D.T.P.S., and advocate that all sections of Irish labour should be organised on similar lines.

However, in the face of the Larkin threat—for so he regarded it—to the realisation of Ireland's national aspirations, he was adamant. I am, of course, referring to the Larkin of the 1913 strike and of the stormy Saturday night torchlight meetings and not to the later Larkin of the Trinity College Debating Society. Larkin, he held, was a disruptive influence. By splitting up the potential forces of the Irish nation into warring factions on class lines, he was postponing any chance of Ireland regaining her freedom, quite apart from the fact that the only logical outcome of the success of his movement would be to set up a dictatorship of the worst kind. Later, he said to me of the Russian Soviet system, then in process of formation, "A dictatorship is bad enough but a proletarian dictatorship is infinitely worse. If there is to be a dictatorship, let it be one by the cultured classes." " The propertied classes ? " I said. " No," he replied, " not the propertied classes—the cultured classes." Many years earlier, in Enniscorthy, we were discussing a speech made by Michael Davitt—one of his last. " Davitt," he said, " visualises a socialist movement in which the Irish proletariat will march arm-in-arm with the English proletariat. What is to become of our distinctive nationality ? Already the so-called upper classes of the two countries are marching arm-in-arm. If Davitt's ideas were to prevail, there would be the end of the Irish nation. The union would be complete."

This attitude of Griffith's towards Larkin was well known and one day we got some fun out of it in Gloucester Jail. I had started out somewhat earlier than usual one morning after breakfast for the exercise ground. On the ground floor of the prison, I found the warders supervising the cleaning out of some cells not previously occupied. I asked a few questions but got no information and, having found there were fifteen cells being prepared, I ran back upstairs to the cell where Joe McGuinness and Griffith were still at breakfast. I told them what I had seen and said that I was going to start the story that Larkin had returned from America and had landed in Dublin the night before, that he had attempted to hold a meeting and there had been a riot in the course of which Larkin and fourteen of his comrades from Liberty Hall had been arrested and that they were on their way to Gloucester. Griffith gleefully agreed he would be furious when he heard the news.

I strolled around the corridor and looked into Tom Hunter's cell. Tom was putting on his boots.

"Aon sgeul ? " he asked.

" No," I said, taking one of his cigarettes.

" What's up with you ? " asked Tom, noticing my heavy preoccupation.

" Nothing."

" You've heard something ? "

I was silent.

" What is it ? "

Only those who have been imprisoned under such conditions can realise the thirst there is for news of any sort.

"Aw, maybe there's nothing in it," I said, looking more and more depressed.

" Where did you get it ? " he asked. " Was it from Thompson ? "

Thompson was the warder who had at times given me some news. I nodded.

" What is it ? "

I closed Tom's door and swore him to secrecy.

" Jim Larkin," I said, " arrived unexpectedly in Dublin last night. There was a riot and Larkin and fourteen of his men were arrested and put on a boat for deportation to England."

Tom began to laugh.

" That's a pretty tall one," he said.

He searched for and found a hand-ball.

"Are you coming out ? " he asked, hopping the ball.

" No," I said, " I've a letter I haven't read."

I went back to my cell and in a few moments Tom passed my cell door and ran down the iron stairs. I heard him going toward the yard and then stop. He paced the hall and a minute later he came stumbling up the steps and burst into my cell.

" They're cleaning out the empty cells below," he said.

" What ? " I asked, absent-mindedly, without taking my eyes from the letter I was reading.

" They're cleaning out the cells downstairs."

" Try another one, Tom," I said, without getting up.

" Honest," he said, " come and see for yourself."

" It's early in the morning, Tom," I said.

He nearly dragged me from the cell and down the stairs. We counted the cells, open-mouthed. There were fifteen, we agreed. Without a word, I turned and walked back up the stairs to my cell, Tom following.

" It looks like it," he said.

" I'm afraid so."

" Well, what is there to be down in the mouth about ? "

" It's Griffith I'm thinking of," I said, " you know how he feels about Larkin."

" Damn it. I never thought of that," said Tom.

He was itching to leave the cell to share the news with someone else. He went to the door.

" Look, Tom," I pleaded, " don't give me away."

" Oh, Lord, not at all," he said.

" You know it's on account of Thompson."

" Sure," said Tom as he went off.

In a few moments I heard excited whispers here and there in the corridor and, after a little while, Sean McEntee came in.

" Did you hear anything ? " he asked.

I had not, I said. He told me the story about Larkin, the riots and the preparation of the cells. I was very sceptical. He assured me it was true. Where had he heard it ? I asked. He was not in a position to tell me, but I could take his word for it that it was absolutely true. Manahan came along just then and he had the story also, but with some additional details. Tommy Dillon, who came on the scene, wanted to know, in voluble Irish, why they couldn't send Larkin somewhere else. I asked meaningly if Griffith had been told and, without a word, they all made for Joe McGuinness's cell. I followed them. Griffith, with an absolutely wooden face, was listening to Jim Dolan telling the story.

"And they're sending him here ? " he asked, pulling at his moustache.

" That's what we're told," said Dolan helplessly.

Griffith turned his back on us and picking up a book, he idly flicked over the leaves. Each of the others looked as if he alone were responsible for the catastrophe. I ventured the opinion that it was all a yarn and brought down on my head a violent and unanimous denunciation. It was clear that in my attitude of doubt, I was in a minority of one. I found myself beginning to believe the story myself. Ginger O'Connell rushed in with the story afresh. He had the added detail that Larkin would arrive in the small hours of the following morning. There was an atmosphere of gloom.

" I don't see," said McEntee, " why we should take it like this. After all, we are all Irishmen and victims of the same foreign tyranny."

Griffith turned on him.

" Larkin is not an Irishman," he said.

" Even if he is not," said Joe McGuinness, " surely we could arrange to carry on without an open break."

Griffith was muttering under his breath words like " communist," " syndicalist," etc.

" Look here," said Dolan, " in spite of everything, and I've no love for Larkin, we should not show a disunited front in face of the enemy."

" That's right," I agreed, " and moreover, whatever A.G. thinks of him, Larkin has done a lot for the working man."

Griffith interrupted me savagely and accused me of being a Larkinite. He said I had taken Larkin's side in the Wexford strike. I retorted warmly that I had taken the side of the workers because they were badly treated, but that did not mean I was a Larkinite.

" Of course," said Griffith loftily, looking at me, " if anyone wants to hobnob with him, that's his own affair, but I will not willingly associate with a man I regard as a destructive force in Irish nationalism."

All day long the discussion went on, even in the exercise ground. After supper the argument grew so hot that a couple of the lads nearly came to blows. Just before lock-up, Griffith came to my cell, chuckling with glee.

" Do you think we ought to tell them ? " he asked,

" Good lord ! " I answered, " we'd be murdered."

In the morning we learned that the new prisoners for whom the cells were being prepared were old friends of ours from Usk prison, and we all breathed freely once more.

Many of the prisoners took advantage of their incarceration to study, but Griffith insisted on regarding his internment as a holiday, having never taken a vacation outside. Life in the world was sometimes grim, occasionally terrible for him, but in jail he refused to take life seriously. I helped him to think up jokes which were often considered a dreadful nuisance by the other prisoners. A number of them had started to play bridge—a slow game at any time, but doubly so for beginners. Griffith and I pointed out to the players that the game was a sad waste of time, that for a card game it had not even the rapid fire delivery of nap or solo or even forty-five to redeem it, that it had all the baneful effects of a drug and was therefore demoralising. The players patiently stroked their budding moustaches—they were all growing them—and tried to reach even deeper depths of concentration on the cards they held. They ignored us as long as they could but finally they abandoned the effort to continue the game in the hall and they retired to one of the cells. Even then, we could not leave them in peace. We walked noisily up and down the corridor outside the cell, talking loudly of the iniquity of card-playing in general and of bridge in particular. We deplored the fact that this insidious vice had found its way into our little world and predicted the dire consequences that would ensue if it were not rooted out. As this had no effect, we decided on trying conundrums which had then been raging in the prison for some time. Someone would propound a ready-made conundrum and challenge the house for an answer. Generally, the more inane the answer, the better the chance of its being right. So we appeared at the door of the card-players' cell.

"Ah, here's a good one," cried Griffith, pointing dramatically at the card table. " How is that pack of cards like a basket of oranges ? "

I tried several silly answers, the most brilliant being that there were several deuces (juices) in it. At each attempt,

Griffith would cry out that it was wrong and exhort me to try again. At last I gave it up.

"It's because there are so many pips in it," he cried and we both laughed so uproariously that the players rose *en masse* and charged at us. We took refuge in the other cells and, when I emerged from my hiding-place, I found Griffith again outside the card players' cell, the door of which had been closed. He had taken off his shoes so as to deaden his footfalls and was carrying out the stools from the adjoining cells. These were piled high against the door and when all was ready we started yelling. As we expected, the door was wrenched open and the stools all fell into the cell, creating an unholy clatter.

All very childish, of course, but all helping to offset the tedium of confinement.

His chess games, however, Griffith took seriously. He was extremely good though he played very rapidly. We played nearly every night and I remember beating him only once.

There was plenty of time to think up and carry out schemes designed to harass one's comrades. Someone gave me one day a copy of the *Dundalk Democrat,* one of the provincial newspapers which was hostile to Sinn Féin. There was a great deal of post-election news, amongst the items being a letter from Sean McEntee thanking the electors of Monaghan for having chosen him as M.P. One of the passages in the letter was a quotation from a speech of President Wilson's, prefaced by the words "As another spokesman has said in another place, etc." I brought the paper to my cell and with a pin I worked at it for half an hour until I had changed the word spokesman into statesman. It was good enough to deceive the naked eye. Then I brought the paper out and showed it to Denny McCullough. He was so tickled that he started reading the letter aloud to all and sundry. McEntee came rushing out of his cell, indignantly denying he had written the "statesman" paragraph. He read the paper for himself and declared his words had been altered by the editor of the *Democrat* to hold him up to ridicule. He retired to his cell, vowing he would write a flaming letter to the editor. I confessed to Griffith and McGuinness what I had done and asked them to try to get Sean to refrain from writing the letter. They merely took it all as a joke, but when Tommy Dillon came in and gave us details of what McEntee was writing, they realised that the letter would have to be stopped. I was deputed to try to reason with Sean. I put the case to him as strongly as I could and said that, as an old newspaper man, if I were the editor of the *Democrat* and received from a political opponent such a letter as he was writing, I would make a hare of him with a headline : " McEntee says he is not a statesman like Wilson." It was all no use. Sean was adamant. Of course, I did not know at the time, that it was I who was being made a hare of because Tommy Dillon had given me away by telling McEntee the whole story. All day long the comedy went on and, finally, it was agreed that when Sean handed the letter into the Governor's office, I should try to get an opportunity to retrieve it. At length, shortly before six o'clock, watching from my cell, I saw McEntee going to the Governor's office with a letter in his hand. Returning, he stopped to chat with a couple of the lads just opposite my cell, while I was in a fever for fear the Governor would turn up and enter the office before I could get the letter. Eventually, Sean went to his cell and I ran across to the Governor's office. There was a letter on the table, addressed to the *Dundalk Democrat*. I picked it up just as I was aware someone had come to the office door. It was the Governor.

" Good evening," he said, looking, as I thought, suspiciously at the letter in my hand. I was so confused that I could not think of a word to say.

" Did you want anything ? " he asked.

" Why, yes," I answered, " there was a parcel sent to me from Dublin and it should have arrived two days ago."

" Well ? "

I wondered if the parcel had come.

" No," he said, " you know very well that all parcels are delivered the day they are received."

" I was going to post this letter," I said, " but I have changed my mind," and I pushed past him out of the office.

All the fellows were in the corridor as I made my way

back and McEntee asked me loudly how I had got on. I knew then, of course, there was something wrong. I went straight to Sean and proferred him the letter.

" I took this back," I said as a preliminary to making a clean breast of the whole thing.

" Open it," said Sean. I did so and found inside only a blank sheet of paper. This time the laugh was on me.

I have often wondered how the monks in a monastery can go on day after day, and year after year, seeing the same people and hearing the same things and retain their mental balance. Of course, their voluntary renunciation of the world in the spirit of self-sacrifice has a great deal to do with it. Certainly in Gloucester Jail, and the same was true of all other internment jails, few of the prisoners kept an absolutely level mental balance and Griffith was one of the few. Only in his dealings with the Governor did he show signs of an irritation which the others of us felt and often expressed towards one another.

Sean McEntee had the quickest temper of any man in the bunch, but at the same time he was quick to forgive and his generosity never failed. I remember how humiliated I felt when only a few days after I had had a fierce row with him over a kettle of boiling water and a frying pan—a row in which all the right was on his side—I came down with a feverish cold and Sean came to my cell at least once every hour to minister to my needs. Every parcel he got was shared with everybody.

Chapter Twenty-three

Sean T. O'Kelly went to Paris as the Envoy of Dail Eireann. For many months he tried to secure a hearing for the Irish delegates at the Peace Conference, but he found that British influence was too strong.

The cells were unlocked at six o'clock but most of us lay on in bed for an hour or so longer. Sean McEntee was always up early to get the half-dozen English newspapers we subscribed to. One morning I could not sleep and I was waiting to come out when the door was opened. I found the papers at the entrance to our wing and my first glance at them showed me that the news was sensational. I hastily picked up all the papers and brought them to my cell. The news featured in ribbon headlines on the front pages was to the effect that de Valera had escaped from Lincoln Jail. I read the account in the *Daily Mail*. After a while, McEntee came out, filled his kettle and put it on the gas ring to boil. Then he went down for the newspapers and returned empty-handed to his cell. I went on with my reading until I had absorbed the whole story and then I concealed all the newspapers under my mattress. I strolled out into the hall and found Manahan assisting Sean, who was frying bacon and eggs. Sean told me the papers had not yet arrived. He was going to make another complaint about the late delivery. I went on to Griffith's cell.

"Are you awake? "

" Yes."

" Listen," I said, " Dev escaped from Lincoln Jail yesterday morning. It's front-page news in all the papers."

He jumped out of bed.

" Where are the papers? "

" They're all concealed in my cell."

"Are you serious? "

"Absolutely. I'm not going to give out the papers till I first tell the story and see the reaction. So don't give me away."

Some of the lads were moving about and the warders were coming on duty when I left Griffith. I went to McEntee's cell. Manahan and he were at breakfast.

" Say, Sean, did you get any explanation about the newspapers ? "

" No."

" I know the reason they're late. There's news in them."

" Well, think of that," said Sean.

" Dev has escaped from Lincoln," I said.

Manahan began to laugh.

" That's a good one," he said.

" I suppose," said Sean, " you got it from one of the warders."

" That's right."

Sean stood up and looked out in the corridor.

" Listen, boys," he said to all and sundry. " Dev has escaped from Lincoln Jail. Who says so ? Brennan says so, Haw, haw, haw ! "

" Haw, haw, haw ! " they all chorused.

I started to prepare breakfast and they all crowded around kidding me. The more I tried to convince them the story was true, the more they laughed.

" You'll have to think up something better than that," said McCullough. " It's not up to your usual standard."

I brought the breakfast along to Joe McGuinness's cell. Griffith had told him the news.

" I don't believe it," said Joe. " You shouldn't play a trick like that on us."

To convince him, I went back to my own quarters and brought back one of the papers, concealed under my coat. They looked at the headlines.

"Aw, this is too good," said Joe, " let them have the papers."

" No," I said, " I want to teach them that they will have to believe me some time."

After breakfast, they all raced out to the exercise yard and I got a chance to distribute the papers in the various cells. When they came in for dinner, there was an uproar. One of the first to burst in on me was McEntee.

" Dev has escaped," he said.

" Didn't I tell you that hours ago ? "
" But you were only codding. Here it is in the papers."
I pointed out sadly that they were willing to believe the
English papers while they would not believe me.

That night the Governor stopped me on the bridge.
" That was very sad news we had this morning," he
said.

I looked very astonished.
" I mean, you boys have my sympathy. That a leader
should desert his followers is terrible."
" You're speaking of Mr. de Valera ? "
" Yes, I think it was mean of him to escape and desert
his men."
" Yes," I said, grinning openly, " it's very sad."
" I know," he said, " none of you gentlemen would think
of doing that."
" It's the last thing we'd think of," I said and went back
to making my rope.

This rope I had been making for many weeks. It was
the outcome of a survey we had made of the prison in the
hope of happening on some means of escape. One day,
when a handball had gone over a wall into the adjoining
yard, Griffith surprised us all by the ease with which he
scaled the ten-foot wall on which there was apparently no
foothold. He had amazingly strong muscular arms, which
he attributed to his early gymnastic training and his regular
daily swim. From the upper windows in our quarters, we
could see a corner of the outer exercise ground where the
walls made an acute angle and A.G. confessed he would
have no trouble in scaling the sixteen-foot wall at this angle.
Outside, at a distance of ten or twelve feet from the wall,
was a tall telegraph pole, conveniently fitted with metal
steps for the repair men. Our plan was that A.G., having
got out of his cell and out of the building by means which
we were to devise, would scale the wall, make fast a rope
to one of the spikes on top and, in case there was some
obstacle like a moat outside, lasso the telegraph pole to
which he would cross, hand over hand, along the rope.
Physically he was quite capable of doing this. Another
length of rope from the top of the wall to the exercise ground

would enable any of the rest of us who could get out, to follow. Without waiting for the other details to be worked out, I decided to make the rope. I had got up early one morning at Pierce McCann's urging, to have an early morning cold bath in another wing of the prison. Pierce and Joe McBride went through this ritual every morning, even when the snow was on the ground. Concealed under my clothing, I had brought back from the baths one of the heavy coarse linen towels. I found that cut into strips and plaited six-fold, it made an excellent rope. Thereafter, I went to the baths three or four mornings each week, bringing back each time a couple of towels. My rope was nearing the prescribed fifty feet in length when the dreadful flu epidemic struck the prison.

One evening I was talking to my friendly warder and I found him very depressed. The 'flu had reached the city, he said, and people were dying like flies. He feared he would take it and that he would not survive. He was a big, strong, healthy fellow and I tried to laugh him out of his fears. He refused to be comforted and he wondered what would happen to his wife and five young children if he was taken away. When he was locking up for the night I tried to rally his spirits but he shook his head dolefully as he bade me good-night. Next day he did not turn up and we learned that he had died at four o'clock that morning. As soon as he had reached home he was taken ill and never rallied. The same day we saw one of the lags being carried out on a stretcher and that night Tom Hunter was down with the dread disease. He was taken off to the hospital and one by one several of the lads followed. The prison stank with the odour of the plague. By the doctor's order, we were allowed to exercise in a larger ground where we could play rounders and we were served with doses of a particularly potent tonic each evening just before lock-up time. On the second night of this performance, J. K. O'Reilly, a genial, elderly man who loved to hear the resounding echoes of his fine baritone voice in the prison hall, indignantly protested against taking the tonic, stating that the doctor had ordered him a glass of whiskey instead.

National Museum of Ireland

American and Irish delegates to Paris Peace Conference, April, 1919. *Sitting* : M. J. Ryan, Philadelphia ; Governor E. Dunne, Illinois ; Frank P. Walsh, Kansas City. *Also in the photograph* : W. T. Cosgrave, Eamon de Valera, and J. Greenlake, secretary to the delegates.

Group taken at Sinn Fein Headquarters, 6 Harcourt Street, Dublin, October, 1918. *Back row*—Sean Milroy, Robert Brennan. *Second row*—Diarmuid Hegarty, Michael Nunan, Dan McCarthy, Michael Collins, Vera McDonnell, Desmond Fitzgerald, Anna Fitzsimmons Kelly, Brian Fagan, W. Murray. *Front row*—Joe Clarke, Barney Mellowes, Jenny Mason, Seamus Kavanagh.

" Where's my whiskey ? " he asked indignantly.

The orderly explained that he had heard nothing about the whiskey, whereupon J. K. protested violently, and we all backed him up. The warders were all grouped around, waiting impatiently to lock up so that they could go off duty.

" Come on, boys," said one of them, " into your cells."

A.G. said it was outrageous to expect us to go into our cells when our men had not got the medicine the doctor ordered.

" Where's my whiskey ? " repeated J. K.

" I don't know anything about it," said the doctor's orderly.

" I know," said J. K. " You drank it."

The orderly now became indignant and there ensued a heated argument in the course of which the Chief Warder, urgently summoned, came on the scene. He tried, in vain, to get us to retire quietly.

" It's no use arguing," said J. K. " Where's my whiskey ? "

" I know nothing about it," said the chief warder.

" I know," said J. K.

" He drank it," we all said.

The Chief Warder, usually a mild-mannered man, got very mad and begged us not to compel him to use force. A.G., who was thoroughly enjoying the scene, said very sternly that the threat to use force was outrageous and one that would have to be reported. He said the doctor should be brought on the scene. Finally, the Chief Warder said he would send for the doctor and, while we were waiting for him, we decided to beguile the time with an impromptu concert, to which J. K. contributed " In Cellar Cool." After a while, a warder came to say that the doctor was not at home and, when pressed for information, he added that he had gone to a dance somewhere ten miles off.

" It's disgraceful," said A.G., " that this man should go off wining and dining and dancing while we are here hovering between life and death. Why should he not be sent for ? "

The Chief Warder decided, very much against his will, to send for the Governor and the latter appeared, wearing an overcoat over a dinner-jacket. He was very worried and frightened but he tried to bluster. He admitted, however, that he knew the doctor had ordered J. K. a glass of whiskey, but there were certain formalities to be gone through before he could procure it. We pointed out that the prescription had been made out two days previously and there was no excuse for the delay. The Governor started a long explanation, but J. K. pulled him up by starting the formula all over again :

" Where's my whiskey ? " he asked.

" I'm trying to explain," said the Governor.

" I know," said J. K.

" He drank it," we said.

The Governor took this quite seriously. He pointedly asked A.G. if he thought he had taken the whiskey.

" Well," said A.G., judiciously, " we are willing to consider any evidence to the contrary."

The Governor stormed and pointed out that it was now ten o'clock, two hours beyond the lock-up time.

" That's another thing," said A.G. " We should not be locked up at all while this epidemic lasts."

The Governor, fearing further demands, suddenly capitulated.

" I'm going to do an unprecedented thing," he said, " I'll supply a glass of whiskey from the prison stores without waiting for——"

The rest of what he had to say was drowned in a very hearty cheer. If the poor man had had any sense, he would have gone off and brought back a glass of whiskey and that would have been the end of the incident. Instead, however, he went to his own office and brought out a full bottle of whiskey from which he proceeded to measure out J. K.'s jorum. The moment I saw the bottle, I slipped over to Sean McEntee.

" Sean," I asked, quietly, " didn't someone send you a bottle of whiskey for Christmas, which you did not get ? "

" Sure," he said.

" Well, take a look at the label on that bottle," I said.

" Right enough," said Sean. He stepped to the Governor's side and took the bottle from him.

" This is Dunville's whiskey, Belfast," said he. " Where did you get it ? "

The Governor began to stammer.

" This is my whiskey," said Sean, " it was sent to me at Christmas."

" I was keeping it for you till you were to be released," said the Governor, who was now behaving like a bad little boy caught stealing the jam. We all crowded around.

"And how dare you give Sean McEntee's whiskey to J. K. ? "

" It's all right, boys," said Sean, " go and get your mugs."

So we got our mugs and made a grand night of it because, fortunately, the majority of the fellows were teetotallers.

One morning, while the flu raged, when our numbers had been reduced by one-half, A.G. did not turn up for breakfast. I went to his cell and found him half awake. One glance showed me he had it.

" How are you feeling ? "

" I'm all right," he said, starting to get up.

" Stay where you are," I said. " I'll bring you your breakfast."

" No, I'm getting up," he said.

My eye caught the tonic bottle the orderly had left the night before. It was empty.

" What happened this ? " I asked.

" I drank it in the night."

"All of it ? "

" Yes."

" You were to take only three tablespoonfuls a day."

" Well, if a spoonful is good, a bottle is better," he said, trying to grin. " That's the stuff to give 'em."

In spite of all I could say he got up and came down to the table. The lads, appalled at his ghastly appearance, tried to prevail on him to go back to bed, but he refused and, when they persisted, he got cross and said he was all right. It was obvious that he had a high fever, but he came out on the exercise ground and even tried to play a game of rounders. He gritted his teeth and put the thing over him on his feet. In three days he was his old normal self. When the fellows began to twit him with having worn an overcoat for the first time, he neatly diverted the conversation, saying :

" I think Bob Brennan should tell us the story of the man who never wore an overcoat."

And I, always glad to be called on for a story, complied.

It was a man from Belfast who never wore an overcoat, the reason being that he could not afford one. A tactless friend of his, whom we will call Jim, happened to remark one day, in his clipped northern accent :

"Ah notice, Tom, that you never wer an overcoat."

" No," said Tom, "Ah never was."

Jim, who was rather slow in his mental processes, kept thinking of this reply on his way home. He said to himself over and over " You never wer "—" No, ah never was."

" Well, well," he said, " that's a clever one. He knew what ah meant all right, but he pretended to misunderstand me. ' You never wer '—' No, ah never was.' Ha, ha, that's a good one."

By the time he got home, he thought the joke so good that he decided to try it out on someone else, so he went out without his overcoat next day, and though it was rather cold, no one said anything to him about it. He went without an overcoat the following day, although it was raining, and still no one said anything to him. So he continued to go without an overcoat in the hail, rain, sleet and snow and during storms and thunder and lightning, and still no one said anything to him. At last, when eight years had passed, and when he had become quite accustomed to going without an overcoat, a friend said to him one day :

"Ah notice, Jim, that you never wer an overcoat."

" No," replied Jim, " right enough, ah never do."

One day about this time, I got a letter from Harry Boland which puzzled me. It was a long letter, written on a double sheet of ruled foolscap, one page and a half covered with writing. What I could not understand was why Harry had written it. There was practically no news in it and it was quite unlike Harry to do something that had no meaning. I read the letter to A.G., and Joe and they were equally puzzled. Suddenly the solution came to me. I recalled having told Harry once of a simple method of writing in invisible ink. You took a new pen and dipped it into your mouth and wrote with the saliva. When it dried there was no trace of handwriting, but if you spilled ink over the paper, what you had written appeared white on the black background. I spilled a bottle of ink over the blank space in the letter and there was Harry's message :

" We want to arrange Griffith's escape. You are to come out on parole on account of your father's illness so we can fix up plans."

I showed the message to A.G. and it was decided I should apply for parole at once. I had received by the same post a letter from my mother telling me my father was very ill, as indeed he was, and enclosing a doctor's certificate. I left the prison next day, taking with me all my possessions, for I had an idea I might not be coming back. The rope, however, I gave to Joe McGuinness and he afterwards brought it out with him.

On my journey home, I again had a long time to spend in Birmingham. I found the name of Peter Moloney's firm in a directory and made my way to the place. From the street I walked straight into a factory, where a lot of girls were working at benches. A young woman looked at me doubtfully when I asked for Mr. Moloney and she went off to make enquiries, while the girls amused themselves discussing me openly and very frankly. One of them thought I would be better for a haircut, and this led to further and more ribald remarks, until a young Amazon with luminous, homely features and flaming red hair, took me under her protection and told them to lay off.

" He's mine, anyway," she said—" I saw him first. " You needn't be afraid of them," she added, " I won't let them touch you."

The others warning me not to trust her, said that her reputation was not spotless and that all she sought was my moral downfall, only those were not the words they used. I was very glad, indeed, to get out of the place when the young woman returned and told me I should go to the managing director's office in another quarter of the city.

I was looking for the office when I saw Peter himself in the street. I hailed him.   Up to that moment, I had not realised that after five months in prison, my one suit of clothes was anything but presentable.   Peter was, as usual, spick and span. He ran over to me, his eyes wide open with surprise and pleasure.

" Have you escaped ? " he asked.

" No, I'm out on parole."

His face fell.

" I'm disappointed," he said.   " I had it all arranged that if you had escaped, I was to put you on a canal barge for one of the Welsh ports where you could get a schooner sailing to Wexford."

I told him to keep the scheme under his hat, for we might find use for it later. It turned out otherwise, however, for on the following day, March 6th, 1919, Pierce McCann died in the prison hospital and, before my week's parole was up, all the other prisoners interned in England were released and I never returned. The poor prison Governor kept writing to me for months asking for the return half of my rail and boat ticket, which I had lost.

Chapter Twenty-four

With one dissentient the Senate of the U.S. passed a resolution requesting President Wilson to secure a hearing for the Irish representatives at the Peace Conference. Wilson sadly told the Irish-American delegation that the British vetoed the hearing of Ireland's claim and that he could do nothing about it.

As FAR back as 1918, the British authorities had issued a proclamation to the effect that Sinn Féin was a dangerous organisation and that meetings held under its auspices were illegal. The elections had shown that nearly seventy-five per cent. of the people supported this illegal and dangerous organisation. Acting in accordance with the election manifesto, the Sinn Féin deputies refused to attend the British parliament and those of them who were at liberty met in Dublin and set up Dail Eireann, the Government of the Irish Republic.

The British Government of the day, foolishly as it now appears, not merely refused to accept the decision of the Irish people in accordance with the principle of national self-determination, but actually decided to bludgeon the people into surrendering to Britain's will. The policy of raids, arrests and suppression of popular meetings, in the endeavour to smash Sinn Féin, was continued and intensified.

In spite of the proclamation outlawing the organisation, the Sinn Féin headquarters at Number Six Harcourt Street remained open. It was realised that the Dublin Castle authorities deliberately refrained from closing the premises in order to enable its spies to track down all those who frequented the place.

De Valera who, since his escape from Lincoln Jail, had been in hiding in England, decided to return openly to Dublin. As soon as this was announced, a great reception was planned for him. The Lord Mayor and Corporation arranged to meet him at Baggot Street Bridge and present him with the Keys of the City, preliminary to a triumphal procession.

Apart from his already wide popularity, his dramatic escape from an English jail had invested him with additional glamour, and Dublin, always renowned for its jubilant demonstrations, was in a mood to excel itself.

Not unexpectedly, however, Dublin Castle proclaimed the whole affair and it was announced that formidable British armed forces would man the bridges and adjoining streets. It was believed that Sinn Féin could not retreat from its decision and a clash seemed inevitable. On the eve of the reception, however, a special meeting of the Sinn Féin Executive was convened and Collins turned up with a proposal that the reception and demonstration be called off. There was an angry debate, in the course of which we had the odd spectacle of the so-called gunmen in favour of retreat, while many of the moderates apparently wanted to make a stand. To the surprise of everyone, Darrell Figgis faced Mick and accused him of trying to get the Sinn Féin Executive to father the decision of the Volunteers, which he termed cowardly. He wanted to go out and defy the British forces. He seemed to be greatly daring, but he knew quite well there was no risk involved since we could not go on without the Volunteers. The Executive could, of course, do nothing but fall into line, but some members made a great show of indignation.

After the meeting, Mick and Harry Boland came to my office and Mick indulged in sulphurous language about Figgis. Then he and Harry had a bout of their customary horseplay. Harry was standing with his back to the fire and Mick shouldered him aside. Harry retaliated and soon they were engaged in a vigorous rough and tumble, giving evidence of the great reserves of surplus energy both of them had. The incident itself was an indication of Harry's attachment to Mick, because he disliked having his clothes tousled while, at that time, Mick gave little attention to his clothes.

Dev arrived quietly and, as usual, he was rather cross at the fuss we made over him. Cathal Brugha and he and I journeyed to his home in Greystones in a motor car. As we were passing Harcourt Street station, Dev wanted to get out to travel by train. He complained about the extravagance of the car. But Brugha, in brusque good humour, told him to have sense.

Dev turned to me and asked me who had written the Election manifesto. I told him I had and explained that three people, Father O'Flanagan, Harry Boland and myself, had been asked by the Executive to submit separate drafts of a manifesto and that mine had been adopted.

" You made it strong," said Dev, " I wouldn't have gone so far."

" Why not ? Because of the voters ? "

" Yes. I was afraid it might frighten them."

" Well, it worked out all right."

" Fortunately."

Next day I encountered Collins in Harcourt Street.

" Look here," he said, " who authorised you to publish *De Valera's Case Against Conscription* ? "

" Nobody."

" Dev says he gave no authority for it."

" I said nobody did."

" You take a lot on yourself, don't you ? "

" Why not ? "

I was vexed about this, not so much on account of Dev's presumed resentment, but because he had voiced his resentment to Mick and not to me. I asked him about it a few days later.

" No," said Dev, " I didn't say I resented it. I was only afraid that Tim Healy and the other members of the Mansion House Conference might think badly of it."

" They didn't," I said. " They were rather glad of it."

" Well, that's all right."

I told him that Father Tim Corcoran, his collaborator, had been keen on having it published and that in the original version I had referred to Father Corcoran's help. The latter had asked me to leave this out in the published version, but he carefully placed the original in a safe.

Only then did it occur to me that Dev would resent the fact that I had lodged the small royalties received from the publication to Mrs. Dev's account and I hoped he would not find out about it.

Early in May, the American Delegation arrived in Dublin.

It consisted of three well-known American gentlemen :
M. J. Ryan of Philadelphia ; Governor Dunne of Illinois
and Frank P. Walsh of Kansas City. They had been
selected at a great Irish Race Convention in Philadelphia,
to go to Paris to try to secure a hearing for Ireland's case
at the Peace Conference. The calculation was that President
Wilson would not dare to flout Irish-American opinion and
would force Lloyd George to admit the Irish spokesmen.
When they got to Paris, however, Wilson stalled them off,
saying that he would require a couple of weeks to study the
matter and they decided to utilise this time by seeing Irish
conditions for themselves at first hand.

They had with them a secretary, a young man whose
name I have forgotten, and from him I gained my first
experience of the Americans' voracious appetite for docu-
mentation and statistics. I was giving him an outline of
the methods of the British Government as shown by the
number of raids on houses, arrests and shootings there had
been during the previous year. These had all been carefully
listed and indexed by Frank Gallagher. This was not
enough for our American friend. He wanted as much
further details of each individual case as we could give him
and he wanted ten copies of each document. Moreover, he
wanted ten copies of every reference to the Delegation's
visit that appeared in all the Irish papers.

I went downstairs to Griffith's office and told him of the
situation.

" I don't have the staff to do all this work," I said.

" I know," he answered, " but because they want it,
we must get it done. Get a few people in for a week or
two. We'll get the Executive to foot the bill."

I did succeed to the extent that I gave that young man
enough material to keep him busy for the rest of his life,
but he seemed quite pleased.

The first Sunday the Delegation was in Dublin, we all
went to Mass in the Pro-Cathedral. As we were coming
out, Dev pulled me aside and asked me to ride in his car.
He said that two of the delegates, Governor Dunne and
Mr. Ryan were to be with him. By way of explaining why
he wanted me, Dev said :

" You know I'm no good to talk."

So I did the talking, pointing out the Post Office, Trinity College, the old Parliament House, and so on. When we came out of Grafton Street, I gave them the history of Stephen's Green. As we were passing the College of Surgeons, one of them asked me to identify the statue of the man seated in the Green facing the College. I said, without thinking :

" That's old Stephen Green himself ! "

Mr. Ryan and Dev both laughed heartily but Governor Dunne showed his displeasure. I had not realised that, having been educated in Dublin, he probably knew who the figure immortalised in marble really was. Afterwards Dev asked me whom the statue did represent. I said quite truly I did not know.

After one very tumultuous and enthusiastic meeting in the Mansion House which had been addressed by the American delegates, most of the people had dispersed when I saw a lady literally chasing Griffith around a settee. He was trying to avoid her, but as unostentatiously as possible. The lady was a Miss D——, usually called Miss French D—— because she always spoke English with a strong French accent. Whenever any prisoners were released she was always in evidence welcoming them and bestowing hearty kisses on one and all. She caught up with Griffith finally and, throwing her arms around him, she gave him a hearty smack.

A little while later, I joined Griffith in the Bailey. He was chuckling so much he could hardly speak.

" So you like the lady," I said.

" It wasn't that," he replied, " but my wife was down at the end of the hall enjoying the whole performance. Near her were two girls and one of them said : ' Look at what that one done. She kissed Arthur Griffith.' Whereupon the other replied : ' Good Lord, I'd as lief kiss a granite wall.' "

.   .   .   .   .

Dev, Griffith and I were walking through the streets after a Mansion House Conference one day, when Dev said :

"Of course, if we only had something to work on, it would be much easier."

I waited and as Griffith said nothing, I asked :

"What do you mean by something to work on?"

"Well, for instance, if the Irish Party had got Home Rule."

A.G. was frowning heavily.

"Don't you think," he said, "it would have had strings to it, strings they could not break."

"Yes," said Dev, "but that would not tie us. We could break them."

Griffith was uncomfortable and Dev sensed it. He said :

"Don't you agree that if we had the resources Home Rule would have given us, we would have ground to consolidate and work on?"

"But," said A.G. "can't you see that the English are too clever for that. If the Party had got Home Rule there would have been nothing to work on. They would have withheld control over Customs and Excise, police and army."

"Well, then, it wouldn't have been Home Rule."

"Of course not," said Griffith, coldly.

"Look," I said to Dev, "you're looking pretty tired. You'll have to take a holiday."

"Yes," said Griffith, "Bob and I were talking about that."

"Not at all," said Dev, becoming cross in his turn.

"You'll have to take it," I said. "James O'Mara has just bought a grand place on the edge of the sea in Connemara and he's going to bring you down there for a few weeks, and he can bring your family, too, if you like."

Dev blazed out : "That's enough," he said, "I'm not going to have my personal life interfered with in this way."

"Well, that's all right," said A.G.

"But he's foolish" he said to me afterwards. "He's overdoing it. He never relaxes at all."

Dev's remarks about Home Rule recalled an earlier observation he had made to me which I thought it wise not to repeat to A.G. He had said :

"There was one drawback in taking our representation

away from Westminster. Westminster gave us a platform
we do not now have from which we could present our case
the world."

In other words, Dev was not a Sinn Féiner at all in
Griffith's sense of the term.

But he was to gain a wider platform than Westminster.
Within a few weeks he had had himself smuggled across the
Atlantic to the United States of America where he used to
advantage a forum far more telling than that of Westminster
to present the Irish case to the world.

Chapter Twenty-five

After their apparent defeat in 1916, the Republicans everywhere had been subjected to arrest, raids and baton charges. They did not begin to strike back until the Spring of 1919, when they made sporadic attacks on Constabulary barracks, as a result of which several Irish counties and, later, nearly all Ireland was placed under British military control.

"Good morning, Mr. Brennan. May I interrupt you?"

I looked up from my desk to see a spare, worn, prematurely aged man with clear, kindly eyes, youthful and alert. He was rather nervous and apologetic.

"I have a note from Robert Barton for you," he said. "He told me to see you. My name is Childers, Erskine Childers."

I, of course, knew of him. I had read his *Riddle of the Sands* and I was aware that he had been connected with the Howth gun-running and with the abortive Dominion Home Rule Conference.

"I am delighted to meet you," I said, giving him a chair. "I hope you are going to write something."

I showed him an article in that day's *Daily Mail*, which called for refutation, and told him I had the material to deal with it. He said he had had a talk before he left England with the editor of the *Daily News* and he thought he could get some articles printed in that paper.

"I want to tell you straightway," he said, "that after a great deal of thought, I have decided that Sinn Féin is the right policy for Ireland. I have come over to give a hand any way I can help. You may not believe it, but the English people do not realise what is going on here. For instance, when I came ashore this morning, I noticed a curious contraption on that overhead railway bridge facing Liberty Hall. There was a soldier in khaki there. I should not be surprised if there was a machine-gun there."

I told him there was a nest of six machine-guns there directly across from Liberty Hall. He said that that was a direct attempt by the military to overawe labour and asked why we had not told the world about it. I told him of the difficulty of getting anything published. The Irish papers were at the mercy of the censor and the English papers, in the main, published only what suited the British authorities, I promised to get him a photo of the machine-gun nest. When we had talked for some time, I asked him if he had met Griffith.

" I haven't," he said. " I would very much like to."

I am aware that most of the writers on the period have said that Griffith resented the appearance of Childers on the Irish scene, that he hated him from the start because he was an Englishman. That is not true. I know, because I introduced the two men.

I went downstairs and told Griffith that Childers had arrived and repeated what he had said ; that he had become convinced that Sinn Féin was the right policy for Ireland, and that he had come over to live in Dublin and do whatever he could. Griffith asked if he meant that he was throwing in his lot with us and I said that that was what I had gathered. Griffith was obviously pleased.

" He's a good man to have," he said. " He has the ear of a big section of the English people."

I brought Childers down and introduced him. I remained only a few minutes as I had a pile of work on my desk. The greeting between them was cordial. Griffith was never demonstrative and neither was Childers, but it was quite plain that Griffith realised the value of Childers and the latter was quite pleased at his reception. It was over an hour later when Childers came back to me.

" How did you get on ? " I asked.

" Fine," he said.

" He doesn't talk much," I said.

" No, but I understand him perfectly. He told me you had some figures regarding raids on private houses."

I gave him the figures and found, at this early stage, that he was very meticulous about any material that he used. Every statement had to be checked and double-checked, verified and re-verified. Later, this trait of his was, at times, exasperating ; but he was always so patient

246246246 ALLEGIANCE

and courteous that one could not get angry with him. I
saw a good deal of him from that time on and so did A.G.,
and there was never the slightest trouble between the two
until nearly two years later. Childers took a house in
Wellington Road and there, and subsequently at his residence in Bushy Park Road, he and Mrs. Childers entertained
French, English and American visitors who were likely to
influence opinion in their respective countries. Every other
day some of us were being brought along to explain the
situation to some foreign public representative or inter-
nationally-known publicist. Later on, when I had to go
on the run, Childers told me that if I was stuck for a stop
at any time, to go to his house. When the place I was
staying in on the north side got too hot, I stayed in Childers'
house at Bushy Park off and on for a few weeks. He was
working at the time on some articles for the *Daily News*
and each evening we checked and re-checked facts and
figures for these articles. Occasionally, he relaxed and
then he became a most delightful companion. One night we
were discussing mystery stories and I mentioned *The Wrong
Box*. He jumped up, with eyes dancing with delight,
crying :
  "Are you a Wrong Boxer ? "
  I looked my astonishment and he explained that several
years earlier *The Wrong Box* was so popular in London that
when one person met another he asked enthusiastically :
"Are you a Wrong Boxer ? " He took down the book and
read several chapters, to our great amusement.
  Another night we got talking of Lady Gregory and he
read several of the Kiltartan stories. When he came to the
place which recounts the Connacht peasants' descriptions
of Queen Elizabeth's supposed love affairs, he was very
embarrassed for the two boys, Erskine and Bobby had not
yet retired. It did not seem to occur to him to alter the
text and there followed an awkward few minutes.
  I had been sleeping badly and he advised a hot bath
before retiring. I was getting out of the bath when there
was a knock and Childers said through the bathroom door :
  " There's a lorry pulled up outside. Do you think they're
after you ? "

A typical street raid by Auxiliaries and " Black and Tans " in Dublin.   The scene is Middle Abbey Street.

During the Truce, 1921. Arthur Griffith and Eamon de Valera leaving a Mansion House meeting.

" More likely they're after you," I replied.

" I don't think so. Would you think of slipping on some clothes and getting out through the back ? "

" If they're after me," I said, " I'm sure they'll have the back covered."

At that moment there came a thundering knock at the door.

" There's no time now," I said. " You'd better open the door or they'll break it in."

He was quite calm as he went downstairs.

" It's all right, Mary," he said to the maid who had come up into the hall, " I'll open the door."

The knocker moved into action again. Childers opened the door.

" What's the meaning of this ? " he asked.

" Who are you ? " enquired a loud, English voice.

" I'm Major Erskine Childers, who are you ? "

" Can you tell us where we will find No. 8 Victoria Road ? "

" I'm sorry, I can't."

" You mean you won't."

" I said I'm sorry I can't. Would you mind giving me your name and regiment. I intend making a complaint to the Commander-in-Chief about your conduct."

The officer mumbled something and backed out and shortly afterwards the lorry drove away. We had great fun later as Childers and I staged the imaginary interview with the Commander-in-Chief.

He was a tireless worker. It was often after midnight when he came down from his study looking white and drawn from long concentration, and bearing the far-away look of the intense mental worker. When he came to his breakfast at eight o'clock, he had already put in an hour at his desk. His extraordinary patience was shown by his gentleness with Mrs. Osgood, his mother-in-law. She was devoted to him but, in her American downright way, she could not see that by her denunciation of the I.R.A. she was wounding him to the quick. A woman of extraordinarily strong character, she was an untiring advocate of peace and love as a solution for the ills of the world.

I knew she was compiling an anthology, but I did not know till many years later that it was to be that really beautiful book *The City Without Walls*.

Mrs. Osgood talked incessantly of William Pitt and his policy of peace when faced by the hostility of savage Red Indians. Each morning she brandished the daily paper, which nearly every day now had news of bloody encounters between the I.R.A. and the Royal Irish Constabulary.

" It's murder," she would cry, " foul, horrible murder. These policemen are being murdered."

" But, mother," Childers would protest, " these men are members of an army of occupation. They are armed. They occupy fortified barracks. They are paid agents of England, holding Ireland in subjection."

" It's murder, I tell you," she would reply and launch into a diatribe on the Commandments, the sacredness of human life and the power of love to conquer all.

I kept out of these arguments as much as I could, but Childers patiently replied to them, going over the ground again and again, courteously and politely, never so much as showing the slightest temper. One day, following such a debate, I remonstrated with him.

" Why not let her have her say ? " I asked. " You can't alter her views."

" What ? Oh, yes," he said. " She's a dear old soul and there's a lot to be said for her point of view."

" But it's a waste of time to be arguing with her."

" Yes, yes, quite so."

But the next morning the argument would start all over again.

One night I arrived at Childers' house at a quarter to ten, fifteen minutes before curfew. The maid who opened the door seemed very frightened. I learned that they had had a very thorough and disagreeable raid and they were expecting the raiders to return. We all agreed I should not stay and they were anxious to assure themselves I had some place to go to and that I could reach it in time. I reassured them on the point and I cycled to a house in the Rathgar area. I had been told I would be welcome there any time. It was seven minutes to ten when I knocked at the door.

The face of mine host when the door was opened showed me I was not welcome.

" I'm stuck," I said, " I should be out on the north side but the bridges are held and the people I went to near here have had a raid."

He closed the door behind me, but very doubtfully. Suddenly a thought struck me.

" You've someone staying already ? " I said.

" No, but——"

" Oh, that's all right," I said, turning towards the door.

" I'm terribly sorry," he said, " but you know I must think of my job."

" That's all right," I said.

" Have you a place to go to ? " he asked.

" Sure," I said, " dozens of places. I'll be all right. Good night ! "

It was the first and only time I had such an experience in all the years from 1917 to 1924. It was almost universally true that no door was closed to us in those days. The man was timid, anyway, and he couldn't be expected to jeopardise his job—he had a big Government job—but theoretically he was a rebel. I got my bicycle and wheeled it out on the roadway. My watch showed me it was three minutes to ten. For fear he might be looking, I got on my machine and cycled to the corner and turned into Kenilworth Square. There I dismounted. I was completely stuck. The places I could think of to go to were too far away. The curfew hour would strike any minute and I would be almost certain to run into a patrol. There was no one about, but there came the sound of a measured tread from the direction of Harold's Cross. I got on my machine and cycled to Terenure Road, where I dismounted again. The city was dead. Not a soul was stirring and I heard the Rathmines chimes telling the hour. Presently, from Rathgar Road, there came the sound of running feet. They belonged to a young man and woman. She was panting and murmuring in terror—

" We'll be caught ! We'll be caught ! "

They raced past me, almost without a glance, and the young man tried to quieten her. Presently I saw the blaze of headlights on Highfield Road and heard the roar of a motor. I heard the girl crying.

"Jesus have mercy on us. Here they are!"

For the first time I remembered I had papers on me which could get me hanged and which I could not destroy. The lorry was roaring up Highfield Road towards us. I pushed open the little gate of a lawn in front of a house. The gate was stiff and the hinges creaked and the headlights were on me. I put my bicycle on the grass and lay down behind the little hedge fronting the road. The lorry roared past and screeched to a halt a hundred yards ahead.

"Halt there! Halt!"

I heard the girl's hysterical voice saying something and I peeped out and saw the pair halted in the glare of the headlights, with the soldiers milling about. There was a medley of hoarse voices and a ribald laugh as the two were hoisted into the lorry, which presently roared off into the direction of Terenure. I lay on the grass for some time wondering whether I should spend the night in the open and, suddenly, I remembered I had a friend in the immediate neighbourhood. He was a Latvian, named Martinson, who worked in Kapp and Petersen's factory and he lived, he had told me, over a butcher's shop at the cross of Rathgar. Several months before, when I had met him in Fred Cogley's flat, he made me promise that if ever I was stuck, I would go to him. I was now not more than a couple of hundred yards from his place. I got to my feet and quickly dropped to my knees again. A car was passing, bearing no lights, the engine so silent one could hardly hear it purr. It was one of the prowlers. Slowly it crawled down the road and turned into Orwell Road. For all I knew, it had stopped round the corner which would be just opposite the butcher's shop. I waited for five minutes and then, unable to bear the suspense any longer, I got up and opened the creaking gate. I mounted the bicycle and free-wheeled down the footpath. I could see no sign of the prowler. There was the butcher's shop all right and the rooms overhead were lighted, but there was no means of entry. The shop was closed with a roller door in which there was no wicket, no bell and no knocker. I looked everywhere and was about to give up in despair when I heard another lorry coming from the city. Intending to repeat my previous manoeuvre, I opened the gate of the garden next to the butcher's shop. There was a concrete path leading to a hall door. As there was no hedge, and no shelter, I walked up this path and suddenly came to a doorway in the side wall of the butcher's shop. I pressed the bell and flattened myself in the doorway as the lorry roared past on the road outside. After a minute or so someone came to the door.

" Who's there ? " came a whisper.

"A friend," I whispered back. " Please open the door."

The door was opened and there was my bearded Latvian friend.

" You are Mr. Martinson," I said. " My name is——"

" Your name is Brennan," he said in guttural accents. " Come in."

He grabbed me by the shoulder and pulled me in. Shoving my bicycle to one side, he closed the door. This done, he appeared to think that all need for caution was at an end, for he began to yell in a voice which I feared would wake the neighbourhood :

" Maria ! Maria ! Yohan ! Yohan ! Look ! Come, see who we have here ! "

A tall girl with a ruddy complexion and a mass of beautiful, untidy brown hair, appeared at the top of the stairs, looking very much frightened. Behind her, I saw a tough-looking, small, swarthy man. Martinson introduced me boisterously to Mr. and Mrs. Yohan Climanis. In his enthusiasm, he made me Vice-President of the Irish Republic. The girl smiled shyly as she took my hand, while Yohan's broad face broke into a grin which disclosed a beautiful set of strong teeth. I was puzzled by the girl's appearance for she seemed just a typical Irish country girl, and so indeed she was. Climanis, who was also a Latvian, had arrived in Ireland only a year before. He went to work in a fish-and-chip shop which wasn't doing well. The proprietor decided to move to another place and he sold Yohan the stock and good-will of the shop for a pound. Yohan, apparently, was a better business man than his

predecessor. He throve so well in the fish-and-chip shop
that in a few months he was able to buy a motor-bicycle and,
on this, he went careering around the country on Sundays.
On one of these excursions he got caught in a storm in a
remote part of Tipperary and he got shelter for the night
in a farmhouse. The moment he caught sight of the
farmer's daughter, he fell in love and, thereafter, all his
Sundays were spent in Tipperary till he brought Maria
back to Dublin as his bride. All this, Yohan and Martinson
explained to me loudly and delightedly while the blushing
Maria prepared a meal. The couple were as happy as
children and Martinson, who was a widower, rejoiced
volubly in their happiness. Maria brought to the table a
huge dish of mixed grill for the four of us. My host was
very disappointed at my poor appetite.

" You Irish will never beat the English," he cried,
" until you can eat as much as they do. Eh, Yohan, you
know, you tell him."

Yohan, whose English was very limited, launched into
voluble Latvian, grinning broadly all the while.

" He says," shouted Martinson, " you will beat the
English because your drinks are better. Bravo, Yohan !
You shall see ! " and he produced a bottle of whiskey with
the air of a conjurer pulling a rabbit out of a hat.

They told me of their fight against the Czars and Yohan,
in the most terrible jargon, dramatised scenes of terror and
bloodshed he had witnessed. I was dead tired but I tried
to keep my eyes open as long as I could. At three o'clock,
Martinson roused me and apologised in stentorian tones
for his thoughtlessness in keeping me up so long. Even
after I got to bed, I could hear them still reminiscing. Yet,
when I got up at seven o'clock, they were already up and
about and I had to eat a huge breakfast before they would
let me go. I was to come back again any night, or every
night, but I have never seen them since.

It was during the period of the truce that the bad feeling
between A.G. and Childers developed. I had never seen
any sign of it before that time and, when I did see it, it
was entirely one-sided. Childers was incapable of entertaining a bitter feeling towards anyone working in Ireland's

cause, however, he might differ with him. At first, it was
merely irritation on Griffith's part, not because he considered Childers an Englishman, or that he doubted his
loyalty, but because of Childers's meticulousness. An instance occurred in connection with the address to the elected
representatives of the various countries throughout the
world. I had, at de Valera's direction, drawn up a series
of statements and statistical tables annotating this document
which was signed by the President and translated into
practically every European language, as well as Japanese,
Chinese, etc. It had already been transmitted to our
foreign offices and had actually been printed in some
countries before Childers called my attention to what he
considered to be a serious flaw in it. This was the use of
the word " police " in a few instances, instead of "constabularymen." Childers rightly pointed out that this
would be misunderstood in countries where police meant
not an armed political semi-military force but a body of
inoffensive and helpful traffic officers or law enforcement
agents ; he went on to protest that this mistake had ruined
the whole case stated in the address and demanded that
cables should be sent out holding up its distribution. This
was going too far, and I said so. Griffith came on the scene
and, having listened to both of us, he laughingly said it
was making a mountain out of a molehill. There was more
annoyance than mirth in his laughter. When Childers
turned away, Griffith said to me :
" Childers would jeopardise the freedom of Ireland
defending the purity of the English language," which, of
course, was not at all the point at issue.
For A.G.'s subsequent bitter attacks on Childers, there
is, of course, no excuse, even though we know the explanation. A.G. had dedicated his life to Ireland. In the face
of heart-breaking difficulties and disappointments, he had
built up a great national organisation. He had sacrificed
his worldly prospects, the ease, and even the wealth, that
might have been his. His was no sudden conversion to the
cause. It had been his through many lean years and he
never thought of turning back when the road grew so hard
that it was almost torture to pursue it. He was the father

of an idea which had materialised into a national creed. And now, with victory almost within his grasp, he was going to be robbed of it by a man who had given the greater part of his life to the service of England, whose manners and accent were English, who had even fought against the liberty of a small nation in the Boer War, and who had been so loyal to England that his services in the Great War had been rendered in England's Intelligence Service. To those of us who knew the two men, the clash was a frightful tragedy. Griffith, unselfish as he was, was not more so than Childers, nor was he more wholehearted or unsparing in the service he gave. Neither of them outranked the other in lack of personal ambition, in sincerity, devotion, or single-mindedness. We could all of us easily understand Griffith's acceptance of the treaty. Not all of us who differed with Griffith, could understand Childers's utter rejection of it. His attitude puzzled many merely because it was so simple. He had sworn an oath of allegiance to the Republic and he meant just that, and nothing more. I saw a good deal of him in the days succeeding Griffith's bitter attack on him and he never had a hard word to say of his opponent and detractor. He was puzzled by the bitterness of the attack, but he did not even complain. His stoicism was almost unearthly. Once during the Civil War, I spoke to him about Griffith. We were travelling through a pleasant countryside in Cork in a military lorry. I said it was surely the irony of fate that A.G., who had always set his face against physical force, should now be waging war against his own countrymen.

" You people," remarked Childers, " have always under-estimated the British."

" What has that got to do with it ? "

" Griffith was deceived by Lloyd George."

" I can see that," I said, " but I still can't understand what bearing that has on the Civil War."

Childers was very patient.

" The British," he said, " can sign and find a way to repudiate their signatures. They've done it over and over again. You need not go back to the Treaty of Limerick. You have Malta and Egypt, for instance. They can always find high moral reasons for such repudiation. They are opportunists. Griffith, however, having given his word, would stick to it whatever the consequences, even though it meant the disaster of a civil war. They knew that."

" You've no hard feelings against him ? "

" No, not at all," he said. " He was unfair, but I can see his point of view."

" I wish I could achieve your detachment," I said.

" Do you really ? " he asked, wrinkling his forehead and looking at me quizzically. " I don't believe you do."

" No, I'm afraid I don't," I conceded, " but I do wish I had your courage."

" Oh, that's different," he said, " anyone can gain that. You just make up your mind to do it. It's all a matter of training."

" You don't mean to say that a craven can become a brave man ? "

" I do. When I was a young fellow, I was terribly afraid until I realised that, apart from its demoralising effects, fear was unworthy of a man. I decided to conquer fear. That is, of course, what differentiates man from all other living creatures—the will to conquer nature. You have me preaching."

" No, go ahead."

" So I said : the thing I am afraid to do, that I will do ; and the thing I am afraid not to do, that I will not do ! Look here, Brennan, let us get back to Carlyle."

We had been discussing Carlyle's *French Revolution*.

" No," I said, " let us get on with this fear business."

"All right," he said, " get hold of someone who is afraid of the dark, or afraid of high places. Get him to go and meet the thing he fears and he will conquer it."

" Or be annihilated ? "

" Or be annihilated."

While he could find excuses for Griffith, he had none for Collins and this was all the more remarkable as he had been very fond of Mick.

" One can understand Griffith," he said, " but who can excuse Mick. Griffith, after all, had said he could consider a working arrangement based on a dual monarchy, but

Mick would have nothing to do with anything short of the Republic."

One night in Fermoy Military Barracks, I woke up and heard someone coughing violently outside in the corridor. I looked across the room, crowded with sleeping figures, and saw that Childers's bed was empty. I got up and went outside. Childers was standing there in his pyjamas. I looked at his bare feet on the cold flagstones.

" My God," I said, " you'll catch your death of cold."

Unable to speak, he motioned to me to close the door. I got him an overcoat and his shoes. When the spasm had subsided somewhat, he said :

" I was afraid I might wake the boys."

I persuaded him to go back to bed, but twice during the night I heard him return to the cold hall when the fit of coughing seized him. In the morning, he looked so worn and pale that I appealed to him to see a doctor and take a rest. He merely smiled somewhat impatiently and shook his head.

" I'll be all right," he said.

I even got Liam Lynch, who was then in command, to appeal to him, but it was all in vain. He had discovered that we could take over the wireless and cable stations at Waterville and Valentia and he was eager to get permission for the two of us to go to Kerry. Later in the day, however, it was decided that I should go to Cork City to edit the *Cork Examiner*, which our fellows had taken over, and from there I was to write despatches on the general situation which Childers was to send by cable to America.

I never saw Childers again.

Chapter Twenty-six

During the year 1919 *Dail Eireann, the Government of the Irish Republic, despite bitter and bloody opposition, continued to function and to extend its sway. The clashes between the British forces and the I.R.A. gradually developed into guerrilla warfare. In September the British prohibited Dail Eireann as a dangerous association.*

A COLONIAL soldier who wished to be assigned a task by Sinn Féin was one of the visitors to Number Six in April 1919, and he was the forerunner of several others. Micheal Nunan told me that the man was downstairs and that he wanted to see me.

" What about ? "

" He wants to be given a task."

" What sort of a task ? "

" He'd like to go to London and shoot Lloyd George."

Micheal was grinning broadly.

" You've heard of Lloyd George," he said, " the joker who's trying to make England a land fit for heroes to live in."

I told him that Andrew Dillon had said that the same Lloyd George was trying to make Ireland a land fit for nobody but heroes to live in.

" Well, this is your man," said Micheal, " not only will he kill Lloyd George, but also the whole British Cabinet if we like."

We were laughing about this when Madame Markievicz came in breathless, as usual. She said she had given shelter to two other colonial soldiers and put them into civilian clothes. They also wanted to be assigned a task, but their predilection was for British Generals rather than Cabinet Ministers. They would undertake to dispose of any number of them.

No one took this matter seriously except Madame, who continued to agitate the question until Cathal Brugha said we were to have nothing whatever to do with these men ; so the colonials left.

Visitors who were not so easy to get rid of were certain members of Casement's Brigade. Sir Roger had tried to recruit a Brigade from amongst the thousands of Irishmen in the British Army who had been captured by the Germans. The title Irish Brigade remained, although Sir Roger had managed to recruit less than enough to make up a full company. We had all heard a great deal about the Brigade and had seen in the Irish-American papers photographs of them arrayed in really beautiful uniforms the Germans had designed for them. When I was in Germany later, I heard what a tough lot they had been.

Frau Grabisch was an Irish-American lady married to a German living in Berlin. When the Brigade was being formed she undertook to look after the personal comforts of the men. She told me that after the revolution in Berlin she one day received from the German Foreign Office a frantic message summoning her there forthwith. She hurried to the Foreign Office and found, in an outer room, practically every member of the staff, including the Foreign Minister. In the Minister's office were two members of the Irish Brigade. They had ordered everyone out of the place at pistol point and they were eating sandwiches and drinking beer, which they had compelled members of the staff to supply them with. They said they were going to hold the place till their rights—whatever they were—were conceded. They refused to listen to any arguments and even Frau Grabisch's blandishments were in vain.

"Ah," said the Minister sadly to Frau Grabisch, " those Irish ! Think of the poor English with four millions of them on their hands ! "

The first member of the Brigade I met was a handsome and dashing young non-commissioned officer in khaki, named Quin. He came into my office and identified himself. I had known some of his people. He wanted to get out of his uniform as quickly as possible and join the Volunteers. I put him in touch with Sean O'Muirthuile, who took him off and gave him a civilian outfit. Thereafter he was constantly to be seen wtih Sean and his companions. One of them told me they were a bit uneasy about him, not because they distrusted him, but because he took no precautions whatever. He had a way with the girls. A few of the lads would go off to Bray or Dunlaoghaire on a Sunday afternoon and before they were half an hour on the Esplanade, Quin had got off with the best-looking girl in the neighbourhood. A fellow like that might inadvertently give something away.

I saw Quin from time to time. He was always immaculately dressed and one would have said that with his good looks, his self-assurance and general *bonhomie*, he would have got anywhere. He liked to give me the impression that he was in on all of Mick Collins's secrets.

Suddenly there was a change. Quin came in after several weeks' absence and asked me where he could find Mick. I said I didn't know but that O'Muirthuile should be able to tell him.

"That's the trouble," he said. "I can't find O'Muirthuile either. I can't find any of them. Do you know if there is anything up?"

"I don't," I said, "I expect they are all lying low for some reason or other." Which, of course, I did not believe.

I reported this to Mick in the afternoon and asked him what was wrong with Quin. He looked up from his desk and said simply:

"Go easy with him."

A few days later Griffith came up and told me that Quin had stopped him in Stephen's Green and asked him where he could find Mick. A.G. was plainly worried and went off to see Mick about the matter.

That night Henry O'Connor, a leader-writer on the *Freeman*, brought me galley proofs of a long letter which had been sent to the *Freeman* for publication. It was written by Quin and it summarised his life story and stated that when he had arrived in Dublin he had been approached by the Castle Authorities and introduced to Superintendent Brien of the G Division, who asked him to act as a spy on the I.R.A. At this time, the Volunteers were being generally referred to as the I.R.A., or Army of the Republic, though they were not officially declared to be such until de Valera returned from America a year and a half later.

In his letter, Quin said he had indignantly spurned

Superintendent Brien's offer and he denounced the Castle Authorities. He also said he had been specifically asked to lead Collins and O'Muirthuile into a police trap in College Green.

Henry O'Connor had stopped publication of the letter. He gave me the proofs and I sent them on to Mick. About a week later Quin's body was found in a field outside Cork City. He had been shot to death and a spy label was attached to his clothing. Mick told me that the wretched man had actually enrolled in the Castle Service and had undertaken to deliver Mick and some others into the hands of the G-men. There was a trap laid for him. He was led to believe that Mick had gone to Cork and he betook himself there to find him. The first Volunteer Quin approached said he would conduct him to Mick and, actually, he conducted him to a secret court-martial and his death. Mick told me that pay dockets, countersigned by Superintendent Brien, were found in his pockets.

When Bob Barton escaped from Mountjoy Jail, in March 1919, all Ireland smiled because he had left behind him a polite note for the Governor, thanking him for his courtesy and hospitality and adding that since he did not like the place, he was leaving. As a street ballad which was being sung shortly afterwards had it :—

> The next was Bob Barton
> When he was departin'
> He wrote out a note his politeness to show.

All Ireland roared laughing a few days later when, in broad daylight, no fewer than twenty prisoners escaped over the twelve-foot-high wall of the same jail.

It had been borne in on me that something big was afoot that morning. Sean Nunan had asked if he might get off for a couple of hours and, a little later, his brother Micheal did likewise. Then Frank Kelly went off. I went downstairs to find the offices almost deserted. Fitz, as everyone called Miss Anna Fitzsimons, the chief stenographer, was walking about restlessly.

" It must be something very big," she said, " when they are all called out like that."

She said she was going out to see what was up and went off. A few hours later, I met Fitz in Grafton Street and she was chuckling with delight.

" Twenty prisoners got over the wall out of Mountjoy ! Can you beat that ? "

The news had spread quickly. Everyone we met was smiling joyously and perfect strangers were shaking hands with one another. It reminded me of Seumas O'Sullivan's poem :

> And all the world went gay, went gay
> For one half-hour in the street to-day.

I wish Fitz would write her reminiscences. Amongst her other activities, she had been secretary to George Moore and she worked in Maunsell and Roberts when that firm was publishing the work of most of the Irish writers of the period. She was at Sinn Féin Headquarters in the most lively period of the movement and, later, she was in the Publicity Department till long after the Civil War had ended. She is one of the wittiest conversationalists I have known.

During the Civil War she used to send me from time to time, racy accounts of the difficulties she and her husband, Frank Kelly, were encountering from day to day. The two were, at that time, printing the weekly Republican News on a platen press, working for the most part in stables, or garages. Once the house where they were working was entered by a bailiff who had come to take away all the furniture. Fitz's hilarious account of their endeavours to proceed with the printing of the outlawed sheet under the nose of the bailiff, while the landlady attempted to raise the necessary cash to pay the bailiff's demands, was something I should have been able to preserve.

Two or three Republican soldiers arrived at her hide-out one night late and asked her to keep " this " for them till morning. " This " was apparently a tin of petrol which they shoved in under her bed. She slept soundly enough and was glad that she did not learn till morning that " this " was a land mine.

On one occasion when the place she and Frank were staying at was raided in the middle of the night, they both escaped by the back. Fitz crossed a field and coming on a mansion, she climbed in through a window, only to discover it was a maternity hospital. To the astonished matron she said : " It's not twins. It's politics."

Superintendent Smith of the G Division, who had been particularly active against Sinn Féin, was waylaid and shot on his way home and thereafter the G-men who had been rather conspicuously hovering around Harcourt Street, were not so much in evidence. When a couple more of them had been shot down in the streets, John Clarke, the butter merchant, came in and told me that four of the G-men had called to his house the previous night and said they wanted to get out of the country because they were fed up with the work. They wanted a safe conduct from the I.R.A. They were to meet John again that night. I reported this to Mick and he decided to go to John Clarke's and see the men himself. I warned him it might be a trap, because one of the men was the sinister Wharton, whom I have mentioned previously.

" I know about Wharton," said Mick, grimly, " and I'll see that if it's a trap, it won't work."

He arranged to see the men individually and three of them he induced to remain on in the force and to work for him. He told Wharton he could do nothing for him. One of these three men, whose name I think was Brennan, was later discovered bringing out documents for Mick and the Black and Tans gave him a cruel death.

The increasing tempo of the executions, alarms and raids convinced us that Number Six was no longer a place where it was safe to work, but before we left it for good and went underground—which was towards the end of the year 1919—we had one raid that was memorable. A big force of constabulary men, headed by the G-men, came suddenly one morning and took away all our files, including the irreplaceable indexed press clippings which Frank Gallagher and I had so carefully compiled. They arrested Paidin O'Keeffe, the General Secretary, and Earnan de Blaghd.

Collins had a close shave on this occasion. He was working in an office he had set up in connection with the

Dail Loan, just across the corridor from my office. When Joe Clarke ran up to say there was a raid on, we both ran into Mick's office to warn him.

" God blast it ! " he said and ran to a window, which he opened as if he were thinking of jumping the thirty or forty feet to the back yard. Fintan Murphy suggested that the roof over Joe Clarke's rooms at the top of the house would be safer. Mick dashed up the stairs just before the first of the G-men appeared on the landing.

The raiders took a long time on this occasion. It was a couple of hours later when I was standing on the landing outside my office that I saw Mick coming down the stairs. I tried to signal to him that there was a G-man on the landing below me, but he did not catch my signal.

" That was a good one," shouted Mick.

The G-man, hearing the voice, looked up at me and I laughed, hoping he would think it was my voice he had heard.

" What do you mean ? " asked the G-man. " What was a good one ? "

" Why," I said, "you damn' near cleaned the whole place out ! "

" You're lucky," he said, " we are leaving you behind."

" Thanks," I said.

Mick was still poised on the stairs. He had somehow got the impression that the raiders had gone and he was puzzled. The G-man began to walk up the stairs. I turned as leisurely as I dared and made a grimace at Mick. He took the hint and vanished. The G-man followed me into my room, looked casually around and strolled out again. When the coast was finally clear, Mick came down off the roof.

Chapter Twenty-seven

The people transferred their allegiance to the institutions set up by Dail Eireann, which continued to function underground. The British outlawed Sinn Féin, the Volunteers, the Gaelic League and Cumann na mBan (the Women's auxiliary of the Volunteers).

AFTER a few more such raids we quitted Number Six. Mrs. Larry Nugent generously gave us the use of a whole floor of her big house in Upper Mount Street and here we carried on the work of the Publicity Department for many months, unmolested, though the Castle authorities who had become aware of the importance of the *Irish Bulletin* were searching all over the town for the office whence it originated.

I had issued the first number of the *Bulletin* on the 11th of November 1919 and thereafter it never missed a single day's issue till the time the Treaty was ratified over two years later. I wrote the first volume of the *Bulletin*; the other three were written by Frank Gallagher, but now and again Erskine Childers substituted for him. The *Bulletin* was a mimeographed issue of two or three sheets giving our version of the conflict. It was delivered by hand to all the Dublin newspapers and all the foreign correspondents in Dublin and mailed to hundreds of addresses abroad. This publication was doing such damage to England's presentation of the Irish case that, in time, its attempted suppression became one of the major objectives of the British Military Government.

The work of collecting material for the *Bulletin*, its production and, over and above all, its distribution involved, of course, many contacts, and yet the Castle authorities never succeeded in interrupting its issue for a single day. Failing in their attempts to stop the *Bulletin*, the Castle issued a fake " Irish Bulletin " in which they reproduced our format down to the last detail, but Frank Gallagher in the *Bulletin* very neatly turned the tables by exposing the fraud and telling readers how to distinguish between the real *Bulletin* and the false.

During our stay in Mount Street, Harry Boland turned up. He had been in America helping Dev to float the Irish Loan. He breezed into Mount Street and gave us all a lively account of how he had been twice smuggled across the Atlantic. He had arrived only that morning and the first man to meet him was Mick Collins.

"And I'm sure," said Fitz, " that the first thing he said to you was come and have a ball of malt."

" You said it, babe," replied Harry.

His main object in coming to the office was to get me to go to America. I asked him if it was an order, because in that case I would go. He said he had no orders. It was only that he thought the American organisation needed a man like me. I turned down the proposal and Harry left.

Word came down that Mrs. Nugent's house was no longer safe, so I got Michael Noyk to rent an office for us in Molesworth Street and we moved in there. We were ostensibly an insurance agency. We did not know until we were well installed that Mr. Henry, who occupied the office beneath us was not, as we had thought, an ordinary solicitor, but the Crown Solicitor. In other words, he was someone who must be in close touch with the Castle. We realised that we would have to be very circumspect indeed, but we realised, too, that the building, because of his presence, would be less suspect.

We were very circumspect. We even, when Armistice Day arrived, observed the two minutes' silence. It was Fitz who remembered it was Armistice Day and told us all to keep silent for two minutes after eleven o'clock. When the two minutes were at an end, we were all somewhat hilarious until the door opened and Mr. Henry himself walked in. He said he had heard from the caretaker that we had a spare set of fire-irons and he wondered if we would sell them to him.

We were all a bit dazed because we realised that Mr. Henry had only to look around him to see the nefarious work we were engaged in. But he did not look about him.

His eyes were on the brass fire-irons and I sold them to him for thirty shillings. He went off very pleased with his bargain, not knowing that I would gladly have given him the fire-irons for nothing to get rid of him.

Mick sent me a photograph of a man who was suspected of spying and who was supposed to be a Wexford man. I went out to tell him that none of my people had been able to identify him. He was working at the time in what had been an outhouse in the grounds of St. Enda's on Oakley Road. Just as I got to the gate, there was a " stop press " being shouted and Mick came out, coatless and hatless.

" Get a copy," he said.

I got the paper and saw the big headlines announcing the attack on Lord French, the Governor-General. We walked back to the office together. Even in those surroundings, Mick's office was the last word in neatness and order. There was apparently little or no attempt to conceal anything. As he had no filing cases, his files were hanging on nails driven into the walls. Most of them had to do with the internal Loan and they were all duly labelled " Wicklow," " West Limerick," etc.

Mick was scanning the newspaper.

" He got away," I said.

" Easy for you to say that. He had three armoured cars and machine guns. We've got a handful of lads with revolvers. Easy to talk."

" I wasn't reflecting on you."

"And who the hell is responsible ? "

That was just like him. Though we had a Minister of Defence and a Chief of Staff, he considered the Army and, indeed, every other Department, as a personal matter he should attend to. It was this trait which first brought him into conflict with Brugha and, afterwards, with Stack. These were both individualists, too, who took their duties very seriously, though they were too slow for Mick's liking. So, when he reached over to do their work, they naturally got mad.

"All right," I said, " Lord French was lucky."

" You're bloody well right, he was lucky. He won't be so lucky the next time."

Someone had suggested a plan by which French might be kidnapped. He was reputed to be fond of the ladies. The plan was to let one of our girls, whose brother was in prison, go to French and appeal to him to have her brother released. She would lead him to ask for an assignation and lure him to an available house in Waterloo Road, where our fellows would be waiting for him. Mick grinned.

" It might be worth trying," he said, " keep it under your hat."

The plan was never tried. I was pretty sure that some of our people at headquarters would have scruples about adopting it.

The mere job of carrying on became more and more difficult as the days passed. Like everyone else engaged in the struggle, I changed my sleeping quarters frequently. I stayed in my own home at rare intervals. On one such occasion, Una and I were talking over the fire when suddenly at five minutes before the curfew hour, which, at that time, was ten o'clock, I got the impression I should not stay.

" I'm sorry I came," I said, " I've an idea they may come to-night."

" If you feel like that," she said, " you ought to go. But they haven't been here for months now."

" I know, but still I have a presentiment."

Looking at my watch, I said :

" I've only five minutes. I wish to God there was some place near."

Una said : " What about Coghlan's ? "

The Coghlans lived only two doors away. They had often offered me shelter, but they had several small children and I hated to bring trouble on them. Still—

" I'll try them," I said.

The Coghlans, Sighle and Seumas, were glad to see me and made me feel at home. We talked till after eleven before we went to bed. I awoke from a sound sleep to find the room flooded with light. There was an enormous cat purring somewhere. I rolled out of bed and crept to the window. The light came from the headlights of a lorry and the purring noise from the powerful Rolls Royce engine of an armoured car. The road from end to end was lined with armed men. There was a second lorry in front of my house. This was the dreaded raid. Men in uniform moved to and fro in the headlights and I heard an English voice cry : " How many men have you got there ? " and the reply was, " Two, sir." This made matters worse, for the reply had come from the direction of No. 13, the last house in the row. It seemed to indicate that two men had been taken from No. 13, which was the home of Dr. Tommy Dillon, and that every house in the street was being searched —in which case, of course, my turn was not far off.

I thought of getting out and trying to escape, though I knew it was pretty hopeless because the rear was sure to be covered also. After a few minutes, it became clear to me that all the activities were centred on my house. I thought of Una and our three little girls and bitterly realised I could do nothing for them. Hours passed and it was obvious they were making a very thorough search.

At length, when dawn was beginning to break, they went away. I made my way to the rear of the house and crossed the intervening garden into my own.

When I got over the wall I saw Una standing at the window, pale and silent. I had never seen her so near a break. She had been crying. They had kept her downstairs all night away from the children and they had grilled her and our eldest child, Emer, aged nine, for hours, on my activities and whereabouts. Una had very narrowly missed having a bayonet run through her at the foot of the basement stairs in the dark. The rooms looked as if a herd of wild cattle had been through them. The two younger children, Maeve, aged three, and Deirdre, one and a half, were hysterical, which was not to be wondered at. It was of this raid that Erskine Childers wrote : " This is not civilised war."*

A few days later, A.G. sent me to London to make arrangements for getting out the *Bulletin* there if it should happen that it was suppressed in Dublin. He had already arranged that in such a contingency we could surreptitiously use the private wire which the *Freeman's Journal* had with

Military Rule in Ireland (The Talbot Press).

London. I made the necessary arrangements with Art O'Brien, but, as it happened, there was never any need for them, because, as I have said, the British did not succeed in stopping the issue of the *Bulletin* from Dublin.

I was walking in Tottenham Court Road one day when I ran into Frank Carney, who was over on a mission for the I.R.A. Frank was a small, slight man from Enniskillen, who had been in the British Army. He had been gassed in France and had been invalided home. On his recovery, he had joined the Volunteers, subsequently becoming Brigade O/C for County Fermanagh.

As neither of us had anything particular to do that evening, Frank and I went to a music hall to see George Robey. While awaiting the appearance of the comedian, we adjourned to the bar. After a while, there was a great deal of applause and, thinking it was time for Robey's entrance, I returned to my seat. It was not Robey, but a sketch in which two men in British uniform were reminiscing about the war. A caricature of an American swaggered on to the stage, spitting right and left. One of the British soldiers said :

" You know where that fellow comes from ? "

" No, where ? " said the other.

" It's a place called America. . . . It was discovered by Christopher Columbus."

" Why ? "

This provoked loud laughter. The American said :

" Did I hear youse guys discussin' the war ? You know, we won that war for you."

One of the British soldiers said to the other :

" This fellow must be very hard of hearing ! "

" How come ? " asked the American.

" Well, that war was going on for two years before you heard of it."

Now, I believed the British would have lost the war but for the intervention of America and that this sketch showed a want of gratitude. I stood up and said so. The people on the stage stopped and stared down at me. The audience in the pit thought it was part of the show and laughed, but when they realised I was in earnest, they began to yell ;

" Shut up ! " " Sit down ! " " Throw him out ! " The noise was such that the show stopped. Frank Carney joined me and yelled, " What's up ? "

" I'm objecting to this show," I said, " because . . ."

"All right," said Frank, " I'm objecting to it too," and he yelled, " who's going to throw us out ? "

We were soon to know. Several ushers came running and they dragged us out and threw us into the street. We picked ourselves up, tried to brush the dust from our clothes and went into a pub. After some time, Frank said :

" What was all that about ? "

" They were sneering about the American's claim that they won the war, and I protested."

Frank laid down his glass and looked at me in astonishment.

" Do you mean to say that that's what we were thrown out for ? "

" Sure," I said.

" Well, by God," he said, " you are a mug."

" And what about yourself ? "

" Never mind about me. I did not know what it was about. I've a good mind to go back and apologise to these people for interrupting their innocent pleasures."

" They would only throw you out again."

" I suppose so," he said, " people are very unreasonable."

Next day Frank told me he was to meet John Chartres, whom he did not know, and he asked me to go with him. I had, years before, met Chartres several times in Griffith's office in Dublin. He was in charge of the Index to the London *Times* and he was a very valuable under-cover agent for Sinn Féin.

We went along to a very select and conservative club in the vicinity of the Houses of Parliament. Here, in a cloakroom, Chartres opened a bag and showed us a very serviceable-looking machine-gun. Frank just glanced at it and said :

" Yes, that will do."

Chartres locked the bag and we adjourned to the lounge for coffee, where Chartres, quietly amused, indicated several important members of the Conservative Party. Frank said :

"A bomb dropped in this place would dispose of a goodly number of Ireland's enemies."

" Make sure and give me warning," said Chartres, " I spend quite a lot of my time here."

" What about that gun ? " asked Frank. "Aren't you going to let me take it with me ? "

" No," said Chartres. " They might take it off you. You were merely to vet it. They're to go by the ordinary channels."

I went one morning to the office of our official representative in London, Art O'Brien. There was a strange man sitting at a table. Fintan Murphy, who was standing with his back to the fire, said something which sounded like : " This is a friend of Art's."

" He's welcome," I said, as I hung up my hat and coat. Fintan was looking at me with his eyebrows raised.

" I said that this was a friend from Scotland Yard," he said.

" He's welcome," I repeated innocently, smiling at the man. " How are you ? "

" I'm pretty well," he said.

It transpired that Art's house was being raided and this man had been sent to keep an eye on the office. I judged the man was a native of Clare and said so and he admitted I was right. He was ill at ease and he obviously did not relish this particular job. After a while, I asked him what time Art was likely to be free to come to the office. He said he had no idea and that it might be a long time. I stood up leisurely and said I could not wait for him all day and that I would call again. I took up my hat and coat and, to my surprise, I found I was allowed to walk out.

On the way downstairs, however, I remembered that I had seen a couple of men lounging in the street near the entrance. I did not look at them but walked slowly into the Strand. I stopped at a shop window and saw one of the men apparently interested in another window. I repeated the operation and saw, indeed, that I was being followed. I became an innocent countryman on his first visit to the big city. I gawked at the shop-windows and stopped to stare at every unusual spectacle. I nearly got run over crossing the streets in the wrong places, and I made many enquiries of passers-by. I got to the Tube Station at Charing Cross and bought a ticket to a destination which necessitated two changes. My guardian was at my elbow. Instead of taking the elevator, I walked down the stairs and my shadow followed suit. At the first stop, I got out and took a wrong turning and spent a long time getting to the right platform. I was beginning to enjoy the experience. I noticed that my sleuth did not get into the same queue with me to board the train. He took the queue above me or below me. At the second change I lined up in the longest queue and thus it was that the detective stepped into the train before I did, whereupon I stepped back and the door closed on him. I had the satisfaction of seeing the look of bewilderment on his face as the train swept past and I allowed that the ability of the Scotland Yard men was over-rated.

I reported this incident to Dublin and said that the job I had come to London for was carried out as far as it could be at that stage. So I was told to return. As the Holyhead-Dunlaoghaire route was considered very dangerous, I decided to take the Fishguard-Rosslare route. On the boat a Wexford sailor named Lacey recognised me and beckoned me aside.

" You're walking right into it," he said.

" How is that ? "

" There's three detectives from Dublin at Ballygeary (Rosslare Pier) and there's two policeman out of Wexford Barracks with them. They're watching out for somebody special. It might be you."

I said that even if it was not so, they would be certain to recognise me and pick me up. He took me below and fitted me out with a sailor's navy blue knitted jersey and a sailor's peaked cap and, when the boat docked, he brought me ashore by the freight gangway. I helped him push a truck past the detectives posted at the passengers' gangway. Acting on his advice, too, I refrained from travelling through Wexford and journeyed to Dublin via Waterford.

Chapter Twenty-eight

In February, 1920, the British imposed curfew in Ireland from midnight to 5 a.m., later extended to 8 p.m. to 5 a.m.

The Black and Tans (so called from their motley uniforms) and the Auxiliaries organised in England to augment the British forces in Ireland, embarked on a campaign of terrorism and destruction designed to break the solidarity of Sinn Féin.

I sought out Cathal Brugha and laid before him a plan which I thought was brilliant. I had visited the House of Commons with a friendly M.P., and I had seen how easy it would be to capture the place if the authorities were taken off guard. The barbed wire entanglements which were later erected about the entrance, were not yet in evidence. I suggested that two hundred men recruited from the Volunteers should be sent to London in batches of ten, each in charge of an officer and provided with arms, British uniforms and military lorries. On a day when there was a full dress debate in the House of Commons, several squads of those men would drive to the Houses of Parliament, close the doors, hold the exits and make prisoners of all within. At the same time, other squads were to take the principal railway termini, Croydon airfield, the wireless station in the Strand and the principal newspaper offices. A proclamation was to be issued purporting to be signed by certain left-wingers of the Labour Party proclaiming the establishment of the British Republic, calling on the workers throughout Britain to seize the industries, bestowing freedom on India, Egypt, Arabia, etc., and calling on the friends of freedom everywhere to rally to the support of the triumphant proletariat. There was a mad grandeur in the plan, but I pointed out that the initial coup was fairly easy of accomplishment. There was no guard whatever on the Houses of Parliament. At best, the scheme might have an initial success which would cause infinite harm to our mighty neighbour before matters could be brought under control. At worst, it would provoke confusion for a few days and perhaps shake the foundations of the Empire and it would certainly bring the Irish question to the attention of the world. Considering the horrible dragooning the Irish people were undergoing at the time, the cost was comparatively small.

I thought I would have had trouble in selling the scheme to Brugha. He listened with his customary patience and quiet humour.

" I like that plan," he said, " and I think it will work. It just fits in with something else I have in mind."

The plan was never tried, however. Brugha told me later that more cautious counsels had prevailed. The scheme was too ambitious for the time.

Maurice Bourgeois had come over from Paris ostensibly to collect material for the French War Museum and incidentally to write a few articles for a French newspaper. In reality, though we did not know this till later, he was an agent for the French Government and his mission was to observe the Irish scene in the interests of France. Relations between the British and the French were rather strained at this time.

Bourgeois had a considerable book knowledge of Ireland. He had written an able book on Synge, whose plays he had translated into French. I was later to see him in the Opera Comique on the occasion of the first production of an operetta based on his translation of *Riders to the Sea.* It was, in the words of a lady sitting near me, " *magnifique mais épouvantable.*"

When he arrived, Bourgeois was rather hostile to Sinn Féin. The memory of 1916 still rankled. The Rising had been a stab in the back for the Allies. This attitude was soon to undergo a change. I was supplying him with all the material I could get for his War Museum and I saw him constantly. He asked me if he could see the Volunteers in action. I told him that would be difficult and dangerous, but he persisted, and I made the necessary introduction. About a week later, he was returning from the Dublin hills when the car he was riding in was stopped by the Tans. It was unfortunate for Bourgeois that the car was being driven by Sean MacBride and that Madame Markievicz was a fellow-passenger. All three were brought to the Castle.

"They threw me into a filthy cell," Bourgeois told me
later, "and when I protested, several bullies in uniform
threatened to beat me up and shoot me. When I produced
my diplomatic passport, they said they were about to provide me with a passport to hell and they reviled France and
the French people in the most revolting language."

It was two days before Bourgeois managed to get word,
of his plight to the French Consul and secure his release.
When I met him he was still white with rage over the treatment he had received. He said he was still being followed
and, right enough, when we were crossing Stephen's Green
park, he pointed out two men who were obviously British
officers in plain clothes. They followed us to Harrington
Street, where Bourgeois had his lodgings. I told him I
could easily rid him of his shadowers.

"How?" he asked.

"I can pass the word along and they will be quickly
dealt with."

"You mean to have them assassinated. Oh no, no!
That would create terrible complications for me. I beg
of you do nothing of the kind."

He had ceased to be anti-Sinn Féin. Indeed, he became
one of our stoutest champions.

Seumas Coghlan, whom I have previously mentioned,
came to me with a strange story. He had encountered,
during a train journey, a man who, after a great deal of
preliminary talk, said he wanted to get in touch with the
leaders of Sinn Féin. He had, he said, taken on a job for
the British Secret Service and he wanted to see the Sinn
Féin leaders to tell them all about it and double-cross his
paymasters. Seumas had told him he could not put him
in touch with the people mentioned but that he would
make enquiries and see what could be done. The man was
to call at his house at nine o'clock that night.

We arranged that as soon as the man had arrived, I
should casually drop in and be introduced as Mr. Kerr, the
ostensible object of my visit being to sell a motor car. When
I arrived, I started talking to Seumas about the motor car,
but the stranger butted in, asking Seumas:

"Who is this? Is he one of the boys?"

He was a middle-aged man, of stocky build, respectably dressed. He spoke in a low, husky voice, his accent being English. As he continued to enquire whether I was one of the boys, I asked him what he was talking about.

"About Sinn Féin," he said. " Are you one of them ? "

" I've better sense," I said.

" Well, don't you know Collins, or Mulcahy ? Couldn't you tell me how to get in touch with them ? "

As I continued to put him off, he continued to plead. He had something to say which the Sinn Féin leaders would be glad to hear. He said his name was Hardy and, though he was an Englishman, he was practically one of the boys himself. He had been on a job with them up in the North and he had been captured and sent to Derry Jail. When he got out, he undertook a mission for a Captain Thompson who, he said, was the head of the British Secret Service in Ireland. The job he got was to locate and trap Michael Collins. Instead, what he really wanted to do was to trap the trapper, in other words, he wanted the Sinn Féiners to trap Captain Thompson.

I told him finally that he could easily get in touch with Arthur Griffith. All he had to do was to go to the reporters' room in the *Freeman's Journal* office and anybody there would tell him where to find Griffith. This was safe enough because A.G. had refused to go on the run. He was still working openly every day in his office in Andy Clarkin's premises in Brunswick Street—(now Pearse Street).

Early next morning I told A.G. about Hardy. I said he might expect a call from him and that he could dodge it if he liked, but that I thought he should see him. A.G. readily agreed to do so. Hardy turned up in the afternoon and had a long talk with A.G. in the course of which he told A.G. all that he had told me, and much more.

" Did you notice his eyes ? " A.G. asked me later.

" Yes," I said. " They are bad eyes."

" That is what I thought," said A.G. " He said he was in Derry jail in December, 1918. I want you to go to the Library and find out whether he was tried and what was his offence."

I looked up the file in the Library and found that in

December, 1918, he had received a five years' sentence for various frauds and that he had a long criminal record. It was obvious that he had been released from jail for his present mission. When I gave the details to A.G. he was in high good humour.

" We'll play a trick on him," he said. " What about getting a group of journalists in here and letting him talk to them in the belief he is addressing the Sinn Féin leaders ? "

I agreed the plan was brilliant and set out to invite a selected list of journalists to assemble in A.G.'s office on the following morning. The outcome was a first-class journalistic sensation. Following is the account which appeared in the *Irish Independent* on September 17th, 1920 :

PRESSMEN'S UNIQUE EXPERIENCE.

INTERVIEW WITH AN ALLEGED SPY.

AMAZING STORY.

MR. GRIFFITH SPRINGS A SURPRISE.

WHAT SINN FEIN KNEW.

"The people who are playing your game are scoundrels, but you are not as a great scoundrel as the people who employ you."

This statement was made yesterday by Mr. Arthur Griffith, T.D., at a close of a dramatic exposure of an Englishman whose mission was said to be to help Sinn Féin. The exposure took place before a party of French, American, English and Irish journalists.

The man, who was introduced by Mr. Griffith, thought he was addressing a secret meeting of Sinn Féin leaders, and, after an elaborate statement in which he disclosed his plans for aiding Sinn Féin, Mr. Griffith produced what he described as the man's record, which included two sentences of 7 years and one of 5 years penal servitude.

Acknowledging the record, the man urged that this was a reason why he should " get even with the Government." When he found he was addressing a meeting of journalists and was ordered by Mr. Griffith to leave the city that night, the man was quite crestfallen, pressed for time, and, protesting that he had never given any information against Sinn Féin, slunk out of the room.

DRAMATIC SCENE.

THE MAN'S STATEMENT.

At brief notice and without any hint as to the part they were to be called upon to play in one of the most remarkable episodes of the many amazing affairs that have recently happened in Ireland, the

French, American, British, and Irish journalists assembled in the offices of " Young Ireland " yesterday.

An " Irish Independent " representative was asked yesterday afternoon to call at a certain address on a most important mission. On going there he was met by a gentleman who asked him to be at Great Brunswick Street at 4.30 p.m. where he would meet Mr. Arthur Griffith and Mr. Desmond Fitzgerald. The object of the request was not disclosed, but it was obvious that a mysterious, and, as it turned out, a sensational drama was about to be enacted. He was asked to make certain alterations in his clothing and to an extent disguise himself.

THE MEETING.

On entering a room at the address mentioned he found there seated about a table Mr. Griffith and a number of journalists, including French, American and English. After some time, and when the curiosity of those present was getting the upper hand of their patience, Mr. Griffith explained the object of the assemblage. A gentleman, he stated, who had described himself as a journalist, but who was in the Secret Service of England, had called on him some days previously, and professing sympathy with the Sinn Féin movement, made certain suggestions and offers which were not considered.

Eventually, after further visits, an agreement was arrived at by which this Secret Service agent undertook to attend a secret meeting of Sinn Féin leaders. " You gentlemen," Mr. Griffith concluded, " are the Sinn Féin leaders for the occasion, and you will have an opportunity of hearing what he has to say." To the two Irish Press representatives present he delegated the work of interrogation, explaining that the accents of their colleagues might arouse the suspicions of the agent.

THE AGENT ARRIVES.

After a further interval, the appointed time arrived, and punctually, the mystery man was ushered into the room. Displaying traces of nervousness, he at once took a seat at the table. A well-set man of middle age, clean-shaven, and dressed in a neat blue serge suit, he immediately entered into fluent converse. Starting with the statement that he was an Englishman, he said that he had been a journalist and done work for the " Daily Chronicle," " Daily Mail," and other journals. He had spent eleven years in Canada and America, and was for a time city editor of a paper in Toronto. " I don't mind telling you," he went on, " that I am a bit of a sport, and I was in Ireland attending race meetings in 1918."

He also said that he got into touch with some Sinn Féiners in Derry, and took part in a raid for arms at a place a short distance from that city. They were arrested, he said, and he was charged, not with raiding for arms, but with burglary, and sentenced to five years' imprisonment. He was sent to Maryboro' prison, and was in the next cell to a Sinn Féin prisoner named Moran. A man named Fleming, who smashed up his cell, was also in the same ward. After serving nine months, he was released on a ticket-of-leave.

Michael Collins during the Truce, 1921.

At Croke Park, during the Truce, 1921, Arthur Griffith, Eamon de Valera, Larry O'Neill (Lord Mayor of Dublin), and Michael Collins watch a hurling match.

J. Cashman

PRETENCE OF ENMITY.

During his incarceration, he said, his favourite child died and he would never forgive the British Government for his enforced absence from home at the time. That and other things embittered him against the Government. He returned to England and some time ago, when out of employment, a friend recommended him to call on " Capt. —— " (giving a name and an address at Charing Cross Road, London). He called and learned that that gentleman was " the head of the Secret Service." " Capt. —— he said, asked him if he would do work for the Government. He said he would and asked what was its nature. The Captain said, " You know Ireland pretty well, don't you ? " He replied that he did. Capt. —— then said that he wanted him to go to Dublin to do secret service work. He asked him if he knew Michael Collins and he replied in the negative. "As a matter of fact," said the man, " I didn't know that he was the Minister of Finance until today." Capt. —— said that the Government would give £10,000 for the capture of Michael Collins and that if he gave information that would lead to his apprehension a large share of that would be his. His share, he added, would run into four figures.

He got instructions to go to Dublin and was informed that he would be allowed 30s. a day subsistence money, and would receive bonuses for any information of value to the Government that he supplied. It was arranged that Capt. —— would send him a telegram to meet him at Harcourt St., and that that would mean that he was to meet him at the pier at Kingstown.

HIS " ROLE " IN DUBLIN.

His work in Dublin, Capt. —— told him, was to be quite independent of the police and military in that city. He said that various important coups had been made a mess of by these departments, and he was not to have anything to do with them. Capt. ——, however, said that he would have the power to call on them at any moment, and, if necessary, they could draw a cordon around a whole area where the men sought for were located.

Continuing, the agent said he did meet Capt. —— on the pier at Kingstown. He stopped to explain to his audience that there were no people present at the time, and that it would be a very easy matter for Sinn Féin " to get him."

Capt. —— and himself again discussed the capture of Michael Collins. He asked how was he to know him, and was given a photograph of Mr. Collins in military uniform. It was obviously, he said, taken from a group, and that even those who knew him could not identify him by means of the picture.

INVISIBLE INK.

He was also supplied with powders which when mixed with water made an invisible ink. The procedure he was told to adopt was to write a formal letter in ordinary ink and to intersperse any secret information he had obtained between the lines in invisible ink. He was directed to forward communications to Mr. C——, at any of three addresses—at Pulborough Road, Southfields, London, S.W.; Charing Cross Road, London, W.C.2, and Newington Buildings, London, S.E. (The agent gave precise addresses.) He explained that he had written these addresses on a page of a diary which he produced (apparently a recent purchase), but Capt. —— tore out the page, stating that it was dangerous to keep such information in his diary.

The Captain at an interview, he continued, produced £45, which he offered to him. He declined to accept it, saying that he could draw on his own account for the present. The Captain said he would lodge it to his credit in any bank he might mention, but he again refused. His first interview in London with the Captain, he said, was on August 21, and that he came to Dublin on August 30, and had not yet drawn any money, but a month's payment would soon fall due. At this stage he placed a fountain pen case—also apparently new—on the table. He also donned gold-rimmed spectacles.

" VALUE OF INFORMATION."

Resuming, he took pains to emphasise the value of the information he had so far imparted would be to Sinn Féin. They could intercept the letters, he pointed out, going to the addresses mentioned, and thereby become cognisant of the moves made against them by having the invisible lines photographed. He also took care to mention that in order to work successfully for Sinn Féin he could supply some fairly correct information to the English agents.

For instance, he said, if he reported that Michael Collins was in Tipperary, information might be supplied from another and more reliable source that he was in Dublin, and in that way he would come under suspicion.

AGENT AND THE " CAPTAIN."

Questioned as to Capt. ——'s appearance, he said he was a young man of slight build, and usually went about in civilian dress. He had been to Galway last week, he said, but he was at present in London. He was expecting him back in Dublin in a few days' time, and he would give ' the tip ' as to when he was coming.

He was asked as to what remuneration he would require for his services in Sinn Féin interests, and he replied that he would leave that to the people who engaged him.

" SHADOWING TACTICS."

Interrogated as to who Capt. —— was in touch with in Dublin, he professed ignorance. While prepared to leave the question as to what would be done with Capt. —— to the judgment of the " Sinn Féin leaders," he explained the chances of securing valuable information by allowing him at large and adopting " shadowing tactics."

He also explained how he himself could be useful in other directions.

For instance, he said, there was a report that there was an arsenal in " Paul Power's " farm in Tramore.

If the military got word of that he could supply information as to when the visit was to take place, and men could be ready to turn the tables on the soldiers when they arrived in lorries.

He also mentioned the names of some prominent Carsonites concerning whom he could supply information. He had supplied particulars already, he said, to the British authorities, of two Unionist quarters in Derry where arms were stored. Capt. ——, he said, took a note of this information, but subsequently said that no action would be taken, as the parties were loyalists.

THE TICKET-OF-LEAVE.

In the earlier stages of the interview the man mentioned that when undertaking the secret service work his ticket-of-leave was withdrawn. He had no longer to report to the police every week, but, he said, if he was found out in anything he might have to go back to prison to finish his sentence.

Asked if he was prepared to take risks, he replied in the affirmative, and smilingly remarked that he had read of a secret society that tested its members' sincerity by asking them to shoot some person. " Of course," he added, " I would not like to have that test imposed."

At the conclusion of his interview he also mentioned that he had been requested to secure information about Bob Brennan. He was told that he had something to do with the Sinn Féin official paper, and that it was very important he should be got.

THE ANTI-CLIMAX.

When the man had concluded Mr. Griffith remarked that all that he had been saying was very interesting, but he begged to inform him that the gentlemen he was conferring with were not Sinn Féin leaders, but journalists, representing American, French, English and Irish newspapers.

HIS CRIMINAL RECORD.

Mr. Griffith then asked him to listen to the reading of the following document, which was an extract taken from the " Belfast News-Letter" of Dec., 1918 :

"A middle-aged man of respectable appearance was put forward for sentence, and in reply to his lordship said his real name was ——.

" His lordship said the prisoner had had several other names. He had sent in a statement admitting that he had been engaged for some months past in a series of frauds, including a number of cases in Waterford, Carlow, Lisburn, Portstewart, Derry, Liverpool, Leeds, Cardiff, Plymouth, Portsmouth, Wolverhampton, and another place, involving sums amounting to £255. Did that statement disclose all the frauds the prisoner had committed in the last few months ? . . .

(Here followed a statement by prisoner in which he said he had been employed by the Ministry of Munitions and was dismissed on account of this record, that he became desperate and would have committed murder if it had come his way. He concluded with an appeal for mercy, offering to pay 20/- in the £ to those he had defrauded.)

" His lordship said he had the prisoner's record before him. Prisoner talked about getting an opportunity of repaying the money, but as a matter of fact he began his career of crime 32 years ago. In 1886 he got 6 weeks for forgery at the Devon Assizes ; in 1890 he was imprisoned for 6 weeks for stealing a bicycle and neglecting his family, and in the same year at Plymouth he got 3 months for larceny and embezzlement. In 1896 he got 12 months at Winchester Assizes for stealing securities and forgery. In 1897—apparently just immediately he came out, he got 18 months at the London Assizes for fraud. He then got 7 years at Surrey Assizes in 1899 for forgery, and another 7 years in 1910 for forging a bill of exchange and for stealing a cheque book. In face of this it was useless to accept any promise from him. He would not be doing his duty if he left the prisoner to go on in that course, defrauding people at will, and he, therefore, sentenced him to 5 years' penal servitude, which would cover all the offences to which the prisoner had pleaded guilty."

Man's Coolness.

At the moment Mr. Griffith explained that those present were journalists there was an interruption by the entry of some other representatives of foreign newspapers, and the man apparently missed the observation, for when his record was read he protested that that did not affect the situation. Rather it was a reason why he should get even with the Government which had inflicted such punishment on him.

Mr. Griffith repeated the explanation as to the character of the audience, and the man, who had listened intently to his record being read, looked crest-fallen, and remarked " I didn't know that."

" I will now warn you," said Mr. Griffith, " to leave Dublin to-night."

The man, in a timid voice, said it would be impossible for him to go that night, and was given until the morning to take his departure. Protesting that he had never given any information against Sinn Féin, he took his hat and quitted the room, leaving the journalists discussing the extraordinary drama in which they had unwittingly participated.

Agents-Provocateur.

Turning to them, Mr. Griffith said there were many of this man's type employed in the country as agents-provocateur. They tried to incite young men to acts of violence, while those that employed them issued posters inviting information as to crimes instigated by their agents.

Asked whether Sinn Féin had information that the man was a Secret Service agent other than his own confession, Mr. Griffith assured those present that they had.

Of course, I could not be present at the interview, but I was in an adjoining room and so were two of Mick's men, Tom Cullen and Liam Tobin. Grinning broadly, they addressed me as Mr. Kerr.

" I hope you're not going to shoot him, Tom," I said.

" No," said Tom, " Griffith said there should be nothing of the kind. I'm here to see that he gets on the boat."

Chapter Twenty-nine

In June 1920, *the British forces began to crack. Several units of
the Royal Irish Constabulary refused to obey orders. Many magistrates
surrendered their British commissions. In India a battalion of the
Connaught Rangers mutinied as a protest against conditions in Ireland.*

On a Sunday morning Griffith came to the place where I
was staying and said that a certain Bishop, who was friendly,
was in the Gresham Hotel for the meeting of the Hierarchy,
which was to be held next day in Maynooth. He asked me
to draw up a statement which the Bishops might adopt
giving an overall picture of the reign of terror. I spent
all day over it and in the evening, with A.G., called to see
His Lordship. He read the statement and said it was too
strong and should be watered down. A.G. pointed out
that it contained nothing but facts, every one of which
could be substantiated. His Lordship agreed, but said
that the Bishops knew very well that we were losing the
country, that the people were tired of the fight and that
if they got a chance, they would turn us down in favour
of the Parliamentary Party.

Griffith was quite plainly taken aback at such sentiments
coming from one whom he had considered a rock of strength.
We left early and as soon as we gained the street, A.G.
said :

" What do you think of that ? "

" It's unbelievable," I answered.

" What can have happened to him ? " he said. " I
can't understand it."

It is noteworthy that, though he affected to disbelieve
what His Lordship had said about the people's morale,
A.G. was impressed by it, because one of the arguments
that he later used privately in defence of the Treaty was
that the people had grown tired of the fight and there was
a danger they might turn to the Parliamentary Party.

The morning we got the news that Terence MacSwiney
had died in Brixton Jail after his seventy-three days' fast,
we were all relieved that his long agony was over. One of

284

the Cork prisoners, Michael Fitzgerald, had already died
after a seventy-two days' hunger strike, and while A.G. and
I were still talking of MacSwiney, word arrived that another
Cork prisoner, Patrick Murphy, had died. There were
several other prisoners in Cork Jail on the point of death
and A.G. found ready approval for his proposal that the
strike should now be called off.

Paddy Moylett, an old friend of A.G.'s, was holding
informal conversations with various influential journalists
and people in close touch with Lloyd George. A.G.
insisted that he should make it clear that he had no official
status whatever and, of course, Moylett was careful to do
so. He made considerable progress on a plan for an
armistice and amnesty as a prelude to a conference to
consider terms of settlement. A.G., in a letter to Moylett,
stated clearly that the conference should be unhampered
by any preliminary conditions. A.G. was really hopeful
that a truce might be effected on terms which we could
accept.

Moylett was staying in an hotel at Dunlaoghaire. I
brought him some material which he could use in the
last minute attempt he was making to save the life of
Kevin Barry. It was in vain.

On the evening of the 1st November, 1920, I entered
a little shop at Rathgar to buy cigarettes. The woman
behind the counter was crying.

" I hope there's nothing the matter, ma'am," I said.

She pointed to the evening paper on the counter. On
the front page was a picture of Kevin Barry in football
togs and the news that he had been hanged that morning.

"A boy of eighteen," she said, sobbing bitterly.

I was surprised. The woman did not know me, but I
knew that she was pro-British, as were all her people.

" It's very sad," I said.

" Sad is not the word for it," she said. " It's a crime.
When people have to hang young boys like that, their
cause is lost."

She gave me the cigarettes.

" That is what it has come to," she said. " Their cause
is lost. Their day is over."

I did not tell her that before hanging him, his captors had tortured Kevin Barry in the vain effort to make him divulge information about his comrades. At this time, the torture of prisoners by the Crown forces had become commonplace. Anyone who is interested in the details of such tortures should read the American edition of Ernie O'Malley's book, *Army Without Banners* (Houghton & Mifflin Co., Boston).

It was very seldom that I ventured home to Belgrave Road in those days, but occasionally I met Una and the children elsewhere. We had arranged to go to a football match in Croke Park on November 21st, not knowing, of course, that this day was to be known for a long time afterwards as Bloody Sunday. On our way to the tram, we met Dr. Kathleen Lynn, who said that the town was in an uproar, that the military were careering everywhere because some twenty British officers had been shot that morning.

From the tram we saw ample evidence of the military activities. Armoured cars and soldiers in lorries were patrolling the streets, holding up and searching pedestrians and cyclists. When we got to Nelson Pillar, however, we saw that there were huge crowds going to the football match and we decided that the crowds might be too much for the children, so we went out to Dollymount instead. There was a cold wind blowing on the Bull wall and we set out to return rather earlier than usual.

We were on top of an open tram running in from Fairview when we saw vast numbers of people running from the direction of Croke Park, some of them bleeding from head and face. They were crowding the trams. An old friend, Paddy Devlin, a Gaelic sports-writer, whose pen-name was Celt, came up on top of the tram. I asked him what had happened and he said that the Tans had driven into the Park and opened fire on the football crowd. Some of the players were killed, he said, and a lot of the spectators.

At the Pillar Una left to take the children home and I went to the *Freeman's Journal* office to find out what had happened. The reports that were coming in were dire indeed. The firing in the Park had been kept up for ten minutes. More than a dozen people had been killed and hundreds were wounded. Many more had been trampled in the stampede.

Henry O'Connor, the chief leader-writer of the *Freeman*, told me that the total number of British officers shot that morning was fourteen and that seven others who were sought, had escaped. He said that Dick McKee and Peadar Clancy, the Commandant and Vice-Commandant respectively of the Dublin Brigade, as well as a man named Conor Clune, a visitor from County Clare, had been taken the night before and had been murdered in Dublin Castle.

While Henry and I were talking, word arrived that there was an enormous fire raging in some buildings on Sir John Rogerson's Quays and, indeed, from the windows we could see the flames. Reports spread from mouth to mouth that the Black and Tans were setting fire to the city. These proved to be incorrect.

Next morning, I was waiting for Griffith when he came into his office. He was badly shaken. The slaughter in Croke Park he thought was dreadful but, after all, that was a British crime. You could not expect better from the British, but the killing of the English officers !

" Look, A.G.," I said, " they were not merely English officers. They were special agents——"

" How," he said, " can we justify this. The killing of men on a Sunday morning in their homes in the presence of their wives."

I pointed out that these men were not merely English officers. They were a special squad, recruited for the purposes of spying and murdering. They had themselves, individually and collectively, carried out a number of murders of our men. They had been recruited at the instance of the Chief of the Imperial Staff, Sir Henry Wilson, who, though an Irishman himself, was bitterly anti-Irish. He made no secret of his belief that the way to meet and beat Sinn Féin was by naked terrorism.

Wilson realised that Collins must have men inside Dublin Castle so, in order to insure greater secrecy, this special squad of military officers had arrived without the knowledge of the Castle. They and their wives were located in various houses which were equipped with telephones and

they passed as civilians.   Each was served by a number
of touts who, when they saw a suspect entering a house,
or a number of men gathering for a meeting, immediately
conveyed word to the officer who, in turn, phoned the
Auxiliaries, so that in a matter of minutes the suspected
house was raided.   At the outset, the activities of this special
squad had Collins completely in the dark, until he managed
to secure a list of their names and addresses and then he
struck like lightning.   According to General Crozier, who
was at the time commanding officer of the Auxiliaries,
Collins acted " in the nick of time in order to forestall
similar action by the British authorities."*

A.G. had received several death notices and one had
arrived that morning telling him he did not have twenty-
four hours to live.   He refused, however, to take any precautions whatever.   He had an appointment at Mrs.
Stopford Green's house in Stephen's Green.   I persuaded
him to let me go with him.

" How are you going to stop a bullet that's coming my
way ? " he asked.

" Maybe," I said, " you could stop one coming my way."

He consented to make a slight detour.   We walked down
Brunswick Street (Pearse Street) and by Merrion Street
and Merrion Row to Stephen's Green.   Two caged lorries
of Tans passed us at a giddy pace and I saw several individuals lounging about who looked like would-be assassins.
I was thankful enough when we were safely in Mrs. Green's.

Griffith was arrested a few days later and when we heard
he was in Mountjoy Jail with some of his own comrades,
we all breathed somewhat easier.   At any rate, what the
Castle could do to him now, would have to be done in
the open.

Diarmuid Hegarty's office was located on the top floor
of a building in Middle Abbey Street.   He was the Secretary
of the Dail Eireann Cabinet and his office was also that of
Army Organisation, the work of which was being carried
out by Diarmuid under the direction of Collins.   I was on
my way to Diarmuid's office when I saw emerging from
Abbey Street into O'Connell Street two lorry-loads of

* *Ireland For Ever* (Jonathan Cape).

Auxiliaries. They were travelling slowly, which was unusual, and the Auxiliaries, their revolvers swinging, eyed the passers-by balefully. People hurried into doorways for shelter. The lorries crossed the street and turned south, disappearing into D'Olier Street.

I climbed the stairs to Diarmuid's office. Madge Clifford (now Mrs. John Comer) was sitting at a typewriter. She was a pretty girl from Kerry whose dark eyes could be very merry and gay, or could flash fire as the occasion demanded. Just now she was very pale and she stared at me.

" You," she said.

" Why not ? "

" My heart is pounding fit to burst," she said.

It seemed that the Auxiliaries had been all over the house. The first Madge knew of it was when she looked up and saw an officer in the doorway. She had beside her a file of the very distinctive light blue official notepaper, boldly headed " Dail Eireann." The sheet in the machine was similarly headed.

"All alone ? " said the officer.

Madge smiled her gayest smile as she answered :

" More's the pity."

With her right hand she quietly turned over the top sheet of the pile of notepaper, and with the left, she quietly twisted the roller of the machine till the heading on the sheet was out of sight.

"Are you always all alone ? "

" Oh, no, not at all. The boss is out to lunch."

The officer hovered over her. All around him were files which would have been of immense value to his pay-masters, but his eyes were only on Madge.

" It's a shame to leave a pretty girl like you all alone," he said.

" It's a cruel shame," said Madge.

" What are you doing this evening ? "

" Oh, nothing much."

" What about you and me getting together ? "

At this point, a loud English voice sounded from the stairs :

" Say, Charlie ! Have you got anything there ? "
Charlie started towards the door.
" Not a thing," he said.
" Well, come down here ! "
" See you again," said Charlie as he went out.
" That was a magnificent piece of acting," I said to
Madge. " You have a grand nerve."
" Oh," she said, " but my heart is still pounding. Think
of what would have happened if that dirty murderer had
laid a hand on me. I'd have torn his eyes out and given
the whole show away."

I met Dr. Tommy Dillon, Professor of Chemistry in
Galway University. He told me that on the night Father
Griffin was taken out and murdered by the Tans, they had
come for him also. He had escaped through a back window
when they were at the door. As he was now a marked man,
he had been advised to leave Galway City and so his wife,
Geraldine, and he had come to Dublin. They were looking
for a safe place to stay. I invited him to stay with us in
the house where we were then living.

After Bloody Sunday, we had decided that Belgrave
Road was no longer safe, so Una left the children in her
mother's place, Coolnaboy in Wexford, and we rented
rooms in a house in Rathgar Avenue. Our landlady was
a true blue Unionist and she had no inkling of our activities.
Had she known she was harbouring Sinn Féiners, she would
have died. To her we were Mr. and Mrs. William Kearney,
and I was an official of the Department of Agriculture.

The night Tommy and Mrs. Dillon arrived, we got a
fright. The four of us were playing cards at a table in the
front sitting-room when we heard the roar of a lorry coming
down the street. As it was long after curfew hour, we
realised it must be a military lorry. It stopped outside.

" I wonder could we have been followed ? " asked Tommy.

" It's not unusual for them to stop when they see a light
in a house," I said. Just then, the headlights of the lorry
were turned on the window.

Una was sitting facing the window, on which there was
a venetian blind, the slats of which were only partially
closed. She said :

" There is someone looking in through the blind."

" Go on playing," I said. " Don't pretend you see anything. Keep your eyes on the cards."

We did so. We continued to deal and play the cards, though, of course, none of us knew what cards we were playing. This scene lasted for a full fifteen minutes before Una announced that the eyes had disappeared from the window. Shortly afterwards we heard the lorry depart. Had any of us shown any signs of panic, the raiders would have entered.

We saw plenty of signs of panic in those days. I was in Dr. Farnan's house in Merrion Square looking out through the window at the park. There was a man on the footpath on the opposite side of the road, reading a newspaper as he strolled along. Three lorry loads of Tans whizzed past and then there was a revolver shot, the signal for an attack on the lorries. The bursting of one, two, three hand-grenades in rapid succession reverberated through the Square. Over on the National Gallery side of the Square several people crowded into a doorway. The door opened behind them, they vanished into the house and the door was closed. The man who had been reading the newspaper was standing petrified, his back to the railings. Within a minute, Crossley cars loaded with Tans from Beggars' Bush barracks, came tearing at an incredible speed, their guns barking incessantly. The man, still clutching his newspaper, started running first one way and then another. He stopped uncertainly and then, turning his back to the roadway, he tried to force his body in through the railings, which were only about six inches apart. It was a sickening spectacle. He fell down on the footpath and we thought he had been shot. When we got to him, however, we found that he had collapsed from fright.

I was on the open top of a tram in Upper O'Connell Street, travelling towards the Pillar. From the direction of O'Connell Bridge came the sound of firing. Three hand-grenades crashed in rapid succession, followed by rifle fire. The tram came to a halt just beyond the Pillar. Down on the bridge people were running in all directions. The conductor put his head over the top of the stairs.

" Yez had better all lie down on the flure," he said.

The admonition was disregarded. The majority of the passengers were standing up craning their heads forward trying to see what was happening. Three caged lorries of soldiers dashed up the street at a dizzy pace. In the second I saw a soldier clinging to the cage, his rifle discarded. His head was flung back and he was bleeding from the throat. His companions were crouching on the floor. In the third lorry two soldiers were firing back towards the scene of the ambush, their aim obstructed by the wires of the cage. Two ambulances raced past in the now deserted street.

The tram moved forward. On O'Connell Bridge a man was lying on the footpath with a priest kneeling beside him. Three civilians were lifting a woman into one of the ambulances. A group of Auxiliaries were tumbling out of a lorry and another group was herding a number of civilians against a wall on Burgh Quay.

A hundred yards further on in Westmoreland Street people were moving about freely. As I got off the tram I said to the conductor on the platform :

" Things are very quiet around here."

" Quiet ! " he said, in a tone of disgust. " Sure you'd die of N.U.I. in this town."

I guessed he meant ennui.

Chapter Thirty

De Valera had set up in America an organisation with one million members to further the cause of the Irish Republic and had raised a loan of six million dollars before returning to Ireland by the underground route.

DESMOND FITZGERALD, Frank Gallagher and I were in Miss Gavan Duffy's house in Stephen's Green, discussing something in connection with the *Bulletin*, when Ernie O'Malley stalked in with a trench coat on his arm, underneath which was a parabellum pistol. He had been fighting in nearly every county in Ireland and the fame of his exploits had come back to Dublin. In his bantering way, he was making light of his adventures, when Josephine Ahearne (later Mrs. James MacNeill) ran in to say the Tans were surrounding the area. They were already in the lane at the rear of the house. We looked through the front windows and saw a cordon forming diagonally across from Earlsfort Terrace to the gate of Stephen's Green.

" Time for me to be off," said Ernie lightly. He picked up the gun, threw his coat carelessly over it and walked out. Breathlessly, we watched as he walked straight over to the cordon. It was obvious to us that he had his right hand on the gun ready to shoot. An officer spoke to him and he replied. They both laughed and Ernie passed through the cordon, mounted the steps to St. Vincent's Hospital, which he entered. We heard later that he had said to the officer, much to the latter's amusement, that he was carrying a machine-gun.

One by one the rest of us slipped quietly out of the house. I got my bicycle and cycled towards Harcourt Street, noticing that all the gates into the park were held. There was a cordon forming at Harcourt Street and Cuffe Street and I turned down the west side of the Green. York Street was also closed and, in the distance. I could see that so was Grafton Street.

I dismounted, realising I was trapped. There was a
group of Tans questioning everyone and moving in my
direction. I was opposite a little cigarette shop I had never
been in. I wheeled my bicycle in there and said to the
girl behind the counter :

" Is there a way out at the back ? "

Without a pause, she said :

" Yes, come this way."

I followed her through a little dark room and through
a yard.

" Get over that wall," she said quietly. " Cross the yard
and you can make your way into Mercer Street."

I lost no time in following her instructions and soon
found myself in Whitefriar Street, outside the cordon.
Next morning, I retrieved my bicycle. The girl told me
that the Tans had entered the shop just as she got back
to the counter. They asked for the man who had come in
with the bicycle. She said no man had entered and asserted
that the bicycle belonged to her brother. They searched
the premises and went off. I thanked her and she laughed
and said it was all in the day's work.

Mrs. Stopford Green sent me word that an old friend
of mine was at her house and wanted to see me. I was
surprised to find that the " old friend " was none other than
Alderman George Hadden, a member of the Wexford
Corporation. I would have said that he was a Unionist,
though I had never talked politics with him. I was shocked
to find that the poor man had become completely blind.

He told me he had come up from Wexford to see me,
thinking I had some influence with the Sinn Féin leaders.
He was very much distressed at the state of the country,
at the slaughter and destruction that was going on. He
thought the methods that the British were adopting to
quell the insurrection were shameful. At the same time,
he realised that England could not afford to have Ireland
an independent republic on her flank and he felt the
British would never concede such a status to us. He did,
however, think that the British could be induced to go
much further than they had ever gone before and that a
settlement could be arrived at on the basis of Dominion

Plenipotentiaries and advisers at Holyhead en route to London. October, 1921. *Left to right :* John Chartres, Desmond Fitzgerald, Eamonn Broy, Arthur Griffith, Eamonn Duggan, Robert Barton, George Gavan Duffy.

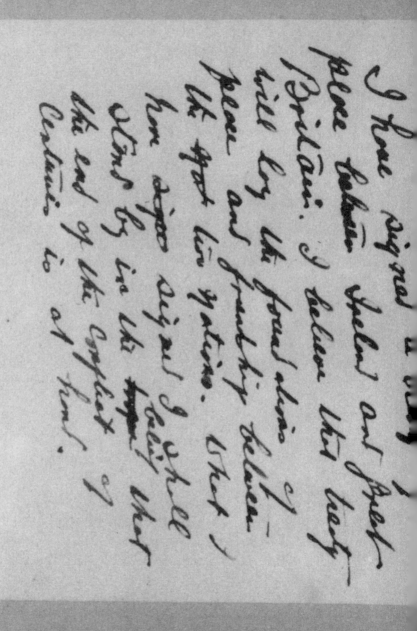

Arthur Griffith's testimony in his own handwriting to his faith in the Treaty to which he had put his hand.

Home Rule. He knew, he said, certain people in England and Ireland who had great influence with the British Government. These people were very anxious to get such encouragement from Sinn Féin as would warrant their using this influence to achieve a settlement. He gave me a document embodying all this and asked me to present it to the leaders.

I said that of course I would do so but I pointed out that a group headed by Sir Horace Plunkett had been working for some time on similar lines and that they had got nowhere.

" But I understand," he said, " that the difficulty lies in the fact that you refuse any settlement short of a republic."

" That is quite true," I said.

" But surely," he said, " your people must realise that the distance my friends and I have travelled from maintenance of the Union to Dominion Home Rule is much greater than yours would be from the Republic to Dominion Home Rule ? "

I said I fully realised how far they had travelled, but they would have to come all the way to the Republic. There would be no going back for us. The poor man was terribly distressed.

" Our country—remember it is my country too—will be utterly ruined," he said.

I promised to give him an official answer in a day or two. I reported the matter to Collins, who was now acting President in the absence of de Valera and Griffith and I returned to Alderman Hadden the next day to say that there could be no negotiations on the basis of Dominion Home Rule. He returned to Wexford very disconsolate.

A few days later, Mrs. Green sent word there was another visitor to see me. This time it was a man who had been secretary to Lloyd George and who was still in the confidence of the Prime Minister. In effect this is what he said :

" I do not want you to think that the Prime Minister sent me here or that he is privy to what I am doing. I am merely one of the people in Great Britain who is acutely conscious of the frightful reputation we British are getting because of the depredations of those scoundrels, the Black and Tans. If they knew why I am here, my life would not be worth a minute's purchase. So I am entirely in your hands. There is a growing body in England wanting a settlement. We think it can be achieved. The first step should be, of course, an armistice ; the second, an amnesty for all prisoners, and the third, a conference to consider the setting up of a Parliament for all Ireland with adequate safeguards for the Unionists in the North. What do you think of that ? "

" Do you mind my asking you why you are saying all this to me ? " I said.

" I told Mrs. Green that I had a plan and that I wanted to try it out on various people. I am trying it out on you."

I knew, of course, that Mrs. Green was in favour of some such plan and I knew, too, that it was substantially the same as that which had been submitted to Griffith through Paddy Moylett. So I said :

" There would be no condition imposed preliminary to the conference ! "

" Not at all."

" For instance," I said, " the All Ireland Parliament you speak of might be the Parliament of the Irish Republic ? "

" Good heavens, no ! " he said. " It would be a Dominion Parliament."

Of course it was no use and I told him so.

At Christmas, Dev arrived back from America. On a bitterly cold night, I cycled from Killester to see him at Loughnavale, a house behind hedges fronting Merrion Strand. He was looking tired, but he was full of plans. He listened to my account of the situation. I told him that, so far as I could judge, the people were standing firm in spite of the terror. He asked what would be the effect if the British made an offer we could not accept. Would it shake the people ? Not, I said, unless there was a break at the top and there was no sign of that.

Father O'Flanagan, who was Vice-President of Sinn Féin, had, on his own initiative, sent a telegram to Lloyd George saying, in effect : " You say you want peace. So

ALLEGIANCE 297

do we. What are your terms ? " At about the same time,
the newspapers reported that a couple of public bodies in
Galway had passed resolutions suggesting that a truce would
be welcomed. This had been construed by Lloyd George as
a sign that Sinn Féin was weakening. He had been con-
templating a peace offer, but now he changed his mind
and decided that an intensification of the reign of terror
would smash Sinn Féin. I told Dev that the lesson of this
had not been lost on the leaders and people alike.

Dev said the Dail had never taken responsibility for the
I.R.A. He was going to get them to do this and to take
the first available opportunity to make it clear to all and
sundry that the Dail took full responsibility for the opera-
tions of the Army.

He asked me what I thought of the suggestion that I
should go to America to help the campaign there. I said
that if it was an order, or if he particularly wanted me to
go, of course, I would do so, but that if I was given the
choice I preferred to stay. It was the second time I had
refused such a trip. (I was to refuse a third offer and to
accept a fourth.) He then asked me if I would be prepared
to set up a Foreign Office in which I would be Under-
Secretary for Foreign Affairs, my work being to co-relate
the activities of our envoys abroad and to keep them better
informed. I said I would gladly do this.

Dev deplored the fact that our communications were not
better. He instanced the case of the British officers killed
on Bloody Sunday morning. This had been represented
in the American papers as brutal murders of British officers
in their homes, merely because they were British officers.
He had had no knowledge of the facts and was compelled,
willy-nilly, to let the reports go uncontradicted until it was
too late. I told him that I had got hold of an Irish agent
for an American firm, who sent and received code messages
every day in the course of his business. He was willing to
let me use his codes and addresses for our purposes.

I noticed that Dev had been reading an English translation of a Greek classic. I told him he should relax and
read something light. I happened to have in my pocket
a copy of a detective story I had had published and I gave

him this but, of course, he never read it. During the whole time he had been in America he had seen only one play, Marc Connelly's *Green Pastures*. Whenever afterwards the theatre was mentioned, he recalled this play with keen delight.

For our new office Una rented a couple of rooms in No. 2 Harcourt Place (now 36 Fenian Street) near Westland Row, under the name of Lewis. We put up a sign " Lewis and Lewis, Insurance Agents."

Kevin O'Higgins, who was assistant minister for Local Government, had an office in Suffolk Street. I went there to try to secure the services of Frank Kelly, who was good at codes and cyphers. O'Higgins told me that he had been held up by the Tans that morning.

" I told them," he said, " that I had nothing more dangerous on me than a safety-razor and I took it out to show them."

" That surely was a clever thing to do," I said.

" Why not ? "

" Wasn't it a clear indication that you were on the run ? "

" Good heavens ! " he said, " I never thought of that."

He agreed to part with Frank Kelly and, in addition, I recruited James Carty, who was later to write his excellent histories ; Mrs. Dr. Jim Ryan (Mairin Cregan), who had not yet written *Old John* and her other famous stories ; James Bolger, now in the Accountant's Section in Iveagh House. George Homan, afterwards Major-domo of Iveagh House, was our special courier.

These couriers were of tremendous importance to the organisation and they had great responsibilities, though they seemed hardly to realise this. They were seemingly carefree messenger boys, flitting here and there on bicycles. Theirs was the job of carrying despatches between the various underground offices and the distribution centre ("The Dump"). They had to make sure they did not attract attention and were not followed. Each of them knew where the various Republican Government departments were located, in case an urgent message had to pass from one department to another. Generally such direct delivery of communications between departments was discouraged, the dump being used to secure greater safety.

There was no instance of even an accidental leakage of information on the part of any of the couriers. There was one amazing case of a courier who was venal in a minor way. A lad I will call Johnnie, was the courier in a department, where the postage bill was very high. It was noticed that the bill was even higher than it should be and then it was found that stamps were disappearing. Johnnie was watched and was caught selling blocks of stamps. By the time he was caught, he had disposed of some fifteen pounds worth of stamps over several months. Now Johnnie had only to walk into any police station and collect ten thousand pounds by giving away the office where Collins worked. The idea had never occurred to him and, indeed, he would have been cut in little pieces before he would have done anything of the kind.

The Foreign Affairs office in Harcourt Place had to be left every evening bare of any evidence of seditious activities. We did not know any of the other tenants of the building, nor did we know anything of the caretaker. Una bought an old wardrobe and, at the top of this, Frank Kelly and I made a secret compartment into which every night we fitted all our files. There was nothing then to show that we were not running a bona fide insurance agency. The desks were covered with insurance promotion pamphlets, which Una and I had collected here and there.

All went well until the caretaker, Mrs. Carey, became suspicious of us. She had noticed that while there was a great deal of work going on in the office, there were no customers. She reported us.

I was leaving the office one evening, when I saw Joe Reilly leaning on a bicycle at the corner of Merrion Square. He called me over.

" Who is in that place you came out of? " he asked.

" I don't know who else is in there," I said, " but my office is there."

" Is it you has the insurance agency ? "

" Yes."

" Well, God blast you anyhow. I came down here to tag you."

Joe laughed,

"Wait till I tell the Big Fella this," he said. "They said they followed you to a house in Rathgar Avenue—a unionist house—and that your name was Kearney and that you worked in the Department of Agriculture."

"That's right, Joe," I said, "that is what I told my landlady."

"Holy bloody Cripes," said Joe, "wait till I tell this to Mick."

It transpired that Mrs. Carey had reported us to the local company of the I.R.A. The D.I. of the company having observed us for some time, reported us to the Battalion and the report went along until it finally reached Intelligence Headquarters which, of course, was Mick Collins.

Chapter Thirty-one

In March 1921, *General Sir Hubert Gough wrote of conditions in Ireland :*

" *Law and order have given place to a bloody and brutal anarchy in which the armed agents of the Crown violate every law in aimless and vindictive and insolent savagery.*"

—Macardle, *The Irish Republic*, p. 448.

MEANWHILE, in order to provide against the contingency of the capture of the Harcourt Place office, I had rented another. This was at 19 Kildare Street, on the first floor. I was disinclined to start another insurance office and was casting about for some other line of business, when Frank Gallagher told me that Jack Morrow, the artist, had invented a wonderful disinfectant, which was called " Iresol." He had put this on the market but the venture had failed. Jack handed over the whole business to me, including the stock in trade consisting of some hundreds of bottles of the stuff. So we put up a brass plate " Iresol, Ireland, Limited " on the door and stacked a lot of the bottles around the room.

Again we had trouble from an inquisitive landlady, who never saw any customers coming in. Mairin Ryan placated her by giving her a few bottles of Iresol, explaining at the same time that we only received wholesale orders, the goods being despatched from the factory at the North Wall.

Neither of the offices was ever captured, though we had many close shaves. I cycled down Merrion Street one morning and saw that the whole section in which my office was located was surrounded by the Tans. Without dismounting, I turned into Clare Street. I saw J. J. Walsh cycling southwards on the other side of the street. Seeing me, he dismounted and called out :

" Come here. I want to see you."

I went across and asked him what he wanted.

" How are you getting on ? " he asked.

" Look, J.J.," I said, " make an appointment for to-night and I'll tell you how I'm getting on. I'm not going to stop here."

301

He asked me why and, as he persisted, I told him the Tans were assembling in strength round the corner and, moreover, we were standing just in front of the cigarette shop over which Willie Cosgrave had his Local Government office. Furthermore, as the Tans were busy in the area, they were sure to have their touts hanging around.

"Where would they be?" asked J.J., looking about him.

"I don't know," I said. "That man over there, standing under the lamp-post might be one for all I know."

"I'll find out whether he is or not," said J.J. He left his bicycle standing by the kerb and approached the man under the lamp.

"What are you doing here?" he asked.

The man started violently and straightened up. He cast a startled glance at J.J.

"Oh, nothing, nothing," he said.

"And what," asked J.J., "do you mean by standing here, doing nothing?"

"Oh, nothing at all, nothing at all."

"Well," said J.J., pointing down Merrion Square, "you walk down that street and don't look to the right or the left of you."

With alacrity the man started off. His hands rigidly at his sides and his head craned forward, he walked down Merrion Square. From his demeanour, it looked as if he was going to walk to Dalkey before looking to right or left. J.J. returned to me and said with a grin :

"That's the way to find out whether they are touts or not."

This was typical of J.J. I remembered that on an earlier occasion he had cycled up to Eccles Street, where he was staying in Miss O'Donnell's house. He saw a couple of lorries and a raiding party of Tans outside the house. He dismounted at the corner and asked a big policeman who was standing there, what was up.

"They're searching for someone," said the policeman.

"Who would they be searching for?" asked J.J.

"I wouldn't know," was the reply.

"I'll tell you," said J.J. "They are searching for J. J. Walsh of Cork and that's me."

Whereupon he mounted his bicycle and rode off. When he had his barber's shop in North Frederick Street, military raiders in a lorry dashed up one day. Before they had time to enter, J.J. had taken his place in the customer's chair, drawn a towel around his neck and put on a heavy lather. He got away with it. In the early days, he was staying in a house in Rathmines, his host being a gentleman who could, by no means, be accused of being connected with Sinn Féin. J.J. was sitting at the fire, in his shirt sleeves, when there came a knock at the door. Restraining his host, J.J. went to the door and opened it. There were two D.M.P.-men outside.

" We are looking for J. J. Walsh," said one of them.

" What for ? "

" Never mind. Is he here ? "

" He's in there sitting down at the fire," said J.J.

The two policemen walked in and J.J. walked out.

On a later occasion, J.J. was making a speech at a public meeting when he noticed in the crowd a notorious G-man named Bruton.

" There's a man down there listening to me," said J.J. " He is in the pay of the enemy of our country. He is now making mental notes of what I am saying so as to report it to his paymasters. Well, here is something for him to make a note of. I advise him here and now, before it is too late, to hand over his gun to the rightful defenders of the liberty of this country—the I.R.A. And if he doesn't, I hope that his paymasters will see to it that his widow is compensated."

Bruton himself arrested J.J. shortly after this and at the subsequent trial, Bruton repeated J.J.'s words advising him to hand over his gun to the I.R.A. From the dock J.J. asked :

" Well, have you handed it over yet ? "

J.J. got a sentence of five years' penal servitude.

After I parted with J.J. in Clare Street, I cycled around the district to try to find out what the Tans were after. They seemed to hold the whole area, which included Westland Row, Brunswick Street (now Pearse Street) and

Denzille Street (now Fenian Street). They visited several houses and made a very thorough search of the Christian Brothers' schools in Cumberland Street. After nearly two hours they went off, apparently empty-handed. They had not entered the house where my office was. I found George Homan in sole possession. He had arrived before the encirclement and had watched the raiders from the windows. The other members of the staff, seeing the raiders, had veered off, as I had. They all turned up shortly afterwards and work was resumed at the Foreign Office.

A despatch from Harry Boland, our Envoy in Washington, said that an American journalist " who was really a British agent " was on his way to Ireland and that we were to be on our guard against him. I will call the journalist Tom Jones. In due course, he arrived and got in touch with me. Perhaps it is just as well to set out here how it was that such people coming to Ireland at this time could get in touch with people who were so badly wanted by the British authorities. It was fairly simple. The visitors, for the most part, stayed in the Shelbourne Hotel. As soon as they arrived they would ask the boots, or the head-waiter, or the doorman, how could they get in touch with the Sinn Féin leaders. As it was extremely dangerous to be in possession of such knowledge and as, moreover, the management abhorred Sinn Féin and everybody connected with it, the boots and everyone else professed ignorance. But one of our agents amongst the hotel staff passed the word along that Tom Jones, say, was making such enquiries and shortly afterwards Tom Jones would receive a visit from an innocent-looking person like Una and be conducted to one or other of our rendezvous.

Quite apart from the fact that Harry had said he was a British agent, I did not like Tom Jones at all. He was entirely too oily. He asked me a dozen questions bearing on the likelihood of a settlement, to which I returned the stock answers. He stressed the importance of the newspaper he represented and said he was anxious to get interviews with de Valera and Collins. I told him I would see what I could do.

Dev had moved to a house in Mount Merrion Avenue, Blackrock, a house standing in its own grounds, approached by a wide avenue. When I was admitted, I saw Dev crossing a landing with a pipe in his mouth.

" Don't tell me you are slipping," I said to him when he appeared.

" How ? "

" You made a vow you wouldn't smoke again."

" I wasn't smoking. Now and again I put an empty pipe in my mouth to pretend to myself I am smoking."

I told him of my interview with Tom Jones.

" Do you know he's a spy ? "

" Not a spy in the ordinary sense. I got the idea he may be here to study the psychology of the leaders. He is very anxious to interview you."

" No, I don't want to see him."

" He says he is in contact with very important people in England—people who can bring about a settlement."

"All the more reason why I should not see him. Tell him my opinion is that the British should publicly offer to negotiate a treaty with Ireland as a separate State. We can meet on this ground."

Mick, on the other hand, said he would meet Tom Jones.

" If he's an English agent, all the better," he said. " We'll see what's in their minds."

With Joe Hyland, our official driver, at the wheel, I drove to Miss Gavan Duffy's house in Stephen's Green and picked up Tom Jones. Joe drove through a bewildering succession of streets and left us down at a house in Ely Place, at the top of which Dora French had a flat. The place was only a couple of hundred yards from the Shelbourne Hotel, though we had driven a couple of miles. I brought Tom Jones up to the flat and returned to the hall to wait for Mick. He came in a few minutes, wheeling his bicycle into the hall. I noticed that his clothes were tighter-fitting than usual.

" You're getting fat," I said.

" I know I am. Is our man here ? "

" He's upstairs."

" Come on up."

I introduced the two men.

" I want to thank you, Mr. Collins," said Tom Jones, " for giving me this interview, particularly as you must be a very busy man."

" It's all in the day's work."

" I've a lot of questions I'd like to ask you."

" Fire away. But I want to tell you that you are not to publish the interview till we have seen the copy and given it the O.K."

" That's all right with me, Mr. Collins. Do you know what I think? You should come to America. You'd make a big splash there."

" Don't you think I'm making a big splash where I am ? "

" You most certainly are, Mr. Collins. Why, your name is becoming a legend."

Tom Jones continued in this strain, indulging in the most unabashed flattery, and Mick laughed heartily.

The interview lasted nearly an hour, at the end of which Mick went off on his bicycle.

" My God, what a man ! " said Tom Jones. " You'd think he hadn't a care in the world. Is he always like that ? "

"Always. Well, nearly always."

Again taking a circuitous route, I brought Tom Jones back to St. Stephen's Green.

The copy of the interview came next day and as there were no mistakes in it, it was O.K.'d.

A couple of weeks later, Tom Jones turned up again. He sent me a note saying he wanted to see M.C. again and he enclosed a poster which I was to show him. The poster had been issued by Tom Jones's newspaper. On it there were reproduced three photographs. The top one was that of Kemal Pasha and the caption said that the latter had been fighting for a long time in the mountains of Ankara, while several armies had tried, in vain, to kill or capture him. " Our Tom Jones went to Turkey and within a week he had secured an interview with Kemal Pasha."

The second photo was that of Lenin and there was a similar caption.

The third was M.C. "A hundred thousand police and soldiers had been trying for two years to kill or capture the elusive Michael Collins. Our Tom Jones went to Dublin and within twenty-four hours he had interviewed Michael Collins."

Now all this was, of course, perfectly justified if, as I do not doubt, Tom Jones had brought off these scoops, but I could not refrain from attaching a sheet of paper to the poster and writing : " T.J. certainly knows how to lay it on."

Mick was furious when he turned up in Ely Place on the following day.

" What the hell do you mean by that gibe about laying it on ? " he stormed.

" You can't take a joke, Mick."

" I don't want any jokes of that kind. Is he here ? "

" Yes. He's above. He did not say outright, but he hints he has been seeing Lloyd George. He thinks the time is ripe for a get-together."

" Well, come on up."

" No. He let me know he would like to see you alone."

" What the hell—oh, all right."

" Will I wait to bring him back ? "

" No. I'll see to that."

I saw Mick next day and he was in high good humour.

" I had a great laugh yesterday," he said. " When the interview was over, I walked out of the flat with him, wheeling my bicycle. We turned the corner and there was the Shelbourne. You should have seen his face. I shook hands with him at the door of the hotel, and roared laughing as I got up on my bicycle and rode away. His eyes and mouth were open like a fish. You should have seen him."

" I'd like to have seen that," I said. " But what about the flat. We may want to use it again."

" No. He won't be back. You'll know why when you see the interview."

" But what about Dora French ? "

" If Tom Jones is the sort of agent I think he is, he won't give the flat away. But I warned Dora French anyway, just in case."

The interview, when it came, showed M.C. as uncompromising as ever. He said that nothing short of an all Ireland republic would satisfy our demands, but the minority in the North would be given any necessary guarantees to ensure fair play.

The air was now thick with rumours of behind-the-scene negotiations. Mrs. Nugent, our former hostess in Upper Mount Street, had introduced Sir James O'Connor to Father O'Flanagan and singly or together, both had paid several visits to London exploring possible avenues for a settlement. Alfred Cope, the British Under-Secretary in Dublin Castle, was a party to these proceedings. Lord Derby had come to Dublin in disguise and interviewed de Valera, and there were numerous other would-be peace-makers coming and going.

Many English newspapers and journals were now violently attacking the British Government for its policy of " spreading ruin and death in Ireland " as the *Nation* put it. The *Manchester Guardian*, the *Daily News*, the *Westminster Gazette*, and even the London *Times* called loudly for a change in policy. Denunciations of the Government were being made by prominent figures such as H. H. Asquith, Sir John Simon, Lord Hugh and Lord Robert Cecil and the Archbishop of Canterbury.

Notwithstanding all this, Lloyd George not merely continued, but intensified the reign of terror, saying he had murder by the throat. The curfew hour was now eight o'clock and, as the days lengthened, it was a weird sight to see the streets completely deserted during the hours of broad daylight. Nothing living was to be seen save the dreaded raiding parties of Black and Tans and Auxiliaries.

Dev sent me a long telegram which I was to send to Sean T. O'Kelly, our Envoy in Paris. I cannot have been functioning very brightly that morning, or I would have realised the message was not for Sean T. I cycled into town and handed in the message in the temporary G.P.O. in O'Connell Street. The G.P.O., after its destruction in 1916, had not yet been rebuilt. When I got back to my office, I saw to my horror, a slip of paper which had become detached from Dev's communication. It said I was to send the message in code to Sean T., who was to cable it to America. I raced back to the office in O'Connell Street and found the clerk who had taken the message from me. I told him I wanted to make an alteration in it. He said I was too late as it had gone down to the telegraph trans- mission office in Amiens Street. I asked him if they would let me have it back there, and he said they might if I could convince them that I was the sender and if it had not already gone.

I hurried down to Amiens Street and saw, with dismay, that there were two soldiers, a policeman and a plain- clothes man guarding the doors of the telegraph office. I walked past them, hoping I was looking nonchalant. I made my request at the window and was referred to another window, where I was told I was too late as the message had gone to the telegraph room.

" Maybe it hasn't gone through yet," I said.

" I can't do anything about it now," said the clerk, " it has been entered."

Seeing my long face, he said :

" Why not send another message with the corrections ? "

" No," I said. " I'll leave it so," and walked out of the building. I immediately turned back and went in again, walking through the front office to the rear, hoping the clerk I had been talking to would not notice me. I ran up a stairs and found myself at a door looking into the telegraph room. There was a large number of operators working machines which clicked merrily away. I saw that my task was pretty hopeless, but I threw my hat on a desk outside the door and walked into the place.

The machines were in rows. I walked behind the backs of the operators, my eyes on the little piles of messages they were working on. My message was distinctive in shape, a larger than foolscap sized sheet. Everybody seemed to be extremely busy and I hoped no one was taking any notice of me but I feared to look around to see if they were. Most of the messages in front of the operators were ordinary telegraph forms. At the sixth or seventh machine my heart gave a leap. The girl was working on a message and beneath it was one that seemed like mine. I lifted the top message and took out the sheet. It was mine. The girl started and turned her head to look at me.

" Excuse me," I said, " this has to be altered."

I saw her eyes widen with suspicion and alarm. I walked away from her, feeling her eyes boring into my back. As leisurely as I could, I walked through the rows of machines, expecting to hear the girl scream. I reached the door and passed through. I did not wait to retrieve my hat. I ran down the stairs but forced myself to walk through the front office. Outside, I found that my bicycle, which I had placed against the kerb, had fallen down. Under the cold eyes of the police and soldiers I picked it up, mounted and rode away. I noticed then that my breathing was painful. I had been holding my breath too long.

I told Dev what I had done. He shook his head as he smiled at me.

" I wouldn't have done it," he said, " I'd have let the damn' thing go."

Chapter Thirty-two

In the early summer of 1921, British Government in Ireland had been brought almost to a standstill. Lloyd George had stated in the House of Commons that " the King's writ no longer runs in Ireland." In June 1921 he called for a truce.

I HAD received a code message from our undercover agent in Germany regarding a proposed landing of arms by a Zeppelin. I thought the scheme was impracticable and I was surprised when Collins showed some enthusiasm for it. Dev had asked me for the details and I met him in Madame O'Rahilly's house in Herbert Park, a rendezvous we sometimes used at this time. Dev asked me if I had been held up and when I said not, he told me he had been stopped by a foot patrol but he had not been searched. We discussed the Zeppelin scheme and Dev said he saw no reason why it could not be worked if a suitable landing-place could be found, sufficiently far from a British stronghold. The Curragh, which had been suggested, was, of course, out of the question.

There were some other matters we had to discuss and before we got through, Madame O'Rahilly came in to say that Mr. Childers had arrived.

" Oh, yes, of course," said Dev, going out with her. Nearly ten minutes passed and I was wondering whether I should go when Dev came in, full of apologies.

" I'm sorry, Bob," he said, " I didn't mean to leave you like that. Come on in here."

We went into a room across the hall, where Childers was standing staring out of a window. Anyone who did not know him would have said he was moody. But I knew him. He was deep in thought on some immediate problem.

" Come on," said Dev, " let us get at this."

We sat at a table and watched Dev with a compass finish a very neat drawing he had already begun. There were five separate and independent circles, all contained within a very large circle. Dev completed the design by drawing another circle outside the large circle, but contacting it.

311

" There you have it," said Dev, " the large circle is the British Commonwealth, having within it these five circles which are members of the Commonwealth. Outside the large circle, but having external contact with it, is Ireland."

This was the first I had heard of the scheme which came to be known as Document Number Two or External Association. Ireland was not to be a member of the Commonwealth, but was to be externally associated with it. I realised at once why the scheme had come into being. There were some of our people, right at the top, who believed that England would never concede an Irish Republic— an absolutely independent nation on her flank. And there were others, the vast majority, who held that nothing short of an absolutely independent Irish Republic would satisfy them or would be in accordance with the aspirations of all Irish republicans since the time of Wolfe Tone.

This plainly was a painstaking, sincere and well thought out plan to reconcile the two schools of thought. Personally, at first glance, I did not like it, but I could not but admire the rare political genius which had brought it into being.

Rightly or wrongly, I got the impression that Childers, at this stage, though willing to accept the plan, was not enthusiastic about it.

While we were still talking, Collins came in. Dev explained the design to him and Mick, who seemed to be thinking of something else, said nothing at all.

I left and walked some distance before I boarded a tram. At Baggot Street Bridge, the tram was held up and the passengers were ordered out to be searched by a mixed party of military and Black and Tans. I was on top of the tram and I was in a panic. Apart from the code messages from Germany, I had several other incriminating documents in my pockets. There was no escape whatsoever and I was beginning to resign myself to the inevitable, when I felt a tap on my shoulder. Looking round, I saw an American journalist, a man named Connelly, whom I had met a few days before.

He said quietly : " Have you got anything on you ? "
" I have."
He pushed his way in beside me.

" What have you got ? "

" These," I said, pulling out the papers.

" Let me have them."

" What about you ? "

" I've an American passport."

I gave him the papers and he stuffed them in his pockets. We went down and took our places in a queue to be searched. There were two lines of passengers being searched and questioned. I looked at the head of the line I was in and saw, to my dismay, that the questioner was the little officer who had had charge of me in Arbour Hill a couple of years earlier, the one who thought everything was so jolly. He was sure to recognise me. I looked about me. It was only three steps to the other line. I took the three steps and got into the other line, surprised that no one had taken any notice. My questioner was a stupid Auxiliary officer, who was half drunk. I got through.

I was back again on the top of the tram and my American friend joined me.

" It's a good job," he said, " they are not looking at you now, because you are giving yourself away."

" I know," I said.

The tram started off at long last and my friend gave me back the papers.

" I feel like a martyr," he said. "Just think of the wonderful copy I am passing up."

It was only a few days later—it was the 22nd June, 1921— when Sean Harling, Dev's special messenger, came into the office, breathless.

" They've got Dev," he said.

" You mean he's been taken ? "

" Yes, they were all over the place before we knew it. I have to tell the others. You are to see Austin Stack at once."

He raced off and I cycled over to Mary Street to see Stack. I was surprised to find that all Stack wanted was to ensure that every department carried on as usual. I thought that this assurance was unnecessary, but I did not say so. It did not strike me, at the time, that what was unusual

was that I was to see Stack and not Collins. At the time
A.G. had been arrested, Collins had become Acting-
President and, of course, he had relinquished this post when
Dev returned from America. Was it the case that Dev had
appointed Stack as Acting-President and not Collins ?

The question had hardly formed itself in my mind, when
to the amazement of everybody, himself included, Dev was
released. He had been told to remain in the house in
Blackrock and there await a letter.

A day or two later Dev received Lloyd George's invitation
to a conference, and thereafter there followed a bewildering
succession of events : Dev's conversations with the Southern
Unionists, the Truce, the prison releases, the protracted
correspondence between Dev and Lloyd George and the
subsequent negotiations which were to end in the ill-fated
Treaty.

Overnight almost, our offices were transferred to the
Mansion House, where we greeted friends we had long lost
sight of because they, too, had been working underground.
There, too, we met friends newly out of jail, A.G., Bob
Barton, Eamon Duggan, Michael Staines. The feeling of
elation which had swept the country following the truce,
permeated the Mansion House to no little extent. Dev
found it necessary to issue a proclamation warning against
undue confidence and calling for a continuance of the
determination and fortitude which had sustained the people
in the struggle. But his words, for the most part, fell on
deaf ears. Few people believed that the fight would be
resumed. Those who remembered that England, often
beaten in the field, had won a victory at the council table,
thought that Dev was a match for any and all of them.
And his tenacity and farsightedness during the correspondence, in refusing to be trapped by Lloyd George into an
abandonment of the Republican position prior to the
conference, strengthened their belief in him.

On the 14th of September, Dev was handed a message.
He glanced at it, half rose from the table and sat down
again.

" Damn, damn, damn ! " he said, and threw the message
on the table. A.G. picked it up, read it and handed it to

me. It was from Gairloch in Scotland, whither Joe
McGrath and Harry Boland had gone to deliver a letter to
Lloyd George. The message sent by Joe and Harry was
to the effect that paragraph two of the letter was unaccept-
able to Lloyd George who strongly urged that the meeting
of the Dail called for that day should be postponed.

" I told them," said Dev, " that they were not to discuss
the terms of that letter with him, didn't I ? "

" Of course you did," said A.G.

Outside in the Round Room the Dail was assembling.

" What are you going to do ? " asked A.G.

" I'm going to do what I told them was the programme.
Get the Dail to sanction the letter and publish it. Don't
you agree ? "

" Of course. It's the only thing to do."

Dev explained the position to the Dail and unanimously
the letter was sanctioned and ordered to be published.
Later, Dev took me aside and said he was worried. He
had had no reply to the protesting telegram he had sent
to Joe and Harry.

" Well," I said, " isn't it obvious that they are on their
way back ? "

" Why ? "

" To have the letter altered."

" They'll have to be stopped," he said. " They must
not be allowed to bring back that letter. How are we
to stop them ? "

I figured out from a map and a timetable, that if they
had left Gairloch after telephoning, they would probably
catch the night boat at Holyhead. The night boat from
Dunlaoghaire would dock at Holyhead an hour before they
were due there. He asked me if I would go over on the
chance of intercepting them. I, of course, said I would.
I had just time to catch the boat.

Dev drove me to Dunlaoghaire and, on the way, we
discussed the plenipotentiaries whom the Dail, on his
recommendation, had appointed that day. They were
A.G., Collins, Barton, Eamon Duggan and Gavan Duffy.
Dev thought it was a good team. Collins and Barton were
a good counter-balance to Griffith.

When I got on the boat I had the idea I might miss my men at Holyhead. I managed to get hold of a steward who knew Joe McGrath and I enlisted his aid. He was to watch one gangway while I took the other. As it happened, there was no need of these precautions for the first people to walk down the pier were Joe and Harry. When I intercepted them, their surprise was comical.

" What's up ? " they asked.

" Have you got the letter ? "

" No."

" Has Lloyd George got it ? "

" Well, he has and he hasn't. He said he would take the attitude he has not received it till it's altered."

" But it's in his possession."

" Yes."

"All right. You can go aboard."

I found a telephone and called Dev and reported. He was greatly relieved. In their stateroom, Harry and Joe were staring at each other. Harry turned to me.

" What's the matter ? " he asked.

" You should not have sent that message."

They both began to swear. There was nothing wrong with the message they sent.

" What happened ? " I asked.

Harry, with his love of the dramatic, re-enacted the scene.

" We arrived at Gairloch, having driven sixty miles in an open car, perished. I said to Joe, ' If he asks me to take a drink, I'll be hard put to it to keep the promise I made to myself.' Outside the house there was a *Daily Mail* man who asked us if we were from Ireland. When I said ' Yes,' he said : ' He'll give you two republics to-day. He's after catching a ten-pound salmon.' Just then Lloyd George came around a corner of the house, a lively little man with pink cheeks like a baby, clear blue eyes and venerable flowing soft white hair. He literally ran to us, crying, 'Are you the boys from Ireland ? ' We said we were and he shook our hands warm-heartedly and impul- sively. ' Wait till I show you the salmon I caught,' he said. He ran off and returned holding the salmon aloft.

' Isn't it grand ? ' he cried. He handed the salmon to
someone standing by and ushered us into a room. ' Have
a drink,' he said, ' I have some good Irish whiskey.' No,
we weren't drinking. ' Sherry ? ' No, no sherry either.
'As you will. Sit down and make yourselves at home.
You know I'm always glad to meet an Irishman. I know
where I am with them, being a Celt myself. I can never
feel the same with these cold-hearted Saxons.' He talked
for a while on the superiority of the Celtic character over
that of the Anglo-Saxon and then turned to us gleefully,
like a boy expecting a new toy.

" ' Well, I hope you've got good news for me.'

" Joe gave him the letter and he began to read it. His
face grew serious as he ran down the page. Still reading
the letter, he sat down frowning. Then he collapsed.

" ' My God ! ' he groaned. ' My God ! He can't mean
this.' He glanced at the letter again and put his hand
wearily to his head. 'After all I said to him he does this
to me. You must alter this letter, boys.' Joe explained
that his instructions were not to interpret the contents of
the letter. Lloyd George sat for a while as if dazed and I
began to pity him. 'A chance missed,' he said and he
repeated this three or four times. 'A wonderful chance
missed.' He was very sad. ' Here we had a unique opportunity. I was at the head of a coalition government with
the Tories in the leash. I could have given de Valera all
the realities he wanted, an Ireland with its own Gaelic
system of education, its own army and police force, its own
flag, its own anthem, the wherewithal to work out its own
destiny as a free and independent Gaelic nation, and this
man spurns it all for a phrase. I asked him not to use that
phrase—" a sovereign nation "—which means nothing at all
if you do not have the essentials. He could have had everything but the name, and he throws it away. He throws me,
too, on the scrap-heap. To-day I was the Prime Minister
of the strongest government Britain has had for generations.
To-morrow, when this letter sees the light of day, I will be
no longer Prime Minister but merely a country solicitor.'
He was pacing up and down the floor, speaking more to
himself than to us, the picture of a man in a desperate fix.

'What's the alternative?' he went on. 'I resign and let loose the dogs of war in Ireland. Now let the Wilsons, the Birkenheads and the Churchills have their way. They boast they'll make Ireland a desert and who's going to stop them? Not de Valera! Not me! My power is at an end.'

"All the time we were getting more and more miserable. Lloyd George turned to us.

'Could you not appeal to him to alter this letter?'

"'It would be no use,' Joe said, 'The Dail is meeting today to sanction it.'

"Lloyd George, who had sat down, jumped to his feet excitedly. 'That must be stopped,' he cried, 'that must be stopped at all costs. You must telephone to him. There is too much at stake in this to have it lost over any pettifogging. We can yet save the day for Ireland and Britain both. We can do it, but that letter must be altered. Look, I'll tell you what I'll do. I'll take the attitude I have not read this letter, you telephone to de Valera telling him to alter it. Get back there and tell him the situation. He must see it. He must see it!'

"We were doubtful and he said—

"'You want to discuss this alone. Very well, I'll go. Ring that bell when you want me!' He went off and left us and there we were with the destiny of a nation in our hands and we had only to ring the bell for the Prime Minister to save it. We decided to telephone Dublin and report what he had said, and we rang the bell. When he came in he was all smiles and encouragement.

"'Send that message,' he said, 'and believe me, boys, we will save the day for Ireland.'

"So that's how it happened," concluded Harry. "Is Dev raging?"

"Well, he's knocked about," I said. "He thought you were bringing back the letter."

"No damn' fear," said Joe.

In Blackrock Harry and I invaded Dev's bedroom. He was asleep, but he woke up as we entered.

"The message was bungled," said Harry.

Dev glanced at his dejected countenance.

"Don't worry," he said kindly.

" Do you know what he said," began Harry, and Dev stopped him.

" I know," he said, " he told you he was a Celt, he wanted us to have our free Gaelic civilisation.   He was holding back the British bulldog from destroying us.   He said all that to me.   He said that if he accepted my terms he would no longer be Prime Minister and I said if I accepted less, I would no longer be President of the Irish Republic."

" If he didn't mean what he said," said Harry, " he must be the greatest actor that was ever born."

" Of course he is," said Dev.   "After all, the man who beat Clemenceau and Wilson and Orlando is no joke.   All right, Harry.   There's no harm done.   Go and get your breakfast." *

*NOTE.—I showed the proofs of this passage to Joe McGrath and his comment was—

" I have a very clear recollection of what occurred.   I handed the letter to Lloyd George, he read as far as ' a Sovereign Nation ' and immediately became enraged and spoke to us on the lines you have written.   My answer was that my instructions were very definite—they were ' do not attempt any interpretation of the document.'

" He suggested I take the letter back which I refused to do ; he then said he would treat the letter as not having been received and left us to talk it over.

" We did so and rang the bell.   When Lloyd George came in we told him his suggestion would not meet the case as the Dail was meeting next day when the document would be made public.   He immediately said there had been a definite agreement that no publication would take place unless and until both parties had agreed to publication.   This I knew to be the case and I suggested that I would convey by telephone his objection to the publica- tion—this was in accordance with my instructions.   Lloyd George again went out, this time to enquire regarding telephone facilities.   When he returned he told us that the nearest was Inverness—80 miles away.   He also told us he had dispatched his personal Press Representative to Inverness by fast car to hold open the lines to Dublin until we reached Inverness.

" He then proceeded to talk like a father to us and wound up by asking what arrangements we had made to return to Ireland as he was in doubt as to whether we would arrive before hostilities were resumed.

" When we arrived after midnight at Inverness I got through to the Mansion House, Dublin.   I spoke with the late Desmond Fitzgerald on a very bad line.   I told him I had delivered the letter.   I repeated four or five times Lloyd George's objection to the publication.   Desmond Fitzgerald asked me had I not told him of the proposed Dail meeting.   I said I had and that it was then he, Lloyd George, raised the objection to the publication.

" I don't know what message was conveyed to Mr. De Valera as a result of the telephone call but I do know that neither Harry Boland nor I discussed the contents of the document with Lloyd George.   He spoke at us rather than to us and we listened."

Chapter Thirty-three

On October 9th, Arthur Griffith headed five Irish plenipotentiaries who went to London with a view " to ascertaining how the association of Ireland with the community of nations known as the British Empire may be best reconciled with Irish national aspirations."

GRIFFITH was plainly worried by the task confronting him as head of the plenipotentiaries. Usually he was very taciturn, but now he kept pelting de Valera with questions. He was aware that the out-and-outers, led by Mary MacSwiney, were holding forth every day about what would happen if there was any compromise. He was aware, too, that many shared his view that the British would never concede the Republic pure and simple and he feared the result of a break.

" Look here," he said one day to Dev, " you said last night we were to manoeuvre the British into leaving over the question of the Crown till last. Supposing they refuse to do this ? "

" Well, you can put it to them that we ought first of all discuss the things there will be no great dispute about."

" But supposing they insist on considering the question of the Crown first ? "

" You can only use your powers of persuasion. After all, they cannot want to have a break the first day."

Griffith persisted and Dev stood up from the table saying :

" Well, there you have the situation. You'll have to make the best of it."

" Oh, wait now, Mr. President. That won't do."

" Why ? "

" It's not enough to say ' make the best of it.' "

" I'm not talking about a settlement," said Dev, " I'm talking about the method of handling the negotiations. You see, if we get them to concede this and this and this and this, and then come to a stumbling-block, like the question of the Crown, which they say is a formula, then

we can put the question before the world and point out
that they want to renew the war on us for a formula."

Griffith smiled wryly.

" It's all right if you can do it," he said.

Larry Ginnell had been sent on a mission to South
America. He sent me a cable from the Argentine saying
that a Dail Eireann loan, if floated there, was certain to
succeed. He asked permission to float the loan. I saw
Mick about this and he took the telegram and said he
would look after it. I cabled Larry saying the matter was
being considered. A week passed and Larry cabled again
urging a quick response. I saw Mick again and he said :

" I told you I was looking after it."

Within a week there were three further cables from
Buenos Ayres. I said to A.G. that the man at least should
get an answer, yes or no.

" Certainly," said A.G., who was just going into a
Cabinet meeting. " I'll bring it up and get a decision."

Over an hour later, I was in the front room of the Mansion
House with a group which included Miss Fitz, Harry
Boland and Frank Gallagher. Collins looked into the
room.

" Where are you ? " he said.

" I'm here," said Harry.

Mick saw me and barged over to me.

" What the hell," he said, "do you mean by butting into
my department ? What do you know about Finance ? "

" Maybe nothing much," I said, as quietly as I could,
" but I certainly know more about Finance than you do
about manners."

Mick opened his mouth to say something but, apparently,
couldn't find words. He turned to Harry.

" Come on," he said and stalked out.

Harry came over to me.

" That's good," he said. " That's the right way to take
him. He'll think over that now and it will do him all the
good in the world."

Mick was unusually nice to me next day.

A few days before the plenipotentiaries were to go to

London for the opening of the Conference, A.G. suggested I should take advantage of the occasion and make a tour of Europe visiting our Envoys. I realised, at once, that this suggestion was as much in the interest of my health as of the service. I had had what was tantamount to a break-down in the previous February and had been forced to lay off for a couple of weeks. Though I returned to my desk, I had been in poor shape all through the Spring and Summer. When the Truce came, instead of getting better, I got worse.

I was glad to avail of A.G.'s generous gesture. Eamon Duggan, who was our liaison officer with the Castle, was arranging for my passport. At the last moment, he told me I would have to pick it up in London. I was to call to a number in Downing Street—I think it was No. 9—and ask for Mr. Alfred Cope. I knew that Cope, who was the Under-Secretary at Dublin Castle, had played a very big part in bringing about the Truce, but no one was quite sure which side he was on.

When I saw him in Downing Street, he was very pleasant. He hoped I would have a very good trip. Where was I going exactly ?

" I'm not quite sure. I'll go to France, Spain and Switzerland and, possibly, Italy and Germany."

" I had thought you might be in on the negotiations here—or is this visit to Europe more important ? "

" Well," I said, grinning at him, " since you want to know, this visit to Europe is very important. I'm going to arrange that when the fight starts again, we will be sure we have adequate supplies of armaments."

" You will have your little joke," he said, and handed me the passport.

I was walking back to my hotel when my eye caught a doctor's name on a door. On an impulse, I said to myself I would hear what he had to say and walked in. The doctor, a big hearty man, asked me what was wrong and I said I didn't know.

" But why did you come to me ? "

" I saw your name outside and I walked in. I haven't been myself for many months."

He made a very thorough examination of me and said he could find nothing wrong. He looked at me for a long time.

" Do you take a drink ? " he said.

" Now and again. Very rarely. Just a bottle of stout at odd times."

" Did you ever get drunk ? "

" Never. At least, not since I was a youngster when I drank a lot of rum thinking it was a temperance beverage."

" That's it," he said, " you're too sober. Go and get drunk, just for once."

" That's about the funniest medical advice I ever heard," I said.

" Isn't it," he said, with a grin, as he pocketed his fee, which was ten and sixpence.

I crossed to France that night and next day rounded up a few Irish friends in Paris. I told them that on the doctor's orders I had something very special to do that night and that was to get drunk. They thought it was a grand idea and they volunteered to help me. We had a wonderful dinner in a restaurant on the Grand Boulevard and my friends proceeded to make me drunk. We had several sorts of wines at the dinner and afterwards a great assortment of liqueurs. I joyously partook of all the drinks and I remained dead sober. I was glad of this because I had to help all my friends home and put them to bed.

The next day, however, I was a new man. The black cloud which had hovered over me for many months was gone and as I walked out into the sunshine, I felt like singing out loud.

Sean T. O'Kelly, our Envoy, was installed in the Grand Hotel. He knew and was on familiar terms with many members of the French Administration and though, of course, he was not officially recognised, he was in touch with the various ambassadors of foreign countries. One of the men he saw very often was a Turkish agent to whom he introduced me. I have, unfortunately, forgotten this gentleman's name. He told us that the people of his part of Turkey claimed to be of Celtic stock and, indeed, he looked like a Tipperary farmer. This was the man who, thanks to the contacts Sean T. had been able to make for him, afterwards concluded the secret agreement with the French Government, as a result of which France withdrew from the Allied invasion of Turkey, leaving England holding the bag, an event which brought about the downfall of Lloyd George.

From France I went to Spain. Here Maire O'Brien was in charge. In spite of the fact that there was not even provision for a paid secretary on her staff, she was doing Trojan work. She had enlisted the support of an enthusiastic body of volunteer workers, mostly university students. She was sending out every day the Spanish version of the Irish *Bulletin* and she had already completed the translation of Ireland's Address to the Elected Representatives of the various countries. This was being sent, not merely to the Spanish deputies, but also to the elected representatives of all the Latin-American countries. Not only that, but almost every day she visited the offices of *El Sol* and *A.B.C.*, and the other Spanish newspapers, keeping the editors in touch with day-to-day happenings in Ireland.

In Madrid, too, I had an opportunity of observing at first hand the ubiquity of the British Intelligence Service. A friend of mine introduced me to an Irish-American, whom I shall call "Coogan." He was very affable and, I thought, well informed on the Irish situation. At our first interview, he completely took me in, though there was nothing serious discussed on that occasion. A few days later, however, he invited me to dinner with a lady friend of his and I noticed he was mixing the drinks in a most amazing manner, while he talked of Sir Roger Casement from whom he had had many letters which he showed me. He produced a handy machine-gun, which he assured me he could supply to us in thousands at a reasonable figure. After dinner, when we had left the lady home, he led the way to a little café, where he ordered more drinks. He told me of contacts he had had with friends of mine in London and Dublin and then he began to wonder how we managed to get our guns and ammunition through the British blockade. Now all my suspicions were awakened and I amused myself by giving him voluminous details regarding the supplies of arms we received and how they were delivered, mainly through the instrumentality of various British officers whom I named, and who, of course, had no existence. He left me now and again under some pretext, but really to make notes. I have often wondered since what his employers thought of the report he made.

A couple of days later—I had been avoiding Coogan in the meantime—I came out of my hotel bedroom one morning to find on the landing a young man exquisitely dressed, reading a printed notice on the wall. He turned to me and said in an English accent :

" Say, have you read these regulations ? "

I looked at him in surprise and then, thinking he was addressing someone else, I made to pass him.

" It's important," he said, " these are police regulations."

" Well, what has that to do with me ? "

" You are very obviously a stranger," he said. " I thought you were English, but now I can tell by your accent you are Irish. I'd advise you to register with the police, if you have not already done so."

By this time, he was accompanying me down the stairs. " You see, if you stay more than twenty-four hours you are supposed to register. The Spanish police can be very nasty. For instance, I had an experience this morning. I got into a row with a fellow named Coogan—a country-man of yours—you know him, no doubt."

" I can't say I do," I lied.

He expressed surprise and went on to talk disparagingly of Coogan. By this time, we were in the street and he was offering to accompany me to the police station. I stopped abruptly, and said :

" I thank you for trying to assist me, but I'm not interested. Goodbye."

He left me with a very ill grace. During the rest of my stay in Madrid, I was followed all the time. When I got back to Ireland, I found my suspicions regarding Coogan were justified. Sean T. told me he had heard of his activities in New York. He was surprised to hear he was alive, because he had been told that Coogan had been shot as a spy in America.

Chapter Thirty-four

The Anglo-Irish Treaty was signed in London on December 6th, 1921. De Valera immediately denounced its terms as being in violent conflict with the wishes of the Irish nation. Dail Eireann recommended the acceptance of the Treaty by a vote of 64 to 57.

EVERYWHERE I went on the Continent I had evidence that we had broken through the paper wall with which England had surrounded us. Everywhere people recalled the story of " Le pauvre Lord Maire," Terence MacSwiney, and I was pressed for particulars of Ireland's struggle for freedom. At Salamanca the students in the College of The Noble Irish were hungry for news from the homeland. With Father Fitzgerald, the Vice-Rector of the College, I visited many historic places—the door whence St. Teresa emerged from making her first confession, the gate through which Columbus entered to kneel and pray before setting out on his voyage of discovery. In the grounds of the Franciscan monastery, we stood on a hillock and gazed on the beautiful city, its spires, towers, minarets and cupolas all shining like old gold in the setting sun. If the ancient city was no longer the centre of European learning, it was still the loveliest sight I had seen in Spain, except, perhaps, Toledo, sitting aloft embattled on its mighty crag over the Tagus.

In Barcelona, a watchmaker who repaired my watch, refused to accept any payment when he learned I was from Ireland. In Geneva, Michael MacWhite introduced me to an Egyptian gentleman who was full of plans to break the power of the English in Egypt, one of them being the introduction of Irishmen to lead a revolt. They were to be camouflaged as students. The talk was more or less general. I did not like the Egyptian, but I told him I would have the plan considered in Dublin.

In Berlin, I was met by Miss Nancy Power who, with John Chartres, was looking after our interests there. Chartres

The Change-over. British troops leaving one of their strongholds : Portobello Barracks, Dublin, May, 1922.

[*National Museum of Ireland*]

The Change-over. Irish troops entering Portobello Barracks, May, 1922.

[National Museum of Ireland]

had been called to London to advise the Plenipotentiaries.
Nancy told me that John T. Ryan was anxious to see me
without delay. This was the first time I had heard the real
name of our under-cover agent in Berlin. He had always
been referred to as Mr. Jetter. Ryan was a well-known
Irish-American, who had had to fly from New York to
escape arrest for his anti-British intrigues with the Germans.

He was an unprepossessing man with a large, unsmiling
face and he was dressed in rumpled homespuns. He asked
me how the London business was going on. I told him all
that had happened up to the time I left and said I had had
no inside information since. I asked him if he knew anything about Coogan but he could not remember anything
about him. When, however, I mentioned the Egyptian
gentleman in Geneva, he consulted a notebook and said :
" He's dangerous. What did you tell him ? "
" Nothing at all," I said. " I did not like him."
" I'll tell you all about him to-morrow," he said, and he
did. He turned up with a complete dossier on the activities
of the Egyptian for two years. He was a very active British
agent. At the end of the recital, I began to have more
respect for the German Secret Service.

Ryan was scathing about the manner in which our people
had handled the purchase of arms in Germany and showed
me a list of thousands of machine-guns and rifles which
were to be had at very low figures. He had a plan for
shipping these on a German boat with an Irish pilot,
through the port of Hamburg, the harbour master there
being the famous Hans Spindler, formerly captain of the
Aud, the German ship which had been captured by the British
in 1916 and later sunk by its crew while being escorted to
Cobh. Captain Spindler was willing to do anything to help
and Ryan assured me that the German authorities would
wink at the proceedings. I took notes for a very full report.

Ryan introduced me to two gentlemen from India, for
whose bona fides he vouched. The first was a very big
and prosperous gentleman (Mr. A.), who told me he
belonged to the constitutional wing of the Indian Nationalists. He owned a lot of chain stores in India. He assured
me he was willing to fall in with any plan the second Indian,

whose name was Bomanji, and I agreed to. He did not
know what Mr. Bomanji had in mind and he did not want
to know. The less he knew the better. He then withdrew
and Mr. Bomanji came in. He was a small, quick, intelli-
gent gentleman and he told me at once that he belonged
to the militant group in India. His plan was twofold.
Firstly, the Indian Moslem League and the All Indian
Congress Party were, for the first time, holding their annual
conventions in the same town and on the same date. It
had been agreed between the leaders that at a pre-arranged
signal, a motion would be put forward simultaneously in
both conventions that the rival sects would join hands for
the purpose of ending the British occupation. They were
then to meet jointly and set up a Provisional Government
for India and, thereafter, carry on on Sinn Féin lines.
Our part was to send one or two advisers who would,
behind the scenes, guide the movement. It was necessary
that these advisers should get to India as soon as possible
before the day set for the Conventions. The other plan
of Bomanji's was to prepare for a guerrilla war against the
British. For this purpose, he needed a number of Irish
guerrilla leaders, twenty or thirty to start off with. They
would ostensibly be employed in the chain stores owned
by Mr. A., but their real work would be to train companies
of selected men in the science of guerrilla warfare.

Ryan, who was present all the time, assured me that
German aid was available to enable the men from Ireland
to get to India without having to utilise British routes. I
agreed to convey all this to the proper quarter. It was
arranged that I was to give my answer to Mr. A. before
the 21st of December. I was then to meet him in the very
exclusive and Tory Carlton Club in London.

On the following day when I called to see Ryan, he was
in a towering rage. In his ill-fitting homespun clothes, he
was striding up and down the room, his usually lardy face
and bald dome crimson with fury. There was froth on his
lips as he kept hurling at me phrases such as "A god-damn'
parcel of traitors "—"A pack of weak-kneed backsliders "
" They're worse than the snakes Saint Patrick drove out
of Ireland." Finally, when I managed to ask him for an

explanation, he turned on me so savagely that I thought he was going to strike me.

" I sacrificed everything for you swine," he said, " and now you've sold us all down the river."

With great difficulty I managed to keep my temper and said I didn't know what he was talking about. He handed me a telegram, of which the following is a copy :

POSTAL TELEGRAPH—COMMERCIAL CABLE
Delivery NO C H
DINY K   105 AM   44 VIA RADIO
   Berlin NOV 8 (1921)
McGARRITY
   923 Walnut St. PHILA
   ONLY GREAT PRESSURE ON TRUSTEES IN L. BY DIRECTORS AT HOME WILL SAVE SURRENDER OF FREE TITLE TO OLD HOMESTEAD.   ALL TRUSTEES WEAKENING INCLUDING M.C.   TOPMAN STANDS FIRM AND STRONG.   CORRECT OFFICIAL INFORMATION FROM INSIDE
JETTER

Jetter was the name Ryan used in cabling to Joe McGarrity in Philadelphia. The meaning of the telegram was that the five plenipotentiaries in London, including Collins, were weakening and that Dev was standing firm.

" This was sent over three weeks ago," I said.

" Yes."

" Why didn't you tell me about it yesterday, or the day before ? "

" I wanted to see whether you would tell me what is going on over there."

" Where did you get this information ? "

" From the people who know what they're talking about —the German Foreign Office."

" I think their information is wrong," I said. " I don't believe one word of it."

Next day, John Chartres arrived from London. I discussed with him the contents of Ryan's cable. He said the report was exaggerated but, at the same time, he was very gloomy over the expected outcome of the negotiations.

" The British," he said, " are more adroit than we are.

They've split up the plenipotentiaries. I was disgusted at the cynical and ribald conversations I heard between Churchill and some of our people. I'm afraid we are going to lose."

On the train from Basle to Berlin, I had met a Mr. Weiner and his wife. He was a German who had spent several years in America where he had an interest in a whole lot of trade journals. He and I had discussed a plan for setting up a world news agency to combat the influence of Reuters. I saw him a few times after I arrived in Berlin and one night in the Hotel Eden I had him and his wife, as well as Nancy Power and John Chartres, to dinner. Halfway through the dinner, Nancy said the newsboys were calling a special edition and, at her request, a waiter brought a paper.

On the front page was the announcement that a treaty had been signed in London on the basis of Dominion Home Rule and exclusion of the Six Counties. I set out for home that night. In Paris, I found Sean T. O'Kelly, our Envoy, Leopold Kerney, our Consul, and all the office staff bewildered and furious at the turn of events. In Dublin I found the split. Sneering and cynical gibes at the diehards on the one hand, were met by ready taunts of " traitors " and " treachery " on the other. Dev had denounced the Treaty and all the newspapers were belabouring him. Almost the first person I encountered when I went to the Mansion House, was Griffith. He came over to me, smiling and cheerful.

" What do you think of it ? " he asked.

" I think you've made an awful mistake."

He flushed.

" Have you read the terms ? "

" I have."

" Do you realise what we've got ? "

" I do," I said. " You got a great deal, but you've also got British sovereignty and partition."

" It does not mean partition," he said stiffly. " Under Clause Twelve we'll get at least two of the six counties, Tyrone and Fermanagh and possibly other areas, such as South Armagh and South Down."

He said that Lloyd George was convinced that this was the case. The Boundary Commission was to allocate such territories in accordance with the wishes of the inhabitants.

He could not, of course, have then foreseen that the Boundary Commission, which was set up long after he was in his grave, was to interpret Clause Twelve as meaning that the boundary which separated the Six Counties from the rest of Ireland was to be rectified by transferring a townland here and there from one or the other side of the Border to the opposite side.

Nor did he or I know that this same Lloyd George had sent to Sir Edward Carson a secret letter saying that " We must make it clear that Ulster does not, whether she wills it or not, merge in the rest of Ireland."

I could see that A.G.'s heart was torn by the thought that his signature to the Treaty might be repudiated. He asked me if I realised that the alternative was war.

" I don't believe that."

" Would you accept the alternative of war ? "

" I know it's a frightful choice, but at least we would all be together."

" The person who talks like that is a fool," said he.

" Well, A.G.," I said, " I don't care what names you call me. I'll never call you any."

He smiled wryly and went out, but he continued to treat me on the old terms, though he was very sore at everyone else who opposed the Treaty. During the heated Dail debates over the settlement, when the bitterness of party feeling was in full tide, he came over to me one day during an adjournment. He was searching the jumbled contents of his pockets.

" I'm bringing a man, some American, to lunch," he said, " and I have no money."

I gave him a couple of pounds. It was several months afterwards when he sent the money back to me with a note of apology for the delay. Many months later, after the outbreak of the Civil War, my house was being raided by a party of Free State soldiers and they came upon this note. Seeing it, they decided they had come to the wrong house and they promptly left.

After the Dail had approved of the Treaty, Dev had resigned the Presidency and he had been proposed for re-election. He was defeated by a very narrow margin—58 for, 60 against—and Griffith was elected in his place.

In his capacity as President, Dev had occupied a house in Kenilworth Square. He decided to vacate this and he asked me to tell Griffith (they were now working in separate rooms in the Mansion House) that he wanted someone to call at the house next day to receive the keys. A.G. pulled his moustache and fidgeted with his tie.

" What does he want to do a thing like that for ? " he asked. " Tell him he can stay in that house as long as he likes."

I went back to Dev, but he was adamant. He asked me to tell Griffith that he would definitely leave the house next day. A.G. was genuinely distressed. He said he would send no one for the keys and asked me to make a personal appeal to Dev to change his mind. I went back to Dev and told him this and added : " Why not talk to him yourself ? "

" What's the use ? " said Dev.

" You never know," I said, " it might do some good."

" Who's with him ? "

" Nobody."

"All right, tell him I'll come in to see him."

I went back to A.G., and he was frankly pleased.

" I'll go to him," he said. He came back with me and the meeting between the two was cordial. I was about to leave but both of them asked me to stay. We sat around a table and for nearly fifteen minutes the talk was on generalities. There was no mention of the house in Kenil-worth Square.

" Look here, Griffith," said Dev, " the way I feel about all this is that we are going from bad to worse if we don't get together."

" That's certainly so," said Griffith.

" It shouldn't be impossible for us to find a formula to enable us to work together."

" I agree."

" It's a great opportunity," said Dev, " and what I feel

about it is that we have the game in our hands if we handle
it right."

" True."

" We have the ball at our feet, so to speak," said Dev,
" and we can win for Ireland with the whole team playing
as one." He paused a moment. " Suppose we try to find
a basis? "

" But we have it," said Griffith, " we have it in the
Treaty."

" You mean the basis is acceptance of the Treaty ? "

" Sure."

Dev threw up his hands and the conference was at an end.

Chapter Thirty-five

The Republican forces were split, pro-treaty and anti-treaty. The pro-treaty (Free State) Volunteers occupied Dublin Castle and the military barracks, vacated by the British. The anti-treaty (Republican) Volunteers occupied the Four Courts and other buildings.

I WAS busy preparing for the Irish Race Congress in Paris. The date of this had been fixed a long time before there was any thought of negotiations with England. The idea had been to mobilise Irish help throughout the world in the struggle for independence, as well as to establish a world organisation for the fostering of cultural and economic relations with Ireland. Now it had become obvious that dissension at home would jeopardise the scheme. Matters reached such a stage that the delegation appointed by the Dail to attend the Congress was divided into two groups, one representing the pro-treaty party and the other the anti-treaty. I found that I even had to divide the finances for the expenses of the delegation, each section insisting on having its own treasurer. One evening I went down to Westland Row Station to see Madame Markievicz and some others of the delegates off to Paris. Outside the station there was a huge crowd and the volunteer police were busy keeping the crowds in order. I wondered if the crowd was there to see the delegates off, but when I had, with some difficulty, made my way to the platform, I learned from some of our friends that the crowd had assembled to hurl final insults at the departing Black and Tans. When the train pulled out, I accompanied half a dozen of my friends to the street. The crowd still lingered and I noticed a boy running beside us, peering into the faces of some members of our party. Suddenly, he turned and ran back to the crowd, crying : " It's them ! " I thought the boy had taken one of the ladies in the group for the Countess and that we were in for a demonstration, but, on looking back, I saw that they were anything but sympathetic. Then I heard a cry :

334

" Down with the Black and Tans ! Down with the bloody Tans ! "

We were being taken for some of the people who attended to give the Black and Tans a friendly send-off. I saw there was no time to be lost and I shouted to my friends to hurry along. I faced the mob hoping to reason with them. None of the Volunteers was in sight and the angry crowd came rushing on. A stone whizzed past my head. Turning, I saw my friends standing bewildered at the corner of Merrion Street. I ran towards them and herded them into a little shop. I had barely got the door closed when the mob charged. Amid cries of " Kill the bastards " the door was bombarded and the windows smashed. The lady proprietor of the shop was terrified for our safety. She had wanted to eject us, until we convinced her we were anything but friends of the Black and Tans. The siege continued for some time, until a Volunteer Officer turned up. We explained the situation to him, but all his endeavours to explain it to the mob were of no avail. Finally, he managed to secure a couple of cabs and an escort and he contrived to get us through the angry populace amid a fusillade of stones.

It had been taken for granted that I should go to Paris to manage the Congress and I was disagreeably surprised when the new Minister for Foreign Affairs, Gavan Duffy, began to put forward reasons why I should stay at home. I read in the *Sunday Independent* an announcement to the effect that Desmond Fitzgerald, who was not a member of either delegation, had been specially sent to Paris on the instructions of the Government. This seemed to be clear proof that the matter was being taken out of my hands and, furthermore, it appeared to me that an attempt was about to be made to sabotage any plan to show a united front at the Congress. I called on Gavan Duffy immediately. He hemmed and hawed. I wrote out my resignation as Under-Secretary for Foreign Affairs straightway and handed it to him. I left for Paris that night.

Any idea I had, however, of trying for a united front vanished the first day. Already the Congress was a hotbed of intrigue, with each side canvassing the delegates for support of their respective stands on the Treaty. What

might have become a great movement was being wrecked
on the rocks of party bias. Roughly as matters developed,
the delegates from America, Britain, Chile and the Argentine
were ranged on one side, while those from the British
Dominions were on the other. To my surprise Eoin
MacNeill, who headed the pro-Treaty section of the
delegation from Ireland, managed to inject an atmosphere
of distrust and suspicion into almost every phase of the
discussions.

For instance, there was a resolution moved to the effect
that the object of the organisation was " to assist the people
of Ireland to attain to the full their national ideals, political,
cultural and economic." As originally drafted, the words
" to the full " were not included. MacNeill insisted that
the insertion of these words constituted an attack on the
people who supported the Treaty.

The old Duke of Tetuan, whose Irish title was The
O'Donnell, since he was the lineal descendant of Hugh
O'Donnell, Prince of Tyrconnell, who had left Ireland in
1601, had come from Madrid to preside at the Congress.
He was frankly puzzled at the whole proceedings.

Ultimately the Congress decided to establish a world-
wide organisation of the Irish race, to be called Fine
Ghaedheal, the objects of which were to assist the people
of Ireland to achieve their national ideals, political, cultural
and economic, to secure for Ireland her rightful place
amongst the nations of the world, to foster amongst the Irish
everywhere a knowledge of the Irish language, history,
literature and general culture and to promote the trade,
industry and commerce of Ireland. My appointment as
Secretary of the permanent organisation caused a minor
row. MacNeill's party held that this was a breach of the
non-political status of the organisation, a contention which
was subsequently found baseless by a committee of enquiry
set up by the Dail. The damage was done, however. The
Cabinet refused to give the grant that was necessary to
tide the organisation over the period pending the receipt
of funds from the far-flung units of the organisation. It is
probable, however, that it could not have survived the civil
war, which was now looming closer every day.

The Republican army formally threw over the authority of the Dail and Mulcahy was busy recruiting a professional army to enforce the will of the Free State Government. The republicans seized the Four Courts and other buildings and then sat down and waited to be attacked. Night was made hideous by a futile sniping at the Beggars' Bush Barracks, which was occupied by the Free State Army. Each side blamed the other for this. Notwithstanding this, there were frequent parleys between the political leaders on the one hand and the military leaders on the other, all trying to find a way by which civil strife might be avoided.

One day Harry said to Dev : " Look here, you'll have to attack these fellows. They're getting ready to attack you." To which Dev replied that civil war would have to be avoided at all costs. He had refused to associate himself with the I.R.A., in their new activities, but he later bitterly regretted that he had not gone further and condemned Rory O'Connor's action in repudiating the authority of the Dail. He and I were crossing Suffolk Street one day when we encountered Oscar Traynor and Joe O'Connor, one in charge of the Dublin Brigade and the other commandant of the Third Battalion. They told Dev that at a meeting of the Headquarters Staff the previous night, the question of making Dev commander-in-chief had been discussed. Dev shook his head and refused point blank. He said he should be free to try to find a solution.

All this time Harry was very busy. Owing to his continued friendship with Collins and his undoubted loyalty to Dev, he was particularly suited to act as a go-between in the negotiations being carried on in the Mansion House in a desperate effort to avoid civil war.

One day Harry came into my office and threw his revolver on the mantelpiece.

" It's going to be war," he said, " and I'm not going to fire on Mick. So I can't fire on any of Mick's men."

He meant it at the time, but no sooner were the Republican positions attacked than he joined up at once.

I well knew how unprepared the Republicans were for

the attack. A few weeks before the bombardment began, Liam Mellowes sent for me and I went to the Four Courts. Liam asked me if I would take on the post of Director of Publicity. I said I would not, because there was no publicity I could do. They had thrown over all authority except that of the gun and no publicity could alter that fact.

Liam did not like my answer.

" The Republic is being undermined," he said. " What else could we have done ? "

" Possibly nothing," I said. " Your job is to get the other fellow to submit or submit yourselves. The time for publicity is passed."

" Well, we're going to act."

" How ? "

" By attacking the British."

" But they are going out."

" We'll attack them before they leave."

I thought this policy was crazy, and I said so.

" It's not as crazy as you think. It's the only way we can unite the army."

Just then, Ernie O'Malley came in.

" Say, Liam," he said, " what about digging some tunnels to provide a getaway from this place."

" I'm looking into that," said Liam.

I left, thinking the situation was pretty hopeless. These were grey days for Ireland as the menace of civil war crept closer and closer. Suddenly and unexpectedly, however, Collins and de Valera got together and signed a Pact by which it was agreed that a national coalition panel of candidates should be presented to the electorate by Sinn Féin, the number from each party representing their then strength in the Dail. When the Pact was unanimously adopted by the Dail, the feeling of relief was profound because the shadow of civil war had been lifted. This feeling was short-lived, however, because the British so-called statesmen denounced the Pact. They cried out that its implementation would violate the Treaty and they again used the threat of immediate and terrible war by which they had compelled the plenipotentiaries to sign the Treaty.

A young man, whom I knew very well, came into my

office with a sensational report. He had been present at a secret meeting of an Independent group that morning. Darrell Figgis, who was not a member of the group, had attended and made a speech urging the group to put forward candidates in opposition to the Sinn Féin panel of candidates, at the election. This was treachery, because Figgis, as a member of the Sinn Féin Executive, was bound in honour to uphold the Pact.

My visitor, whom I will call Dan Smith, handed me a verbatim report of the meeting. He thought it should be published right away. I took the report to Suffolk Street, de Valera's headquarters, and Dev called Austin Stack and Erskine Childers into conference on the matter. They decided to issue the report in a special edition of *An Poblacht*, and Childers went off to get this done. I returned to my office in O'Connell Street and found my friend placidly awaiting me. He was quite elated at the thought of the scoop he had made, but when I told him of the special edition of *An Poblacht*, he got into a panic.

" They'll know," he said, " it was I took these notes. I'll get into a hell of a row."

" Why didn't you think of that before ? " I asked. " It was your own idea the report should be published."

" But you're not giving me time to cover up my tracks. I'll be ruined."

" Can't you make up some story about losing the notes ? "

" They wouldn't believe it."

" Can't you say you were held up by the Republicans and the notes taken from you ? "

" Too thin. Too thin altogether. That publication will have to be stopped."

I told him that was impossible. Everyone who had been a party to the decision would have to be consulted and, by the time we could get that done, the papers would be on the streets. He paced up and down in desperate apprehension, while I tried to think of a way out. Suddenly he wheeled on me.

" What time will the paper be out ? "

" In about an hour or so."

" That would work out all right," he said. " I left my

place two hours ago and no one has seen me since. Have me arrested ! "

" What ? "

" Get the fellows from the Four Courts to arrest me. I can then say they found the report in my pocket."

I said it might not be easy to manage that, but I would do what I could. I went downstairs to Brennan and Walsh's drapery store, which occupied the ground floor of the building and explained the position to Tom Walsh. Tom went off to the Four Courts at once to try to arrange for an escort. By the time I got back, Dan had worked himself into a real panic. Was I sure they would send an escort ? Maybe they would arrive too late and the paper would be out in the streets. Why did not Tom Walsh come back ? How would they effect the arrest ?

The situation had become so comical that my secretary, Maire O'Brien, left the office hurriedly. I found her in an outer room, almost in hysterics.

" I can't go in there again," she said, " I'll die if I do."

At last, Tom Walsh returned. He said that an escort would be along right away.

" But how are they going to take me ? " asked Dan.

" That's easy," said Tom, " as soon as the lorry pulls up outside, you walk out and they'll grab you."

" But they won't hammer me, will they ? Will they know I'm a friend ? "

" I don't know about that," said Tom. " I saw Rory O'Connor and he said he's sending an escort, but I don't suppose he's going to tell them you're a friend."

" They'll beat me up. I'm sure they will. Couldn't you do something about it ? Couldn't you go back and——"

" Look here," said Tom, " I don't know where you get these notions about beating up. They won't lay a hand on you unless you get rough."

" There's another thing," said Dan, " if anyone sees me leaving here they'll know it's a plant."

" I see," said Tom. He could stand it no longer and he left.

" Listen," said Dan, " supposing I was walking up the street and the lorry overtook me, it would look more like the thing wouldn't it ? "

"All right," I said. " You can walk up the street."

" But how will they know it's me they want ? "

" Tom or I will point you out," I said.

He was jumping up every now and again to peer out of the window.

" It's a wonder they don't come."

" Oh, they'll be here all right."

" Listen," he said, " I'd better put on some disguise before I leave here in case anyone who knows me sees me leave. If they did, they'd know it was a put-up job."

" What sort of a disguise ? "

" I'll leave my hat here. You go down to Tom Walsh and get me a cap."

" What size do you wear ? "

" Seven and a half and, look—bring me a muffler, too, a great big muffler."

Down in the shop I found Tom Walsh and Maurice Brennan in fits of laughter. I got them calmed down sufficiently to give me the cap and muffler. An hour later, there was still no sign of the lorry. Dan had reached the groaning stage. I got him to agree to accompany Tom Walsh to the Four Courts and coaxed Tom into taking him. They set off and when they reached their destination, Tom announced to the sentry that he had a prisoner. The sentry summoned an escort and opened the gate. The soldiers formed up beside Tom.

" Wait," said Dan, " he's not the prisoner. I'm the prisoner."

They complacently took him into custody and marched him off. Tom stayed to have a chat with some of his friends in the garrison. An hour later, he was leaving when he heard his name called. He saw Dan behind the bars.

" They won't bring me my tea," he said to Tom, " will you go up to Rory and tell him to tell them——"

" Shut up ! " shouted his guard.

" Is he dangerous ? " asked Tom.

" He has a hell of a lot to say," said the guard.

" Make sure he doesn't escape," said Tom.

On the following day, I found Dan waiting for me near my home.

" Oh, you got out ? " I said.

" I had a job of it," he said, " but I managed it. Blarney, you know, the old blarney ! "

I did not tell him I had made sure he would be released that morning. He was all smiles again and assured me that the trick had worked. His story about his arrest had been believed.

The blowing up of the Four Courts, Dublin, 30th June, 1922.

Erskine Childers, 1922.   A characteristic attitude.

Chapter Thirty-six

On the 28th June 1922 the Free State army opened fire on the Four Courts, the headquarters of the Republican forces. The Civil War spread throughout the country and continued until May 24th, 1923, when the Republicans, hopelessly beaten, were ordered by de Valera to cease fire.

ON the morning of the 28th June, a little after four o'clock, Una and I were awakened by the noise of heavy explosions. We both said : " They have attacked the Four Courts." I cycled into town. The streets were quiet till I reached the quays, where I found groups of people looking on at the bombardment. Later in the morning, I went to Suffolk Street. Stack and Brugha were there already and de Valera arrived just as I entered.

" Is it true they are attacking the Four Courts ? " he asked.

" It is," said Brugha.

" I was stopped on the way in by Free State troops," said Dev. " They recognised me but let me pass. Well, will we try to stop it ? "

" Stop it ? " said Brugha. " Stop it ? What do you mean by stop it ? "

" No," said Stack, but rather half-heartedly, " it's too late now."

" I was thinking of trying to get hold of the Lord Mayor," said Dev. " Don't go, Cathal," he added, as Brugha started for the door.

" It's no use," said Cathal, " these fellows have gone over to the British. We're going to fight back."

He went out, but came back in a few minutes and told Dev he was joining up.

" I'm going to issue a short statement, Cathal," said Dev, but Brugha went out. I never saw him again.

I went to my office in O'Connell Street and tried to put things in some sort of shape so that it could be carried on in my absence. Then I went home and told Una I was going to join up.

343

" It's terrible," she said, " but there's nothing else to be done." She added she would go in to Suffolk Street and see if she could give a hand.

All day the noise of the guns sounded like a death knell. Each time I crossed the river, the curious crowd of sightseers was bigger. At nightfall, I went to the headquarters of the Third Battalion in York Street and was directed to go to Jack Baird's house in Mercer's Street. The place was ill-lighted but I saw Joe O'Connor, the Commandant, inside and told him I wanted to join up. Now, Joe and I had long been friends and he called me Bob and I called him Joe, but on this occasion, I found I was talking to the Commandant. He asked me, as if I were a complete stranger, if I knew what were the objects of the Volunteers and, when I assured him I did, he solemnly administered to me the Volunteer oath. I was very self-conscious because I was aware that there was someone sitting in the corner who I sensed was grimly amused. It was Dev. When I sat down beside him, he laughed.

" He did the same to me," he said.

Joe told me to report at York Street, where I was attached to the Battalion Headquarters staff, with some vague duties. I spent the night receiving reports from scouts and trying to put them in some sort of order. In the morning I was sent with a special report to Oscar Traynor's headquarters in Barry's Hotel and there I found a lot of old comrades, some of whom I had not seen since 1917.

On Friday, the Four Courts fell and the fighting was transferred to O'Connell Street, where Oscar Traynor had set up his headquarters in the Hammam Hotel. On Sunday morning I got a message that Dev wanted to see me and I was directed to a house on the canal bank, at the end of Harcourt Terrace. The house was garrisoned and sandbagged. I found Dev in an upstairs sitting-room. He had drawn up a peace proposal, which he showed me. He wanted the Lord Mayor to carry this to the other side, but first of all he had to get the consent of the Republicans. My job was to find out if there was a route clear to the Hammam Hotel and report how he could get there. I set out on my bicycle and found, as I expected, that

O'Connell Bridge was impossible owing to the cross-firing.
A few idlers sheltering in D'Olier Street warned me that
Burgh Quay was dangerous, so I made my way through
empty streets to Butt Bridge, which I crossed without
difficulty. The intersection of Gardiner Street and Talbot
Street, however, was a no man's land, swept by incessant
fire. I traversed the lane behind the Abbey Theatre, which
was quiet, but no sooner did I appear in Marlborough
Street than I had to duck out of sight. A couple of bullets
clipped the wall over my head. By a devious route, I
regained O'Connell Street, through Sackville Place. Here
I knew I was in full view of the Free State troops in Elvery's.
I started wheeling my bicycle towards a builder's barricade
in front of Clery's. I had only gone a few yards when
someone took a shot at me and missed. He cannot have
been trying very hard because I was an easy mark, but I
covered the last few yards in a hurry. There was a man
sitting down inside the barricade. He started up as I
entered. He was evidently badly scared.

"Who are you?" he cried. "What are you doing
here?"

"It's all right," I said, "I just want to get up the street
a bit."

"I shouldn't be here at all," he said. "I want to get
home and I can't get out of here."

From the end of the barricade it was about thirty yards
to Earl Street—too far to make a dash for it.

"What are you going to do?" asked the man.

"I'm going to try and get into Earl Street."

"They'll shoot you."

"Maybe they won't if I walk."

"You don't know them," he said.

"Do you?"

"Oh, no I don't," he said hastily, "no, I don't. Listen,"
he went on, "will you take a message to my wife."

"Why?"

"I'm not going to get out of this. I feel that way."
He was pulling nervously at his moustache. "She doesn't
know where I am. I shouldn't be here at all. I live out
Cabra way. Listen! I went to Navan yesterday to buy a

few cattle. I got drunk and someone drove me into town.
I woke up this morning on the steps of the Theatre Royal.
She won't know what has happened to me. She'll think
maybe I've gone away on her or something. God, I'd
give a lot for a glass of malt. Will you bring her a message
for me ? "

"Sure I will."

"Listen; may be I'd better go with you."

"As you like."

"I've been bad to her. I know I have. I wish to God
I could tell her so."

"Never fear, you'll be able to tell her."

"You think they won't fire on us ? "

"Maybe they won't if we walk."

"I'm afraid I'll run if they do."

"Don't run. Just try and take cover."

"Maybe I'd better stay here."

"Maybe it would be best."

"No, go ahead."

He followed me as I walked as casually as I could to
Earl Street corner. To my surprise, we were not fired on.
Further progress up O'Connell Street was, however, impossible. There were constant bursts of fire exchanged
across the street. I turned down Earl Street and my
companion followed. Suddenly, a machine-gun opened
fire and my companion started to run. I shouted at him
to take cover, but my words were drowned in the sharp
loud swish of bullets on glass. I turned my head to see a
large plate-glass window falling to the street just behind
me. I sheltered in an all-too-shallow doorway. I saw my
companion a dozen yards ahead stumble and fall to his
knees. He got up and turned round, but suddenly dropped
as if felled by an axe. His face was towards me and I saw
blood seeping from two bullet wounds in his forehead.

"And now," I heard myself saying audibly, " I won't
be able to tell his wife because I didn't get his name and
address." After a while, in little runs, sheltering from door to
door, I got into Cathedral Lane. In the yard at the rear
of the Hammam Hotel there were several young Volunteers, but none of them knew me and I was not admitted

till Barney Mellowes chanced to come down and brought me in. I found Oscar Traynor looking surprisingly fresh and buoyant. He was astonished to hear I had been fired on in Marlborough Street. He asked an officer to make an investigation and the latter returned and assured us that Marlborough Street was clear. Oscar grinned.

" It must have been our fellows tried to get you," he said. He turned to the officer : " Make sure," he continued, " they don't get Dev."

I managed to get back without molestation and I sketched the route for Dev. He and Joe Begley cycled off.

A few days after the fall of the Hammam Hotel, Stack sent for me and told me Dev wanted me to join him at Clonmel. I was to travel with Childers, Kathleen O'Connell and Dorothy Macardle. As all the roads around Dublin were by this time held by the Free State troops, we were to travel by train and chance getting through. Una came with us as far as Waterford. The journey was uneventful till we reached Clonmore, Co. Kilkenny. The train could proceed no further because the railway bridge ahead had been blown up. We were told to make ourselves as comfortable as we could in the train and we tried to sleep. In the morning, the dozen bedraggled travellers betook themselves to a near-by farmhouse, where we breakfasted on tea and bacon and eggs. The farmer's wife apologised because there was only one egg apiece. A red-haired, jovial fellow growled that the only priest in the party had got two eggs. He solemnly told the farmer's wife that she had undermined his faith and that he was going to turn Protestant. The lady pounded him on the back and said he was not going to imperil his immortal soul for the sake of an egg. " It's not for an egg," he said, " it's the principle of the thing." No one mentioned the civil war. Everyone was distrustful. We hunted around and found a boy with a pony and trap. We offered him a pound to bring us to Waterford. He demurred at the figure and we finally agreed on thirty shillings. The six of us squeezed into the car. It was what used to be called a conversation car. The driver was very taciturn, but he knew his way. The country we were passing through was a sort of no man's land between the opposing forces and the roads were blocked every few hundred yards. The driver detoured through fields, for miles it seemed, and gained the road every now and again. I saw a village off to the right.

" What place is that ? " I asked.

" That's Clonmore."

" We left Clonmore hours ago."

" That was the station. This is the town."

In an endeavour to be friendly, I told the old story of the man who asked why the railway station at Ferns was a mile from the town, and the reply was " Because they wanted to have it near the railway line." Our driver took no notice of the joke. I tried to draw him out about the feeling of the local people about the civil war. He had nothing to say but, after a while, he volunteered this statement about Clonmore.

" There's no public-house there, and no policeman and no Protestants."

Childers, who was a Protestant, laughed heartily.

" It must be heaven on earth," he said.

Our driver lapsed into grim silence again. One of the party made the mistake of addressing Childers by name but the driver still remained impassive. As we were now in Republican territory we felt safe. When we arrived outside the Metropole Hotel in Waterford, I took the driver aside and said :

" If you heard anything you shouldn't have heard, you might forget it."

He said nothing but glanced significantly at Childers's mackintosh, which he was handing to me. I followed the direction of his eyes and saw the label on the inside of the coat, " Erskine Childers."

" So you knew all the time," I asked.

He was severe.

" It was lying like that across my knees."

" Well," I said, " for your own sake———"

"All right," he said, " I saw nothing and heard nothing. I never saw you people in my life, nor heard of you."

We reported to Pax Whelan at the military barracks, where I said good-bye to Una as she was returning to

Wexford. Pax said he was to get us to Clonmel with the utmost despatch. He drove us at a furious pace through the beautiful country of the Comeragh Mountains. We pulled up on the barrack square of Clonmel in a cloud of dust. An hour later, I was wondering what all the hurry had been for, because there was nothing for us to do. Liam Lynch was putting the finishing touches to a flagged map showing the territory held by the rival forces. The line of flags extended from Waterford to Limerick. The territory south of the line was held by the Republicans, that north and east of it was in the hands of the Free State forces. Dev studied the map for a while and then brought Childers and myself into another room. He said that this was the right time to make a peace offer when we still held territory we could hand over without fighting, and he suggested terms which he was thinking of putting forward. Childers said nothing, but it was quite clear from his expression that he thought little of any offer of peace right then. My view was that the Free State forces were winning all along the line and they were not inclined to listen to anything but an offer to surrender, which was now out of the question.

We were told there were no quarters for us in the barracks and we were to go to one of the hotels, so an escort accompanied Kathleen O'Connell, Childers and myself through the streets. When we reached the hotel and found the door closed, the man in charge of the escort began to belabour the door with the butt end of his rifle. Childers and I remonstrated with him. He grew very angry and told us the people of the hotel were a lot of so-and-so Free Staters. We told him if he did not desist, we would return to the barracks and report him. He looked furious enough to turn his weapon on us but, fortunately, the door opened and a very frightened waiter admitted us. At first he could give us nothing to eat but, finally, he brought us some tea and eggs. While we were eating, a man who was at another table approached me and reminded me that I had met him at a Sinn Féin meeting in Dublin. He was from Thurles, which was held by the Free State troops, and he was going back there next day. All Thurles, he said, was pro Free

State. He was quite evidently badly frightened and, consequently, I thought all the more of him when later that
night he offered to aid us when he thought, and we thought,
we were going to be shot.

I was in bed only a couple of hours when I was awakened
by a thundering knocking which shook the house. It ceased
and I was about to go to sleep again, when there was the
sound of heavy tramping in the corridor. There was a knock
on a door and a rough voice cried, " Is Childers there ? "
I heard Kathleen O'Connell replying that it was her room.
There was a knock at another door.

" Is Childers there ? "

" Yes."

" You're the man we want. Come out."

" My God ! " I said to myself, " it's a murder gang," and
I tumbled out of bed and opened the door. A man, unkempt
and wild-looking, plunged at me, rifle in hand.

"Are you Brennan ? "

" Yes."

" Come along with us quick."

Kathleen O'Connell in a dressing gown, and Childers
in his pyjamas, came out. In all our eyes was the same
question : " Was it the murder gang ? "

" What's up," I asked. Several people joined us and the
man from Thurles pushed his way in front.

" What are you going to do with these men ? " he asked.

" Nothing. We've to get them out of this. We're leaving the town. The lorries are waiting outside. Hurry up ! "

Hastily dressing, we made our way downstairs, only to
find the door locked and no one in attendance. We made
our way through a broken window and over a spiked railing.
The lorries were crowded and uncomfortable and, as we
whirled through the early morning air, we were all miserably
cold. Moss Twomey, who was on our lorry, sang " Sean
O Duibhir a Gleanna " and the doleful refrain " You're
worsted in the game " seemed to fit in with the circumstances
of our trip. We gathered that the hasty evacuation was
due to a report that the Free State troops in Thurles were
advancing to surround Clonmel during the night. We
found out next day that there was no truth in the report.

The first thing Childers did when we reached our destination, Fermoy, was to write a letter to the proprietor of the Clonmel Hotel apologising for our hasty departure and enclosing a bank-note to pay for our bills and the mending of the broken window.

Liam Lynch surprised me by the measure of his distress over a statement Mulcahy had published to the effect that when he (Lynch) was arrested in Dublin, he had been released on condition that he would not join the " irregulars " and that he would use his influence to stop the armed resistance in the south.

" I gave no promise of any kind," said Liam. " They wanted me to, but I refused. How can they tell such lies ? "

He was a strange young man to be at the head of a rebel army, especially a rebel army in Cork. He was handsome, in a boyish, innocent way. His large blue eyes and open countenance indicated his transparent honesty. His looks, bearing and presence might have belonged to a single-minded devoted priest. He had come to be the chief warrior in the most turbulent section of the country through his fearlessness and daring and his ability to command respect. He had been a draper's assistant before the fight started and, without any training or experience, he had discovered in himself wonderful military qualities. But his heart was not in this fight of brothers. There had been something glorious and holy in the fight against the British but now——. When some prisoners were brought in, Liam ordered they should be served the same food as we had. He gave them the freedom of the barrack parade ground. He refused to have them questioned as to troop movements. He would be ashamed to think they would give their chums away.

" They wouldn't do it anyway."

" All very magnificent," said Moss Twomey to me, " but it's not war. We're losing because the fellows are not fighting. We're firing at their legs."

At the mess table we heard the reason for the Clonmel debacle. Liam Lynch had sent a company of men, fully equipped to take Thurles. They had been ambushed and captured. The courier who had brought this report also said that the Free Staters were on their way in strong force to attack Clonmel. So far was this from being the case that Lynch sent back a detachment to reoccupy the town.

Despatches from Kerry reported there would be no difficulty in taking over the cable stations at Valentia and Waterville. It was arranged that Childers should look after this, while I was to go to Cork to edit the *Cork Examiner*, an opposition paper which our fellows had taken over, and also to prepare daily despatches which Childers would put on the cables. In Cork there was no lack of publicity personnel, amongst my helpers being Donal Corkery, Frank O'Connor and Sean O'Faolain.

I stayed in Mary MacSwiney's house and she was as full of fight as ever. She roundly denounced me for suggesting that the Free State forces could capture Cork. There was no use in pointing out to her that Waterford had already fallen and our right wing thereby turned, that we had been unable to take the offensive anywhere and that the idea of holding the line with our present forces was hopeless. We might have had a chance, at this stage, if we abandoned the towns and embarked on such a guerrilla war as we had carried on against the British. That, too, would have been difficult because the majority of the people were against us. In Fermoy, Mallow, and other towns, the people looked at us sullenly, as if we had belonged to a hostile invading army. Dev had seen all this, as I had, and that was one of the reasons he was so desperately trying for peace while he had still some bargaining power.

Cork City was deceptive. Here, life seemed to go on as usual, just as if there was no war. At Union Quay barracks, however, there was tremendous activity and there seemed to be no lack of guns and supplies. One day when I was there a big, strapping fellow arrived from Limerick, where a terrific fight for the city had been in progress for days. He had been in the thick of it and he was going back next day. He had come down to Cork to play with his team for the Cork County hurling championship ! Everybody, including the men who were filling hand-grenades, joined in a terrific argument as to which team was going to win the match.

With Peter MacSwiney, I visited Cobh and Seumas Fitzgerald took us over the defences of the harbour. Apart from his riflemen, he had a few machine-guns here and there on the Barrymore estate, mainly on Fota Island. The positions were based on the idea that the Free State forces would land at Cobh, but that was no fault of Fitzgerald's ; when the Free State forces did arrive some weeks later, they landed at Passage across the river and met with practically no resistance.

Fitzgerald, for no reason but to beguile the time, thought that the loss of a night's sleep would do me no harm and he asked me to accompany a squad of men who were going out on the tender to meet an American liner on which he said guns were expected. We met the liner, but there were no guns. On the return journey in the tender, we had about a dozen American passengers. Most of them, when they learned of the disturbed state of the country, took the position philosophically enough, but one lady was very irate. She denounced de Valera and his confederates with terrific zest in beautifully picturesque American language.

When I went into the hotel dining-room for my breakfast, there was only one solitary waiter there and no guests. He was in a very bad humour and he grumbled as he arranged the table.

"A nice state of affairs," he said, " the whole country thrown into a yury ary ! Bridges down and roads blocked ! No god-damn travellers. A nice bloody state of affairs ! "

"Are you talking to me ? " I asked severely.

" Oh, no," he said, " I'm talking to myself."

The vociferous lady who had been on the tender came in and sat at a table, to the music of peals from her golden bangles. She immediately launched out. She was coming back after twelve years to see her people in Limerick, though she wouldn't have come back if she didn't have to. And what was her welcome ? No buses or trains. The roads all blocked, the bridges all blown up. She was talking to the waiter and, as he did not reply, she asked him point blank :

" Don't you think this is a scandalous war ? "

" God damn it," he said, " sure it's better than no war at all anyway."

Dev summoned me to Carrick-on-Suir and told me he wanted me to go back to Dublin and start a publicity department. Accompanying me was Dev's son, Vivion, and a lady with whom the boy had been staying in Cork. A Ford car brought us from Carrick-on-Suir to Kilkenny and, though the distance is only thirty miles, the journey occupied a whole day. The route lay through a country which was daily the scene of encounters between the rival forces. We passed through the section held by Dan Breen who, jovial as ever, accompanied us to the limits of his territory. Thereafter, we left the main highway and, travelling through fields and byways, made a wide detour so that we entered the city from the north instead of the south. Darkness was falling when the driver pulled up in front of a small hotel.

" I'll drop you here," he said, " you'll have to fend for yourselves now. I'll have to go back."

The landlord himself came out and helped us with our two small bags. There were a number of Free State soldiers lounging about, but none of them seemed to take any notice of us. At about midnight, however, I was awakened by a loud knocking. I jumped out of bed, pulled on my pants and rushed downstairs. The landlord was in the hall.

" Who is it ? " I asked.

" It's them," he said.

" Are they friends of yours ? "

" I'm on no side," he said.

I led him back to the rear hall.

" Stay there," I said, " I'll open the door."

I had not made up my mind as to what I was going to do. The knocking was shaking the house as I took the chain off the door. There were several soldiers outside.

" It takes you a hell of a long time to open up," said the officer.

" I was in bed asleep," I said. " What's the matter ? "

" We want to interview three travellers who came here to-night."

" You're making a mistake," I said, " no one came here to-night."

The officer glanced over his shoulder.

" You hear that, Jemmy," he said. A private spoke up :
" I was told three people came here."

" There's some mistake," I said, " you can search the
house if you like, but I'd rather you wouldn't because everyone is in bed. Three people stopped here looking for rooms,
about nine o'clock, but I wouldn't take them. I said there
was no room. I don't like taking people with no luggage."

" They had no luggage ? "

" Just one little bag."

" Did you know them ? What were they like ? "

"A man, a woman and a boy. I didn't know them."

" Where did they go ? "

" Down the street. There was a car waiting for them.
The woman said something about pushing on to Callan."

The officer looked doubtful and rubbed his chin.

" Come on in and have a drink," I ventured.

" No, no thanks. Sorry for disturbing you."

They went off and I closed the door. The landlord
emerged from the rear hall. He was shaking and so was I.

" Will they come back, do you think ? "

" I don't know," I said. " I'm going to have that drink
they refused."

We groped our way to the bar and he poured a glass of
whiskey for me and one for himself.

" I don't know who you are," he said, " but here's to you
anyway."

We drank in the dark. On the way upstairs, I heard
doors being furtively closed.

" Fear stalks abroad," I said to myself, " I'll be awake
all night."

I fell fast asleep, however, as soon as I got into bed. In
the morning, through glorious sunshine and busy streets,
we made our way to the railway station. We got to Dublin
without further alarms.

That evening I saw Austin Stack in his hideout in Upper
Mount Street. He said I was to organise a Publicity
Department, of which I was to be the Director.

I agreed to do so and I went underground.

APPENDIX

The following ex-prisoners appear in the photograph facing page 182.

Ashe, Tomas

Beasley, Pierce
Bevan, Charlie
Bevan, Tommy
Boland, Harry
Brady, Michael
Brennan, Maurice
Brennan, Robert
Brennan, Seumas
Brooks, Fred
Brosnan, Tadhg
Burke, James J.
Burke, Joseph
Byrne, Joseph

Carrick, Chris
Carrick, John
Clancy, Peadar
Clarke, James
Collins, Con
Coleman, Dick
Corcoran, Eamon
Corcoran, John
Corcoran, Liam
Corrigan, Willie
Cosgrave, Phil
Cosgrave, William

Davies, Dick
De Lacey, Michael
Dempsey, James
Derrington, J. J.
Derrington, William
De Valera, Eamon
Doherty, John
Donohue, Dick
Downey, John
Doyle, Gerald
Doyle, Peadar
Doyle Seumas
Doyle, Thomas

Etchingham, Sean
Fahy, Frank

Fahy, Padraig
Faulkner, John
Fitzgerald, Desmond
Flanagan, Patrick
Fleming, Michael
Fleming, Michael, junr.
Fogarty, Patrick
Fury, Patrick
Fury, Thomas
Fury, Thomas Fred

Galligan, Paul

Hehir, Michael
Higgins, Michael
Howley, Joseph
Hughes, Seumas
Hunter, Tom
Hussey, William

Irvine, George

Joyce, James

Kelly, P.
Kelly, R.
Kent, Davy
King, Dick

Lawless, Frank
Lawless, James
Leahy, Denis
Levins, George
Loughlin, James
Lynch, Diarmuid
Lynch, Fionan

Macardle, Jack
McEntee, Sean
McGarry, Sean
McGinley, Conor
McGuinness, Joe
McMahon, Phil
McNeill, Eoin
McNestry, Patrick
Marks, James
Martin, Francis

Meehan, William
Melinn, Seumas
Mervyn, Michael
Molloy, Brian
Morrissey, Seumas

Norton, J.

O'Brien, John
O'Callaghan, Denis
O'Connor, Fergus
O'Dea, William
O'Donovan, Con
O'Gaora, Colm
O'Hanrahan, Harry
O'Kelly, Thomas
O'Neill, Charles

Peppard, T.
Plunkett, George
Plunkett, Jack
Poole, Vincent

Quinn, John

Rafter, Seumas
Reid, John J.
Reynolds, Michael
Roach, E.

Sally, James
Scully, Michael
Shouldice, Jack
Slattery, James
Stack, Austin
Sweeny, Patrick E.

Thompkins, John
Thornton, Frank
Tobin, Liam
Toole, Michael

Walsh, J. J.
Walsh, Tom
Williams, John
Wilson, J.
Wilson, P.
Wilson, W.

INDEX

Abbey Street, 288.
Abbey Theatre, 345.
A.B.C., 324.
Æ, 18 ; 19.
Ahearne, Josephine, 293.
Aherne, Father, 145 ; 149.
Alice T., 31.
Allies, The, 274, stab in the back.
All Ireland Football Championship, 157.
America, 29 ; 41 ; 94, effect of executions on ; 96, Tom Ashe ; 103, Britain needs ; 156, warnings from ; 175, self determination for nations ; 265 ; 278 ; 293 ; 296, de Valera's return from ; 297; 298, de Valera ; 308 ; 336, Irish Race Congress.
America, South, 321.
American Delegation, 239.
American liner, 353.
American Navy, 20.
American opinion, 147, To be deceived.
Amiens Street, 309.
Ancient Roman, 215.
Anglo-Irish aristocracy, vi.
—— lords, v.
Anglo-Normans, v.
Ankara, 306.
Arabia, 273.
Arbour Hill, 38 ; 84 ; 187 ; 313.
Ard Fheis 1917, 155 ; 216.
Argentine, 321 ; 336, Irish Race Congress.
Arklow, 65.
Arklow District Inspector R.I.C., 69.
Armada, Spanish, 31.
Armagh, South, 330.
Armed agents of the Crown, 301, " violate every law."
Armistice 1918, 182 ; 265.
Army organisation, 152, Collins ; 288.
Army without banners, 286.
Asgard, The, 33.
Ashbourne, battle of, 95, Tom Ashe.
Ashe, Tom, 90, Kilmainham ; 95, Mountjoy ; 96 *et seq.*, journey to Jail ; 129, Lewes Jail ; 132, removal from Lewes ; 151 ; 161.
Asia Minor, 188.
As I roved out, 97.

Asquith, H. H., 75 ; 88 ; 94, new Departure; 98, jig-saw puzzle; 308.
Astronomer Royal, 117.
Athenaeum, Enniscorthy, 64 *et seq.* Republican H.Q.
Athlone, 34.
Aud, The, 327.
Auxiliaries, 288, Bloody Sunday ; 289 ; 292 ; 308.

Bachelor's Walk, 43.
Baggot Street, 237 ; 312.
Bailey, The, 207 ; 241.
Baird, Jack, 344.
Balfe, 203.
Balfour, Arthur, 178.
Ballygeary, 272.
Banba Hall, 36.
Bannow, Co. Wexford, 60.
Barber of Seville, The, 203.
Barcelona, 326.
Barker, John, 10 ; 53.
Barntown, Co. Wexford, 57.
Barry, Jack, 20 ; 22.
Barry, Kevin, 285 ; 286.
Barrymore Estate, 353.
Barry's Hotel, 344.
Barton, Robert, 244 ; 260 ; 314, release ; 315, plenipotentiary.
Basle, 330.
Bealadangin, 86.
Beasley, Pierce, 118.
Beaumont & Fletcher, 203.
Beggar's Bush, 291 ; 337.
Begley, Joe, 347.
Belfast, 20 ; 39 ; 171 ; 218.
—— Jail, 174.
—— *Newsletter*, 281.
Belgium, 48 ; 171.
Belgrave Road, 286 ; 290.
Berlin, 326 *et seq.*
Bevan, Charlie, 122 ; 134 *et seq.*
Bevan, Tommy, 122 ; 134 *et seq.*
Birkenhead, Lord, 147 ; 318.
Birmingham, 196 ; 198 ; 235.
—— Carbines, 36.
Black & Tans, 27 ; 212 ; 262 ; 273, Campaign of Terror ; 286, Bloody Sunday ; 287 ; 290, murder of Father Griffin ; 291 ; 296, 298 ; 301, *et seq.* Westland Row raid ; 308 ; 334 *et seq.* Hostile Demonstration.

357

358 ALLEGIANCE

Blackrock, 318.
Bloody Anarchy, 301, General Gough.
—— Sunday, 286 ; 290 ; 297.
Boer War, 254.
Bohemian Girl, The, 4.
Boland, Harry, 81 ; 95, Mountjoy ;
99 *et seq.*, Dartmoor ; 120 *et seq.*,
Lewes Jail ; 132, removal from
Lewes ; 153, on Mick Collins ;
165 ; 172, on the run ; 174,
elections ; 176 *et seq.*, Peace Con-
ference ; 183, the Armistice ; 234,
235, code letter to Gloucester ;
238, horseplay ; 239, election
manifesto ; 265, visit to Mount
Street ; 304, envoy at Washing-
ton ; 315 *et seq.*, Gairloch ; 321,
and Collins ; 337, prelude to Civil
War.
—— Jerry, 24 ; 153, on Mick Col-
lins.
—— Mrs., 133.
Bolger, Jim, 37 *et seq.* ; 41 ; 187 ;
298.
Bomanji, 328.
Borris, Co. Carlow, 54.
Boundary Commission, 331.
Bourgeois, Maurice, 274 *et seq.*
Braddon, Miss M. E., 108.
Brady, James, 144.
Bray, 259.
Breen, Dan, 210 *et seq.*, Soloheadbeg ;
354.
—— Jem, 21.
Brennan & Walsh, 340.
—— Jimmy, 132.
—— Maurice, 149 ; 341.
Bride Street, Wexford, 85.
Bridewell, Dublin, 187.
Brien, Superintendent, 259 ; 260.
Brighton, 134.
Britain, 94 ; America alienated ; 274,
strained relations with France ;
336, Irish Race Congress.
Britannic Majesty, His, 74.
British, 48 ; 56, reinforcements ; 61 ;
95, showed wisdom ; 175, self-
determination for nations ; 227,
influence at Peace Conference ;
237, outlaw Sinn Féin ; 237, veto
Irish representatives ; 244, military
control ; 254, underestimated ;
257, forces clash with I.R.A. ; 275,
plain-clothes officers ; 276 *et seq.*,
Secret Service ; 334, evacuation.
—— Admiralty, 42.
—— agent, 304.
—— Ambassador in Washington, 94.
—— Army, 27 ; 32 ; 34 ; 258, Irishmen in.

British, artillery, 61.
—— Authorities, 288, forestalled.
—— Cabinet, 257.
—— Chief Secretary for Ireland, 41.
—— Commonwealth, 312, external
association with.
—— Dominions, 336, Irish Race
Congress.
—— Empire, 34 ; 39 ; 143 ; 274 ;
320.
—— fleet, 44.
—— forces, 63 ; 64 ; 65 ; 66 ; 72 ;
73 ; 284, cracking.
—— Generals, 257.
—— Government, 43 ; 156, Con-
scription ; 164 *et seq.*, Conscrip-
tion ; 202 ; 237, decide to smash
Sinn Féin ; 240, raids ; 295,
Dominion Home Rule.
—— Home Office, 130 *et seq.*
—— House of Commons, 1 ; 167,
Conscription Act for Ireland passed
16th April, 1918.
—— Intelligence Service, 38 ; 324.
—— Labour Party, 273.
—— Lancers, 81.
—— Liberal Party, 2.
—— Military Government, 264,
hunting *Irish Bulletin*.
—— Officers, 287, Bloody Sunday.
—— patrol boats, 106.
—— propaganda, 297.
—— Republic, 273.
—— statesmen, 338, denounce pact.
Brixton Jail, 158 ; 284.
Broadmoor Jail, 137.
Brugha, Cathal, 153, and Griffith ;
155 ; 166, Chief of Staff ; 179
et seq., "Jean Christophe" ; 215
ets eq., Griffith and ; 238-9, with
de Valera ; 257, Colonial soldiers ;
266, clash with Collins ; 273 *et
seq.*, campaign in England ; 343,
civil war.
Brunswick Street, 276 ; 288.
Bruton, G.-man, 303.
Bryan, Paddy, 23.
Buenos Ayres, 321.
Bull Wall, 286.
Burgh Quay, 292 ; 345.
Bushy Park Road, 246.
Butt Bridge, 345.
Buttle, Mr., 66.
Byrne, Pierce, 157.

Cabra, 345.
Cadogan, Seumas, 47.
Callan, 355.
Callanan, J. J., 40.
Cambridge magazine, 116.

Camolin, Co. Wexford, 68.
Campaign of terror, 273.
Campbell, Joe, 17, *The Gilly of Christ*.
Canada, 278.
Canterbury, Archbishop of, 308.
Capitol, 18.
Cardiff, 281.
Carey, Mrs., 299 ; 300.
Carlow, 14 *et seq.* ; 281.
Carlton Club, London, 328.
Carlyle, 255.
Carney, Frank, 269.
Carson, 331.
Carsonites, 281.
Carty, James, 298.
Casement, Roger, 37 ; 53, landing in Kerry ; 151 ; 258 ; 324.
Castlebridge, 9.
Cathedral Lane, 346.
Cathleen Ni Houlihan, 11.
Cavan by-election 1918, 175.
—— East, 202.
Cecil, Lord Hugh, 308.
—— Lord Robert, 308.
Ceithre Sgealta, 6.
" Celt," 286.
Censor, 245.
Centenary of '98 celebrations, 1.
Chamber music, 17.
Chaplain, Dartmoor, 105.
—— Lewes Jail, 121 *et seq.*
—— Parkhurst Jail, 132.
Charing Cross, 272 ; 279.
Charlemagne, 215.
Charters, John, 270 *et seq.* ; 326 *et seq.* ; 329.
Chief of Staff, 50 ; 266.
—— Warder in Parkhurst, 143 *et seq.*
Childers, Erskine, 33 ; 244 *et seq.* ; 245, meeting with Griffith ; 246, Wellington Road ; 252, and Griffith ; 256, illness ; 264, the *Irish Bulletin* ; 268, *Military Rule in Ireland* ; 311–312 External Association ; 339, *An Poblacht* ; 348, Civil War ; 349, Waterford ; 350–351, Clonmel ; 352, Fermoy.
—— Mrs., 246.
Chile, 336.
Christ Church, 182.
Christian Brothers, 5 ; 304.
Christophe, Jean, 178 *et seq.*
Churchill, Winston, 318 ; 330.
Citizen Army, 53 ; 54 ; 55 ; 118.
City Without Walls, The, 248.
Civil War, 254 ; 261 ; 331 ; 343, the start of.
Claidheamh Soluis, 19.
Clancy, George, 158 ; 160 *et seq.,* hunger strike.

Clancy, J. J., 202.
—— Peadar, 287.
Clare election, 154.
—— 271 ; 287.
—— Street, 301.
Clarke, Joe, 165 ; 186 ; 263.
—— John, 262.
—— Tom, 34 ; 35 ; 36 ; 41 ; 44 ; 45 ; 52 ; 81 ; 137.
Clarkin, Andy, 276.
Cleary, Jim, 37 ; 67.
Clemenceau, 319.
Clery's, 345.
Clifford, Madge, 289.
Cliffs of Moher, 97.
Climanis, Yohan, 251.
Clonmel, 347 *et seq.*
Clonmore, 347 ; 348.
Clontarf, 36 ; 208.
Clune, Conor, 287.
Cobh, 353.
Coghlan, Seumas, 267 ; 275 *et seq.,* Hardy.
Coghlan, Sighle, 267.
Cogley, Fred, 14 *et seq.* ; 250.
Cole, Walter, 13.
College of Surgeons, 241.
Collins, Con, 103.
—— Mick, 45 ; 151 ; 152, my first impression of ; 154, the I.R.B. ; 155 *et seq.,* the 1917 Ard Fheis ; 166, Brugha ; 167, German Plot arrests ; 170, guns Mayo coast ; 171, German emissary ; 172, election candidates ; intelligence officer ; S.F. National Executive ; 173, " gunmen " ; 176, Peace Conference ; 178 *et seq.,* Jean Christophe ; 238, horseplay ; 239 ; 255, Childers on ; 256, the Republic ; 259 *et seq.,* Quin ; 262, enrolls G.-men ; 263, escape in No. 6 ; 266, attack on Lord French ; 276, Hardy ; 279, £10,000 reward ; 287, 288, Bloody Sunday ; 295, Acting President ; 300, Intelligence H.Q. ; 304 *et seq.,* " Tom Jones " ; 306, becoming a legend ; 311 *et seq.,* arms for Germany ; 315 plenipotentiary ; 321, South American loan ; 329, in London ; 337 friendship with Harry Boland ; 338 *et seq.,* the Pact.
Collopy, Sergeant, 73 ; 74 ; 162.
Colloquiem in Dublin, 117.
Colman, Visiting Justice, 107 ; 108.
Colonial Soldiers, 257.
Columbus, Christopher, 269 ; 326.
Colum, Padraig, 17.

Comer, Mrs. Dr. John, 289.
Comeragh, Mountains, 349.
Commandant Dublin Brigade, 287.
Commissioner D.M.P., 43.
Communications, 152, Collins.
Congress of U.S., 166.
Congreve, 203.
Connacht, 246.
Connelly, American Journalist, 312.
Connelly, Marc, 298.
Connolly, James, 53 ; 90 ; 105.
—— Seumas, 9.
Conscription, 164, Act passed ; Irish
  Party leave House of Commons ;
  Mansion House Conference ; 166,
  Irish Volunteers ; 167, Conscrip-
  tion Act never enforced ; 209.
Conservative Party, 270.
Constabulary barracks, 244, attacks
  on.
Constitution of 1782, 14 ; 216,
  Arthur Griffith.
Constitution Wexford, 213.
Convict Q 103, 99.
Conway, Father, 138 et seq.
" Coogan," 324 et seq.
Cope, Alfred, 308, 322.
Corcoran, Father Tim, 239.
Corcoran, William, 53.
Cork, 39 ; 157 ; 254 ; 260 ; 285 ;
  351, Liam Lynch ; 352, Mary
  MacSwiney.
—— County Hurling Championship,
  352.
Cork Examiner, 109 ; 110 ; 256 ; 352.
—— Jail, 44 ; 156 et seq.; 161, release.
—— Mid., 202.
—— Post Office, 37.
Corkery, Donal, 352.
Corporation of Dublin, 237.
Corrigan, Willie, 127.
Cosgrave, Nicky, 5 ; 6.
Cosgrave, William, 302.
County Inspector R.I.C., 47 ; 73.
Couriers, 298.
Cousins, Eva, 214.
Cregan, Mairin, 298 et seq.
Crofts, Gerard, 111 ; 122.
Croke Park, 36 ; 286, Bloody Sun-
  day ; 287.
Crossley Cars, 291.
Crown Forces, 286, torture.
Croydon Airfield, 273.
Crozier, General, 288.
Crubeen Patch, 25.
Cuffe Street, 293.
—— Tom, 9.
Cullen, Tom, 163 : 283.
Cumann na mBan, 64 ; 164 ; 264,
  outlawed.

Cumann na nGaedheal, 14.
Cumberland Street, 304.
Curfew, 273 ; 308 in daylight.
Curragh, The, 63 ; 311.
Curtis, O'Leary, 13 ; 170.
Customs and Excise, 242.
Czar, 196.
Czarist Russia, 195.
Czars, 188 ; 252.

Dail Eireann, 207, established ; 227 ;
  237 ; 257, " a dangerous associa-
  tion " ; 264, underground ; 288,
  Cabinet ; 289 ; 326, recommends
  Treaty ; 332, approval of Treaty ;
  334 et seq., Irish Race Cingress ;
  337, authority repudiated.
Dail Eireann Loan, 263 ; 321.
Daily Chronicle, 278.
—— Mail, 227 ; 244 ; 278 ; 316.
—— News, 244 ; 246 ; 308.
Dalkey, 302.
" Dan Smith," 339.
Dante, 119.
Dara, William, 17.
Dartmoor Jail, 78 ; 98 et seq. ; 124.
Davis, Thomas, 6.
Davitt, Michael, 219.
de Blaghd, Earnan, 262.
Deeps bridge, 24.
Defence of the Realm Act (D.O.R.A.),
  185.
Deirdre, 268.
de Lacey, Larry, 37 ; 39.
de Lacey, Michael, 65 ; 72, sur-
  render ; 78 ; 84 et seq., court-
  martial ; 92, death sentence ; 95 ;
  96 code ; 98 ; 104 et seq.
Department of Agriculture, 290.
Derby, Lord, 308.
Derry Jail, 276 et seq.
de Valera, Eamon, 90, Kilmainham ;
  95, Mountjoy ; 103 et seq., Dartmoor Jail ; 112, hunger strike ;
  113, removed to Maidstone ; 116
  et seq., Lewes Jail ; 118, Einstein
  and relativity ; 119 et seq., Lewes
  Jail ; 128, becomes leader in
  Lewes ; 131, mutiny in Lewes ;
  132, removal from Lewes ; 142,
  " a fellow called de Valera " ; 153,
  and Harry Boland ; 154, Clare
  Election ; 154, leaves I.R.B. ; 155
  et seq., the 1917 Ard Fheis ;
  162, Sinn Féin Press Bureau ; 163,
  middle of the road ; 164, Conscription ; Mansion House Conference ; 166, Ireland's case against
  Conscription ; President of the
  Volunteer Council ; 167, arrested

for " German Plot " ; 181 ; 182 ; 194 ; 216, 1917 formula ; 227 *et seq.*, escape from Lincoln Jail ; 237 *et seq.*, return to Dublin ; 238, 239, his parsimoniousness ; 239, Election manifesto ; 240, American delegation ; 242, Irish Party ; 242, representation at Westminster ; 243, United States ; 253 Address to Elected Representatives Abroad; 259, Army of the Republic ; 293, American organisation ; 296, return from America ; 297, Dail responsibility for I.R.A. ; 298, *Green Pastures* ; 304, *Tom Jones* ; 305, not smoking ; 308, Lord Derby ; 311, arms from Germany ; 312, External Association ; 313, arrested ; 314, released—correspondence with Lloyd George ; 315 *et seq.*, Gairloch ; 319, on Lloyd George ; 320, advice to Griffith ; 329, standing firm ; 330, denounces Treaty ; 332, 333, Kenilworth Square ; 337, " civil war must be avoided " ; 338 *et seq.*, the Pact ; 339, H.Q. in Suffolk Street ; 343, Four Courts ; 344, Volunteer oath ; 344, Hammam Hotel ; 352, trying for peace ; 354, Carrick-on-Suir.
—— Vivion, 354.
Devereux, Dinny, 5.
Devlin, Paddy, 286.
Devon, 98 ; 188 ; 282.
Dickens, Charles, 194.
Dick the Dandy, 213.
Dillon, Andrew, 257.
Dillon, Geraldine, 290.
Dillon, John, 165.
Dillon, Tom, 172 ; 217 *et seq.* ; 268 ; 290.
Diogenes, 77.
Director of Elections, 167, appointment of.
—— of Publicity, 338, position refused ; 355.
District Inspector R.I.C., 74.
Document No. 2, 312.
Doherty, Jim, 193.
Dolan, Jim, 221.
D'Olier Street, 289 ; 345.
Dollymount, 286.
Dominion Home Rule, 244 ; 295 ; 330.
Donnelly, Eamon, 168 ; 181 *et seq.*, Partition.
Donnybrook, 45.
Donovan, Con., 115 ; 119.
" Dooley, Mr.", 76.

Dostievsky, 188.
Downing Street, 322.
Down, South, 330.
Doyle, Anthony, 87 *et seq.*
—— John L., 33 ; 47.
—— John, Railway Guard, 55.
—— Phil, 56 ; 57.
—— Seumas, 54 ; 56 ; 64 *et seq.* ; 68, journey to Dublin ; 71, interview with Pearse ; 72, surrender ; 75 ; 84 *et seq.*, courtmartial ; 92, death sentence and commutation ; 120, Lewes Jail ; 151.
—— Seumas, organiser, 168.
—— Tom, 128.
Drinagh, Co. Wexford, 87.
Dublin, 6, Gaelic League founded ; 9, Griffith's cycle party ; 11, St. Teresa's Hall ; 13, No. 17 Fownes Street ; 13, D.B.C. ; 14, Lennox Street ; 15, Stephen's Green ; 17, The National Library ; 20 ; 27, Mountshannon Road ; 28, Harcourt Street Station ; 30, strike ; 31, Larkin ; 33, Volunteers ; 34, Broadstone Station ; 35, Forresters' Hall ; 38, newspapers ; 38, Arbour Hill ; 43, Metropolitan Police ; 43, Bachelor's Walk ; 44, Tom Clarke ; 45, Sinn Féin H.Q. ; 49, route to ; 50, courier from ; 53, MacNeill's countermand ; 53, the Rising ; 54, train from ; 55, fighting in ; 57 ; 61 ; 63 ; 64 ; 67 *et seq.*, surrender ; 77 ; 79, prisoners for ; 94, ovation for deportees ; 116, Rowan Hamilton ; 133, handbill ; 151, reception in ; 153 ; 163 *et seq.*, No. 6 Harcourt Street ; 274, Maurice Bourgeois ; 275 *et seq.*, Hardy.
—— Brigade, 337.
—— Castle, 3 ; 56 ; 57 ; 67 ; 156 ; 211 ; 237 ; 238 ; 264, search for *Irish Bulletin* ; 274, bourgeois ; 286, Bloody Sunday ; 308, Cope ; 334, occupation of.
—— Corporation, 80.
D.M.P., 303.
Dublin Parliament, vi.
—— Typographical Provident Society, 218.
Duggan, Eamon, 132 ; 314 ; 315 ; 322.
Duncannon line, 57.
Dundalk Democrat, 224 *et seq.*
Dundalk Jail, 158.
Dun Laoghaire, 259 ; 285 ; 315.
Dunne, Governor, 240 ; 241.

Dunsink Observatory, 117.
Dunville's, Belfast, 233.
Dwyer, Danny, 146.
Dyan, Principal Warder, 134 *et seq.*

Earlsfort Terrace, 293.
Earl Street, 345 *et seq.*
Easter Sunday, 1916, 50.
Easter Week Rising, 67 ; 153.
Eccles Street, 302.
Echo, Enniscorthy, 24 ; 25 ; 37 ; 63 ;
  80, entire staff arrested and paper
  suppressed ; 86.
Economic Case for Irish Indepen-
  dence, 206.
Edenderry, 165.
Edgbaston, 198.
Egypt, 254 ; 273 ; 326.
Egyptian, 327, a British agent.
Einstein, Albert, 117 ; 118.
Election machinery, 1918, 167 *et seq.*
—— manifesto, 239.
Elizabeth, v.
El Sol, 324.
Elvery's, 345.
Ely Place, 305.
Emer, 268.
Emmet, Robert, vi ; 62 ; 187.
England, v ; 27 ; 30 ; 31 ; 56 ; 82,
  concentration camp ; 84, indiga-
  tion over executions ; 94, deportees
  to ; 188.
England's Intelligence Service, 254.
English Bibles, 94.
—— Catholic soldier, 84.
—— guns, 85.
—— newspapers, 308, castigating the
  Government.
—— prisons, 44 ; 207.
Ennis, Co. Clare, 182.
Enniscorthy, 20, the Féis ; 24, Con-
  vention ; 37, pike making ; Larry
  de Lacey ; *Echo* ; 51, Easter Sunday, 1916 ; 52, rendezvous ; 53 ;
  54 ; 56 ; 60, march to ; 61 ; 62
  et seq., occupation of ; 66, threat
  to shell ; 67, Irish Republican
  H.Q. ; 72 ; 75 ; 77 ; 79, every
  man arrested ; 86, men wrongly
  arrested ; 95 ; 96, news from ;
  151 ; 156.
" Enniscorthy Emily," 72 ; 73.
Enniskillen, 269, Frank Carney.
Epping Forest, 188.
Esmonde, Sir Thomas, 24.
Etchingham, Sean (Patsy Patrick), 64
  et seq. ; 68, journey to Dublin ; 71,
  interview with Pearse ; 72, surrender ; 73 ; 75, " First Offender " ; 76 *et seq.* ; 84 *et seq.*,

courtmartial ; 92, death sentence
  and commutation ; 107 *et seq.*,
  Dartmoor Jail ; 119 *et seq.*, Lewes
  Jail.
Euclid, 117.
Executions, 84.

Fáinne, the, 118.
Farnan, Dr., 291.
Farrell, Stationmaster, 54 ; 55.
Faust, 203.
Fenian Rising, vi.
Fenians, 145.
Fenian Street, 298.
Fermanagh, 269, Frank Carney ; 330.
Fermoy, 256 ; 351 ; 352.
Fernand, Luigi, 214.
Ferns, Co. Wexford, 65.
Ferrycarrig Bridge, 65.
Fianna Eireann, 26.
—— Fail, 182.
Fielding, John, 57.
—— Tom, 56.
Figgis, Darrell, 155 ; 163 ; 204 *et*
  seq. ; 238 ; 339.
Finance Department, 152, Collins.
Fine Ghaedheal, 336, aims of.
First Offenders' Act, 75.
Fishguard, 272.
Fitz, Miss (Anna Kelly), 172 ; 260
  et seq. ; 265 ; 321.
Fitzgerald, Desmond, 112 ; 162 ;
  202 ; 278 ; 293 ; 319 ; 335.
—— Father, 326.
—— Michael, 285.
—— Seumas, 353.
Fitzhenry, Rev. Father, 66.
Fitzsimons, John, 34.
Fleming, Paddy, 278.
Flood, Jim, 168.
Foggy Dew, The, 97.
Foley, Ned, 11 ; 43 ; 46.
Foreign Office, 297 *et seq.*
—— visitors and publicists, 246.
Foster, Stephen, 4.
Fota Island, 353.
Four Courts, 334 ; 337 *et seq.*, Re-
  publican Army H.Q. ; 343, at-
  tacked ; 344, fall of.
France, 188 ; 274, strained relations
  with Britain ; 275 ; 322 ; 323.
Frazer, Major, 215.
Frederick Street, North, 303.
Freeman's Journal, 259 ; 268 ; 276 ;
  286 ; 287.
Free Press, 22 ; 53.
Free State, 216.
—— Army, 182 ; 337 ; 343,
  attack Four Courts ; 343 *et seq.*
—— Government, 337.

Free State Soldiers, 331.
—— —— Volunteers, 334.
French, Colonel, 66 et seq. ; 84.
—— Consul, 275.
—— Dora, 305.
—— Government, 274 ; 324, secret agreement with Turkey.
—— Lord, 266 ; 267.
—— Peter, 48.
—— prisoners, 103.
—— Revolution, 255.
—— War Museum, 274.
Friend, Major, 190.
Furlong, John, 56 et seq.
—— M. J., 5 ; 21 ; 22.
—— Mrs., 58.
—— Pat, 37 ; 59 et seq.

Gaelic Athletic Association (G.A.A.), 10 ; 34 ; 35 ; 172.
—— Classes, 158.
—— League, 1 ; 5 ; 6 ; 7 ; 11 ; 12 ; 19 ; 20 ; 67 ; 96, Tom Ashe ; 108 ; 209 ; 264, outlawed.
Gaiety Theatre, 17.
Gairloch, 315 et seq.
Gallagher, Frank, 167, publicity ; 172, Mountjoy Jail ; 176 et seq., Jean Christophe ; 240 ; 262 ; 264 ; 293 ; 301 ; 321.
Galligan, Paul, 64 ; 65 ; 135.
Gallop, Warder, 120.
Galway, 28, Mellowes ; 101; 107 ; 280 ; 290.
Galway public bodies, 297.
—— University, 290.
Gardiner Street, 345.
Gavan Duffy, George, 315, plenipotentiary ; 335, Minister for Foreign Affairs.
Gavan Duffy, Louise, 293 ; 305.
G. Division, 259.
Geashill, 200 ; 201.
General Election, 1910, 20.
—— —— 1918, 196, Sinn Féin Victory.
General Post Office, 241 ; 308.
Geneva, 176 ; 326 ; 327.
George's Street Barracks, Wexford, 73.
German Foreign Office, 258 ; 329.
—— H.Q., 171, emissary with questionnaire.
—— landing, 209.
" German Plot," 167.
Germans, 37 ; 48 ; 49 ; 175, losing the war ; 258.
German submarines, 42.
Germany, 27 ; 33 ; 44 ; 82, arms from ; 103 ; 258 ; 311 ; 322.

Gilbert and Sullivan, 214.
Gilly of Christ, The, 17.
Ginnell, Larry, 321.
Gloucester Cathedral, 202, 203.
—— Jail, 167 ; 179 ; 196 et seq.
—— Police Station, 200.
G.-Men, 34 ; 35 ; 82 ; 185 ; 260 ; 262, shot down.
God Save Ireland, 132 ; 134.
Goldsmith, 203.
Gonne MacBride, Maud, 11, the I.R.B. ; 11, Cathleen ni Houlihan.
Gorey, Co. Wexford, 77 ; 157.
Gorki, 188.
Gorman, Tommy, Sergeant Major, 81.
Gougane Barra, 39 ; 40.
Gough, General, 301.
Government of the Irish Republic, 257, bloody opposition.
Governor Cork Prison, 161.
—— Dartmoor Prison, 100 et seq. ; 108.
—— Lewes Prison, 115 et seq.
—— Parkhurst Prison, 139 et seq.
Grabisch, Frau, 258.
Grafton Street, Dublin, 183 ; 209 ; 241 ; 261 ; 293.
Grand Dissolving View, The, 61.
—— Jury, 2.
—— National, 107.
Great War, the, 209 ; 254.
Green Flag, 118.
Gresham Hotel, 284.
Greystones, 238.
Griffin, Father, 290.
Griffith, Arthur, 2, The United Irishman ; 9 ; 12, the Sinn Féin Party ; 13, No. 17 Fownes Street ; 14, Cumann na nGaedheal ; 23, North Leitrim Election ; 152 ; 153, " moderation in everything " ; 154 et seq., 1917 Ard Fheis ; 163, publicity ; 167, arrested for " German Plot " ; 200 et seq., Gloucester Jail ; 202, 203, a typical Dubliner ; 203, Cathleen ni Houlihan ; 204, et seq., Figgis ; 208 et seq., storm of 1903 ; 209 et seq., the Rising ; 210, I.R.B. ; 211, physical force ; 212, Black and Tans ; 215 et seq., and Cathal Brugha ; 216, Constitution of 1782 ; 218, attitude to Labour ; 218 et seq., attitude to Larkin ; 219, on dictatorship ; 229, physical strength ; 233, influenza ; 235, arrange escape ; 240, American Delegation ; 241, " a granite wall " ; 242, Home Rule ; 245

et seq., meeting with Childers ; 252 *et seq.*, and Childers ; 259, Quin ; 270, John Chartres ; 276, Hardy ; 284, hierarchy ; 285, negotiations ; 287, Bloody Sunday ; 288 death notices ; 288, arrested ; 296, Moylett ; 314, release ; 315, plenipotentiary ; 320, head of the plenipotentiaries ; 321, South American loan ; 322, suggests European tour ; 330, " Treaty does not involve partition " ; 331, " Lloyd George is convinced " ; 332 elected president.
Guerrilla warfare, 257.

Hadden, Alderman George, 294 ; 295.
Hague, The, 176.
Haifa, 188.
Hamburg, 327.
Hamilton, Rowan, 116 ; 117 ; 118.
Hammam Hotel, 344 ; 346 ; 347.
Hanrahan, Harry, 155.
Harcourt Place, 298 *et seq.*
Harcourt Street, 163 *et seq.*, No. 6 ; 293.
—— —— Station, 238.
—— Terrace, 344.
Hardy, 276 *et seq.*
Harling, Séan, 313.
Harold's Cross, 249.
Harper, Father William, 20.
Harper's Lane, 23.
Harrell, Sir David, 43.
—— William Vesey, 43 *et seq.*
Harrington Street, 275.
Hastings, Stephen, 30.
Hawke, Warder, 123 *et seq.*
Hayes, Dr. Richard, 96, journey to jail ; 106 *et seq.*, Dartmoor Jail ; 112, removed from Dartmoor ; 121, Lewes Jail.
—— Thady, 212.
H.Q. Irish Command, 38.
Healy, Tim, 39 ; 165 ; 239.
Heffernan, James, 33.
Hegarty, Diarmuid, 288.
—— Jack, 37 *et seq.*
Henley, 188.
Henry, Crown Solicitor, 265.
Herbert Park, 311.
Hibernian Military Academy, 27.
Hierarchy, 284.
Higgins, 30 ; 31.
Highfield Road, 250.
Hindenburg, 143.
Hindu prisoner, 147.
Hobson, Bulmer, 36.
Holbrook, George, 88.

Holbrook, Matt, 67.
Holyhead, 194 ; 315 *et seq.*
Homan, George, 298.
Home Rule Bill, 1 ; 12, Bill of 1912 20 ; 23 ; 30, Act passed ; 94 95 ; 103 ; 242.
Hotel Eden, Berlin, 330.
Hound of Heaven, The, 109.
House of Commons, 149 ; 273.
Howth gun-running, 33 ; 244.
Hughes, Ben, 5 ; 212.
Hughes, Seumas, 122.
Hunger strike, Cork Jail, 159 *et seq.*
Huns, 48.
Hunter, Tom, 200 ; 217 *et seq.*
Hyde, Douglas, 5 ; 6.
Hyland, Joe, 305.

Immediate and terrible war, 338.
Imperial Government, 20.
Imperial Staff, Chief of, 287.
In Cellar Cool, 231.
Independent, 53.
India, 273 ; 327 ; 328.
Indian Congress Party, 328.
Indian Moslem League, 328.
Indian Nationalists, 327.
Institute of Advanced Studies, 117.
Intelligence Department, 152, Collins.
—— Division of British Admiralty, 42.
—— H.Q., 300.
—— Organisation, 167.
—— Service, 35 ; 201.
Intermediate Examinations, 4.
Inverness, 319.
Invisible ink, 171, German formula ; 235, Irish formula.
Ireland, 84, indignation over executions ; 288, *Ireland for Ever* ; 311, " King's writ no longer runs in."
—— *Germany and the Freedom of the Seas*, 37.
Ireland's Address, 324.
—— *Case Against Conscription*, 166 ; 239.
" Iresol, Limited," 301.
Ireland's Own, 25.
Irish American, 96 *et seq.*, Tom Ashe.
—— —— opinion, 240.
—— —— papers, 258.
—— Brigade, 258 *et seq.*
—— *Bulletin*, 264, started 11th Nov., 1919 ; 265, false *Bulletin* issued by Castle ; 293 ; 324.
—— coast, 42.
—— Envoy to U.S., 128.
—— Government, 117.
—— *Independent*, 277 *et seq.*, Hardy.
—— newspapers, 121.

Irish, Parliamentary Party, Irish Nationalist Party, Redmondite Party, Irish Party), 1 ; 2 ; 3 ; 10 ; 12 ; 13 ; 20 ; 48 ; 57 ; 112, two elections lost to Sinn Féi ; 164, conscription ; 202 ; 242 ; 284.
—— *Press*, 218.
—— prisoners, 147.
—— Question, 147 ; 274.
—— Race Congress, 334 *et seq.*
—— —— Convention, 218 ; 240.
—— Republic, 14 ; 53 ; 72 ; 82 ; 155 ; 175, backed by 80 per cent. ; 207 ; 237, Government of the ; 293, American aid ; 295 ; 296 ; 312 ; 338, undermined.
—— Republican Army (I.R.A.), 75 ; 248, bloody encounters ; 257, clashes with British forces ; 259, Quin ; 262, " safe conducts " ; 269 *et seq.*, Frank Carney ; 303, J. J. Walsh ; 337, Dail authority repudiated.
—— —— Brotherhood, 9 ; 10 ; 11 ; 12 ; 27 ; 34 ; 41 ; 153 ; 154, orders from ; 155 *et seq.* ; interference in Volunteer movement ; 166, Brugha and the ; 180 ; 209 ; 210, Griffith and the ; 211, Joe Poole.
I.R.B. Supreme Council, 154.
Irish Republican H.Q., Enniscorthy, 67.
Irish Times, 42 ; 43 ; 72.
—— Volunteers, 28 ; 30 ; 33 ; 43 ; 45 ; 48 ; 50, Executive ; 51, G.H.Q. ; 52, G.H.Q. ; 53 ; 54 ; 64 ; 68 ; 131 ; 140 ; 153 ; 156, lacked arms ; 156, interference from I.R.B. ; 166, Conscription threat ; 167, arrested in " German Plot " ; 183, 3rd Battalion, Dublin ; 209 ; 238 ; 264, outlawed ; 273 ; 274, Maurice Bourgeois.
—— whiskey, 208.
Irwin, C. J., 80 ; 86.
Isle of Wight, 135 ; 137 ; 150 ; 188.
Italian Literature, 119.
Italy, 322.
Iveagh House, 298.

Jackets Green, The, 97.
James I, v.
Jameson, 208.
" Jetter, Mr.", 327.
Johnson, Dr., 188.
Joyce, James, 17 ; 18.
Judge Advocate, 86.

Kapp and Peterson, 250.
Karsavina, 188.
Kavanagh, Warder, 157 ; 162.
" Kearney, William," 290.
Keegan, Pat, 37 ; 45 ; 67.
Kehoe, Father Owen, 68 ; 69 ; 70.
Kelly, Alderman Tom, 173.
—— Frank, 260 ; 261 ; 298.
—— *of Killann*, 158.
Kemal Pasha, 306.
Kenilworth Square, 249 ; 332.
Kent, Davy, 106.
Kerney, Leopold, 330.
Kerr, Mr., 275 *et seq.*
Kerrigan, Sarsfield, 17.
Kerry, 53, Casement ; 158 ; 161 ; 256 ; 289 ; 352.
Kerrymen in Cork Jail, 159.
Kew Gardens, 188.
Kildare Street, 301.
Kilkenny, 51 ; 63 ; 354.
Killester, 296.
Killurin, Co. Wexford, 61.
Kilmainham Jail, 87 *et seq.*
Kilmashogue, 86.
Kiltartan, 246.
King, Dick, 72, surrender ; 75 ; 84 *et seq.*, courtmartial ; 92, death sentence and commutation ; 115 ; 124.
—— Lords and Commons, 217, Griffith on.
Kingsbridge, Dublin, 79.
Kingstown, 62 ; 279 *et seq.*, Hardy.
Kurdistan, 188.

Labour, 209 ; 218 *et seq.*, Griffith's attitude to.
Lacey, Jack, 67 ; 68.
—— (Wexford sailor), 272.
Lady Emissary from German H.Q., 170 *et seq.*
—— Gregory, 246.
Land war, vi.
Larkin, James, 30 ; 31 ; 218 *et seq.*
Latin America, 324.
Latvian, 250.
Law, Bonar, 149.
Leader, The, 2 ; 13 ; 17.
le Blanc, Maurice, 160.
Leeds, 195 ; 196 ; 281.
Leinster Football Championship, 157.
—— *Leader*, 183.
Leitrim North Election, 23.
Leix, 174 ; 201.
Lenin, 306.
Lewes Jail, 108 *et seq.* ; 115 *et seq.*
" Lewis & Lewis," 298.
Liberals, 20.
Liberator, 212.

Liberty Hall, 220 ; 244.
Liffey, 30 ; 210.
Light on the Broom, The, 17.
Limerick, 45 ; 349 ; 352.
—— West, 266.
Lincoln Jail, 227.
—— memorial 19.
Lisburn, 281.
Little Red Lark, 97.
Liverpool, 281.
Lloyd George, 103 ; 147, Home Rule
  Convention ; 240 ; 257 ; 285 ;
  295 ; 296 ; 297 ; 307 ; 308, reign
  of terror ; 311, Truce ; 314, cor-
  respondence with Dev ; 315 *et seq.*,
  Gairloch ; 324, downfall of ; 331,
  Boundary Commission; 331,
  secret letter to Carson.
Local Government, 298.
—— —— Inquiry, 24.
—— —— Office, 302.
London, 115 ; 138 ; 150, arrival in
  Pentonville ; 268 ; 273, Houses of
  Parliament ; 282 ; 308, secret
  negotiations.
—— Conference, 322.
Longford, 122 ; 202.
Longshoremen, anti-German, 42.
Lord Mayor of Cork, 158.
—— —— —— Dublin, 164 ; 237 ;
  343 ; 344.
Loughnavale, 296.
Louth, 154.
Love Songs of Connacht, 7.
Lucan, 210.
Lynch, Diarmuid, 111 ; 154, the
  I.R.B.
Lynch, Liam, 256 ; 349 *et seq.*
Lynn, Dr. Kathleen, 286.

Macardle, Dorothy, 72 ; 82 ; 196 ;
  301 ; 347.
—— Jack, 112 ; 114.
MacBride, Sean, 274.
—— Joe, 230, Gloucester Jail.
McCann, Pierce, 202 ; 212 *et seq.*,
  Gloucester Jail ; 236, death of.
MacCarthy, Dan, 80, 168.
McCullagh, Denny, 224 *et seq.*
MacCurtain, 158 ; 160 *et seq.*, hunger
  strike.
MacDermott, Sean, 13 ; 14 ; 44 ;
  80 ; 81 ; 82 ; 89 ; 90, execution ;
  210.
MacDonagh, 81.
McEntee, Sean, 103 ; 119 ; 200 *et
  seq.*, Gloucester Jail ; 222 *et seq.*
McEvoy, Jack, 32 ; 33.
McGarrity, Joe, 329.
McGovern, Barney, 69 ; 70 ; 71.

McGrath, Joe, 315 *et seq.*
McGuinness, Joe, 122 ; 151 ; 201 ;
  219.
McInerney, Limerick, 160.
McKee, Dick, 287.
McMahon, Phil, 108.
MacMurchadha, Fergus, 215.
MacNeill, Eoin, 50 ; 51 ; 52 ; 53,
  countermanding order ; 72 ; 82 ;
  103 *et seq.*, Dartmoor Jail ; 119,
  lectures on Irish History ; 128 ;
  133 ; 153, and de Valera ; 210 ;
  336, the Irish Race Congress.
MacNeill, Mrs. James, 293.
MacSwiney, Mary, 320, 352.
—— Peter, 353.
—— Terence, 158 ; 160, hunger
  strike in Cork Jail ; 284 ; 285,
  death of ; 326.
MacWhite, Michael, 326.
Mackensen, 188.
Mackenzie, Compton, 204.
Madrid, 324 ; 325 ; 336.
Maeve, 141 ; 268.
Magistrates, 284, resigning commis-
  sions.
Madhi's Camp, 115.
Maidstone Prison, 118 ; 133.
Mallow, 352.
Malta, 254.
Manahan, Liam, 221 *et seq.*
Manchester Guardian, 308.
—— Martyrs, The, 20.
Mansion House, Dublin, 130 ; 151 ;
  162 ; 164 *et seq.* ; 182 ; 239 ; 241;
  314 ; 319.
Marino Crescent, Dublin, 133.
Markievicz, Madame, 26 ; 56 ; 76 ;
  257 ; 274, Bourgeois ; 334.
Maritana, 4.
Marlborough Street, 345 ; 347.
Marseillaise, The, 4.
Marshallstown, 65.
Martin from Wexford, 85.
Martinson, 250 *et seq.*
Martyn, Edward, 18.
Maryboro' Prison, 278.
Mass in Lewes Jail, 131.
—— in Parkhurst, 139.
Maunsel, 166.
—— & Roberts, 261.
Maxwell, General, 84.
Maynooth, 165 ; 284.
Mayo, 170.
Mazurian Lakes, 188.
Meath Street, Dublin, 80.
Mellowes, Barney, 28 ; 29 ; 81 ; 82 ;
  347.
—— Fred, 28.
—— Jenny, 28.

Mellowes, Liam, 27 ; 28 ; 29 ; 30 ; 31 ; 49 ; 78 ; 338.
M.P.'s in Gloucester Jail, 202.
Menapia, 214.
Mercer Street, 294 ; 344.
Merrion Row, 288.
—— Square, 291 ; 299.
—— Street, 288 ; 335.
—— Strand, 296.
Military Barracks, Wexford, 73 ; 75.
—— Rule in Ireland, 268.
Minister of Defence, 266.
—— —— Finance, 279.
Ministry of Munitions, 281.
Molesworth Street, 265, Publicity Office.
Moliere, 214.
Moloney, John, 14 et seq.
—— Peter, 14 et seq. ; 198 ; 235 ; 236.
Monaghan, 224.
—— South, 202.
Mooney's, 207.
Mooney, Joe, 80 ; 81.
Moore, George, 17 ; 261.
Moore's Melodies, 4.
Moran, D. P., 2 ; 13 ; 17.
Morrow, Jack, 301.
Morris, Mike, 30.
Mountjoy Chaplain, 95.
—— escapes, 260 ; 261.
—— Jail, 94 ; 288.
—— manners, 95.
Mount Merrion Avenue, 305.
Mount Street, Upper, 264 et seq., 355.
Moylett, Paddy, 285 ; 296.
Mulcahy, Richard, 276 ; 337 ; 351.
Mulvey, Anthony J., 63.
Murphy, Fintan, 271.
—— Fred, 212 et seq.
—— Nick, 25.
—— Patrick, 285.

Napoleon, vi.
Napoleonic wars, 103.
Nation, The, 308.
Nationalists, 33 ; 41.
Nationality, 217.
National Council, 9.
—— Executive, 154.
—— Gallery, 291.
—— Library, 17 ; 166 ; 276.
—— University, 18.
Native chieftains, v.
Navan, 345.
Nelson Pillar, 286.
New Ross, 20, the Féis.
New York, 96 et seq., Tom Ashe ; .325.
Norman Invasion, 214.
Normans, v.

North Sea, 106.
—— Star Hotel, 36.
—— Wall, 192.
Norton, of North Co. Dublin, 144.
Noyk, Michael, 265.
Nugent, Mrs. Larry, 264 ; 308.
Nunan, Michael, 171 et seq. ; 185 ; 186 ; 257 et seq.
Nunan, Sean, 260.

Oakley Road, 266.
Oath of Allegiance, 254.
O'Brien, Art, 269.
—— Jack, 147.
—— Maire, 324 ; 340.
—— William, 164.
O'Byrne, Rev. Mark, 74.
O'Connell Bridge, 191 ; 345.
—— Daniel, 5 ; 212.
—— General, 51, footnote ; 52 et seq. ; 212 et seq.
—— Kathleen, 347 et seq.
—— Street, 288 ; 291 ; 308 ; 339 ; 344 ; 345.
O'Connor, Batt, 45.
—— Fergus, 122 ; 123.
—— Frank, 352.
—— Henry, 259 ; 260 ; 287.
—— Joe, 337 ; 344.
—— M. J., 50.
—— Rory, 176 ; 337 ; 340 ; 341.
—— Seumas, 9.
—— Sir James, 50 ; 308.
O'Donnell, Hugh, 336.
—— Miss, 302.
—— The, 336.
O'Donovan Rossa funeral, 44.
O'Duffy, General, 130.
O'Faolain, Sean, 352.
Offaly, 165 ; 174 ; 201.
O'Flanagan, Father, 239 ; 296 ; 308.
O'Gaora, Colm, 143.
O hAodha, Tomas, 9.
O'Hara, District Inspector, R.I.C., 76.
O'Hegarty, P. S., 176.
O'Higgins, Kevin, 174 ; 298.
Oireachtas, 154.
O'Keeffe, Paidin, 262.
O'Kelly, Sean T., 10 ; 11, I.R.B. ; 19, Gaelic League ; 44, Rossa funeral ; 45, Collins ; 227, Envoy in Paris ; 308 ; 323 ; 325 ; 330, Treaty.
O'Kelly, Seumas, 183.
Old John, 298.
O'Mahony, John, 12.
O'Malley, Ernie, 286 ; 293 ; 338.
O'Mara, James, 168 et seq., election machinery ; 175, silver shortage ; 176 ; 242.

O'Mara Opera Company, 122.
O'Muirthuile, Sean, 258 *et seq.*
O'Neill, Larry, 164.
—— Moira, 65.
Opera Comique, 274.
O'Rahilly, Madame, 311.
Orange Society, 20.
Orangemen, 33.
O'Reilly, J. K., 230 *et seq.*, Gloucester Jail.
—— M. W., 156.
Orlando, 319.
Osgood, Mrs., 247 ; 248.
O'Sullivan, Gearoid, 81.
O'Sullivan, Seumas, Captain, 45.
O'Sullivan, Seumas, the poet, 9 ; 184 ; 261.
Oylegate, Co. Wexford, 64.

Pact, the, 338 *et seq.*
Paris, 176 et seq. ; 240 ; 323 ; 334 *et seq.*
Parkhurst Jail, 132 *et seq.*
Parliament for All Ireland, 296.
Parnell, Charles Stewart, 1 ; 62.
—— Square, 35 ; 154.
Partition, 30 ; 103 ; 330.
Passage, 353.
Patsy Patrick (Sean Etchingham), 76 *et seq.*
Pavlova, 188.
Peace Conference, 156 ; 175 *et seq.* ; 218 ; 227 ; 237 *et seq.*
Pearse, Padraic, 19, *An Claidheamh Solus* ; 45, lecture in Enniscorthy ; 46, order from ; 51, order for the Rising ; 52 ; 53, Rising postponed ; 66, surrender ; 67, verbal order ; 68 ; 69 ; 71, in Arbour Hill ; 72 ; 81, execution ; 82 ; 85 ; 190.
—— Street, 276 ; 288.
Pembroke, Co. Dublin 202.
Pentonville Prison, 149 *et seq.*
Persia, 188.
Philadelphia, 218 ; 240 ; 329.
Phillips, *Irish Times*, 42 ; 43.
Philpotts, Eden, 98 ; 188.
Phoenix Park, 38 ; 187 ; 208.
Plenipotentiaries, 320.
Plunkett, Count, 157.
—— Countess, 190.
—— George, 139, mutiny in Parkhurst Jail.
—— Jack, 119 ; 147.
—— Sir Horace, 295.
Plymouth, 98 ; 281.
Poblacht, 339.
Poblacht & Saorstat, 216.
Poincare, 116.

Police Commissioner for Ireland, 130.
Poole, Joe, 35 ; 211.
—— Vincent, 118 ; 119.
Portland Convict Prison, 118.
Portobello, 209.
Portsmouth, 281.
Portstewart, 281.
President of the Irish Republic, 319.
President of U.S., 166.
Price, Major, 38 ; 39.
Prime Minister, 319.
Prince of Tyrconnell, 336.
Princetown University, 117.
Prisoners' Council, Lewes, 119.
Prisoners of War demand, 131.
Prison releases, 314.
Prison Board, 100.
Publicity Department, 261, Fitz ; 264, Mrs. Nugent ; 355.

Quaternions, 116.
Queen Elizabeth, 246.
Queen's Theatre, 203.
Quin, 258 *et seq.*
Quinn, John, 208 *et seq.*

Raid on No. 6 Harcourt St., 262.
Rafter, Seumas, 37 ; 64 ; 72, surrender ; 79 ; 84 *et seq.*, courtmartial ; 92, death sentence and commutation.
Rathangan, Co. Wexford, 60.
Rathgar, 248 *et seq.* ; 285.
Rathgar Avenue, 290 *et seq.*
Rathmines, 184 ; 209 ; 249 ; 303.
Rebellion of 1798, v ; 1.
Redmond, John, 1 ; 13 ; 22 ; 23 ; 33 ; 48 ; 50 ; 56 ; 103.
Redmondite Volunteers, 34 ; 73.
Redmond, Myley, 52 ; 53 ; 61.
Reilly, Joe, 299.
Relativity, theory of, 117.
Renunciation Act of 1782, 217.
Republic, 64, proclaimed ; 94, cheers for the.
Republican clubs, 35.
—— forces, 334, split ; 337, unprepared.
—— *News*, 261.
—— Volunteers, 334, Four Courts.
Resident Magistrate, 74.
Resurrection of Hungary, The, 13 ; 217.
Return from Fingal, The, 97.
Reuter's News Agency, 330.
Reward of £10,000, 279.
Richmond, 188.
Richmond Barracks, 28 ; 79 ; 87 ; 88.
Riddle of the Sands, 244.
Riders to the Sea, 274.

INDEX

Rising, 29 ; 36 ; 45, preparations for ; 49 ; 50 ; 51, orders for ; 53, postponed ; 59 ; 61, begins in Dublin ; 67, no informers ; 71 ; 72 ; 103 ; 109 ; 156 ; 209, Griffith ; 274, French reaction.
Rising of 1848, vi.
Robey, George, 269.
Robinson, Seumas, 210 et seq., Soloheadbeg.
Roche, The Castle, Enniscorthy, 65.
Rogerson's Quay, 287.
Rome, 178.
Rooney, William, 52.
Rosslare Harbour, 56 ; 63.
Royal Irish Constabulary (R.I.C.), 41 ; 54 ; 211 ; 248, bloody encounters ; 284, units revolting.
Royal Irish Regiment, 87.
Royal University, 4.
Russia, 122 ; 188 ; 191 ; 196.
Ryan, John T. (" Mr. Jetter "), 327 et seq.
Ryan, M. J., 240 ; 241.
Ryan, Mrs. Dr. Jim, 298.
Ryan, Paddy, 168.

Sackville Place, 345.
Safeguards for Unionists, 296.
St. Enda's, 266.
St. Germain the Deathless, 215.
St. Teresa's Hall, 11.
St. Vincent's Hospital, 293.
Salamanca, 326.
Salford, 105.
Sankey & Moody Band, 39.
Sappho, 17.
Scotland Yard, 271 ; 272.
Sean O Duibhir a Ghleanna, 350.
Sears, William, 24 ; 80 ; 86.
Self-determination, 218, Ireland's right to.
Selskar Abbey, 215.
Settlement offer, 296.
Shakespeare, 203.
Sheehan, Paddy, 176.
Shelbourne Hotel, 304 et seq.
Shelley, 188 ; 203.
Sheridan, 203.
Shouldice, Jack, 81.
Siberia, 188.
Simon, Sir John, 308.
Sinn Féin, 3 ; 9 ; 11 ; 12 ; 13 ; 14 ; 20 ; 23 ; 24 ; 50 ; 152 et seq. ; 156, organisation unequalled ; 163, Figgis, honorary secretary ; 164, Conscription ; 167, substitute Executive ; 209 ; 217 ; 237, proclaimed ; 244, Childers ; 264, outlawed ; 273, solidarity of ;

274, Maurice Bourgeois ; 275 et seq., Hardy ; 287, Sir Henry Wilson ; 328, methods for India.
—— —— Ard Comhairle, 162.
—— —— Ard Fheis, 154, the battleground.
—— —— daily paper, 12.
—— —— Deputies, 207.
—— —— Executive, 167, German Plot arrests ; 172, meeting in Croke Park ; 238 ; 339.
—— Feiners, 48, ; 53 ; 55.
—— —— in London, 115.
—— Féin Headquarters, 206 ; 237 ; 261.
—— —— leaders, 277 et seq., journalists posing as.
—— —— Notes, 163 ; 164.
—— —— Press Bureau, 162, appointed director.
—— —— Publicity Bureau, 45.
—— —— Rising, vi.
—— —— Volunteers, 34 ; 216.
Sinnott, Sean, 26 ; 27 ; 43 ; 45 ; 51 ; 52 ; 53 ; 56 et seq. ; 73 ; 157.
Six Counties, 330, exclusion of.
Skeeterpark, Co. Wexford, 56.
Slaney River, 24.
Slattery's Loom, Lewes, 119.
Sligo, North, 202.
Sloan, Detective Officer, 54 ; 55.
Smith, Superintendent, 186 ; 262.
Soldier's Joy, The, 157.
—— Song, The, 158 ; 195.
Solicitor General, 50.
Solitary confinement, 101.
Soloheadbeg, 210.
South Dublin Union, 29.
Southern Unionists, 314.
Sovereign nation, 319.
Spailpín a Ruin, 97.
Spain, 322 ; 324.
Spanish police, 325.
Spindler, Hans, 327, Captain of the Aud.
Stack, Austin, 103 ; 108 et seq., Dartmoor Jail ; 158 ; 174 ; 266, clash with Collins ; 313 ; 314 ; 339 ; 343 Civil War ; 347 ; 355.
Stafford's workshop, 53.
Stafford, Tom, 59 ; 60.
Staines, Micheal, 133 ; 134 ; 166 ; 314.
Stephen's Green, 186 ; 241 ; 275 ; 288 ; 293.
Stephens, James, 17.
Stone, Thomas, Principal Warder, 104 et seq. ; 109 et seq. ; 126 et seq.
Stopford Green, Mrs., 288 ; 294 seq.

Storm of 1903, 208.
Strongbow, 214.
Suffolk Street, 298 ; 339 et seq.
Sullivan, John, 18.
Summerville, 42.
Sunday Independent, 335.
Supreme Council I.R.B., 34 ; 35 ;
  38 ; 43 ; 44.
Surrey, 282.
Sussex, 116 ; 188.
Switzerland, 322.
Synge, 203 ; 274.

Taghmon, 50.
Tagoat, 9.
Tagus, 326.
Talbot Street, 345.
Tavistock, 115.
Terenure, 249 ; 250.
Tetuan, Duke of, 336, Irish Race
  Congress.
Thames, 188.
Theatre Royal, 346.
Third Battalion, 337 ; 344.
Thompson, Captain, 276 et seq.
—— Francis, 109.
—— guns, 37.
—— Warder, 220.
Thornton, Frank, 113.
Three Rock Mountains, 56 ; 59; 213.
Thurles, 349 et seq.
Times, The London, 270.
Tipperary, 183 ; 252 ; 280 ; 323.
Tipperary, Mid-, 202.
Tithe War, vi.
Toledo, 326.
Tolstoy, 188.
Tom Jones, 304 et seq.
Tommies, 196.
Tories, 20.
Toronto, 278.
Tory Party, 30.
Tottenham Court Road, 269.
Tramore, 281.
Traynor, Oscar, 337 ; 344 ; 347.
Treanor, Tom, 46.
Treaty, 326, Dáil recommends ac-
  ceptance ; 330 ; 338.
Treaty of Limerick, 254.
Trinity College, 117 ; 219 ; 241.
Truce, 311, Lloyd George.
Turgeniev, 188.
Turkestan, 188.
Turkey, 306 ; 324.
Turkish agent, 323.
Twomey, Moss, 350 ; 351.
Tyrone, 63 ; 330.

Ukraine, 188.
Ulster Provisional Government, 20.
—— Volunteers, 30 ; 33.

Under Secretary for Foreign Affairs,
  128 ; 297 ; 335.
Unionists, 202.
Union Quay Barracks, 352.
Union, The, vi.
United Irishman, The, 2 ; 9 ; 17.
United States, 124, enters war ; 128 ;
  166 ; 218, self-determination for
  Ireland ; 237, the Senate ; 243.
Usk Prison, 223.

Valentia, 256 ; 352.
Vinegar Hill, 72.
Visiting Justices—Dartmoor, 107.
Volunteers in England, 171.
Volunteer Oath, 344.
—— Police, 334 ; 335.

Wakefield Prison, 205.
Walker, Captain, 24.
Wallace, 203.
Wallace, Henry, 19.
Wandering Jew, The, 215.
Walsh, Frank P., 240.
—— J. J., 151 ; 301 et seq.
—— John M., 25.
—— Nicholas O'Hanlon, 5.
—— Tom, 340 ; 341.
Washington, D.C., 18 ; 165 ; 304.
Wasp, the, 110.
Waterford, 63 et seq. ; 76 ; 154 ;
  202 ; 272 ; 281 ; 347 et seq.
Waterloo, vi.
Waterloo Road, 267.
Waterville, 256 ; 352.
Webb, Mrs., of Gorey, 119.
Weiner, Mr., 330.
Welsh Ports, 236.
Westland Row, 334.
Westminster, 243.
—— Gazette, 308.
Westmoreland Street, 292.
West's Awake, The, 136.
Wexford, 1 ; 3 ; 5 ; 20, the Feis ;
  26, Summerhill ; 26, Hackett's
  Spout ; 28, Mrs. Mellowes ; 30,
  schooner ; 34, football team ; 36,
  arming ; 36, Brigade ; 37, pike
  making ; 37, pro-German notices ;
  42, correspondent ; 42, Summer-
  ville ; 45, White's Hotel ; 45,
  Captain O'Sullivan ; 47, Main
  Street ; 48, Redmond Monument ;
  50, Selskar Street ; 61 et seq. ; 67,
  British forces in ; 72, deputation
  to ; 73, prisoners ; 77 ; 96, news
  from ; 146, John's Gate Street ;
  151 ; 161, return from Cork Jail ;
  166, guns for ; 185 ; 214, Assembly Room ; 272 ; 290, Coolnaboy.

Wexford, Battalion, 51 ; 156.
—— Brigade, 156.
—— Corporation, 10 ; 186 ; 294.
—— County Council, 212.
—— Feis, 9 ; 20.
—— football team, 157.
—— *Independent*, 212.
—— Kilmore, 44.
Wexfordmen, 49.
—— in British uniform, 88.
Wexford, North, 65.
—— Park, 51, mobilisation.
—— Police Officers, 84.
—— prisoners in Cork, 158 *et seq.*
—— Quarter Sessions, 84.
—— schooner, 236.
—— soldier, Kilmainham, 87.
—— South, 60.
—— station, 63.
—— strike, 222.
—— warder in Cork, 157.
Wharton, the G.-man, 185 ; 262.
Whelan, Pax, 348 ; 349.
Whitefriar Street, 294.
White, Mary, 65.
White's Hotel, 45.

Whitman, Walt, 183.
Wicklow, 163 ; 203 ; 266.
Wild Earth, 17.
Wilson, President, 49 ; 78 ; 218 ;
    224 ; 237 ; 240 ; 319.
Wilson, Sir Henry, 287 ; 318.
Winchester, 282.
Windsor, House of, 155.
Wind that Shakes the Barley, The, 97.
Wolfe Tone, 86 ; 312.
Wolverhampton, 281.
Women in the I.R.B., 10.
Wrong Box, The, 246.
Wyse Power, Charlie, 39 ; 84.
—— —— Nancy, 326 *et seq.*

Yeats, W. B., 11, *Cathleen ni Houlihan* ;
    17, *Dana* ; 203.
York Street, 344.
Young Ireland, vi ; 278.
—— Irelanders, 5 ; 212.
—— Men's Debating Society, 21.

Zeppelin, 311.
—— raid on London, 150.

ACKNOWLEDGMENTS

I wish to thank Dorothy Macardle for giving me permission to quote from her book *The Irish Republic* ; Dr. G. A. Hayes McCoy of the National Museum, James Carty of the National Library, Liam McGowan, Angus O'Daly and Thomas Bevan for their help in securing some of the illustrations and verifying certain details ; and the Proprietors of Independent Newspapers Limited for allowing me to quote from the columns of *The Irish Independent*.